Mental Disability and the European Convention on Human Rights

International Studies
in Human Rights

VOLUME 90

Mental Disability and the European Convention on Human Rights

By

Peter Bartlett
Oliver Lewis
and Oliver Thorold

Foreword by

Sir Nicolas Bratza
Judge of the European Court of Human Rights

Arts & Humanities
Research Council

MARTINUS NIJHOFF PUBLISHERS
LEIDEN / BOSTON

A C.I.P. record for this book is available from the Library of Congress.

Printed on acid-free paper.

ISBN 0924-4751
ISBN-13: 978-90-04-15423-0
ISBN-10: 90-04-15423-X
© 2007 Koninklijke Brill NV, Leiden, The Netherlands.

Koninklijke Brill NV incorporates the imprints Brill, Hotei Publishers, IDC Publishers, Martinus Nijhoff Publishers and VSP.

Printed in the Netherlands

To Edith and Kurt Bauer

Contents

About the Authors

Peter Bartlett is Nottinghamshire Healthcare NHS Trust Professor of Mental Health Law in the School of Law at the University of Nottingham in England. He is author of *Blackstone's Guide to the Mental Capacity Act 2005* (Oxford University Press, 2005) and, with Ralph Sandland, of *Mental Health Law: Policy and Practice* (2nd ed., Oxford University Press, 2003). Professor Bartlett has served on the board of the International Academy of Law and Mental Health, and on the editorial board of the *International Journal of Law and Psychiatry* and the *Journal of Mental Health Law*. He is a board member of the Mental Disability Advocacy Center in Budapest, and is also a member of the bar of Ontario, Canada.

Oliver Lewis served for five years as Legal Director of the Mental Disability Advocacy Center in Budapest before becoming its Executive Director in 2006. MDAC is an international legal advocacy organisation which promotes and protects human rights of people with mental health problems and intellectual disabilities across central and eastern Europe and central Asia. Mr Lewis trained as a barrister in the United Kingdom and is an associate member of Doughty Street Chambers, London. He teaches mental disability law and advocacy at the Central European University, Budapest, and is a fellow of its Center for Ethics and Law in Biomedicine. He also serves on the board of Amnesty International Hungary.

Oliver Thorold became interested in mental health law during a placement at the Center for Law and Social Policy, Washington D.C., in the early 1970s. Mental health law formed a major part of his practice at the English Bar thereafter. Between 1978 and 1981 he worked in the legal department of MIND (the National Association of Mental

Health), amongst other things helping to formulate its amicus brief submitted in support of the applicant in *X. v. the United Kingdom*, the first British case to reach the European Court of Human Rights. Mr. Thorold recently retired from full-time practice, but remains an associate member of Doughty Street Chambers, London.

About the Artists

The cover of this book shows one of the fabric paintings of Đorđina Budimić, who was born in 1953 in Rijeka, Croatia. Until 2001 she lived at the Centre for Rehabilitation Stančić, a large residential institution for people with intellectual disabilities, just outside Zagreb. She now receives support and lives in an apartment in Zagreb and currently involved in a project aimed at transforming the residential institution Stančić into a community-based service provider.

Acknowledgements

Inevitably, a work of this scale is the product not only of the authors, but of a wide variety of colleagues. This book is no exception.

Throughout the development of the book, we have benefited through discussions with our colleagues, in particular Dmitri Bartenev, Jan Fiala, Gábor Gombos, Yuri Marchenko, Marit Rasmussen, and David Zahumensky at the Mental Disability Advocacy Center in Budapest; and Ralph Sandland at the University of Nottingham.

Peter Bartlett's contribution was greatly assisted by the grant of sabbatical leave from his duties at the University of Nottingham and the Nottinghamshire Healthcare NHS Trust. This leave was extended by one semester through the terms of the Research Leave Scheme of the [United Kingdom] Arts and Humanities Research Council. That sabbatical was spent as a visitor in the School of Law of Birkbeck College, University of London. Our thanks are expressed to all these organisations for their respective contributions.

We are grateful to Alan Yoshioka for the preparation of the index, table of cases and table of authorities, and also for a considerable amount of copy editing. We would also wish to thank Jane Shvets for research on the ECHR and costs, and Matthew Francis for more general research assistance.

The team at Martinus Nijhoff Publishers has dealt with us with considerable patience and consistent professionalism. In particular, we would wish to thank the section editor for law, Lindy Melman, and our production editor, Leonieke Aalders.

At a relatively late stage in the process, we were fortunate to receive assistance from a variety of colleagues, who very generously read and commented on all or part of the manuscript: Kees Blankman, Luke Clements, Sarah Green, Georg Høyer, Fabrice Kellens, Anna Lawson, Jill Peay, Vadim Pak, Nikolay Pomazkin, Genevra Richardson, Ralph Sandland, and Graham Thornicroft. The intelligent and detailed commentary that many of these colleagues provided takes considerable time, and we are very grateful indeed for the assistance of these experts. All errors, of course, remain our responsibility.

We also wish to thank Sir Nicolas Bratza, Judge of the European Court of Human Rights, for providing the foreword to the book. As we discuss in the conclusion, the workload of the Court has been exploding in recent years, and we are thus particularly grateful that Judge Bratza took the time to help us in this way.

Finally, the completion of this book would not have been possible without the support and encouragement of our partners. Many thanks, therefore, to Gen, Isti and Rick.

Foreword

It was in 1979 that the former European Court of Human Rights delivered its landmark judgment in the case of *Winterwerp v. the Netherlands*, laying down the three essential requirements for the lawful detention of persons of "unsound mind" under Article 5 of the Convention. While one might have expected that this judgment would lead to a flowering of the Court's case-law on the Convention rights of persons with mental disabilities, the contrary proved to be the case: the jurisprudence of the Court in the succeeding twenty years is notable for the almost complete dearth of judicial decisions in this vitally important area. This gap is a reflection not of adequate safeguarding by member States of the Convention rights of those with mental disabilities but rather of the acute practical and legal difficulties faced by an especially vulnerable group of persons in asserting those rights and in bringing claims before both the domestic courts and the European Court.

The past few years have witnessed a change, the Strasbourg Court receiving if not a flood, at least a steady flow, of applications from those with a mental disability, mainly related to the lawfulness and conditions of detention in psychiatric and other institutions. The increase in the Court's case-load has spawned a corresponding and welcome increase in academic writings on the topic of mental health and the Convention. But what has been lacking until now is a comprehensive and systematic treatment of the subject. This work admirably fills that gap.

Written by authors with an unrivalled knowledge of the subject, the book provides a clear, readable and authoritative analysis of the Convention provisions of particular relevance to those suffering from mental disability and of the Court's developing case-law, focusing on the key areas of detention, treatment and guardianship. In addition, it contains a valuable summary of the practice and procedures of the Strasbourg Court, as well as addressing the special and complex problems faced by lawyers representing persons with mental disabilities.

The advances made in recent years in the protection of persons with a wide diversity of disabilities and with widely differing needs are readily acknowledged. The Court is commended for its progressive judgments extending the reach of the Convention, particularly in the area of procedural safeguards under Article 5. But the examination of the Court's case-law is by no means uncritical. The authors identify a number of areas in which in their view the protection afforded by the Court has, as yet, proved deficient: an over-cautious incremental approach, in which cases have been decided on the narrowest basis, leaving unresolved issues of general importance; the over-strict interpretation given to the concept of 'victim' and the consequent restriction on effective access to the Strasbourg Court by those not capable of lodging complaints on their own behalf; and the excessively broad margin of appreciation granted to national authorities, both in the determination of what constitutes unsoundness of mind justifying detention and in deciding on the necessity for the continued detention of those suffering from mental disability. Whether or not one agrees in all respects with the authors' assessment, the case is compellingly argued and merits careful study.

So, too, do those parts of the book dealing with institutional standards and controls, highlighting with reference to the reports of the European Committee for the Prevention of Torture the often lamentable conditions of detention and treatment in psychiatric hospitals and similar facilities, as well as the reluctance of States and domestic courts effectively to apply Convention standards and to implement judgments of the Strasbourg Court.

While concentrating on what might be described as the classic Convention rights of liberty, freedom from abuse and procedural protection, the book also ventures into the relatively uncharted territory of rights of persons with mental disabilities in broader civic society. In a stimulating discussion, the authors address the issue of the barriers to full integration in the community. They consider the use which might be made of the Convention in furthering such participation and in better fostering the rights of those with disabilities to education, to work, to vote, and to marry and found a family.

The authors' closing observation in their conclusion deserves to be quoted:

> For too long, people with disabilities, and people with mental health problems and intellectual disabilities in particular, were left at the margins of human rights discourse. A change has commenced, but only commenced.

In this they are surely correct. There still remain wide, unexplored areas in which imaginative use of the Convention could give life to the rights of persons with mental disabilities and ensure their more effective protection. It is difficult to overestimate the contribution which this book will make to this process. The authors are to be congratulated on producing a work which will become essential reading for judges and practitioners, as well as for others concerned with the rights of a large and often-ignored section of society.

I warmly welcome the publication of a book which will, I know, become an indispensable part of every library on the Convention.

Sir Nicolas Bratza
European Court of Human Rights
Strasbourg

Table of Cases from the European Court of Human Rights and the European Commission of Human Rights

Table of Cases from the European Court of Human Rights and the European Commission of Human Rights

Table of Cases from Domestic Courts and the European Court of Justice

England and Wales

European Court of Justice

Canada

United States

Table of Standards of the European Committee for the Prevention of Torture and Inhuman or Degrading Treatment or Punishment

Table of Domestic Statutes and Rules

Table of International Instruments and Documents

Council of Europe

1950, Convention for the Protection of Human Rights and Fundamental Freedoms
(European Convention on Human Rights) as amended by Protocol 11

List of Abbreviations

COE	Council of Europe
CPT	European Committee for the Prevention of Torture and Inhuman or Degrading Treatment or Punishment
CTO	Community treatment order
ECHR	European Convention for the Protection of Human Rights and Fundamental Freedoms ['European Convention on Human Rights']
ECT	Electro-convulsive therapy
ECtHR	European Court of Human Rights
EHRR	European Human Rights Reports
ETS	European Treaty Series
EU	European Union
NGO	Non-governmental organisation
UN	United Nations
UNESCO	United Nations Educational, Scientific and Cultural Organisation
WHO	World Health Organization

Note on Language and Terminology

The labels which are used to describe the people whose rights are the subjects of this book have long been experienced by those people as stigmatising. Such stigma flows not merely from informal language – words such as 'nutters', 'psychos' or 'retards' – but also from more formal and professional language. Quite appropriately, terminology has become subject to considerably political controversy. Terms such as 'mental illness' and 'patient', for example, are criticised as adopting an uncritically medical model of disability.

The medical model is argued to be inappropriate for at least two reasons. First, controversially, some people deny its applicability entirely. They take the view that mental disabilities are not essentially medical. Regarding intellectual disability, for example, this is a coherent objection. People with an intellectual disability may have different abilities to others in society, but it is difficult to see that someone with such a disability is 'sick'. Second, even among those who accept a medical model of some forms of mental disability, it is argued that the medical model focuses attention on the medical aspects of the individual, to the exclusion of the remainder of the individual's situation. The people affected by diagnoses and conditions relevant to this book experience difficulties that are by no means medical in nature, and these experiences may be as central to the problems they face as anything medical in their condition. Prejudice is a clear example: to be known to have a psychiatric history may well significantly affect how an individual is treated in society and by administrative bureaucracies, even if the manifestations of the condition are now entirely in the past. The problems of people at issue in this book are at least not merely medical: they are also social, cultural and environmental.

These issues of terminology pose difficulties for this book. It is not merely that the acceptable language changes, although that is certainly the experience of those of us who have been active in the 'mental disability' field for some time. It is also that this is a book in part for people who wish to develop an interest in the human rights of people with mental disabilities, and they will not necessarily be aware of what the most recent language actually refers to. The fact that this book is aimed at an audience across Europe merely adds to this problem: we cannot assume that our readers will be first language English, and unduly complicated language may lead to incomprehension or misunderstanding.

While we are sympathetic to the political concerns regarding the use of terminology, some sacrifices have been necessary for clarity. We are using the term 'mental disability' as a broad umbrella term, to include the conditions of all those that are the subjects of this book. This includes people with intellectual disabilities and people with difficulties related to mental health. 'Intellectual disability' is the term we adopt for the condition previously called 'mental retardation', 'learning disability', or 'developmental disability' and related conditions such as Autism. It also includes (depending on context) conditions traditionally associated with old age, including senile dementia and Alzheimer's disease.

We have been less successful at finding an appropriate term for people with mental disabilities related to what has traditionally been called 'mental illness'. 'People with psychosocial disabilities' has found favour with the disability rights movement at the United Nations level, and we use it occasionally, but it has not yet entered common usage, and a reader new to the field is likely to find it baffling. 'Person with a psychiatric history', 'person diagnosed with a mental illness' and such-like phrases are also used, but they are cumbersome, and make for overly long sentences. We have on occasion referred to 'patients' and 'mental illness', simply because they are terms that are commonly understood, notwithstanding their exclusively medical resonances.

There is some variance between chapters. People living in institutions are sometimes referred to as 'residents', and persons detained in institutions as 'detainees', for example. The object in using such terms is to focus on the aspect of the individual's situation that is relevant in the context of the chapter in question.

The choice of language has been the subject of considerable debate between the authors, and none of us is entirely happy with the result. Our overall approach is shared, however: we have felt obliged to use terms which allow the reader to focus as far as possible on the human rights questions in the text. Those questions are, after all, at the core of the book, and unduly complicated phrasing which would draw focus from those questions would undermine our fundamental concern, instilling an understanding of the rights of people with mental disabilities under the European Convention on Human Rights.

Chapter 1

Introduction: The European Convention on Human Rights and Mental Disability

Mental disability has come of age as a subject of concern under the European Convention on Human Rights (ECHR). It was only in 1979 that the first significant decision of the European Court of Human Rights (ECtHR) was decided on the subject, and after that, cases were relatively few for many years. It is only recently that this has begun to change. Between 2000 and 2004, there were over forty judgments of the European Court of Human Rights relating to mental disability or to detention in psychiatric and related facilities.[1] In some areas, such as the law relating to detention of individuals with mental health difficulties, it is possible now to speak of a jurisprudence of the Court. In others, the increased profile of disability rights internationally combined with the broader jurisprudence of the Court makes it possible to articulate likely patterns of future development in the Court's case law.

With the rise of the Court's caseload in this area has been a corresponding increase in academic literature.[2] Further, the importance of human rights is increasingly accepted by

---

[1]   This figure refers to Court judgments, and does not include admissibility decisions.
[2]   See, for example, P. Fennell, 'Convention Compliance, Public Safety and the Social Inclusion of Mentally Disordered People', 32 *Journal of Law and Society* (2005) 90, L.O. Gostin, 'Human Rights of Persons with Disabilities', 23 *International Journal of Law and Psychiatry* (2000) 138; L.O. Gostin and L. Gable, 'The Human rights of Persons with Mental Disabilities: A Global Perspective on the Application of Human Rights Principles to Mental Health', 63:1 *Maryland Law Review* (2004) 20; D. Kingdon, R. Jones and

mental health and social care professionals. As yet however there is no systematic and detailed analysis of the topic as a whole, focussed specifically on the ECHR. That is the primary purpose of this book. It is written with two groups of readers in mind: those with an interest in the ECHR who have an interest in how cases relating to mental disability may shape the ECHR jurisprudence, and those with an interest in the rights of people with mental disabilities who have an interest in discovering what the ECHR may bring to those people. With those readers in mind, this first chapter is intended to provide introductory information about 'mental disability' and people affected by it within the countries of the Council of Europe, an introduction to the ECHR and its place among human rights instruments, and an introduction to the European Court of Human Rights.

'People with mental disabilities'

Statistics would suggest that roughly one in four of the population will experience mental disorder at some time in their life. For the majority of those people, the disorder will be relatively minor. Nonetheless, one tenth of the population will be subject to a serious neuropsychiatric condition such as schizophrenia, depression, addictive disorders, and dementia at some time in their life. These figures are relatively constant internationally, and do not appear to vary markedly based on wealth or distinctions between urban and rural environments.[3] The human rights questions regarding people with mental disability are therefore not marginal questions, but rather directly relevant to a significant proportion of every country's population.

People with mental disabilities are not a homogeneous group. To take an example, it is fair to wonder what if anything a person with an intellectual disability will have in common with a person with schizophrenia, other than the label 'mental disability'? They have quite different disabilities with different manifestations, and different needs. While language such as 'symptoms', 'treatment' and 'illness' can apply (albeit controversially in some circles) to people with problems relating to mental health (or 'psychiatric disorders', 'mental illness'), they are difficult to apply to the people with intellectual disabilities,

J. Lönnqvist, 'Protecting the human rights of people with mental disorder: new recommendations emerging from the Council of Europe' 185 *British Journal of Psychiatry* (2004) 277; O. Lewis, 'Protecting the rights of people with a mental disability – the European Convention on Human Rights' 9 *European Journal of Health Law* (2002) 293; G. Richardson, 'The European Convention and Mental Health Law in England and Wales: Moving Beyond Process' (2005) 28 *International Journal of Law and Psychiatry* 127; O. Thorold, 'The ECHR and UK Mental Health Legislation', *European Human Rights Law Review* (1996) 619. Particular note should be made of Philippe Bernardet, Tomais Douraki, Corrine Vaillant, *Psychiatrie, droits de l'homme et défense des usagers en Europe* (Ramonville Saint-Agne: Editions Erès, 2002). This book contains a wealth of information and analysis of domestic legislation within Europe, and some significant discussion of the European Convention on Human Rights.

3   World Health Organization, *The World Health Report 2001: Mental Health: New Understanding, New Hope* (Geneva: WHO, 2001), p. 23 and studies cited therein. This publication is available electronically at http://www.who.int/whr/previous/en/index.html.

(sometimes called 'learning disabilities', 'mental retardation', or 'mental handicap'),[4] which fit much more closely into the language of disability. While both may well live in the community, either in their own home or in some form of supported housing arrangement, if admitted to a more controlling institution, it will be likely to be a different institution – a hospital for the person with schizophrenia, and a group home or social care home for the person with the intellectual disability. If they are subject to legal controls, they may well be different legal controls, with the person with schizophrenia under a Mental Health Act or similar legislation, and the person with the intellectual disability under a guardianship régime. While this is perhaps a particularly clear example of the diversity of the 'mentally disabled', it is by no means the only one. Similarly, people affected by 'mental illness' may differ in similarly fundamental ways. The label 'mental disability' creates the illusion of homogeneity in a diverse spectrum of people. The phrase 'people with one or more of a variety of psychosocial or intellectual disabilities' would be more accurate in reflecting this diversity. The use of the phrase 'mental disability' in this volume is used as a matter of practicality to refer to this diverse collection of conditions, but not without reservations.

Mental disorders are classified according to a variety of international instruments. Most relevant within Europe is the World Health Organization (WHO) standard, the International Statistical Classification of Diseases and Related Health Problems, currently in its tenth edition (ICD-10).[5] The WHO World Health Report for 2001 contains a readable introduction to this classification structure, and a number of the significant specific disorders contained in it.[6] In some situations, diagnoses may be of considerable assistance. Some people affected find it comforting that their difficulties have been placed in a coherent medical framework, which often allows the possibility of treatment. Others find the diagnoses unhelpful and stigmatising.

A diagnosis may change for a given individual in many cases. Sometimes, this has to do with comorbidity of disorder – two or more disorders existing in the same individual – or a change in the disorder over the course of time. It is good practice for the physician to re-visit the question of diagnosis periodically, but it can nonetheless be frustrating for the patient when such changes occur, particularly when the doctor changes his or her assessment retrospectively.

In any event, it is appropriate to be clear what the diagnostic structures do, and what they cannot do. They are frameworks through which doctors categorise mental disabilities. Such a diagnosis is a condition precedent for detention to be justified under Article 5 of the ECHR, but the mere fact of a diagnosis does not of itself create sufficient conditions for legal intervention. The ICD-10 does not purport to determine whether a

---

[4] Regarding terminology in general, see introductory note to this book.
[5] Also significant internationally is the American categorical structure, the Diagnostic and Statistical Manual of Disorders, currently in its fourth edition (DSM-IV-TR).
[6] World Health Organization, *The World Health Report 2001: Mental Health: New Understanding, New Hope* (Geneva: WHO, 2001), chapter 2.

specific disorder warrants detention or mandatory treatment: that will depend on the nature and severity of the individual case, and whether specific legal safeguards both in domestic law and the ECHR are met. The specifics of these safeguards are dealt with in later chapters of this book. For now, the point is that the presence of a psychiatric diagnosis is not necessarily sufficient justification for legal intervention.

The presence of a mental disability must be distinguished from the determination of the mental capacity of an individual. The former is determined by a medical assessment; the latter is a question of an individual's ability to make a particular decision. Frequently, people with even quite severe mental health problems or intellectual disabilities may nonetheless have capacity to make decisions. The most detailed study on this question compared people admitted to psychiatric institutions to people living in the community and to those hospitalised for a cardiac disorder. The study tested understanding of information relevant to treatment decisions, appreciation of that information, and reasoning ability. It showed that about half of people diagnosed with schizophrenia, and approximately three-quarters of people diagnosed with depression, showed no impairment on any of these tests.[7] It is simply wrong to assume that people with mental disorder are necessarily unable to make decisions: most can.

Further, it cannot be assumed that because an individual lacks capacity for some decisions that he or she lacks capacity for all. From a human rights perspective, the issue is whether the individual sufficiently understands and appreciates the information relevant to the specific decision to be made. If so, he or she has capacity to make the decision.

Capable decisions may nonetheless be overridden if domestic law allows. Domestic law in most European jurisdictions currently allows the detention of individuals even if they continue to have capacity. More controversially, most European jurisdictions allow the forced psychiatric treatment of people who have capacity to consent to treatment. Similarly, and also controversially, some guardianship régimes lack the precision to ensure individuals retain legal authority for decision-making in their areas of capacity. The degree to which such compulsion of individuals with capacity is permitted by the ECHR will be discussed in the chapters that follow.

Nonetheless, lawyers, advocates, courts and others involved in decision-making regarding people with mental disabilities should engage with the person who is subject of the decision. Still, throughout Europe, people with mental disabilities are routinely stigmatised as having little to bring to decisions regarding their care, or subjected to other stereotypes. There is still evidence of lawyers failing even to meet their clients before hearings or failing to meet even basic standards of legal representation in a way that would be unthinkable for a client who did not have a diagnosis of a mental disability.[8] This is indefensible: standards of professional conduct do not cease simply because a client has (or

---

[7]   T. Grisso and P. Appelbaum, 'The MacArthur Treatment Competence Study III: Ability of Patients to Consent to Psychiatric and Medical Treatments', 19(2) *Law and Human Behaviour* 149 at 169.

[8]   See, for example, Mental Disability Advocacy Centre, *Liberty Denied: Human Rights Violations in Criminal Psychiatric Detention Reviews in Hungary* (Budapest: Mental Disability Advocacy Centre, 2004). This report is available online at http://www.mdac.info.

is alleged to have) a mental disability, and professional associations should take urgent action to ensure that their members meet appropriate standards of representation. Failure by lawyers to meet appropriate standards of representation may itself give rise to a breach of the ECHR.[9]

Care and treatment of people with mental disabilities will occur in a variety of settings. Internationally, it is increasingly the case that people will remain in the community, either in their own homes or in small community facilities, rather than be admitted to a large institution. These community solutions are favoured by the WHO.[10] Ideally, their ethos is one of 'least restrictive alternative': the individual is left in the least restrictive legal and physical situation that is appropriate for his or her needs. Medical treatment, if necessary, may be offered through out-patient services at a local hospital, by the individual's general practitioner, or by community health teams visiting the individual in his or her home. Social services such as assistance with budgeting, shopping and cooking may be provided by local authorities. Where appropriate, drop-in centres or workshops may be offered, to provide activities during the day. Employment opportunities should be sought and assistance given for a person to hold down a job. Ideally, the providers of formal services should work in close liaison with any family or other informal carers. In this ideal, community care is buttressed by a legal policy of non-discrimination: people with mental disabilities cannot be refused employment or services because of a disability.

This rosy picture must be viewed with some scepticism. Certainly, when appropriate for the affected individual, good community care services are vastly preferable to other forms of care. As the WHO acknowledges,[11] however, the realities do not necessarily measure up to the intentions, often because of under-funding by governments. The result of such under-funding may be a lack of provision of programmes such as day centres or home support, with a resulting marked depreciation in the quality of life of affected people. In other cases, community care remains heavily regimented. Individuals may awake in a group home, be bussed to a day-care centre or sheltered workshop during the day, and be returned to the group home at night. Their time may be as regimented as in a traditional asylum, with little interaction with the broader community in which they live. If one of the ideals of community care is integration with the broader community, some experiences of users would suggest at best very qualified success.

At the other extreme from community care are large facilities devoted exclusively to the care of people with mental disabilities. The historical basis of these facilities lies in nineteenth-century practices of institutionalisation, at that time focussing primarily on people with mental illness as then understood, rather than intellectual disabilities. At

---

[9] See further chapter 9, below.
[10] World Health Organization, *The World Health Report 2001: Mental Health: New Understanding, New Hope* (Geneva: WHO, 2001), chapter 3, especially at p. 50; WHO European Ministerial Conference on Mental Health, *Mental Health Action Plan for Europe: Facing the Challenges, Building Solutions*, EUR/04/5047810/7 (14 Jan 05), pp. 6–7.
[11] World Health Organization, *The World Health Report 2001: Mental Health: New Understanding, New Hope* (Geneva: WHO, 2001), p. 51.

their peak, generally in the middle years of the twentieth century, many of these facilities contained over 1000 people. They are generally much smaller now, although Italy is notable as the only European country to have done away with them completely. Instead, psychiatric wards of general hospitals have grown in prominence.

Whatever reservations one might have about how community care has been implemented, the criticisms of the large old institutions were compelling. Both symbolically and literally, they drew a divide between those deemed able to participate in society and those who were identified as mentally disabled, who were not. Frequently, they were considerably removed from an inmate's family, making visits difficult, and the walls that tended to surround them emphasised an almost other-worldliness of the people they contained. The movement of people out of these institutions into general hospital wards and community alternatives is therefore to be encouraged. In countries where resources are strictly limited, the evidence is that investment in these community programmes provides the best results, although where resources allow, as in most of Europe, the evidence would seem to suggest that a range of community and hospital-based services is desirable.[12]

Typically, a given geographic jurisdiction will offer institutional facilities of varying levels of intensity and security. Some particularly high security institutions may bear considerable resemblance to high security prisons: high walls surmounted with razor wire, numerous locked doors between the inmates and the outside, body searches of all visitors, and intrusive surveillance by officers who resemble prison guards as much as traditional nurses. At the other extreme, some wards are not merely unlocked, but allow or indeed encourage patients to spend time outside them in the community. Indeed, in some countries patients are permitted to go on long-term leave from hospitals, so they live in the community. For them, being a patient in the hospital may mean little more than an administrative entry on the hospital register, and perhaps attending the hospital for treatment as if they were an out-patient.

Increasingly, hospital wards and similar psychiatric institutions seem to be used primarily for short-term care of people with mental disabilities or people who present particular behavioural difficulties. Other people who require long-term care and support, such as people with more severe intellectual disabilities or some people with chronic mental illness, tend to be accommodated elsewhere. Sometimes, this will be either in their own homes, in small-scale sheltered housing or in other accommodation in the community. Particularly in central and Eastern Europe, however, they may be accommodated in a social welfare institution or 'social care home'. These have much of the institutional nature of traditional psychiatric facilities, but without their hospital ethos. While medication is certainly normally provided to residents of social care homes when considered appropriate by a medical professional, the expectation is that the individuals will remain

---

[12] For a survey and assessment of the studies, see G. Thornicroft and M. Tansella, 'Components of a modern mental health service: a pragmatic balance of community and hospital care', 185 *British Journal of Psychiatry* (2004) 283.

in these facilities for many years rather than be treated and released in a relatively short time.

The elderly may be housed in these same institutions, particularly if they have a history of chronic psychosocial disabilities, but in cases of senility and similar disorders, they are often accommodated in different institutions, designed for elderly people. These institutions differ from those discussed previously, as they may well contain a mixture of people with and without mental disabilities. Nonetheless, they are often the accommodation chosen for people with Alzheimer's disease and other degenerative disorders associated with ageing. They therefore form an important part of the constellation of places where people with mental disabilities are cared for. They further raise a number of issues overlapping with other institutions. In some, questions arise as to whether medication is provided in part to sedate individuals. Many have locked wards, for example, or people who lack the capacity to decide whether to consent to admission to the institution, raising issues of detention under Article 5 of the ECHR.[13]

This is by no means a complete list of places where people with mental disabilities may be found. It does however include many of the most important loci of care. It is significant because it serves again to remind of the diversity contained within issues related to mental disability. It is also significant because cases regarding human rights of those contained in different facilities must take into account the differences between facilities: as an obvious example, the standard of censorship of mail that would be justified under Article 8 of the ECHR will not be the same in a high security institution as in an old people's home or community-based group home. The ECHR must be interpreted with this diversity in mind, and the Court's judgments must be read with reasonable attention to their facts in this regard. A case about a high security institution may perhaps not apply straightforwardly to a less secure environment and vice versa. Finally, the diversity serves as a reminder that the ECHR is not a human rights panacea. It will be clear that for the individual, the specific institution in which he or she is detained may be of profound importance. The choice by the State to detain an individual in one facility rather than another does not generally raise an issue under the ECHR. While the ECHR imposes requirements against arbitrary detention under Article 5, the placement within the system of an individual who has been found to be rightly detained has been held not to be within the scope of that Article.[14]

Programmes offered for the care and rehabilitation of people with mental disorders may include pharmacological interventions, psychotherapy, and psychosocial rehabilitation. Electro-convulsive therapy (ECT) is also used in most countries of Europe. The Council of Europe expects that each individual should receive an individualised

---

[13] See, for example, *H.L. v. the United Kingdom*, Application No. 45508/99, judgment 5 October 2004, (2005) 40 EHRR 32, discussed in chapter 2 below.

[14] See *Ashingdane v. the United Kingdom*, Application No. 8225/78, judgment 28 May 1985, (A/93) (1985) 7 EHRR 528, para. 41–2. Regarding the possibility that the right to the least restrictive alternative might raise an issue under Article 3, see chapter 3, below.

treatment plan.[15] Treatment should only be provided with the consent of the patient if that individual is capable of making the decision, although as discussed below, some derogation from this principle is permitted when mandated by domestic law and with the provision of appropriate safeguards.[16] The specific programme of treatment offered will of course vary between individuals, depending on their mental state and diagnosis. Particular issues relating to the ECHR and psychiatric treatment will be discussed in chapter 4 below, but a few general comments are appropriate by way of introduction.

While they certainly have beneficial effects in many cases, pharmacological interventions are not unproblematic. Adverse effects are common. The adverse effects for antipsychotic drugs such as risperidone and olanzapine, used to treat disorders such as schizophrenia, include obesity, diabetes, and dizziness. While less common and less severe than was the case under older psychiatric medications, these antipsychotic drugs are still known to cause 'extrapyramidal symptoms', including parkinsonian symptoms (including tremors), dystonia (abnormal face and body movements), akathesia (restlessness), and tardive dyskinesia (rhythmic involuntary movements particularly of the tongue, lips, face, hands and feet). In some parts of Europe, older antipsychotic drugs are still used. In those cases, the extrapyramidal symptoms are more frequent and more severe. Depression is normally treated with either tricyclic medication or selective serotonin re-uptake inhibitors (SSRIs). Tricyclic medication can cause heart problems, and deaths from heart attacks of those receiving this medication are not unknown. SSRIs can cause nausea, and gastro-intestinal problems. Vascular problems are also known, although occur less frequently. Medication may interfere with the individual's lifestyle as well: much anti-psychotic medication has sedative properties, leaving an individual feeling drowsy or apathetic, and some additionally may cause impotence.[17]

These adverse effects are not necessarily an argument against such medications. Severe depression and psychotic disorders such as schizophrenia can also be extremely unpleasant, and the medications do ameliorate the unpleasant effects of those disorders in a significant number of people. Large numbers of people take the drugs in spite of the adverse effects, because of these benefits. It is rather a reminder that the decision as to whether or not to consent may involve a balancing between wanted and unwanted effects of the medication, and a patient's decision to refuse medication does not necessarily flow from delusions or an inability to understand the benefits of the proposed treatment. It is further a reminder that an individual refusing some medication will not necessarily refuse all medication: different drugs can treat the same disorder, and it may

---

[15] See for example Committee for the Prevention of Torture and Inhuman or Degrading Treatment of Punishment, The CPT Standards, 'Substantive sections of the CPT's General Reports', CPT/Inf/E (2002) 1, Rev 2004, p. 56, para. 37; and COE Committee of Ministers Rec (2004) 10, Article 12.1

[16] See further chapter 4, below.

[17] Medical information drawn from Joint Formulary Committee [United Kingdom], *British National Formulary*, 49th ed. London: British Medical Association, 2005, sections 4.2 and 4.3. The *British National Formulary* is available online free of charge at http://www.bnf.org.

be possible for a drug to be found that will both treat the individual's condition and have adverse effects that the individual is prepared to tolerate.

ECT also warrants a particular mention. This procedure involves the introduction of electricity to the individual's brain to induce a seizure broadly similar to a grand mal epileptic episode. While it is a recognised form of treatment, particularly for severe depression, it is expected that it will be performed only in its 'modified' form, that is, with the use of muscle relaxants and anaesthetics.[18] Even in this form, it is highly controversial among some users of psychiatric services, who report short- and long-term memory loss. The fact that a client is resisting ECT, therefore, again does not mean the individual lacks capacity, or is suffering from relevant delusions, or is averse to all medical interventions.

All of this leads to a variety of conclusions. First, and perhaps most important, is that people labelled as having a mental disability are not a distinct and separate 'group' in society. 'They' constitute one in four of all of us. 'They' constitute individuals with disparate life experiences, wishes, desires and needs, the same as people who do not have labels of a mental disability. People with mental disabilities cannot be assumed to be mere passive recipients of care, but are often entirely capable of full involvement with their care, and able to articulate their wishes and preferences. The options open to them are likely to be complex, with various advantages and disadvantages attached to each. The selection between those options will vary between different individuals. The role of health care professionals in this decision-making is therefore not simple. Certainly, doctors, nurses and social workers may well be part of the professional team working with the individual and, often, other informal carers such as family members. These professionals should be expected to have appropriate training and experience, and therefore particular areas of expertise. Most users of the mental health system will wish to take the professional opinions seriously in those areas of expertise (although they, like other users of health or social services, are not obliged to do so). In the end, however, the opinions are only advice. Wherever possible, it is for the person with mental disabilities himself or herself rather than the professionals to weigh up the advantages and disadvantages of the available options, and to make a choice as to what care or treatment to accept or reject. Any departure from that must be clearly justified under domestic law, and subject to the human rights safeguards described in the chapters that follow.

Applicable Domestic Law

The human rights issues related to domestic law will be discussed in the chapters that follow, but at this stage it may nonetheless be useful to describe overall frameworks of domestic law, to give a general context for that later discussion. The legislative régimes

---

[18] See, eg., CPT Standards, CPT/Inf/E (2002) 1, Rev 2004, p. 56, para. 39.

fall conveniently into three categories: statutes allowing detention of people with mental disabilities, statutes allowing their involuntary treatment, and guardianship laws relating to people found to be lacking capacity.

Admission to a psychiatric hospital or other institution will be either on an informal or involuntary basis. It is only the latter set of patients that are detained in law. In many European countries, most admissions are informal, and those patients have the right in law to leave the institution just as any patient with a somatic disorder may discharge himself or herself out of a regular hospital. The realities of these admissions are not so clearcut, however. Empirical research suggests that roughly half of those admitted informally to psychiatric facilities nonetheless felt coerced during the admission.[19] This can be the result of the threat of legal coercion. An individual may be told that if he or she does not agree to informal admission, he or she will be admitted involuntarily, with the added social stigma that implies. Further, in most countries, domestic law allows informal admissions to be converted to involuntary admissions, when the civil committal criteria are met.[20] Informal patients who attempt to exercise their right to leave may therefore find themselves changed into involuntary patients, making their right to leave illusory. Other forms of coercion, no less important, flow from a lack of reasonable alternatives available to the individual. A vulnerable person may have no real ability to find alternative care or housing, and therefore be effectively forced to consent to an admission instigated by a doctor or family member. For this reason, it is perhaps unsurprising that the ECtHR decided in *H.L. v. the United Kingdom*[21] that a person admitted informally who, because of an intellectual disability was unable to make the decision regarding admission, was 'deprived of his liberty' for purposes of Article 5.[22]

Laws allowing for involuntary admission must require a mental disorder of sufficient severity to warrant the admission.[23] The approach to the severity question is normally based on an individual's dangerousness, or his or her need for treatment, or both. Dangerousness approaches are controversial, because they reinforce the stereotype that people with psychosocial disabilities are dangerous. In fact, the statistics show that people with psychosocial disabilities are barely more dangerous than the general popula-

---

[19]   The pioneering study on this question is J. Gilboy and J. Schmidt, '"Voluntary" hospitalization of the mentally ill', 66 *Northwestern Law Review* (1971) 429. For more recent studies, see, e.g., J. Monahan, S. Hoge, et al., 'Coercion and Commitment: Understanding Involuntary Mental Hospital Admission', 18:3 *International Journal of Law and Psychiatry* (1995) 249; H.D. Poulsen, 'The Prevalence of Extralegal Deprivation of Liberty in a Psychiatric Hospital Population', 15 *International Journal of Law and Psychiatry* (2002) 29.

[20]   Norway is an exception. There, patients who admit themselves informally may not later be made subject to the régime of civil detention, even if they meet the other legal requirements for detention.

[21]   *H.L. v. the United Kingdom*, Application No. 45508/99, judgment 5 October 04, (2005) 40 EHRR 32.

[22]   See further chapter 2, below.

[23]   *Winterwerp v. the Netherlands*, Application No. 6301/73, judgment 24 October 1979, (A/33) (1979–80) 2 EHRR 387. *Winterwerp* establishes a variety of human rights safeguards under Article 5 for psychiatric admissions, and will be discussed in detail in chapter 2.

tion.[24] Indeed, people with psychosocial disabilities are more likely to be the victims of violence than the perpetrators. Equally problematic from a civil rights standpoint is that dangerousness is exceptionally difficult to predict. Studies would suggest that between half and three quarters of those predicted to be dangerous by psychiatric professionals do not, in the end, turn out to be violent.[25] Further, many of the criteria used to predict dangerousness are themselves questionable on human rights grounds. Age, sex, race, marital status, social class, criminal record and use of alcohol or drugs are arguably better predictors of violence than mental disorder and may be key to the determination of dangerousness in people with mental disorder.[26] The use of such criteria to make detention decisions is problematic, however. Article 14 of the ECHR precludes discrimination on the basis, inter alia, of race and colour in the interpretation of Convention rights. It is difficult to see how the race of an individual could therefore be used in determining his or her dangerousness, and correspondingly his or her liability to detention. Once such suspect categories are removed, however, predictions as to who is dangerous will be correspondingly worse.

Other statutes define the severity of the mental disorder required for detention in terms of the need for treatment. The difficulty here is how to specify the degree of seriousness in any precise way, as there is no objective scale of severity of mental disorders. *Winterwerp* requires that a disorder be of a 'kind or degree warranting compulsory confinement'.[27] That is surely a narrower criterion than that a treatment is available for the disorder in question, but it is difficult to see how the scope of the criteria can be determined sufficiently clearly to serve as the basis for deprivation of fundamental human rights. The risk is that the severity test becomes one of clinical judgment, with little meaningful law to guide the exercise of clinical discretion. The doctor exercising that discretion will often be well aware of the consequences of civil detention to the person affected and well aware of the human rights implications of his or her determination: clinical discretion does not mean these decisions are necessarily taken lightly. Nonetheless, it is difficult to see that a highly discretionary system offers appropriate protections to civil rights.[28]

---

[24] See, for example, H. Steadman, E. Mulvey, et al., 'Violence by people discharged from acute psychiatric inpatient facilities and by others in the same neighborhoods', 55 *Archives of General Psychiatry* (1998) 393.

[25] See studies surveyed in P. Bowden, 'Violence and Mental Disorder', in N. Walker (ed), *Dangerous People* (London: Blackstone, 1996); J. Monahan, *Predicting Violent Behaviour* (Beverley Hills: Sage, 1981); J. Monahan, 'Risk Assessment of Violence Among the Mentally Disordered: Generating Useful Knowledge', 11 *International Journal of Law and Psychiatry* (1988) 249. More recent attempts by Monahan and his colleagues have improved predictability somewhat, but with a questionnaire that they themselves acknowledge to be too complex to be used clinically: see J. Monahan, H.J. Steadman, et al. *Rethinking Risk Assessment: The MacArthur Study of Mental Disorder and Violence* (Oxford: Oxford University Press, 2001), 127.

[26] V. Hiday, 'The Social context of mental illness and violence', 36 *Journal of Health and Social Behaviour* (1995) 122–37.

[27] *Winterwerp v. the Netherlands, op. cit.*, para. 39.

[28] Regarding the clarity of regulation required for compliance with ECHR standards, see *Kawka v. Poland*, Application No. 25874/94, judgment 9 Jan 2001, para. 49.

The decision to detain is from the human rights viewpoint distinguishable from the decision to treat involuntarily. This difference arises in two contexts. First, it does not follow from the fact that an individual has been detained that treatment should be enforced on him or her. The European Committee for the Prevention of Torture and Inhuman or Degrading Treatment or Punishment (CPT),[29] the Council of Europe inspectorate for places of deprivation of liberty, expressly takes the view that detention should not, in principle, result in a loss of the right to make treatment decisions,[30] a view that is shared by most recent international instruments in Europe and internationally.[31] These views stop short of saying that compulsory treatment of competent people who are detained is never justified, but they do make it clear that detention is not carte blanche for involuntary treatment.[32] Nonetheless, a number of jurisdictions in the Council of Europe allow compulsory treatment of detained individuals on a much more routine basis than would be consistent with these international standards. There is little ECHR jurisprudence on this point at present, but it is reasonable to suspect, given the movement in international law, that it will be an important set of issues for the Court in the future.

The distinction between detention and involuntary treatment is also relevant for people living in the community. The question here involves 'out-patient committal' or 'community treatment orders' (CTOs), legal mechanisms designed to require people who are not detained to comply with programmes of treatment, generally medication. These mechanisms currently exist in a number of European jurisdictions. They are controversial in some quarters, largely because they have the potential considerably to increase the range and numbers of people subject to coercion. While they restrict the rights of people in the community, their efficacy is further the subject of considerable dispute.[33] They have not yet attracted litigation under the ECHR. While Articles 6 and 8 of the ECHR would certainly require that any involuntary treatment in the community be based in domestic law and import appropriate sufficient substantive and procedural safeguards, it is not yet clear how much further the Court would go in regulating CTOs.

The substantive thresholds for the above legislation relating to admission and treatment tend to centre on the severity of mental disability. Guardianship legislation instead

---

[29]   The composition and role of the CPT will be discussed in detail later in this chapter.

[30]   CPT Standards, CPT/Inf/E (2002) 1, Rev 2004, p. 57, para. 41.

[31]   Rec (2004) 10, Article 18. Involuntary treatment in the short-term in emergency situations is also envisaged by Article 21, and treatment of those convicted of offences by Article 34(1). Principle 11 of the UN Mental Illness principles is broadly to the same effect as the Council of Europe Recommendations. The Convention on Human Rights and Biomedicine and the 1999 Incapable Adults Recommendations of the Council of Europe are of similar effect, although they allow involuntary treatment only in cases of serious risk to the health of the patient himself or herself, not for the benefit or safety of others: ETS 164, article 7 and R (1999) 4.

[32]   See further chapter 4, below.

[33]   See S. Kisely, L. Campbell, N. Preston, 'Compulsory community and involuntary outpatient treatment for people with severe mental disorders', 2005: 3 *The Cochrane Library* (2005). This publication is available electronically at http://www.thecochranelibrary.com. The authors of that study conclude that the evidence does not show that compulsory community treatment results in no significant difference in service use, quality of life, or social functioning of people with severe mental disabilities, compared to standard care.

looks to the capacity of individuals, whether they are able to make decisions about their lives, rather than the severity of their disorder per se. Traditionally, continental legal systems have seen such legal capacity as creating a boundary to legal personhood,[34] an approach that continues in a number of European jurisdictions. As a result, guardianship becomes an all or nothing affair: either the individual has authority to make the full range of decisions about his or her life, or the authority to make no decisions. In the latter case, a person appointed by the domestic court will assume responsibility and authority for all decisions relevant to the incapacitated individual. The discussion of capacity above will make it clear that this is an unsatisfactory situation, as people with mental disabilities often continue to have the ability to make some decisions but not others. Even in areas where they may formally lack capacity, they may nonetheless have important contributions to make in decisions regarding their care.[35] Consistent with this, the 1999 Council of Europe Recommendation, 'Principles Concerning the Legal Protection of Incapable Adults' envisages that people under such plenary guardianship arrangements should nonetheless not be treated without their consent, if they have capacity to make the treatment decision.[36] This, sadly, is not always complied with, although there is potential for ECHR litigation in the area.[37] Also of concern is that the individual may lose authority over other decisions that he or she may have capacity to make. Of particular relevance in this volume is the authority to retain and instruct counsel, and to commence and be heard in legal proceedings. If the person lacks legal personhood, he or she may not be accorded standing before domestic courts. The result is highly objectionable: even if the individual has the capacity to litigate and also has a winning case, he or she may be precluded from bringing that case in domestic courts. We take the view that this would not preclude such an individual from taking a case to the ECtHR, and indeed that the inability to take proceedings domestically may constitute a violation of Article 6 of the ECHR, the right to judicial process.[38]

The existence of different legal régimes for people with mental disabilities creates the possibility of overlap. Guardianship legislation, for example, will generally allow the guardian to determine where the individual will live. The decision of a guardian that the individual will live in a psychiatric hospital, for example, may have the same consequences to the individual as detention under mental health legislation. In many instances, this may pose no practical problem, if the guardian is appropriately involved with the situation and robust in his or her decision-making ability. If the guardian lacks that involvement or ability, however, the individual lacking capacity may be left in essence detained, but without

---

[34] See, for example, the German *Bürgerliches Gesetzbuch*, paras. 6 and 1910, concerning guardianship and curatorship. This is a descendant of the *cura furiosi* in the Twelve Tables. See especially I.1.23.3.4 (Justinian).

[35] For legislation taking a different approach, allowing the individual authority over all decisions he or she is capable of making, see the English *Mental Capacity Act 2005* (United Kingdom, 2005).

[36] Council of Europe Recommendation R (99) 4, Principle 23(1).

[37] See further chapters 4 and 6, below.

[38] See further chapters 6 and 8. Regarding the right of access in matters related to detention, see also chapter 2.

the procedural safeguards that flow from detentions under mental health legislation. Often, there may be an option as to which legislative mechanism to use. An individual who has severe mental illness may also lack capacity to make decisions about himself or herself. In this situation, it may well be possible to use either guardianship or mental health legislative intervention. The choice may have considerable ramifications for the individual affected, but it is not obvious that it raises issues under the ECHR.

Also of concern is the degree to which the legislation is followed for specific populations. Elderly people are perhaps the obvious example, where decisions regarding their care and treatment are perceived in some cultures as a private matter where legal intervention is inappropriate, not an issue of public law and human rights. There is nothing in the ECHR to support such a notion. Indeed, the anti-discrimination provisions of Article 14 have been interpreted to preclude discrimination on the basis of age,[39] suggesting that the elderly have an equal right to protection of the law. This is as it should be: the vulnerable elderly are as much at risk of physical, emotional or economic abuse as any other vulnerable person, and they deserve the same human rights protections against such abuse.

All of this presupposes that the individual is admitted through civil admission procedures. People with mental disorders are also admitted as a result of involvement in criminal proceedings, or are identified as suffering from mental disorder while serving a period of incarceration pursuant to a criminal sentence. Most if not all Council of Europe countries have special legal régimes for people whose mental disability is a direct cause of their criminal behaviour. These people are then generally moved to psychiatric or similar environments, particularly if there is a likelihood that their disorder may be amenable to treatment. The ECHR makes it clear that if the justification for an individual's confinement flows from his or her mental disorder, he or she must be housed in a therapeutic institution such as a hospital.[40] Depending on the perceived severity of their disorder and, as a matter of political reality, the severity of their crime, they may end up in institutions that range from minimal to very high security, for an indefinite period of time.

Notwithstanding this sort of diversion programme, significant numbers of people with mental disorders do seem to be found in custodial institutions such as prisons and gaols. It is clear from the ECHR that appropriate treatment must be provided to these people.[41] It does not appear however that there is an obligation to move these people to a dedicated psychiatric or medical institution, even if their condition is treatable, so long as appropriate treatment is available in the gaol or prison.

---

[39] *Bouamar v. Belgium*, Application No. 9106/80, judgment 29 February 1988, (1989) 11 EHRR 1, para. 67.
[40] *Aerts v. Belgium*, Application No. 25357/94, judgment 30 June 1998, (1998) 29 EHRR 50, para. 46.
[41] *Keenan v. the United Kingdom*, Application No. 27229/95, judgment 3 April 2001, (2001) 33 EHRR 38, paras. 108–115.

The ECHR requires domestic legal processes to be available to challenge detention at periodic intervals. This must involve a court or court-like body taking evidence in an oral hearing, in which the detained person has a right to representation. Similar fair trial safeguards apply for decisions regarding guardianship.[42] The ECHR requires that both substantive and procedural requirements must be articulated in domestic law, normally in the form of a statute. As a matter of ECHR law, therefore, there must be domestic processes relating to these statutory régimes.

This is intended merely to give an initial indication of the various legal régimes under which a person with mental disorder may find himself or herself. They will be expanded upon in the chapters that follow.

The European Convention on Human Rights

The Basics of Process

The ECHR was the first convention promulgated by the Council of Europe (COE). The COE itself was formed by a treaty signed in London on 5 May 1949. As of January 2006, it is composed of 46 member States, covering a population of roughly 800 million people. The 25 members of the European Union are all members, but the COE also includes 21 other States, primarily from central, south-eastern and eastern Europe. Indeed, Belarus and the Vatican are the only two obvious European countries that are not currently members of the COE.[43] Its objectives include promotion of human rights, social cohesion, harmonisation of legal systems, and cultural harmonisation across its membership. To this end, since its inception, the COE has promulgated roughly 200 treaties or conventions now in effect. The COE itself is governed by the Committee of Ministers, composed of the Foreign Ministers of the 46 member States or their designates. While this is the body with the prime decision-making authority for the COE, there is also a Parliamentary Assembly composed of delegates from the legislatures of the member States, and assemblies for local and regional authorities. The COE is given administrative support by a secretariat, currently numbering approximately 1,800 staff.

The ECHR was signed in Rome on 4 November 1950, and came into effect on 3 September 1953. As of January 2006, it has been extended by fourteen protocols. While all member States of the Council of Europe have acceded to the initial Convention, not all members have done so for all protocols. A complete list of accessions for the protocols can be found at the Court's web site, http://www.echr.coe.int, and at the end of Appendix I, below.

The processes of taking a case to the ECtHR will be discussed in some detail near the end of this book. At this time, however, it may be helpful to summarise some basic

---

[42] See further chapter 6 below.
[43] The Vatican has observer status at the Council of Europe. A full list of Member States may be found at http://www.coe.int.

structural issues. Each member of the COE nominates one judge. While the Judges of the ECtHR are elected by the Parliamentary Assembly for a fixed term, the Court is otherwise independent of the political bodies of the COE. The Court is governed by Rules of Court, and is supported by a Registry.

Any person who believes his or her rights under the ECHR have been violated by a signatory State to the ECHR may apply to the Court for a remedy, so long as all domestic remedies for the breach have been exhausted. The Court's processes changed considerably on 1 November 1998. Formerly, an initial decision regarding admissibility would be made by the European Commission of Human Rights, a body that had jurisdiction to examine the facts of the case. In the event that the Commission considered a case to be admissible, that is, within the jurisdiction of the Court and sufficiently strong as to present a reasonable prospect of success, it would provide reasons both as to why it was of that view, and of the overall merits of the case. The Court was not bound by the Commission's findings of fact but it did normally accept these factual assessments absent cogent reason to do otherwise. Nor, of course, did the Commission's assessment of the merits and proposed disposition of the case bind the Court, and here the Court did depart fairly often from the Commission view. Cases pre-dating the 1998 changes in process should be read with the distinction between the Court and the Commission in mind. Commission decisions were published and form a part of the ECHR jurisprudence; they are however not as persuasive as decisions and judgments of the Court itself.

The Commission was abolished in 1998. Now, if an initial consideration of the material submitted by an individual applicant[44] indicates that the application is inadmissible, it is sent immediately to a committee of three judges of the Court. If those three judges find unanimously that the case is not admissible, then the case proceeds no further. If the initial consideration suggests that the case has some merit, then a single judge of the Court is allocated to investigate the case as 'Judge Rapporteur'. He or she will normally report to a Chamber of the Court, a panel of seven judges. After receiving the observations of the respondent Government, the Judge Rapporteur will provide a view to the Chamber both as to the facts, and the admissibility of the case. If requested to do so by the Chamber, he of she will also provide a provisional view as to the merits of the case at this stage. Otherwise, such a view of the merits will be presented following a decision that the case is admissible – that, is, once it is determined that there is a case for the respondent government to answer. Usually, this entire process is based on the application and subsequent investigations by the Judge Rapporteur: there is generally no oral hearing.

In the event that the case raises a particularly serious question of interpretation might have a result inconsistent with a judgment previously delivered by the Court,[45] the Chamber may prior to reaching a decision on the merits relinquish jurisdiction to the

---

[44] Applications may also be made by one State against another. The procedures for such applications are slightly different.
[45] ECtHR Rules of Court, Rule 72.

Grand Chamber of the Court. The Grand Chamber sits as a panel of seventeen judges of the Court. As one would expect, its decisions carry more persuasive weight than decisions of the regular Chambers.

If the case is held inadmissible by the committe or by the Chamber, the matter ends. A judgment of the Chamber on the merits, however, may be referred to the Grand Chamber within three months of the date of the decision. Applications for such referrals are heard by a panel of five judges.

The decisions of the Court are published in English, French or both. Most are most readily accessible through the Court's web site, http://www.echr.coe.int. Some early decisions are as yet not in the online database, although attempts are ongoing to include the backlog. In addition, major decisions are published in hard copy in the European Human Rights Reporter (EHRR), available at any good law library.

The Basics of Substance

As noted above, ECHR was signed in 1950. There can be little doubt that issues relating to mental disability were not in the minds of the framers of the Convention. The only express mention of mental disability is contained in Article 5(1)(e). This is a qualification of the right to liberty, which allows 'the lawful detention of persons for the spreading of infectious diseases, of persons of unsound mind, alcoholics or drug addicts or vagrants.' The clause on its face seems more consistent with the deprivation of civil rights than with their protection. On this basis, it is unsurprising that the court did not decide its first case on the subject until 1979.

Fortunately, the Court has taken the view that its jurisprudence is a 'living tree'. The approach of the Court is not frozen in time, but developing with a view to progressing attitudes to human rights. The Court has in recent years made considerable progress in the protection of the rights of people with mental disabilities, and as the core of this book shows, there is potential for a good deal more. While certainly not wishing to undercut that trend, a note of caution is appropriate. The 'living tree' approach goes only so far. In the end, the Court must be governed by the terms of the ECHR itself, and there will in the future no doubt be worthy cases where the language of the ECHR cannot adequately fashion a remedy.

The specific articles of the ECHR will be discussed in detail as they arise in the chapters that follow. A copy of the ECHR and relevant protocols is contained as an appendix to this book, but for newcomers to the field, it may be of assistance here to provide brief overview of the substantive articles of the Convention, and an indication as to how they may be relevant to cases involving mental disability.

Article 2 protects the right to life. Ironically, it seems to be successfully invoked almost exclusively when the victim is already dead: cases involving sufficiently substandard conditions that life is put at risk tend to be dealt with under other articles, if the victim is still alive. Article 2 is nonetheless relevant because of the requirements in its jurisprudence to investigate deaths, particularly when those deaths occur in custody or in state institutional environments. When an individual dies in a psychiatric institution, therefore, Article 2 requires a full and prompt investigation by the state into the death. The investigation must be public, and independent from those implicated in the death. The next of kin of the deceased must be able to be involved in the investigation. It must have the power to compel witnesses, and be able to apportion responsibility for the death, if that is warranted by the facts.

Article 3 protects the right to be free from torture, and from other inhuman or degrading treatment or punishment. This is one of the articles that has the potential to provide substantive standards and protections relating to mental health care. As with many of the articles of the ECHR, the acts or omissions complained of must reach a particular level of severity to engage the article. It has been held that for persons who are detained for punishment, this minimum threshold will be reached when more force is used than intrinsically necessary to achieve the purposes of the detention. It is certainly at least arguable that no higher threshold can apply to people in psychiatric facilities, who are after all not detained for punishment. While some use of force may be necessary, for example to protect people in institutions from violence from each other, any indication of violence beyond what is clearly necessary in institutions should be taken to engage Article 3. More problematic are questions of whether Article 3 is engaged by enforced treatment of people without their consent, and at what point physical conditions in institutions are sufficiently poor as to trigger Article 3. We argue below that the Article potentially applies to these situations, but there is as yet no case law providing clear indications of the scope of that application.

Most of the ECHR litigation relating to mental disability has flowed from Article 5, the right to liberty. As noted above, this article expressly allows the lawful confinement of 'persons of unsound mind'. The key case in this area is *Winterwerp v. the Netherlands*,[46] the first case on mental disability heard by the ECtHR. *Winterwerp* lays out a variety of procedural safeguards that must be followed, if the detention is to be allowed under Article 5. The detention must be justified by reasonably clear domestic law. The person detained must have prompt access to a court or similar tribunal to challenge the validity of the detention, and the opportunity to be heard at that hearing and to be represented by counsel. The further articulation of these procedural rights has been central to the development of the Court's mental health jurisprudence since that time. Sadly, *Winterwerp* has been less successful at imposing substantive standards upon detention. It does require that there be a mental disorder, established by objective medical evidence, that is of a 'kind or degree warranting compulsory confinement',[47] but there has been little subsequent litigation to determine precisely what that means. It is now clear that detention of a person with a mental disability must be in a therapeutic environment.[48]

---

[46]   *Winterwerp v. the Netherlands, op. cit.*
[47]   *Winterwerp v. the Netherlands, op. cit.*, para. 39.
[48]   *Aerts v. Belgium, op. cit.*, para. 46.

Also relevant to Article 5 is the meaning of detention when an individual lacks the capacity to make decisions regarding admission. In *H.L. v. the United Kingdom*,[49] the Court held that a person with severe autism who was not able to decide on the issue was detained in a situation where he made no move to leave, but where he would not have been allowed to leave had he wished to do so. This raises interesting and complex questions about the line between informal and involuntary status.

Article 4 prohibits slavery and forced labour. Such forced labour is permitted, however, if it is 'in the ordinary course of detention imposed according to the provisions of Article 5'. The key issues here therefore involve the dividing line between entirely legitimate and therapeutic programmes and exploitative labour for people detained in psychiatric facilities, and if the latter, whether it is in the 'ordinary course of detention'. There is as yet no helpful case law as to how these issues are to be determined.

Article 6 provides the right to a 'fair and public hearing' by an independent and impartial tribunal in determining an individual's civil rights and obligations. This article does not generally affect decisions regarding psychiatric detention: those are dealt with under Article 5. It is very important in other contexts, however, providing safeguards against arbitrary deprivation of legal capacity, and for people who are to be subject to guardianship régimes with the right to challenge a finding of incapacity, or restrictions on other civil rights such as the right to consent to medical treatment. Even more than other ECHR rights, however, this is a process right. It provides a right to a hearing, but no substantive rights as to what law is applied at that hearing.

Article 8 states that everyone has the right to respect for his or her private life, family, home and correspondence. The scope of this article is exceptionally broad. For example, it is engaged by any involuntary medical treatment,[50] and by the decisions removing legal capacity from individuals.[51] It provides a right to correspondence with loved ones. It provides rights to view medical records. The rights it provides are not however absolute. The second paragraph of Article 8 states:

> There shall be no interference by a public authority with the exercise of this right except such as is in accordance with the law and is necessary in a democratic society in the interests of national security, public safety or the economic well-being of the country, for the prevention of disorder or crime, for the protection of health or morals, or for the protection of the rights and freedoms of others.[52]

While this exception is broad, it is not infinitely expansive. First, any violation of an Article 8 right must be in accordance with domestic law: there must be a clear domestic legal standard that applies. Second, there must be a demonstrable connection between

---

[49] *H.L. v. the United Kingdom*, Application No. 45508/99, judgment 5 October 2004, (2005) 40 EHRR 32.
[50] *Y.F. v. Turkey*, Application No. 24209/94, judgment 22 July 2003, (2004) 39 EHRR 34, para. 33.
[51] *H.F. c. Slovaquie*, Application No. 54797/00, judgment 8 Nov 05, para. 47. The Court did not examine the application of Article 8 in detail, and did not consider the scope and effect of Article 8(2) at all in that case.
[52] Article 8(2).

the prima facie infringement of Article 8 and the ground relied upon under Article 8(2). Finally, the infringement of the Article 8 interest must be necessary in a democratic society, and proportionate to the benefit achieved.

Articles 9, 10, and 11 of the ECHR protect respectively freedom of thought, conscience and religion; freedom of expression; and freedom of assembly and association. These apply, of course, as much to people with mental disabilities as to anyone else. An individual in a psychiatric or related facility would, for example, have the right to practice his or her religion under Article 9, and to receive newspapers under Article 10.

Article 12 protects the right to marry and found a family, consistent with national laws governing the exercise of that right. People with mental disabilities therefore have the right to marry. The right to found a family further suggests a particular restriction on sterilisation of people with mental disorders. This is consistent with a number of international instruments that provide that sterilisation should never be a treatment for mental disorder.[53] The Article also prevents an assumption that people with mental disabilities are not worthy to become parents.

Article 14 requires that the other articles in the ECHR be interpreted in a way that is non-discriminatory. While the Article does not preclude discrimination on the basis of disability (or mental disability) specifically, the article quite specifically does not close the list of prohibited grounds, and it is likely that the Court would read it in by implication. Article 14 is not a free-standing right to non-discriminatory treatment, however.[54] It is instead a guarantee that the Convention rights will be interpreted in a non-discriminatory fashion. This considerably reduces the usefulness of the Article. The Court has tended in the past either to find a violation of a convention right without reference to Article 14, or to say that as there is no violation of the other convention right, Article 14 has nothing to add.

The ECHR also has thirteen protocols, which extend the rights in the main Convention. Protocol 1, Article 2 contains a right to education. While this is certainly an important right for people with mental disabilities, we argue that it is an exceptionally weakly worded right as it appears in Protocol 1.[55] Protocol 12 is potentially much more significant, as it creates a free-standing right to be free of discriminatory treatment. This is markedly broader than the non-discriminatory guarantee in Article 14, since the Article 14 guarantee applies only to rights under the Convention. The Protocol 12 right applies to the whole body of the State's domestic law. Like Article 14, it does not specifically preclude discrimination on the basis of disability, but it seems likely that it will be included by implication. Protocol 12 was only signed in November 2000, and the Court has not yet had occasion to interpret it. Potentially, it constitutes an important step forward for the rights of people with mental disabilities.

---

[53] Council of Europe Recommendations, Article 30; UN Mental Illness Principles, principle 11.13.
[54] Such a free-standing right would be introduced by Protocol 12.
[55] See further chapter 7 below.

In all this, the respondent in ECHR litigation is a State, not a private individual, and the articles of the ECHR directly bind only States, not private persons. That said, Article 1 obliges the States to 'secure to everyone within their jurisdiction the rights and freedoms . . . of this Convention', and Article 13 provides people whose rights have been infringed the right to 'an effective remedy before a national authority'. This so-called 'doctrine of horizontal effect' means that States cannot simply turn a blind eye to alleged violations of Convention rights by private persons in their jurisdictions. The use of the police and criminal justice systems to investigate and prosecute alleged violations of rights is the most obvious way that States satisfy this obligation. They are not necessarily the only way, however. As discussed above, people with mental disabilities are diverse. Some will have the capacity and desire to press for their rights, and for them a system such as the criminal justice system that is instigated by the complaint of an affected person may be suitable. Others will lack that capacity, or may be in such a vulnerable position in an institution that the pursuit of a complaint is not practically possible. For them, a process that commences only upon the receipt of a complaint is not helpful. While the Court has not examined the issue from this perspective, it is at least arguable that with those people in mind, other processes such as routine investigation of facilities by independent agencies may be required.

The ECHR and Domestic Law

While the applicant is required to exhaust all domestic remedies prior to commencing an ECHR application, an application to the ECtHR is not an appeal in the usual sense. The other party in the domestic action is unlikely to be the State itself, but rather for example a specific person, institution, health or social services authority or government department. At issue in the domestic action may well be the alleged violation of Convention rights, but there may also be a range of issues under domestic law that require adjudication. It may be difficult to frame ECHR rights clearly in domestic law, particularly when the judge is unfamiliar with the ECHR. In the ECHR action, the respondent is the State itself, and the complaint is instead that the State has failed adequately to protect the applicant's rights under the Convention. That is the only question before the court: in particular, the correctness of the domestic court in its interpretation of purely domestic law is not an issue before the ECtHR.

The ECtHR generally follows the findings of fact made by domestic courts, but it is not formally bound by them. The Court will substitute its own findings of fact when it considers the domestic version to be unconvincing or incomplete.[56] To that end, the Court may request further factual information from the parties. Further, and significantly, when an injury occurs during a period of detention, the ECtHR requires the State

---

[56] See, for example, *Ribitsch v. Austria*, Application No. 18896/91, judgment 21 November 1995, (1995) 21 EHRR 573, para. 33.

to provide a plausible explanation for those injuries.[57] Any failure of the State to provide evidence it possesses relevant to such injuries creates an inference in favour of the applicant.[58] That said, the deference shown by the ECtHR to domestic courts is real. It would for example be highly unusual for the ECtHR to question the domestic court's view of an individual's psychiatric diagnosis, assuming the domestic court had relied on evidence of a suitably qualified medical expert.

While States are required to meet the standards established by the ECHR, the ECtHR allows them considerable latitude (a wide 'margin of appreciation') as to how they do so. For example, *Winterwerp* requires that a detention under Article 5 may occur only if the individual is affected by a mental disability of a 'kind or degree warranting compulsory confinement'.[59] Assuming this threshold is defined with sufficient clarity under domestic law, the ECtHR is unlikely to be perturbed by the particular terms of the definition.

While the ECtHR does not review domestic law except as it impacts directly on ECtHR rights, most COE countries do allow their domestic courts to take into account ECtHR jurisprudence, and allow the ECHR to be pleaded at the domestic level. Justice in these domestic courts may be considerably more expedient and less expensive than at Strasbourg, particularly as the complainants will have to exhaust all remedies in these domestic courts prior to launching their ECtHR applications in any event. Further, the remedy achieved domestically may be preferable. If the objective is a change in the domestic legal régime, for example, a successful case before a domestic Constitutional Court may carry more weight than a decision of the ECtHR, as the former may be directly enforceable where latter may require government implementation. There is further no restriction on domestic courts adopting a standard more protective of human rights than that contained in existing ECtHR case law, when that standard is either implied in domestic law or, in the view of the domestic court, implied in the ECHR itself. The ECHR and the decisions of the ECtHR are in this respect a floor, not a ceiling.

Particular mention should also be made to the interface between ECHR law and the law of the European Union (EU). All member States of the EU are also member States of the COE, and the European Court of Justice, the final arbiter of EU law, takes account of ECtHR jurisprudence in its deliberations.[60] Further, decisions of the European Court of Justice have direct effect, so successful litigation there will have an immediate impact on domestic law and practice. Health care per se (apart from "public health")[61] is not within EU competencies, but nonetheless the EU is moving into that area as a question of provision of services.[62] Further, since the Treaty of Amsterdam, the EU has

---

[57] See, e.g., *Selmouni v. France*, Application No. 25803/94, judgment 28 July 1999, (2000) 29 EHRR 403, para. 87; *Aksoy v. Turkey*, Application No. 21987/93, judgment 26 November 1996, (1996) 23 EHRR 553, para. 61; *Ribitsch v. Austria, op. cit.*, para. 34.

[58] *Nevmerzhitsky v. Ukraine*, Application No. 54825/00, judgement 12 October 2005, para. 75.

[59] *Winterwerp v. the Netherlands, op. cit.*, para. 39.

[60] See, e.g., *Johnston v. Chief Constable of the RUC* [1986] ECR 1651 at 1682.

[61] See EC Treaty, Article 152.

[62] See T. Hervey and J. McHale, *Health Law and the European Union* (Cambridge: Cambridge University Press, 2004).

adopted a policy of non-discrimination based on disability in the interpretation of its core documents and the provision of its services. In the event that a case could fall either under ECtHR or European Court of Justice jurisdiction, there may be cogent reasons for considering the latter.

The ECHR and the Human Rights Context

As noted above, the first mental disability case before the ECHR was decided in 1979. The Convention was not drafted with the rights of people with mental disabilities foremost in the minds of its framers. Instead, the Convention rights have developed, consistent with developing concepts of human rights internationally. As such, the Convention does not exist in a vacuum. While the duty of the ECtHR is to interpret the Convention, other more recent human rights instruments and reports serve as aids to that interpretation in appropriate circumstances. For cases regarding mental disability, an abundance of such documentation has been forthcoming, as disability rights has established itself as a field over the last few decades. The ECHR is a product of the COE, and other COE sources relating to mental disability and human rights are as a result likely to be particularly persuasive. United Nations resolutions and World Health Organization recommendations and studies also serve as important indicators of the broad direction of human rights theory regarding issues of mental disability, although they are likely to be less persuasive than COE documents as they are not specific to the region.

The Committee for the Prevention of Torture and Inhuman or Degrading Treatment or Punishment

The standards and published reports of visits by the European Committee for the Prevention of Torture and Inhuman or Degrading Treatment or Punishment (CPT) are particularly persuasive. The CPT is a COE entity, established by Convention in 1987.[63] It is administratively entirely separate from the ECtHR. Its mandate is 'by means of visits, [to] examine the treatment of persons deprived of their liberty with a view to strengthening, if necessary, the protection of such persons from torture and from inhuman or degrading treatment or punishment.'[64] The reference to torture and inhuman or degrading treatment or punishment is drawn verbatim from the wording of Article 3 of the ECHR. Because of this close connection with Article 3, it is unsurprising that the Court refers routinely to CPT reports, when they are relevant to cases before it.[65]

---

[63] The European Convention for the Prevention of Torture and Inhuman or Degrading Treatment or Punishment (1987).
[64] European Convention for the Prevention of Torture and Inhuman or Degrading Treatment or Punishment (1987), art. 1.
[65] See, for example, *Peers v. Greece*, Application No. 28524/95, judgment 19 April 2001, (2001) 33 EHRR 51 on prison conditions and *Dougoz v. Greece*, Application No. 40907/98, judgment 6 March 2001, 34

Each Party to the Convention has the right to have one member in the CPT, elected by the COE Committee of Ministers. Members tend to have long-established records in human rights or related work. The membership of the CPT usually includes some physicians and psychiatrists. This is significant for the credibility of its work in the psychiatric field; the CPT cannot be viewed as a body alien or hostile to psychiatric institutions per se. The CPT's role is to visit places where people are deprived of their liberty by a public authority, and to report to the State on its findings. 'Periodic' visits generally last between one and two weeks, with a number of institutions visited in that period. The CPT also has jurisdiction to make visits 'required by the circumstances' (ad hoc or follow-up visits), when it receives information as to the existence of particularly severe circumstances within its mandate. In the event that individuals encounter specific institutions that warrant a CPT visit, either as part of a periodic visit or on an ad hoc basis, they may notify the CPT. In the event that an advocate's concern is inhuman or degrading standards overall in an institution, such a notification, if it results in a visit and critical mention by the CPT, may force improvements.

If a State consents to the publication of the visit reports, these reports (as well as the State responses) are published on the CPT web site.[66] Some States agree to publication almost immediately, but others delay, sometimes for several years. The CPT publishes at the end of each year the countries that will be visited in the following year.

The CPT's mandate covers any place within a State's jurisdiction where persons are deprived of their liberty by a public authority. This includes people in psychiatric facilities, and the CPT has been routinely visiting such establishments since its inception. The CPT also started to visit social care homes in 1997[67] and, since 2000,[68] it also visits homes for the elderly. Its concerns include physical standards of institutions, the intrusiveness of rules in the institution, any violence or use of force in those institutions be it between staff and residents or between residents, and any other circumstance that could be considered inhuman or degrading. Its interest is not merely in these actual situations, however, but also in the administrative and cultural environments that allow these situations to fester. Its reports press for routine inspections of institutions by independent authorities, for example, and appropriate mechanisms for complaints to be registered by residents and investigated. Similarly, it considers whether appropriate safeguards for wrongful detention are in place. Its role is not to comment on the entire ECHR, however. While its approach is no doubt informed by the Convention as a whole as well as other factors, its mandate is specific to preventing violations of Article 3, and strengthening safeguards against such violations for those subject to deprivation of liberty.

EHRR 61 concerning conditions in a police headquarters; *Aerts v. Belgium, op. cit.*, concerning conditions in the psychiatric wing of a prison.

[66] http://www.cpt.coe.int.

[67] The first visit to a social care home was carried out in Estonia CPT/Inf (2002) 26 (visit of July 1997), paras. 163–174, and the second in Bulgaria, CPT/Inf (2002) 1 (visit of April to May 1999) paras. 167–191.

[68] The first visit to such a institution was in Germany (see CPT/Inf (2003) 20).

The CPT has published a set of institutional standards, which are updated periodically.[69] These include a section on involuntary placement in psychiatric establishments.[70] These articulate the CPT's expectations regarding living conditions in institutions; scope and availability of treatment; consent to treatment; staffing; restraint and seclusion; and procedural safeguards at admission, during detention, and at discharge. The CPT is not the ECtHR, and its views both in its published standards and its reports are in no way binding on the Court. Nonetheless, these views provide a considered and informed assessment of rights in these institutions in the context of the COE and ECHR. Its views are therefore extremely relevant.

Other Council of Europe Instruments

While the CPT has the most firmly established presence in the jurisprudence of the Court, more recent recommendations of the COE Council of Ministers also speak directly to the rights of people with mental disabilities. These texts are only recommendations to member States: they are not in themselves directly enforceable before the ECtHR or any other judicial body. Nonetheless, they represent the agreed view of the COE's primary decision-making body, and therefore serve as a good indicator of accepted best practice in COE countries.

Two sets of recommendations are of particular relevance. The first is the Recommendation on Principles Concerning the Legal Protection of Incapable Adults.[71] This recommendation extols States both to establish suitable régimes for the protection of people who lack capacity, and also to protect their human rights. Consistent with the trends in disability rights for many years, it proposes that people should be as involved as reasonably possible in the decisions that affect their lives, and that views of the individual should be taken into account even if that person lacks legal capacity.[72] In particular, it protects the individual's right of consent to treatment, if that individual has capacity to make that decision, even if they are under a general guardianship régime.[73] It proposes formal hearings in the event of objection to the use of formal guardianship powers, and specifically requires that the range of people who can apply for such hearings must be broad enough to ensure that the domestic court considers all necessary cases.[74] Hearings would be subject to due process requirements. It is in this last respect that it was relied upon by the ECtHR in *H.F. v. Slovakia* to support a decision that the guardianship hearing in question in that case did not meet the procedural requirements of Article 6.[75]

---

[69] *The CPT Standards*, CPT/Inf/E (2002) 1, available on their web site.
[70] CPT/Inf/E (2002) 1, pp. 52–62. These were originally published as part of the CPT's 8th General Report, CPT/Inf (98) 12.
[71] Recommendation R (99)4, adopted 23 February 1999.
[72] See, for example, Principle 9.
[73] Principles 22 and 23.
[74] Principle 11.
[75] *H.F. c. Slovaquie*, Application No. 54797/00, judgment 8 Nov 2005, para. 39.

More recently, the Council of Ministers has issued the Recommendation concerning the Human Rights and Dignity of Persons with Mental Disorder.[76] This is a more extensive recommendation, covering service provision and standards, specific rights for persons affected by mental disorder, staffing of facilities, the substantive and procedural requirements for detention and for compulsory treatment, seclusion and restraint, persons with mental disorders in the criminal justice system, and systems for the monitoring of quality. It provides a detailed set of indicators as to what constitutes best practice in these areas. While it has not yet been cited by the Court, there can be little doubt that it will be, in cases where it is relevant.

Also relevant is the COE's Convention for the Protection of Human Rights and Dignity of the Human Being with regard to the Application of Biology and Medicine.[77] While negotiated under the auspices of the COE, it is a convention rather than a recommendation. It therefore has more gravitas than the Council of Ministers' recommendations in countries where it has been signed and ratified, but no formal legal effect in countries that have not done so. The Convention is colloquially known as the Convention on Bioethics, or the Orviedo Convention. The former is in a sense a misnomer, since its substance is considerably broader than that name implies. It provides some protections to individuals' right to consent to treatment, although not necessarily as strong a right as that contained in the Council of Ministers' Recommendations.[78] It does deal with a number of circumstances not expressly considered by those recommendations, however. Standards are provided for consent to organ removal, and when this may be done on a patient who lacks capacity to consent. It also, importantly, has a set of rules determining when research may be carried out on people who are unable to consent.[79] These are supplemented by the related Protocol concerning Biomedical Research.[80]

In April 2006, the Committee of Ministers issued its 'Action Plan to promote the rights and full participation of people with disabilities in society'.[81] This is an agenda for action for 2006 to 2015, designed to induce practical advances in the integration of people with disabilities into the broader community. It addresses a wide variety of issues, from involvement in political, public and cultural life to public transport, to protection from violence and abuse. While its suggestions are valuable, and will be discussed in some detail below in chapter 7, it creates a plan for action, not an enforceable set of rights.

---

[76] Rec (2004) 10, adopted 22 September 2004. The United Kingdom alone among COE member states has thus far not agreed to be bound by the terms of this recommendation.

[77] European Treaty Series no. 164, concluded 4 April 1997.

[78] Convention on Bioethics, Articles 5, 6, 7, 17, 20.

[79] Convention on Bioethics, Articles 17 and 20.

[80] Strasbourg, 25 January 2005, ETS 195. This protocol is not yet formally in force, although it may nonetheless serve as a guide for the CPT and for the jurisprudence of the ECtHR.

[81] Rec (2006) 5.

United Nations Instruments

While the reports, recommendations, conventions and other documents of the COE will be particularly relevant in interpreting the scope of ECHR rights as they apply to mental disability, United Nations documentation may also be of assistance. Of particular relevance is the General Assembly resolution on the Principles for the Protection of Persons with Mental Illness.[82] These have a broadly similar scope to the COE Mental Disorder Recommendations, although the documents differ in some of their specifics. The World Health Organization, the UN's specialist health body, has also recently published a resource book on mental health, human rights and legislation, *Stop Exclusion, Dare to Care*.[83] This is less a book purporting to establish standards than a guide to legislative formulation and drafting in the mental health realm. Nonetheless, it contains a good introduction to issues relating to law and mental health, and discussions of a good range of legislative issues.

As we go to press, negotiations are well advanced at the United Nations toward agreement of the text of the International Convention on Protection and Promotion of the Rights of Persons with Disabilities. It seems possible that this will be agreed about the time this book is published, in the autumn of 2006. The draft text currently in circulation[84] contains language which, if adopted, could introduce a significantly different era of disability rights. The definition of disability does not appear to have been finally determined, but assuming it includes mental disability, the landscape of mental disability law will be expected to alter considerably. Article 15(1)(b), for example, would preclude any deprivation of liberty based on disability. Article 17 would specifically preclude enforced institutionalisation intended to correct, improve or alleviate any disability. These articles would apparently prohibit civil detention of people based on mental disability. Article 12 would recognise the legal capacity of people with disabilities, and would require any restriction of that status to be strictly proportional to the degree of support required. This would make many guardianship régimes vulnerable to criticism. Like other United Nations documents, it does not formally bind the ECtHR, and it contains no formal enforcement provisions among its articles. Nonetheless, it would serve as a part of the overall context of human rights in which the ECtHR would exercise its judgment.

---

[82] General Assembly Resolution 46/119, 17 December 1991.
[83] Geneva: WHO, 2005. This publication is available electronically at http://www.euro.who.int/document/E72161.pdf.
[84] The draft is available electronically at http://www.un.org/esa/socdev/enable/rights/ahc7ann2rep.htm. (Accessed: 19 April 2006).

The Potential to Make a Difference

This chapter began with the claim that mental disability had come of age as a subject of concern under the ECHR. So it has; but it would be wrong to suggest the subject has yet reached its full potential. If the challenge of the last quarter century has been to place mental disability squarely in the ECHR framework, the challenge of the next must be continue to breathe life into the Convention provisions as they apply to this client group, and to press for full implementation of the standards that are won through litigation and political advances. This issue of implementation should not be taken for granted. Notwithstanding the victories of applicants under Article 3, there is no shortage of work for the CPT. Notwithstanding the decision in *Winterwerp* more than a quarter of a century ago, reports continue to appear from some COE countries suggesting a failure to meet even basic procedural safeguards. The issues here are of basic human dignity: the right to ensure that the deprivation of one's liberty is consistent with the standards of human rights; and, if one must be detained, the right to be placed in an institution that incorporates physical safety with at least adequate therapeutic and recreational programmes and the right to ongoing contact with the outside world.

The rights already established under the ECHR are but a starting point. As the subsequent chapters of this book show, much is yet to be done. The chapters that follow provide an account of where the law stands and speculation as to how it may develop, but as befits a relatively new field of jurisprudence, much is yet to be determined. The Court has so far shown a willingness to engage with procedural rights, but it is less clear how far it will be prepared to impose substantive standards into rights and the provision of care. The Court's jurisprudence to this point has tended to deal with applicants who have the ability and the motivation to litigate; with the Court's decision in *H.L. v. the United Kingdom*, it has made it clear that people who lack basic capacity are still to receive the benefits of ECHR protection, but it is not yet clear what that will mean if a such a person does not have the basic ability to litigate. In some relatively early case law, the ECtHR relied on medical professionalism as a substantive boundary for ECHR rights; how far will the Court go in allowing thresholds of human rights to be determined by medical discretion? The potential of the Court to make a massive difference in the lives of traditionally marginalised individuals of society is tremendous. It has taken important first steps in this direction; it remains to be seen how it will continue.

This is not the job of the court or indeed the ECHR alone. Meaningful rights happen when litigation is combined with political progress. The political discourse of the disability rights movement in the last decades has been uniformly to greater involvement of users of psychiatric and related services in the decisions related to them, both at the individual level and the political level. Litigation, like other tools to prompt reform, must acknowledge that political shift.

The chapters that follow fall into two divisions. The next six chapters concern substantive aspects of Convention rights. The first concerns issues of detention in institutions, including both substantive and procedural safeguards against inappropriate admission. The next chapter concerns conditions within institutions, including physical standards and overzealous regulation. Chapter four concerns the provision of medical treatment for mental disorder. It asks both how far the ECHR can be used to ensure specific standards of treatment, and how far it can be used to restrict the enforced provision of unwanted treatment. Death in institutions raises specific issues, and these are discussed in chapter five. Chapter six tackles the problems associated with guardianship. The issues here involve how individuals should be protected to ensure that they keep decision-making authority in areas where they continue to have it, while making sufficient structures of care available in areas where they do not. The chapter covers both the assessment of capacity and the appointment of a guardian. Chapter seven looks at the rights of people with disabilities in the community, including rights to education, rights to property, rights to marry, to vote, and to associate.

The final two chapters move to discuss the practicalities of litigation. In chapter seven, the concern is with the nature of the ECHR procedures, and how they apply to the particular circumstances of cases involving mental disability. In chapter eight issues surrounding the representation of a client with mental disabilities are discussed.

A number of appendices are contained at the end of this book. They primarily are the copies of the primary international legal materials of relevance to mental disability rights under the ECHR, including the Convention itself, and the relevant recommendations, and principles from the Council of Europe. In the course of writing this book, however, we became aware that there was little written for a European audience that provided practical guidance to lawyers as to the mechanics of representing people with mental disabilities. With that lacuna in mind, there is also an appendix providing, in step-by-step terms, advice on how to represent such a client.

Chapter 2

Admission to and Discharge from Psychiatric and Related Institutions

Introduction and overview

This chapter analyses admission to and discharge (release) from psychiatric institutions. It is principally concerned with the terms of Article 5 of the European Convention on Human Rights and its associated case law. This is the area that has attracted the most cases taken to the European Court relating to mental disability. While there are certainly many areas remaining to be litigated, it is possible in this area more than most others discussed in this book to describe an established jurisprudence, particularly in relation to the procedural requirements for deprivation of liberty.

Article 5 is 'designed to ensure that no one should be arbitrarily dispossessed of his liberty'.[1] It is the only Article in the Convention that refers explicitly to mental health, by including the now-derogatory term 'persons of unsound mind' in Article 5(1)(e). Such persons can be deprived of their liberty, but subject to the conditions and criteria that the European Court of Human Rights has evolved in its case law. It is of particular significance that persons to whom Article 5(1) applies have the right of access to a court

---

[1] *Schiesser v. Switzerland*, Application No. 7710/76, judgment 4 December 1979, (1979) 2 EHRR 417 at 425.

to challenge the lawfulness of their detention. In the event that the Article is not complied with, there is also express provision for compensation for the violation.

Article 5 is not concerned with degrees of deprivation of liberty. If a person is already detained, additional seclusion would fall outside considerations of Article 5, although it might raise issues under Article 3.[2] However, where someone is in a hospital voluntarily and is secluded, the seclusion would be evidence of detention and therefore Article 5 would be engaged.

The approach adopted by the European Court of Human Rights in Article 5 cases allows countries considerable flexibility in defining the criteria and procedure for involuntary entry into institutions. The Court has construed the words 'unsound mind' very broadly, and so countries have considerable freedom to choose for themselves how they structure their substantive criteria for detention.

The European Court of Human Rights has been far stricter when interpreting the more specific requirements in Article 5(4) that a detained person must be able to apply to a court to test the lawfulness of detention, and that the court must decide on it 'speedily'. There is extensive case law on this provision, dealing with time requirements, legal representation, the fairness of the proceedings, the disclosure of information and the powers that the domestic court must have. The European Court of Human Rights has had no hesitation in finding a violation of Article 5(4) even when it has been satisfied that an applicant has been lawfully detained under Article 5(1)(e). As it explained in the early case of *De Wilde, Ooms and Versyp v. Belgium* in relation to Article 5(4):

> the latter is, in effect, a separate provision, and its observance does not result eo ipso from the observance of the former: "everyone who is deprived of his liberty", lawfully or not, is entitled to a supervision of lawfulness by a court; a violation can therefore result either from a detention incompatible with paragraph (1) (art. 5–1) or from the absence of any proceedings satisfying paragraph (4) (art. 5–4), or even from both at the same time.[3]

This chapter falls into three broad sections. The first concerns the threshold criteria for the engagement of Article 5, and in particular what it means to be 'deprived' of liberty. The second concerns the scope, effect and requirements of Article 5(1)(e), which permits the 'lawful detention of . . . persons of unsound mind'. The third concerns challenges to detention, and particularly the exercise of the right to a hearing under Article 5(4).

---

[2]   See further chapter 3 below.
[3]   *De Wilde, Ooms and Versyp v. Belgium*, Application No. 2832/66; 2835/66; 2899/66, judgment of 18 June 1971, (1972) 1 EHRR 438, para. 73.

'Deprivation of Liberty'

Article 5(1) commences by stating:

> Everyone has the right to liberty and security of person. No one shall be deprived of his liberty save in the following cases and in accordance with a procedure prescribed by law.

Article 5 is engaged only if an individual has been deprived of his or her liberty. This requirement may or may not be met when an individual is admitted to a psychiatric institution. In many parts of Europe, people enter psychiatric and related institutions on a voluntary basis, without the use legal compulsion. In such circumstances, entry to a psychiatric hospital is similar to a person being admitted to a hospital for non-psychiatric matters. The individual may choose to enter, and there may be few practical restrictions other than those necessary for the management of any institutional structure. In particular, the individual may enjoy considerable freedom of movement both inside and outside the institution, and considerable freedom to receive whatever visitors he or she chooses. When this is the individual's situation and the individual is in a position to enjoy those conditions, it is difficult to see that there has been a deprivation of liberty, and Article 5 would therefore not apply.

In practice, however, psychiatric admissions are not necessarily so simple. The academic literature relating to these individuals suggests that roughly half of persons admitted without formal legal compulsion nonetheless feel coerced during the course of the admission and afterwards.[4] This compulsion can be in a variety of forms, including the threat of legal coercion or physical force if the individual does not 'consent' to the admission, or the removal by carers of services necessary to make viable options other than admission. The admission may be the result of the consent of a guardian and be actively opposed by the individual himself or herself. In other cases, it may be that the individual does not have the intellectual capacity to make the decision as to whether or not to consent to the admission.

Admissions without resort to formal legal confinement powers are often referred to as 'voluntary' admissions, but this term may often be misleading, insofar as it suggests the exercise of a free choice by the person admitted. In recognition of the complexity of this situation, this book adopts the more neutral term 'informal admissions' to cover all admissions where formal legal detention is not present.

In some jurisdictions and some institutions, it is the practice to require persons informally admitted to sign a form applying for the admission, or indicating that the

---

[4]   The pioneering study on this question is J. Gilboy and J. Schmidt, '"Voluntary" hospitalization of the mentally ill', 66 *Northwestern Law Review* (1971) 429. For more recent studies, see, eg., J. Monahan, S. Hoge, C. Lidz, L. Roth, N. Bennett, W. Gardner and E. Mulvey, 'Coercion and Commitment: Understanding Involuntary Mental Hospital Admission', 18(3) *International Journal of Law and Psychiatry* 249; For a more recent study of such coercion in Denmark, along with a good survey of the existing literature, see H.D. Poulsen, 'The Prevalence of Extralegal Deprivation of Liberty in a Psychiatric Hospital Population', 15 *International Journal of Law and Psychiatry* (2002) 29.

admission was indeed without coercion. This may be a desirable practice, as it creates an occasion when the legal basis of the admission is addressed and discussed with the individual. The evidential value of such forms must nonetheless be viewed with some scepticism: if the admission itself was the result of coercion, the signing of the form may similarly not reflect the individual's free consent. As would be the appropriate approach in the absence of such a form, it is appropriate to look to the collection of circumstances surrounding these admissions to determine whether compulsion is in fact involved.

What Article 5 of the ECHR means when it refers to an individual 'deprived of his [or her] liberty' is thus a matter of some importance. It does not follow that only those subject to formal statutory controls are within its scope. It is an autonomous concept under the Convention, that is, whether a measure is defined as detention under national law is not the decisive factor in deciding on whether a person's Convention rights have been violated. The European Court of Human Rights clarified the meaning of detention in the case of *Guzzardi v. Italy*:

> In order to determine whether someone has been "deprived of his liberty" within the meaning of Article 5, the starting point must be his concrete situation and account must be taken of a whole range of criteria such as the type, duration, effects and manner of implementation of the measure in question.[5]

The phrase must be considered in the context of the qualified right to liberty of movement in Article 2 of Protocol 4 to the ECHR, and the qualified right to respect for family and private life Article 8 of the ECHR. There are boundary lines to be drawn between these different Convention guarantees. In *Ashingdane v. the United Kingdom* the ECtHR said:

> According to the established case law of the Court, Article 5(1)(e) is not concerned with mere restrictions on liberty of movement, which are governed by Article 2 of Protocol 4. In order to determine whether circumstances involve deprivation of liberty, the starting point must be the concrete situation of the individual concerned and account must be taken of a whole range of criteria such as the type, duration, effects and manner of implementation of the measure in question. The distinction between deprivation of and restriction upon liberty is merely one of degree, and not of one of nature or substance.[6]

Psychiatric regimes can indeed have infinite gradations of control. At one extreme people may be detained in secure hospitals with strong perimeters and close internal prison-like control. But in some countries, people who are 'detained' under national law may be allowed extensive leave of absence from a hospital, making the hospital not much more than a place to sleep at night, and sometimes not even that. Some of these 'detained' people may live in their own homes, but be required to attend therapeutic day centres, either

---

[5]   *Guzzardi v. Italy*, Application No. 7367/76, judgment 6 November 1980, (A/39), (1981) 3 EHRR 333 para. 92.
[6]   *Ashingdane v. the United Kingdom*, Application No. 8225/78, judgment 28 May 1985 (A/93) (1985) 7 EHRR 528, para. 41.

daily or periodically for the purpose, for example, of receiving medication. While still detained in hospital according to domestic law, the relationship of these people to the hospital may be little more than an entry on an administrative register. Such 'long leashes' are generally coupled with a power to enforce actual admission with minimal bureaucracy in the event that professionals consider that admission to be necessary or appropriate. In these countries, the type and extent of control applied can vary according to the needs of the case.

Mr Ashingdane was a person who had been sent to a secure hospital, from which he sought transfer to a local psychiatric hospital as a stepping-stone to release. Due to a labour dispute at the relevant local hospital his transfer there was blocked for several years. Living conditions in the local hospital would have been far more relaxed. Unlike the high security hospital, the local hospital unit was not locked, and patients were free to leave the hospital during the day. Eventually, well after launching his ECHR application, he was moved to the local hospital. For present purposes, the issue in the litigation was whether his continuation in the higher security facility during the period of the labour dispute violated his Article 5 rights.

The Court's approach to this issue establishes two related principles. First, the Court reasoned that the daytime freedom he enjoyed in the local hospital was a privilege not a right, and it could have been revoked. The ECtHR thought that the conditions there still deprived him of his liberty in the local hospital. This suggests that for people subject to formal legal compulsion in their admissions, the threshold of conditions necessary for the engagement of Article 5 is very low. Second, and as a result, for the period under dispute, he would have been detained under Article 5 no matter which facility he had been in, and as a result the Article was not breached. Article 5 allowed the individual to challenge detention; it did not allow the degree of severity of régimes to be challenged, so long as the prerequisites for detention under the Article were met.

Some domestic legal systems have provisions to compel an individual to accept treatment or other care in the community, without resort to the language of detention at all. Whether such compulsion is sufficient to constitute a deprivation of liberty under Article 5 will depend on the specifics of the order in question, but the fact that an individual is living at home does not automatically exclude the Article's application. In *Guzzardi v. Italy*, the ECtHR found that a curfew combined with a very limited range of possible geographical movement constituted Article 5 detention.[7] This case involved concerns about criminality rather than mental disability, but that should not affect the threshold for deprivation of liberty. If a person's daytime hours were largely controlled, the ECtHR may regard the case as Article 5 territory, and not just a restriction on freedom of movement.

More frequently, these 'community treatment orders' mandate psychiatric treatment in the community rather than controlling where individuals will live or how they spend

---

[7]   *Guzzardi v. Italy, op. cit.*

their time. As yet the European Court of Human Rights has not decided a case on such treatment-specific orders, and therefore it is a matter of speculation as to whether constitute a deprivation of liberty under Article 5. The usual cases in which Article 5 has been invoked have concerned physical restrictions on a person's liberty of movement, with incarceration being the most obvious example. Psychiatric medications may have properties that are relevant to this. In the event that an individual's treatment programme results in ongoing sedation rendering the individual unable to leave his or her home, for example, a coherent argument for the engagement of Article 5 could certainly be made. At the very least, however, these community treatment orders are designed to remove the individual's free choice regarding treatment: they remove the civil right of consent and intrude on a person's private life and could be examined under Article 8 (right to private life) and Article 6, which provides the right to a judicial hearing in the determination of an individual's civil rights.

The issues regarding coerced informal admissions to hospitals, social care homes, nursing homes or old people's homes are rather different. At what point do restrictions imposed in hospitals, social care homes and similar institutions cross the line between restrictions on freedom of movement and detention? The fact that the individual is accommodated on a locked unit in the institution would be a strong indicator that he or she is detained. Similarly, if managers of such institutions require residents to spend the night in the institution, and require residents to ask permission to leave during the day, the circumstances strongly suggest detention. The use of physical restraints or sedating medication to control the individual would certainly be relevant to whether Article 5 is engaged. People may lack the finances to live anywhere else, and so they may be forced to accept living in an institution, whilst enjoying a theoretical right to leave. Family and friends of the person in the institution may be prohibited from or restricted in visiting. Restrictions on access to telephones or the sending and receipt of mail would similarly suggest a deprivation of liberty. Institutions may take other probably unlawful measures such as prohibiting lawyers from entering the institution. Social care homes in many countries are in very remote locations, with the result that residents are effectively excluded from society. All these factors are likely to be relevant in determining whether a deprivation of liberty has occurred; in the years ahead it is likely that the ECtHR will have to examine these issues. Though the Court has always insisted that Article 5 is not concerned with the conditions or therapeutic regime within a hospital or other institution, in the sense that it confers no 'right to treatment', those factors can clearly be relevant to resolving whether a person is detained or not.

Particular difficulties arise when considering people who lack capacity to make admissions-related decisions, whether by reason of lifelong mental disability, degenerative disorders related to old age or other disability. This issue has recently been examined in the ECtHR's decision in *H.L. v. the United Kingdom*.[8] The applicant in that case was an adult

---

[8] *H.L. v. the United Kingdom*, Application No. 45508/99, judgment 5 October 2004, (2005) 40 EHRR 32. See also *Storck v. Germany*, Application No. 61603/00, judgment 16 June 2005, which reaches a similar result.

man diagnosed as autistic. He was unable to speak and had a limited level of under-standing. He lived with paid carers, and attended a day centre. It was agreed by all par-ties that he lacked the capacity to consent or object to institutional admission. In 1997, whilst in the day centre, he became agitated, hitting himself on the head and banging his head against the wall. On the recommendation of his social worker he was transferred to an Intensive Behaviour Unit of a psychiatric hospital as an informal patient. There he was compliant and did not try to run away. When his admission was challenged, the High Court (in this case, the court of first instance) in the United Kingdom held that he had not been detained, and that the English common law allowed the admission of people lacking the capacity to make decisions in these circumstances. When the Court of Appeal reversed the decision, his compulsory detention was initiated under the Act, but the House of Lords (the United Kingdom's highest Court) restored the High Court's deci-sion. An application was then lodged on Mr H.L.'s behalf with the ECtHR.

The ECtHR concluded that Mr H.L. had been deprived of his liberty. It noted that he had been under continuous supervision and control, and was not free to leave. It had been conceded by the hospital authorities that, although he had made no attempt to leave, he would have been stopped if he had tried, and legal detention would have been imposed. The evidence was equivocal as to whether the hospital unit on which he had been kept was locked, but the Court held that even if it had not been, the point was not determinative of whether he was detained. It also found that the common law relating to the informal admission of persons lacking capacity was insufficiently precise and pre-dictable to constitute a 'procedure prescribed by law'. It lacked certainty with regard to formalised admission procedures, definition of the purpose of admission, limits of time, or limits concerning the scope of care and treatment. Moreover, although Mr H.L. was in fact unable to make the relevant decisions regarding his admission, the common law did not provide for the appointment of a legal representative for him.[9]

The decision in *H.L. v. the United Kingdom* has major implications for the United Kingdom, and should have significance across all countries which have ratified the ECHR, under the principle of subsidiarity. It greatly expands the population of people for whom access to a court review of the lawfulness of the detention must be provided, with significant resource implications. As will be seen further on, Mr H.L. undoubtedly fell into the class of persons who would require legal representation, though, as will be seen, this is arguably the position of all people who are detained in mental disability settings.

---

[9] *H.L.* may be contrasted with the decision in *H.M. v. Switzerland*, Application No. 39187/98, judgment 26 February 2002, (2004) 38 EHRR 17. That case involved the removal of an elderly person to a foster home, on the basis that necessary basic care by the family was severely deficient. It would seem that Ms H.M. was housed in an unlocked part of the institution, and continued to have free contact with the world outside the institution: para. 45. It would also appear that, at least later on, she made a conscious choice to agree to stay in the institution: paras. 46–7, a point expressly noted by the ECtHR in the later case of *Storck v. Germany,* Application No. 61603/00, judgment 16 June 2005, para. 74. The ECtHR found a deprivation of liberty in *Storck*, but not in *H.M.* (para. 48).

While it is the State that is the respondent in litigation under the ECHR, it does not follow that the right to liberty applies only to State institutions. While the ECHR directly binds only the State, the ECtHR has interpreted the Convention rights to impose duties on the States to secure Convention rights throughout the country. Thus in *Storck v. Germany*,[10] a psychiatric detention had occurred in a private clinic, but Germany was nonetheless implicated under the ECHR for three reasons. First, when Ms Storck had escaped from the clinic, she was forcibly returned by the police. Such involvement was taken to be sufficient to engage the responsibility of the State to ensure that her detention was consistent with Article 5.[11]

Second, the Court held that Article 6 of the ECHR placed domestic courts under a duty to apply domestic law in the spirit of the ECHR rights, in order to ensure that those rights had 'practical and effective' application at the domestic level.[12] This aspect of the case concerned civil litigation pursued against the clinic by Ms Storck following her release. The case had been dismissed based in part on the expiry of a limitation period, that is, the domestic court held that there had been too long a delay between the detention complained of and the commencement of the domestic litigation. The ECtHR held that this approach did not take adequate account of the fact that for much of the limitation period, Ms Storck had been confined in the facility, and both in the facility and for some time afterward, that she had been treated with strong medications that would have affected her practical ability to commence proceedings. The domestic court had dismissed another element of the case based on its finding that Ms Storck had agreed to a contract with the clinic for her care. The ECtHR noted that her capacity to enter such a contract was doubtful, and that on the facts, she had actively opposed her admission to the facility and attempted to flee on several occasions. On that basis, the ECtHR held the finding of a contract by the domestic court to be arbitrary. For both these reasons, the domestic court failed adequately to interpret domestic law in the spirit of the Convention.

Thirdly, the Court held that the obligation upon States under Article 1 of the ECHR to 'secure' Convention rights and freedoms 'to everyone within their jurisdiction' created positive obligations on the State to protect individuals' rights to liberty.[13] The State was obliged under Article 8 of the ECHR to protect of the physical integrity of its citizens, and State hospitals were provided to ensure this standard of care. The protection of that physical integrity was a Convention obligation, and the State could not absolve itself by delegating that provision to the private sector. There was still an obligation to license private psychiatric institutions, particularly those where people could be admitted without court order. The State was under a further obligation to provide 'competent supervision

---

[10] *Storck v. Germany, op. cit.*
[11] *Storck v. Germany, op. cit.*, para. 91.
[12] *Storck v. Germany, op. cit.*, paras. 92–99.
[13] *Storck v. Germany, op. cit.*, paras. 100–108.

on a regular basis of the justification of the confinement and medical treatment.'[14] Inspections that were triggered by court-ordered confinements were insufficient; measures had to be in place to ensure the protection of people admitted to psychiatric facilities without court order. This is consistent with the CPT Standards, which favour routine inspections of psychiatric establishments by an independent body, and the establishment of a complaints process independent of the institution.[15]

Exceptions to the Right to Liberty

The general right to liberty under Article 5(1) is subject to a variety of exceptions. These exceptions are subject to an overriding requirement that they be 'in accordance with a procedure prescribed by law'. The State may of course provide a procedure that includes protections in excess of those required by the ECHR. If it does so, then failure to follow those procedures will still result in a violation of Article 5(1).[16]

Elsewhere, Article 5 provides further safeguards applicable to these deprivations of liberty:

- The right upon arrest to be informed promptly of the reasons for the arrest, in a language that he or she understands [Article 5(2)]; and
- The right to take proceedings by which the lawfulness of the arrest or detention shall be decided speedily by a court, and his or her release ordered if the detention is held not to be lawful [Article 5(4)].

These two points will be discussed later in the chapter.

The exception to the right to liberty that is of prime importance in this book is contained in Article 5(1)(e), which allows 'the lawful detention . . . of persons of unsound mind'. Article 5(1)(a), however, allows 'the lawful detention of persons after conviction by a competent court'. Many people who commit criminal acts are affected by mental disabilities, and the commission of such acts is one of the significant ways that people with mental disabilities are drawn to the attention of authorities, and brought into detention. The specific exception under Article 5(1) under which an individual falls may be a significant point for a number of reasons:

- The ECtHR accepts that the deprivation of liberty under Article 5(1)(a) is by its nature punitive. This is not the case with detentions under Article 5(1)(e).
- The conditions of detention are therefore different. While neither category may be detained in conditions that are inhuman or degrading under Article 3, persons

---

[14] *Storck v. Germany, op. cit.*, para. 103.
[15] CPT Standards, CPT/Inf/E (2002) 1, Rev 2004, p. 61, paras. 53–4.
[16] See, eg., *Tám v. Slovakia* Application No. 50213/99, judgment 10 November 2004, paras. 56–60. See also discussion below, regarding analogous issues relating to the phrase 'lawful detention' under Article 5(1)(e).

detained under Article 5(1)(e) must be detained in an appropriate therapeutic environment. There is no such requirement for people detained under Article 5(1)(a).

- Article 5(1)(a) allows for a fixed period of detention, up to and including for life, determined at the point of trial with no requirement for re-assessment. The justification for the detention is in the past: the sentence, determined by the crime. The ECHR generally offers no right to routine re-assessments of the appropriateness of the length of a criminal sentence. 'Unsoundness of mind' is by contrast understood as a non-static condition that may vary over time. As a result, while both categories have a right to a hearing under Article 5(4) at the beginning of the detention, the ECHR jurisprudence provides a right to periodic hearings under Article 5(4) for people detained under Article 5(1)(e). There is no comparable right for those detained under Article 5(1)(a).
- Because of the different rights to court review under Article 5(4), it is argued below that for people detained under Article 5(1)(e) there is a corresponding *ongoing* right to receive reasons for detention, which is not a right for people detained under Article 5(1)(a).

A comparison of the cases of *Aerts v. Belgium*[17] and *Bizzotto v. Greece*[18] provides some indication as to how the ECtHR draws the distinction between the two categories. Both cases involved men who had committed criminal acts, being a serious assault in Mr Aerts' case, and drug trafficking in Mr Bizzotto's. In both cases, drug addiction appears to have been central to their difficulties, although Mr Aerts was also given a diagnosis of borderline personality disorder. In both cases, medical treatment relevant to their disorders was ordered by the domestic criminal court at the end of their trials. Mr Aerts was not convicted of his offence, but was detained pursuant to the Belgian Social Protection Act. Mr Bizzotto was convicted and given a six year custodial sentence, but with the condition that he be detained either in a prison or state hospital, where he could be offered treatment for his drug addiction. Both were in fact detained in prisons, where appropriate treatment was unavailable. In both cases, this was because of the unavailability of a suitable place for them in a treatment facility. In Mr Aerts' case, this detention lasted for about a year; in Mr Bizzotto's for just over four years. Both applied to the ECtHR, alleging that the conditions of their confinement breached Article 5(1).

Mr Aerts was successful; Mr Bizzotto was not. The difference was that Mr Aerts was held to be detained pursuant to Article 5(1)(e), and Mr Bizzotto Article 5(1)(a). As a result, Mr Bizzotto was appropriately confined in a punitive institution, but Mr Aerts could only be appropriately detained in a therapeutic institution – the second point of distinction noted above.

The ECtHR held that Mr Bizzotto's detention flowed from his conviction as a drug trafficker:

---

[17] *Aerts v. Belgium*, Application No. 25357/94, judgment 30 July 1998, (1998) 29 EHRR 50.
[18] *Bizzotto v. Greece*, Application No. 22126/93, judgment 15 November 1996, *Reports of Judgments and Decisions* 1996–V, p. 1738.

[A] sentence was in fact passed in the instant case for the purposes of punishment. The same court's finding that the applicant was a drug addict and the decision to have him placed – as required by section 14 of Law no. 1729/1987 – in a prison with medical facilities do not in any way affect the main ground for his "detention". Accordingly, only sub-paragraph (a) of Article 5 para. 1 (art. 5–1–a) applies in the present case.[19]

The detention of Mr Aerts, by comparison, was not punitive:

The Court considers that only Article 5 § 1(e) is applicable to the applicant's detention. Although the Committals Chamber of the Liège Court of First Instance found that Mr Aerts had committed acts of violence, it ordered his detention on the ground that at the material time and when he appeared in court he had been severely mentally disturbed, to the point where he was incapable of controlling his actions (see paragraph 8 above). As he was not criminally responsible, there could be no "conviction" within the meaning of paragraph 1 (a) of Article 5, and in any case the Committals Chamber could not give such a ruling.[20]

The distinction is therefore whether the individual is treated by the domestic court as being criminally responsible. The fact of a formal criminal conviction is certainly relevant to this, but it is not necessarily determinative. In *X. v. the United Kingdom*,[21] the applicant had been convicted of wounding with intent to cause grievous bodily harm. He was found by the domestic court to be suffering from paranoid psychosis, and notwithstanding the conviction, he was sent to a high security psychiatric hospital. The fact of the conviction meant that the Article 5(1)(a) applied, but the fact that he had been dealt with by the domestic court as 'suffering from a mental disorder warranting his confinement in a mental hospital for treatment' meant that Article 5(1)(e) also applied.[22] While the Court held that it did not need to distinguish between the requirements of Articles 5(1)(a) and 5(1)(e) in this case, it did note that the fact that the case involved the applicant's recall to a high security facility following a long period of leave in the community made the latter provision more relevant.

While the theoretical dividing line drawn by the Court between *Bizzotto* and *Aerts* is convincing enough, the similarity between the cases is nonetheless striking. The difference appears to be a nuance by the respective domestic courts. In neither case is it obvious that these domestic courts realised the outcomes those nuances would have on the rights of the respective applicants before the ECtHR. Further, the dividing line between criminal and non-criminal detention in domestic legislation varies between countries. The result is that rights under the ECHR may depend to a considerable degree on such divergence in domestic practice. For a document that is intended to provide a floor to rights across Europe, this provides cause for concern.

---

[19] *Bizzotto v. Greece, op. cit.*, para. 32.
[20] *Aerts v. Belgium, op. cit.*, para. 45.
[21] *X. v. the United Kingdom*, Application No. 7215/75, judgment 5 November 1981, (1981) 4 EHRR 188.
[22] *X. v. the United Kingdom, op. cit.*, para. 39.

'Persons of unsound mind'

The scope of Article 5(1)(e), which allows the detention of 'persons of unsound mind', is of central relevance to this chapter. The process of elaborating the meaning of Article 5 in the context of mental disability was begun in *Winterwerp v. the Netherlands*.[23] The ECtHR's judgment has become the cornerstone of the interpretation of the Article as it relates to mental disability, and will be referred to repeatedly throughout this chapter.

In *Winterwerp* the ECtHR acknowledged that the scope of the phrase 'persons of unsound mind' was dependent on developing medical understanding of mental disability and its care and treatment:

> This term is not one that can be given a definitive interpretation . . . it is a term whose meaning is constantly evolving as research in psychiatry progresses, an increasing flexibility in treatment is developing and society's attitude to mental illness changes, in particular so that a greater understanding of the problems of mental patients is becoming widespread.[24]

The case nonetheless establishes the following framework for the interpretation of the phrase:

> In the Court's opinion, except in emergency cases, the individual concerned should not be deprived of his liberty unless he has been reliably shown to be of 'unsound mind'. The very nature of what has to be established before the competent national authority – that is, a true mental disorder – calls for objective medical expertise. Further, the mental disorder must be of a kind or degree warranting compulsory confinement. What is more, the validity of continued confinement depends upon the persistence of such a disorder.[25]

The individual must therefore be suffering from a 'true' mental disorder, and the disorder must be of a kind or degree warranting compulsory confinement.

A 'True Mental Disorder'

A 'true medical disorder' is determined by objective medical expertise, and the Court views this expertise as creating a safeguard to the abuse of Article 5.[26] The (now defunct) European Commission on Human Rights held that this does not require specialist psychiatric assessments; the view of a general practitioner will suffice.[27] The case law appears content to allow a broad reading of the disorders upon which 'unsoundness of mind' might be based. In *X. v. Germany*[28] the Commission held that the term 'unsound mind' was not limited to mental illness, but must be understood in its widest sense, including abnormal personality disorder. Thus it must be taken to include intellectual disabilities

---

[23] *Winterwerp v. the Netherlands*, Application No. 6301/73, judgment 24 October 1979, (A/33) (1979–80) 2 EHRR 387.

[24] *Winterwerp v. the Netherlands, op. cit.,* para. 37.

[25] *Winterwerp v. the Netherlands, op. cit.,* para. 39.

[26] See *Rakevich v. Russia*, Application No. 58973/00, judgment 28 Oct 2003, para. 32.

[27] *Shuurs v. the Netherlands,* 41 D & R 186, 188.

[28] 6 D & R 182.

(sometimes described in statutes as mental impairment or mental retardation in contrast to mental illness), psychotic illnesses, psychopathy, and probably neurotic conditions as well. The Court is equally clear that mere eccentricity is insufficient to constitute unsoundness of mind:

> In any event, Article 5(1)(e) obviously cannot be taken as permitting the detention of a person simply because his view or behaviour deviate from the norms prevailing in a particular society.[29]

In *Rakevich v. Russia*, for example, a person confined was in a deranged state of mind after a night-long emotional study of the Bible. The ECtHR held that this alone would not have been sufficient to constitute unsoundness of mind, although on the facts there was additional medical evidence of mental health difficulties.[30]

The ECtHR has not as yet referred in its analysis of 'true mental disorder' to either the relevant chapter of the International Statistical Classification of Diseases and Related Health Problems (ICD) published by the World Health Organisation or to the Diagnostic and Statistical Manual of Disorders (DSM) published by the American Psychiatric Association. Both of these provide an extensive classification of mental disorders, based on consultation among psychiatrists, and both are revised on a periodic basis to reflect developments in psychiatric knowledge. Certainly as a general guide, disorders contained in one or both of these taxonomies are likely to be considered by the Court to be true mental disorders; conditions contained in neither taxonomy may well warrant considerably more scrutiny. As an obvious example, homosexuality is no longer contained in either taxonomy; detention of people on that basis would almost certainly fall afoul of the requirement for a 'true mental disorder'.

To date, the ECtHR has never disturbed the findings of domestic psychiatrists and courts as to whether an individual suffered from mental disability, and has been at pains to indicate a hesitancy in doing so:

> [I]n deciding whether an individual should be detained as a 'person of unsound mind', the national authorities are to be recognised as having a certain discretion, since it is in the first place for the national authorities to evaluate the evidence adduced before them in a particular case[.][31]

This is consistent with the Court's general policy of reliance on matters of fact as determined in domestic courts, and general deference to medical opinions. Regarding the *Winterwerp* criteria specifically, the Court said in *X. v. the United Kingdom*:

---

[29] *Winterwerp v. the Netherlands, op. cit.*, para. 37.
[30] *Rakevich v. Russia, op. cit.*, para. 29. The evidence was to the effect that on the date in question the person detained also suffered from an acute and rapidly progressing mental condition that manifested itself in disorientation. This was sufficient to constitute unsoundness of mind, and the situation itself constituted an emergency, allowing some derogation from the requirement that a true mental disorder be demonstrated in advance. Re emergencies, see further below.
[31] *Winterwerp v. the Netherlands, op. cit.*, para. 40.

Whilst the Court undoubtedly has the jurisdiction to verify the fulfilment of these conditions in a given case, the logic of the system of safeguard established by the Convention places
limits on the scope of this control; since the national authorities are better placed to evaluate the evidence adduced before them, they are to be recognised as having a certain discretion in the matter and the Court's task is limited to reviewing under the Convention the
decisions they have taken. . . .[32]

While the Court does depart from domestic factual determinations in appropriate situations, it nonetheless seems unlikely that the Court would do so in this context.
Compelling evidence that a diagnosis was made in bad faith or for collateral purpose
might well induce the Court to intervene, but it is difficult to see other examples.

A Disorder 'Warranting Compulsory Confinement'

The ECtHR in *Winterwerp* limited the scope of the power to detain to cases where the
mental disorder is 'of a kind or degree warranting compulsory confinement'. By requiring this level of severity, minor mental disorders would in practice fall outside the permitted justification under Article 5 for depriving an individual of his or her liberty.

The Court has held that this standard may be met either on the basis of the need for
medical treatment for mental disorder, or on the basis that the individual would be dangerous if left at large. These are alternative justifications. In *Hutchison Reid v. the United
Kingdom*,[33] the applicant had been diagnosed with psychopathic disorder. Domestic law
required that such individuals could be detained only if medical treatment could alleviate or prevent a deterioration of their condition. The domestic courts held that there were
treatments that could alleviate the symptoms and manifestations of his disorder, but there
was no way of treating the underlying disorder itself. They nonetheless held that the
domestic threshold for his detention was satisfied. He appealed to the ECtHR, on the
basis that the absence of treatment for his underlying disorder rendered his detention
inappropriate. The ECtHR did not agree:

This argument however turns on the domestic-law criterion applicable at the time, namely,
that detention in a mental hospital was conditional on the illness or condition being of a
nature or degree amenable to medical treatment. There is no such requirement imposed by
Article 5 § 1(e) of the Convention. . . . The Court's case-law refers rather to the applicant
being properly established as suffering from a mental disorder of a degree warranting compulsory confinement. Such confinement may be necessary not only where a person needs
therapy, medication or other clinical treatment to cure or alleviate his condition, but also
where the person needs control and supervision to prevent him, for example, causing harm
to himself or other persons. . . .[34]

---

[32] *X. v. the United Kingdom, op. cit.*, para. 43.
[33] *Hutchison Reid v. the United Kingdom*, Application No. 50272/99, judgment 20 May 2003, (2003) 37
EHRR 9.
[34] *Hutchison Reid v. the United Kingdom, op. cit.*, at para. 52.

Whether a condition warrants compulsory confinement may depend on the services that are available outside the institution. There may be a variety of reasons for the unavailability of these services. In much of Western Europe and North America, developments in policy thinking made community alternatives central to care provision in the 1970s and 1980s. While these developments have received enthusiastic support in the international community,[35] they have not been taken up in some Member States of the Council of Europe. In these countries, the physical and administrative infrastructure has not been developed to support community alternatives to institutionalisation. In other countries that have embraced community alternatives as part of their policy rhetoric, there may nonetheless be a shortage of services in practice.

Reluctance of professional staff to provide community alternatives raises a different set of problems. For some people who would otherwise be incarcerated, community services will have to be relatively intensive to be a real alternative. People who would benefit from such intensive community services are sometimes not easy to manage, and require significant investments of time and emotional energy by medical and social services professionals. In some health systems, it is difficult to require a care team to take responsibility for an individual in the community when the team does not wish to do so. In systems where the provision of services is discretionary in this way, institutionalisation may become necessary not because services do not exist, but instead because no one is prepared to provide them.

Kolanis v. the United Kingdom[36] will serve as an example. The applicant in that case had been convicted of a serious assault, but was detained in a psychiatric hospital rather than a prison because of her mental disorder. Eventually, a Mental Health Review Tribunal held that she should be released to the care of her family, but remain under psychiatric supervision and subject to recall to the hospital should the need arise. Eleven months later, Ms Kolanis was still detained in the hospital, as no psychiatrist had been found who was prepared to supervise her under these conditions. In the psychiatrists' view, the requirement that she would live with her family was not in her best interests, and they were therefore not prepared to undertake the supervision. The case turned primarily on whether the refusals of the professionals effectively thwarted the decision of the tribunal, a matter discussed later in this chapter. Ms Kolanis also argued that the fact that appropriate community treatment would render her detention unnecessary meant that her condition did not warrant detention. The Court did not agree:

> As events in the present case showed, the treatment considered necessary for such conditional discharge may not prove available, in which circumstances there can be no question of interpreting Article 5 § 1(e) as requiring the applicant's discharge without the conditions

---

[35] See, for example, World Health Organization, *The World Health Report 2001: Mental Health: New Understanding, New Hope* (Geneva: WHO, 2001), chapter 3, especially p. 50; WHO European Ministerial Conference on Mental Health, *Mental Health Action Plan for Europe: Facing the Challenges, Building Solutions*, EUR/04/5047810/7 (14 Jan 05), pp. 6–7.

[36] *Kolanis v. the United Kingdom*, Application No. 517/02, judgment 21 June 2005, (2006) 42 EHRR 12.

necessary for protecting herself and the public or as imposing an absolute obligation on the authorities to ensure that the conditions are fulfilled. Nor is it necessary in the present case to attempt to anticipate what level of obligation could arise by way of provision of treatment in the community to ensure the due effectiveness of MHRT [i.e., Mental Health Review Tribunal] decisions concerning release. In the situation under consideration a failure by the local authority to use "best efforts" or any breach of duty by a psychiatrist in refusing care in the community would be amenable to judicial review. The Court is therefore not persuaded that local authorities or doctors could wilfully or arbitrarily block the discharge of patients into the community without proper grounds or excuse, or that this is what occurred in this case.[37]

When the individual is in fact suffering from a mental disorder, the Court has thus far been unwilling to impose obligations on the country to provide community services that would make the detention of the individual unnecessary. The Court's hesitancy in this regard is unsurprising. These are issues about the level and choice of services made by individual countries, and judgments as to their adequacy by the Court could have significant budgetary implications in those countries. At the same time, the finding in *Kolanis* that it was not necessary 'in the present case' to determine the scope of such State obligations suggests that the Court may be prepared to enter this territory in the future. This is consistent with the Court's insistence on standards of provision in other contexts. Places where people are incarcerated must meet certain standards, for example, and appropriate procedural and court protections must be available for people under Article 5 and other provisions of the ECHR. These cost money just as community services would cost money; it is not obvious why the Court would be hesitant on the latter and not the former.

The Court's finding about local decision-making in individual cases is problematic. The Court's view is premised on 'best efforts' being used to provide community care, in an environment where a refusal by a psychiatrist to provide such care is open to judicial challenge. The question is whether judicial review in this situation has the power to ensure reasonable provision of services. If it does, the Court's view makes some sense, as it would return the question of reasonableness of service provision back to the domestic courts, who might well be best placed to balance the interests involved. In *Kolanis* itself, the jurisdiction of the domestic court to make such orders is at best highly questionable.[38] If the domestic court denies jurisdiction in such matters, it is difficult to see the reasoning of the ECtHR in *Kolanis* as convincing.

As noted, *Kolanis* turned on whether the failure to provide services thwarted the decision of a review tribunal. As such, it was primarily about discharge rather than admission standards. Nonetheless, it is not obvious that the Court's approach would differ in determining whether an initial admission met the standards of Article 5.

---

[37] *Kolanis v. the United Kingdom, op. cit.,* para. 71.
[38] See further discussion below regarding *Kolanis* and the power of Article 5(4) courts to enforce their decisions.

'A procedure prescribed by law' and 'lawful'

Article 5 requires that any deprivation of liberty based on unsoundness of mind is pursuant to 'a procedure prescribed by law' and that it is 'lawful'. These restrictions are designed to ensure that a restriction of human rights is not arbitrary.

The Court's classic articulation of 'prescribed by law' is contained in *Sunday Times v. the United Kingdom*, which was not a mental disability case:

> In the Court's opinion, the following are two of the requirements that flow from the expression 'prescribed by law'. Firstly, the law must be adequately accessible: the citizen must be able to have an indication that is adequate in the circumstances of the legal rules applicable to a given case. Secondly, a norm cannot be regarded as a 'law' unless it is formulated with sufficient precision to enable the citizen to regulate his conduct: he must be able – if need be with appropriate advice – to foresee, to a degree that is reasonable in the circumstances, the consequences which a given action may entail.[39]

For the Article 5(1) exceptions allowing detention to take effect, therefore, there must be a domestic law on involuntary detention, and it must be 'accessible' in the sense that its meaning can be readily discovered. Common law (in the United Kingdom and Republic of Ireland) can, in theory, meet this standard, but it is likely that in most cases, this level of certainty must be reached through codification.

'Lawful' means compliant both with the Convention and the domestic code of law, and also implies that 'the deprivation of liberty is in keeping with the purposes of the restrictions permissible under Article 5(1)'.[40]

The effect of these definitions is to provide two separate mechanisms to challenge detentions. First, an applicant can challenge the detention on the basis that the substance of the domestic law is not in compliance with the Convention. Second, since compliance with a 'procedure prescribed by law' is written into Article 5, it follows that any failure to follow domestic law will also be a breach of the Convention.

Van der Leer v. the Netherlands provides an example of the latter sort of breach. The domestic Dutch law on civil detention had required the judge making the order for detention to interview or hear from the person to be detained, unless this would be devoid of purpose or medically inadvisable, and to consult with the spouse of the person to be confined. Neither Mrs Van der Leer nor her husband was given the opportunity to speak with the judge, and no reasons were provided for this failure. The judge's failure to follow the process established by the law itself constituted a violation of Article 5.[41] This is an interesting example, because the failures complained of were not all substantive

---

[39] *Sunday Times v. the United Kingdom*, Application No. 6538/74, judgment of 26 April 1979, A.30 (1979) 2 EHRR 245, para. 49. This statement in this case is in the context of Article 10. For use of the same phraseology in the context of Article 5, see, for example, *Kawka v. Poland*, Application No. 25874/94, judgment 9 January 2001, para. 49.

[40] *Bouamar v. Belgium*, Application No. 9106/80, judgment 29 February 1988, (1989) 11 EHRR 1 para. 50.

[41] *Van der Leer v. the Netherlands*, Application No. 11509/85, judgment 21 February 1990, (1990) 12 EHRR 567, para. 23.

requirements of Article 5 jurisprudence. Thus while Article 5 provides a right to challenge detention before a court or similar tribunal, it does not require a routine court hearing *prior* to the detention. Nor does it require consultation with the spouse of the person to be detained. The essence of the Article 5(1) violation was instead that the domestic procedure was not followed.[42] Breaches of this sort will by definition refer to the specifics of domestic law, and little more can be said about them here.

Allegations that domestic law is inconsistent with the substance of the Convention do allow for broader discussion. The requirement here is to protect the individual from arbitrariness.[43] That in part concerns both the process and the substance of domestic law:

> [T]he domestic law must itself be in conformity with the Convention, including the general principles expressed or implied therein. The notion underlying the term in question is one of fair and proper procedure, namely that any measure depriving a person of his liberty should issue from and be executed by an appropriate authority and should not be arbitrary.[44]

Substantive certainty is particularly important. In *Kawka v. Poland* the ECtHR emphasised the point:

> The Court stresses . . . that where deprivation of liberty is concerned, it is particularly important that the general principle of legal certainty is satisfied. It is therefore essential that the conditions for deprivation of liberty under domestic law should be clearly defined, and that the law itself be foreseeable in its application, so that it meets the standard of "lawfulness" set by the Convention, a standard which requires that all law should be sufficiently precise to allow a person – if needed, to obtain the appropriate advice – to foresee, to a degree that is reasonable, the consequences which a given action may entail.[45]

This language is problematic in cases involving mental disabilities. Certainly, some people affected will be able to understand the connections between their actions and consequences, but it is in the nature of some sorts of mental disability, some psychoses and intellectual disabilities for example, that the individual may not have the ability to make these connections. This cannot be taken as a justification for arbitrariness regarding the detention of these people. Instead, it is helpful to reconsider the last provision of the quotation from the perspective of the person depriving the individual of his or her liberty. The law should be clear enough to provide meaningful guidance to those people as to when detention should occur, and when it should not. The Court in the *Sunday Times* case was keen to balance the need for certainty with the need to avoid rigidity and the need for the law to keep pace with changing circumstances.[46] That is indisputable, but at the same time, the loss of liberty should not be allowed to be determined simply by medical discretion.

---

[42] See also *Tám v. Slovakia*, Application No. 50213/99, judgment 10 November 2004, para. 69.
[43] *Van der Leer v. the Netherlands, op. cit.*, para. 22.
[44] *Winterwerp v. the Netherlands, op. cit.*, para. 45.
[45] *Kawka v. Poland, op. cit.*, para. 49.
[46] *Sunday Times v. the United Kingdom, op. cit.*, para. 49.

The requirement that the individual be suffering from a 'true mental disorder' is not necessarily a problem. As discussed above, reference can be had to international professional taxonomies of mental disorder. The requirement that the disorder be of 'a kind or degree warranting compulsory confinement' is much more difficult to define with precision. The words themselves provide little assistance: they are deliberately flexible, to allow countries to meet the ECHR provision with the standard they think appropriate. Nonetheless, if the ECHR is to provide real safeguards to human rights, it must insist that the domestic standard be articulated with some clarity. Standards based on the severity of the mental disability may prove particularly difficult to draft clearly, as there is no obvious objective measure of this severity, nor any objective measure of mental disabilities. Standards based on dangerousness may be easier to render in sufficiently clear terms, as criminal law provides a language to define the seriousness of behaviours, and the standard could require some form of behaviour related to a sufficiently serious behaviour. Standards that refer simply to 'dangerousness' without further elaboration should be discouraged, however, for how dangerous is dangerous? Are threats sufficient, or is an overt act required? Must the danger be physical, or may the potential of psychological damage suffice?

As yet, the Court has provided no helpful analysis regarding these problems of clarity. When invited to do so, they have declined.[47] If the standards established in *Winterwerp* are to provide meaningful human rights protection, however, it is difficult to see that the Court can avoid these questions in perpetuity.

Place of detention

It was established in *Ashingdane v. the United Kingdom* that the place of detention must bear a relationship to the justification for confinement under Article 5:

> The issue of principle raised by this submission is whether and, if so, to what extent the expression "lawful detention of a person of unsound mind" can be construed as including a reference not simply to actual deprivation of liberty of mental health patients but also to matters relating to execution of the detention, such as the place, environment and conditions of detention.
>
> . . . The Court would further accept that there must be some relationship between the ground of permitted deprivation of liberty relied on and the place and conditions of detention. In principle, the "detention" of a person as a mental health patient will only be "lawful" for the purposes of sub-paragraph (e) of paragraph 1 (art. 5–1–e) if effected in a hospital, clinic or other appropriate institution authorised for that purpose. However, subject to the foregoing, Article 5 para. 1(e) (art. 5–1–e) is not in principle concerned with suitable treatment or conditions[.][48]

A breach of Article 5 was found on this basis in *Aerts v. Belgium*.[49] In that case, the applicant had committed a serious assault, for which he had been found not responsible due

---

[47] See for example, *Van der Leer v. the Netherlands, op. cit.*, para. 24.
[48] *Ashingdane v. the United Kingdom, op. cit.*, para. 44.
[49] *Op. cit.*

to his mental disorder. He was detained, not in a psychiatric institution, but in the medical unit of a prison. There was only a part-time psychiatrist in attendance, and other carers, some without medical qualifications, administered medical interventions such as intramuscular injections. Only doctors were allowed to give intravenous injections, and these were therefore not available because the doctor spent only six hours per week on the unit. There were no nurses, occupational therapists, or psychologists, and only a part-time social worker. There were few therapeutic programmes in place. There was evidence that the institutional conditions were in fact harmful to Mr Aerts. In these circumstances, the Court held that the hospital unit of the prison was not a therapeutic environment, and there for not an appropriate institution for people detained under Article 5(1)(e).[50]

In *Ashingdane* itself, the issue was the failure to transfer the applicant from a high security psychiatric hospital to one where he would have enjoyed considerably more freedom and where the surroundings would be more conducive to his recovery. The Court held that both were appropriate therapeutic environments, and therefore that Article 5 was not violated.[51] This is consistent with the view that Article 5 is concerned with the deprivation of liberty, not with the intensity of that deprivation.

It does not follow that the Convention is irrelevant to the provision of treatment or the intensity of confinement. Either may, in appropriate circumstances, raise issues under Article 3 (prohibition of torture and inhuman or degrading treatment or punishment) or Article 8 (right to respect for private and family life). These issues will be discussed elsewhere in this book, in chapters 3 and 4.

Right to be Informed of Reasons

Article 5(2) of the ECHR provides:

> Everyone who is arrested shall be informed promptly, in a language which he understands, of the reasons for his arrest and of any charges against him.

The Court's general approach to this provision was established in *Fox, Campbell and Hartley v. the United Kingdom*:

> Paragraph 2 of Article 5 (art. 5-2) contains the elementary safeguard that any person arrested should know why he is being deprived of his liberty. This provision is an integral part of the scheme of protection afforded by Article 5 (art. 5): by virtue of paragraph 2 (art. 5-2) any person arrested must be told, in simple, non-technical language that he can understand, the essential legal and factual grounds for his arrest, so as to be able, if he sees fit, to apply to a court to challenge its lawfulness in accordance with paragraph 4 (art. 5-4). . . . Whilst this information must be conveyed "promptly" (in French: "dans le plus court délai"), it need not

---

[50]   This approach only applies if the disorder is central to the justification for confinement. If the justification for the detention is pursuant to a determination that the individual was criminally responsible for the actions giving rise to the confinement, it would seem that detention in a punitive environment is permissible. See discussion of *Aerts v. Belgium* and *Bizzotto v. Greece*, above.

[51]   *Ashingdane v. the United Kingdom, op. cit.*, para. 47.

be related in its entirety by the arresting officer at the very moment of the arrest. Whether the content and promptness of the information conveyed were sufficient is to be assessed in each case according to its special features.[52]

Notwithstanding the references to 'arrest' and 'charges' in Article 5(2), language generally associated with criminal detentions, the Court has held that the provision also applies to detentions under Article 5(1)(e).[53] Nonetheless, the cases in which the provision has received the most meaningful discussion have not concerned mental disability, but regarding criminal charges[54] or, occasionally, extradition proceedings.[55] The pragmatic issues of relevance in cases regarding people diagnosed with mental disabilities are rather different, and it is therefore largely a matter of speculation how the Court will deal with the specific issues that arise in Article 5(1)(e) detentions.[56]

The litigation to date has tended to focus on the scope of information that must be disclosed. In a criminal context, it is insufficient that the detainee be told merely the statutory justification for his or her arrest;[57] some factual information must also be provided. It does seem that the detaining authority is required only to explain in general the criminal acts alleged; it is not required to provide an account of the evidence in support of those allegations.[58] Further, it would appear to be acceptable that persons arrested on criminal charges be able infer these particulars from the questioning they undergo, or from the context of other police investigations known to them and broadly related to them.[59] The Court noted in *Fox*, above, that the purpose of Article 5(2) is to allow the

---

[52] *Fox, Campbell and Hartley v. the United Kingdom*, Application Nos. 12244/86; 12245/86; 12383/86, judgment 30 August 1998, A 182 (1990) 13 EHRR 157, para. 40.

[53] *Van der Leer v. the Netherlands, op. cit.*, para. 27.

[54] See, for example, *Dikme v. Turkey*, Application No. 20869/92, judgment 11 July 2000, *Fox, Campbell and Hartley v. the United Kingdom, op. cit., H.B. v. Switzerland*, Application No. 26899/95, judgment 5 July 2001, (2003) 37 EHRR 52; *Ireland v. the United Kingdom*, Application No. 5310/71, judgment 18 January 1978, (1978) 2 EHRR 25, *Lamy v. Belgium*, Application No. 10444/83, judgment 30 March 1989, (1989) 11 EHRR 529; *Murray v. the United Kingdom*, Application No. 14310/88, judgment 28 October 1994, A 300 (1994) 19 EHRR 193.

[55] See for example, *Bordoviskiy v. Russia*, Application No. 49491/99, judgment 8 February 2005, *Chamaïev c. Géorgie et Russie*, (available only in French) Application No. 36378/02, judgment 12 October 2005.

[56] The CPT Standards require that all persons admitted to a psychiatric establishment ought to receive a brochure detailing the routine of the institution, and the individual's rights in that institution. Assistance should be given to understanding the brochure if it is required. A brochure ought also to be provided to the patient's family: see CPT Standards, CPT/Inf/E (2002) 1, Rev 2004, p. 61, para. 53.

[57] *Ireland v. the United Kingdom*, Application No. 5310/71, judgment 18 January 1978, (1978) 2 EHRR 25, para. 198. This specific case concerned criminal charges related to terrorist offences and a derogation from the provisions of Article 5(2) was permitted pursuant to Article 15 because of the security situation in Northern Ireland at that time.

[58] See for example, *Lamy v. Belgium, op. cit.*, paras. 9 and 32.

[59] See for example, *Murray v. the United Kingdom, op. cit.*, para. 77, where the nature of the questioning to which the accused was subjected, coupled with the knowledge that her brother had been convicted in America of offences relating to procuring arms for the IRA, an outlawed organisation in Northern Ireland, was deemed constitute sufficient compliance with Article 5(2). See also *H.B. v. Switzerland, op. cit.*, paras. 48–50, where the accused was arrested on charges relating to corporate fraud. The nature of the allegations was disclosed only during interrogation. In reaching the conclusion that there was no violation of Article 5(2), the ECtHR noted that he was aware of police investigations concerning the

detainee to determine whether to commence proceedings to challenge his or her detention under Article 5(4). The fact that such a challenge has been effectively commenced, has been held to be evidence that there is no breach of Article 5(2).[60]

It is difficult to separate this approach from the criminal context of the cases in which it arises. In the criminal context, the question of how far and what stage the police must disclose their evidence, the need to protect the sources and integrity of that evidence in the period up to the trial, and the management of disclosure to ensure that further evidence may come to light, may be of considerable significance. This is particularly evident in the terrorism context of a number of the leading cases, but it will apply in any serious criminal investigation.

Whatever the merits of that approach in a criminal context, it is problematic to apply it to detention of people with mental disabilities. The ethos of the latter is care, not punishment, and investigations to justify should be based on medical or social factors, not policing. A detention based on mental disorder is unlikely to be based on a specific and defined incident analogous to a crime; it may instead be based on a mental condition and a broad array of social and practical factors. Relevance thus does not necessarily fall into the neat criteria of criminal investigations. Unlike the usual criminal case, a person detained because of a mental disability may be suffering from a mental condition that makes it impossible for him or her to appreciate the relevant information at the time of the detention. Alternatively, the relevant disability may mean that individual is unable to make the rational assessments during examination that a person arrested for a crime may be taken by the Court to make in questioning by the police. Does this affect the scope of the information that must be disclosed, and does Article 5 import a duty to give the relevant information again at a time when the individual is able to process it? In the event that the detainee is likely to continue to lack capacity for some time, is there an obligation to provide the reasons required by Article 5(2) to someone other than the detainee? The lack of relevant case law offers few clear answers to these questions, but some analysis may provide some possibilities.

Article 5(2) expressly requires that the information be made available to the individual 'in a language he [or she] understands'. Certainly, this means that interpreters must be available to assist persons who do not speak the individual's language, but for people with intellectual disabilities, it must also mean that the reasons must be given using simple vocabulary and sentence structures, consistent with the detainee's ability to understand. The appropriate approach can be understood from the Court's view in *Fox* that a key purpose of Article 5(2) is to place the individual in a position to decide whether to exercise his or her rights to challenge the detention under Article 5(4). For an individual who at that time cannot understand the relevant information, the purpose of ensuring such a real choice means that it is arguable that the information must be re-explained at

---

company for some time, and took into consideration that he was a board member and manager of that company with a specialised financial knowledge of its situation.
[60]   See for example, *H.B. v. Switzerland, op. cit.*, para. 48.

a time when the individual is better able to understand it. It may also mean that the information must be provided in written form, so that the detained person can read the information whenever he or she feels comfortable in doing so.

The relationship drawn by the Court between Articles 5(2) and 5(4) may also be useful in assessing the breadth of information that must be provided. If the information to be provided is to enable the individual to decide whether to proceed to a hearing under Article 5(4), the scope of the hearing can be taken as a guide to the scope of the information that must be provided. *X. v. the United Kingdom* concerned rights under Articles 5(2) and 5(4) following the recall to a high security psychiatric hospital. The Court defined the scope of the Article 5(4) hearing in the following terms:

> The review should, however, be wide enough to bear on those conditions which, according to the Convention, are essential for the "lawful" detention of a person on the ground of unsoundness of mind, especially as the reasons capable of initially justifying such a detention may cease to exist. . . . This means that in the instant case, Article 5 para. 4 (art. 5–4) required an appropriate procedure allowing a court to examine whether the patient's disorder still persisted and whether the Home Secretary was entitled to think that a continuation of the compulsory confinement was necessary in the interest of public safety [public safety being the justification for the recall under the relevant domestic law].[61]

Sufficient information must therefore include that which will allow the detainee, with legal advice if necessary, to decide whether to proceed to an Article 5(4) hearing. The information should contain the hospital's opinion on diagnosis, and the reason why that disability 'warrants' detention in a psychiatric hospital or similar institution. It is a matter of speculation how far the Court will insist on further specificity. If the detainee decides to challenge the detention, however, the evidence for the reasons for detention will become clearer. With a view to developing a relationship of trust between mental health professional and patient, it will usually be good practice for the hospital to provide specifics when they are requested.

As noted above, the Court has been clear that Article 5(2) rights do apply to people detained under Article 5(1)(e). As noted earlier in this chapter, many people enter psychiatric and related institutions without formal legal compulsion. Some nonetheless are deprived of their liberty under Article 5 from the time they enter, because of the intensity of the controls on them and the limited choice they have.[62] Other people will be formally detained after they have entered the institution on an informal basis. This can be an invisible process to the detainee. Unlike criminal detentions, psychiatric detention is not normally achieved by informing the individual that he or she is under arrest, but instead by the completion and filing of the relevant forms, a process about which the detainee may not be aware. This was the situation in *Van der Leer v. the Netherlands*: the detainee was unaware that this process had been completed until ten days later, when she

---

[61]　*X. v. the United Kingdom, op. cit.*, para. 58.
[62]　See further pages 33–4, 36–7, above.

was placed into an isolation room. The Court found that the failure to inform her of her detention and to provide reasons constituted a breach of Article 5(2):

> It therefore appears that neither the manner in which she was informed of the measures depriving her of her liberty, nor the time it took to communicate this information to her, corresponded to the requirements of Article 5 § 2 (art. 5–2). In fact it was all the more important to bring the measures in question to her attention since she was already in a psychiatric hospital prior to the Cantonal Court judge's decision, which did not change her situation in factual terms.[63]

Detentions pursuant to Article 5(1)(e) are unlike criminal detentions, in that there is a *periodic* right to a hearing to challenge the detention.[64] Following *Fox*, if a key factor in the scope of rights under Article 5(2) is to allow a decision as to whether to apply to challenge the detention under Article 5(4), it must follow that the obligation to provide reasons for the detention arises at least as often as the right to apply for a hearing under Article 5(4). It cannot be that it ceases after the initial detention.

Is the right to reasons under Article 5(2) a periodic right, based on the occurrence of a new right to apply to challenge the detention under Article 5(4), or a continuous right to be informed of changes in factors relevant to the detention? If the Court views the sole reason for Article 5(2) as the decision as to whether to apply for a hearing under Article 5(4), then the Article 5(2) right would re-arise each time a new court hearing could be applied for. The Convention does not create an obligation to apply for such a court hearing, however. If a detainee chooses not to apply for such a hearing immediately, the logic of *Fox* would be that the right to reasons would continue so long as the right to apply for the court hearing remains active.

This is not necessarily the sole basis for Article 5(2), however. Article 5(2) is separate from Article 5(4), and the right to an explanation for detention is significant even if the detainee does not choose to exercise rights to challenge the detention. It is also a protection against arbitrariness, an insistence that the State should explain itself to the detainee, and a protection against a Kafkaesque bureaucracy. In that event, the right is easier to understand as an ongoing right, rather than a right which depends on the existence of a right to apply for a court hearing under Article 5(4). Such an approach is consistent with the requirement in *Winterwerp* that the legal authority to detain lasts only so long as the substantive conditions for detention continue to exist.[65] If the right to detain the individual is contingent on the continuing existence of these factors, which are to be kept under ongoing review, it is at least arguable that the right to reasons under Article 5(2) is similarly continuous.

---

[63] *Van der Leer v. the Netherlands, op. cit.,* para. 31.
[64] *Winterwerp v. the Netherlands, op. cit.,* para. 55. See further pages XXX below.
[65] *Winterwerp v. the Netherlands, op. cit.,* para. 39.

Emergencies

The protections contained in Article 5 are significantly reduced in emergency situations. In such situations, it is not necessary to have formal medical evidence of mental disorder prior to detention, and the rights to challenge such detentions is markedly reduced.

Considerable flexibility is permitted to national authorities in defining what constitutes an emergency. In the words of the European Court of Human Rights in *X. v. the United Kingdom*,

> The *Winterwerp* judgment expressly identified "emergency cases" as constituting an exception to the principle that the individual concerned should not be deprived of his liberty "unless he has been reliably shown to be of 'unsound mind'" . . .; neither can it be inferred from the *Winterwerp* judgment that the "objective medical expertise" must in all conceivable cases be obtained before rather than after confinement of a person on the ground of unsoundness of mind. Clearly, where a provision of domestic law is designed, amongst other things, to authorise emergency confinement of persons capable of presenting a danger to others, it would be impracticable to require thorough medical examination prior to any arrest or detention. A wide discretion must in the nature of things be enjoyed by the national authority empowered to order such emergency confinements.[66]

Clearly, then, when immediate intervention is *necessary* to prevent a danger to other people, the State may consider an emergency to exist. It would seem that dangerousness is not a necessary condition for an emergency, however. *Winterwerp* itself was, initially, an emergency detention. In that case, the facts justifying the emergency detention were that Mr Winterwerp had stolen some documents from the local registry office, and, when detained by the police as a result, was later found naked on a bed in the police cell.[67] The psychiatric evidence, obtained some six weeks later, stated that he was 'a schizophrene, suffering from imaginary and Utopian ideas, who has for a fairly long time been destroying himself as well as his family' and that he was 'unaware of his morbid condition,'[68] although how evident these factors would have been to the authorities at the time of the initial detention is a matter of speculation. For present purposes, it is sufficient to note that he was not immediately dangerous at the time of the emergency detention. It must therefore be taken that the Court will not preclude emergency detentions defined primarily on the severity of the disorder.

Any detention, emergency or otherwise, must of course be justified under domestic law. Once again, the ECtHR appears to accord a remarkable discretion to domestic authorities as to how, if at all, this domestic law is to be defined. The applicant in *X. v. the United Kingdom*, for example, was a person with a mental disability who had been convicted of a criminal offence, and following a period of psychiatric detention, had been given leave of absence from the psychiatric institution. For almost three years, he lived

---

[66] *X. v. the United Kingdom, op. cit.*, para. 41.
[67] *Winterwerp v. the Netherlands, op. cit.*, para. 23.
[68] *Winterwerp v. the Netherlands, op. cit.*, para. 24.

with his wife in the community. At the end of that time, his wife informed the authorities that she intended to leave him. Because of concerns as to the effect these marital problems would have on him, the authorities terminated Mr X's leave of absence and recalled him to the psychiatric institution. The relevant legislation permitted such returns to the institution, but provided no criteria as to when those should occur: the matter was entirely within the discretion of a government minister. Nonetheless, in recognition of the emergency context in which the decision might need to be made, the complete absence of such criteria did not bring about a contravention of Article 5(1).[69]

The rights to a court hearing provided by Article 5(4) are similarly limited for emergency detentions. In *X.* it was held that they had been met by the English *habeas corpus* procedure.[70] This allowed for scrutinization of the procedural aspects of the detention to ensure that they were in conformity with domestic law, but required of the detaining authority no material justification for the detention.

Because of the severe limitations to the rights of the detainee in emergency situations, it is of considerable relevance as to how long the emergency can be taken to last. In *Winterwerp*, though admitting to 'some hesitation' the ECtHR was tolerant of a six-week delay being categorised as an 'emergency'.[71] The Court would not be so tolerant today, illustrating the extreme caution of its early jurisprudence. As we shall see, it has found a violation of Article 5(4) on grounds of insufficient speed when a court decision was made 24 days after the detained person applied. Clearly the passage of time since the *Winterwerp* decision has seen a marked shift in the ECtHR's approach to speed.

The view that the Court would insist on a shorter period today does little to assist in determining how long that period would be. The emergency must last long enough that, with reasonable diligence, the detaining authority can fulfil its processes for formal detention, if such detention were found to be necessary. In practice, that may well depend on the facts of the case in question and the complexity of domestic legislation regarding non-emergency detentions. That said, legislation in England and Wales, for example requires both medical evidence and an assessment by a social worker prior to formal detention. That legislation allows only 72 hours for this to be accomplished for individuals found by police officers to be in need of immediate care or control,[72] and this period has proven workable. This would suggest that the appropriate period should be substantially less than that in *Winterwerp*.

Ongoing Detention and the Persistence of Mental Disorder

The *Winterwerp* criteria expressly require that the validity of continued confinement depends upon the persistence of mental disorder. This case draws no distinction between

---

[69] *X. v. the United Kingdom, op. cit.*, para. 41.
[70] *X. v. the United Kingdom, op. cit.*, para. 58.
[71] *Winterwerp v. the Netherlands, op. cit.*, para. 42.
[72] *Mental Health Act 1983*, s. 136.

the criteria for initial admission to a psychiatric institution and continued detention in it.[73] While this provision is still routinely cited by the ECtHR in its articulation of the scope of permitted detention under Article 5(1)(e), its meaning has been complicated by subsequent case law.

The complexity is that current trends in institutional care of people with mental disabilities no longer favour a 'clean break' from the institution at the end of detention. The view is instead that effective social re-integration is most likely to be accomplished if an individual is weaned from control. As a result, there has been a movement to releasing individuals from institutions in stages, subject to conditions that reduce over time.

When the individual's condition still meets the *Winterwerp* criteria, the Court has dealt with this situation by finding that a discharge from an institution subject to certain conditions (typically relating to place of accommodation and conditions of treatment) concerns merely degree of deprivation of liberty, and therefore does not raise an Article 5(1) issue.[74] In the event that a court or review tribunal orders a conditional discharge and the conditions cannot be fulfilled, however, a new right to challenge the detention arises under Article 5(4).[75] As discussed above, the Court has so far refused to impose a positive obligation on States to provide the community services that would allow detention to be avoided for people with mental disabilities. The right to a fresh court hearing does not change that approach, because the fresh court hearing will determine whether detention remains warranted given that the preferred conditions for discharge cannot be met. The court at the new hearing would be faced with an unfortunate choice: continue the detention of an individual who it believes should be released subject to conditions, or release the individual on conditions it thinks inadequate. Neither of these appears a desirable outcome.

The situation is even more controversial if the individual's condition does not meet the *Winterwerp* criteria. This was the case in *Johnson v. the United Kingdom*.[76] Mr Johnson had been convicted of a serious assault in 1984, but because of a diagnosis of schizophrenia and personality disorder, had been sent to a high security psychiatric hospital. When his detention was reviewed by a tribunal in 1989, that tribunal found that he was no longer suffering from a mental disorder. It did not, however, order his immediate discharge:

> The [applicant] had an unrealistic opinion of his ability to live on his own in the community after nearly five years in Rampton Hospital and required rehabilitation under medical supervision and that such rehabilitation (and its associated support) can be provided only in a hostel environment. Further, the Tribunal is of the opinion that the recurrence of

---

[73] *Winterwerp v. the Netherlands, op. cit.*, para. 39.
[74] *Kolanis v. the United Kingdom*, Application No. 517/02, judgment 21 June 2005, (2006) 42 EHRR 12, para. 72.
[75] See *Kolanis v. the United Kingdom, op. cit.*, para. 80, discussed further below.
[76] *Johnson v. the United Kingdom*, Application No. 22520/93, judgment 24 October 1997, (1997) 27 EHRR 296.

mental illness requiring recall to hospital cannot be excluded until after successful rehabil-itation of that nature.[77]

Three and a half years later, he had still not been released. A number of tribunal hearings to review his detention had been held in the interim, and in each instance, the medical evidence continued to be that he was not suffering from a mental disorder. Indeed, at his final hearing in January 1993, the medical evidence was that 'with the benefit of hindsight it appears unlikely that he ever experienced more than a drug-induced psychosis'.[78] He had not in fact been taking medication for a mental disorder since 1988. At that hearing, he was discharged from detention without conditions.

Clearly, an important aspect of this case was the tribunal's inability to enforce the con-ditions it imposed. When the case reached Strasbourg, the European Court of Human Rights held that this created an indefinite deferral to Mr Johnson's release, and found a violation of Article 5(1) as a result.[79]

More significant for instant purposes was that the ECtHR held that even though Mr Johnson was not suffering from a mental disorder, he did not thereby acquire an imme-diate right to immediate and unconditional release:

[I]t does not automatically follow from a finding by an expert authority that the mental dis-order which justified a patient's compulsory confinement no longer persists, that the latter must be immediately and unconditionally released into the community.

   Such a rigid approach to the interpretation of that condition would place an unacceptable degree of constraint on the responsible authority's exercise of judgment to determine in par-ticular cases and on the basis of all the relevant circumstances whether the interests of the patient and the community into which he is to be released would in fact be best served by this course of action. It must also be observed that in the field of mental illness the assessment as to whether the disappearance of the symptoms of the illness is confirmation of complete recovery is not an exact science. Whether or not recovery from an episode of mental illness which justified a patient's confinement is complete and definitive or merely apparent cannot in all cases be measured with absolute certainty. It is the behaviour of the patient in the period spent outside the confines of the psychiatric institution which will be conclusive of this.

   62. It is to be recalled in this respect that the Court in its Luberti judgment . . . accepted that the termination of the confinement of an individual who has previously been found by a court to be of unsound mind and to present a danger to society is a matter that concerns, as well as that individual, the community in which he will live if released. Having regard to the pressing nature of the interests at stake, and in particular the very serious nature of the offence committed by Mr Luberti when mentally ill, it was accepted in that case that the responsible authority was entitled to proceed with caution and needed some time to consider whether to terminate his confinement, even if the medical evidence pointed to his recovery.

   63. In the view of the Court it must also be acknowledged that a responsible authority is entitled to exercise a similar measure of discretion in deciding whether in the light of all the relevant circumstances and the interests at stake it would in fact be appropriate to order

---

[77] Quoted in *Johnson v. the United Kingdom, op. cit.*, para. 18.
[78] Quoted in *Johnson v. the United Kingdom, op. cit.*, para. 31.
[79] *Johnson v. the United Kingdom, op. cit.*, para. 67.

the immediate and absolute discharge of a person who is no longer suffering from the mental disorder which led to his confinement. That authority should be able to retain some measure of supervision over the progress of the person once he is released into the community and to that end make his discharge subject to conditions. It cannot be excluded either that the imposition of a particular condition may in certain circumstances justify a deferral of discharge from detention, having regard to the nature of the condition and to the reasons for imposing it. It is, however, of paramount importance that appropriate safeguards are in place so as to ensure that any deferral of discharge is consonant with the purpose of Article 5 § 1 and with the aim of the restriction in sub-paragraph (e) (see paragraph 60 above) and, in particular, that discharge is not unreasonably delayed.[80]

The scope of these comments are not entirely clear. Certainly, the ECtHR has held that domestic courts may take the time to do proper investigations to satisfy themselves that the release of an individual is appropriate, so long as that investigation is not unduly delayed. That is the point of the paragraph from *Luberti v. Italy*,[81] cited by the Court, but that is a question about delay, not the attainment of the substantive criteria in *Winterwerp*.

Further, the domestic courts can certainly impose conditions that do not reach the level of severity to engage Article 5. As discussed early in this chapter, conditions that do not significantly interfere with the daily life of the individual might well not reach this level of intrusiveness. Subject to the comments regarding *Ashingdane*, below, a condition that the progress of an individual living in the community be monitored on an occasional basis by a professional would for example be unlikely to engage Article 5. Such a condition might well be sufficient to meet the concerns identified by the Court. Such conditions may in practice take some time to organise and it would seem from *Johnson* that detention can continue in that period.

It is unclear how the proposed conditions in *Johnson* itself would have been interpreted in this regard. The key condition was that he live in a hostel, but the facts do not indicate what sort of care and services he would have receive there. It is therefore not clear whether this requirement would have engaged or violated Article 5. The ECtHR specifically declined to make a finding on this point, because of Mr Johnson's success on other aspects of his application.[82]

The difficulty with restricting the Court's reasoning to conditions that do not engage Article 5 is the decision in *Ashingdane v. the United Kingdom*,[83] discussed earlier in this chapter. In this case, the Court found that for people subject to formal powers allowing detention under mental health legislation, the threshold for the engagement of Article 5 is very low. By the time his case was heard, Mr Ashingdane himself was allowed to leave the hospital during the day. As this was a freedom that could be taken away,

---

[80] *Johnson v. the United Kingdom, op. cit.*, paras. 61–63.
[81] *Luberti v. Italy*, Application No. 9019/80, judgment 23 February 1984, Series A no. 75, pp. 12–13, 1984 6 EHRR 441.
[82] *Johnson v. the United Kingdom, op. cit.*, para. 68.
[83] *Ashingdane v. the United Kingdom, op. cit.*

however, it was held that there was still a deprivation of liberty, and Article 5 was still engaged. If the conditions imposed by the court or tribunal were enforceable in this manner, therefore, it might well be the case that they would engage Article 5. If it is the Court's view that it is conditions that do not in themselves constitute deprivations of liberty under Article 5 that ought to be permitted, *Ashingdane* may need to be revisited.

That said, *Ashingdane* may itself provide a solution to most of the problematic cases. *Johnson* raised problems because at the time when conditional release was first considered, the medical evidence was that he no longer had a mental disability. The more usual case is that conditional release will be considered at a time when the medical evidence still suggests the presence of a mental disability, but a disability that a court considers not to justify the intensity of full-scale detention so long as specified conditions are met. Continuing to view these as engaging Article 5 brings them within the scope of the *Kolanis* decision, which guarantees a forum to contest whether the restrictions are appropriate.

The alternative reading is that the ECtHR is prepared to say that individuals may be detained under Article 5(1)(e) on the basis that they once were 'persons of unsound mind', even if there is no evidence that they continue to be so. This would be a rather startling result, but it may be implied in their claim that confirmation of complete recovery from mental disorder is 'not an exact science', and 'the behaviour of the patient in the period spent outside the confines of the psychiatric institution' provides the only conclusive proof.[84] This is a surprising statement in the context of *Johnson* itself, where the undisputed medical evidence at the time of the tribunal hearings that he was not suffering from mental disorder at all. It suggests that, while *Winterwerp* requires medical evidence that there is a mental disorder to support an initial detention, courts and tribunals may be free to reject the contrary medical evidence in deciding whether the individual is to be released.

It is difficult to see that the detention of persons who were once of 'unsound mind' (but are no longer) can reasonably be justified given the wording of Article 5(1)(e). If the ECtHR seriously proposes to allow the ongoing detention of such people for a period longer than that necessary to arrange their release from detention, it should define the permitted parameters of such detention without delay.

An Enforceable Right to Compensation (Article 5(5))

If the ECtHR finds that there has been a breach of the Convention, it has the power to award 'just satisfaction' to the applicant.[85] That includes an award of financial compensation, when the Court thinks it appropriate, as well as legal costs.[86] The right to com-

---

[84] *Johnson v. the United Kingdom, op. cit.*, para. 61.
[85] Article 41.
[86] Regarding financial compensation, see for example *Hentrich v. France*, A.296-A (1994) 18 EHRR 440 (for pecuniary damages) and *Yagci and Sargin v. Turkey*, A.319 (1995) 20 EHRR 505 (for non-pecuniary damages). Regarding legal expenses, see *McCann v. the United Kingdom*, A.324 (1995) 21 EHRR 97.

pensation in Article 5(5) is thus not directed solely to awards by the ECtHR. Instead, the Article provides a right to compensation before the domestic courts for any violation of the right to liberty under Article 5. The right does not guarantee a financial award if there has been no real injury suffered, and, rather surprisingly, it would seem that the ECtHR does not view the infringement of a Convention right in itself as giving rise to a compensable injury.[87] For example, in *H.L. v. the United Kingdom*, discussed above, no award of financial compensation was made, notwithstanding the finding that Mr H.L. had been deprived of his liberty in violation of the Convention.[88] What is provided is instead that if a compensable injury has in fact occurred, there must be a way for a domestic court to enforce the provision of appropriate compensation.[89]

Discharge/Release from Hospital and Challenging Detention

In *Winterwerp* the ECtHR held that the validity of continued confinement depends upon the persistence of a disorder of the required severity.[90] As will be discussed further below, there has been further elaboration regarding these conditions in the context of release. Nonetheless, it is incumbent on the domestic authorities to keep the detention of persons with mental disability under review, and to terminate the detention when the relevant conditions are no longer met.

In addition, Article 5(4) provides the detainee with the right to apply to an independent court or court-like body to challenge his or her detention.

Challenging Detention under Article 5(4)

Article 5(4) further provides the detainee with the right to challenge his or her detention:

> Everyone deprived of his liberty by arrest or detention shall be entitled to take proceedings by which the lawfulness of his detention shall be decided speedily by a court and his release ordered if his detention is not lawful.

In *Winterwerp* the ECtHR took the opportunity to say that this is a periodical right, on the common sense basis that mental disorder can be a changing condition.[91] Later case law has gone a considerable way in clarifying the scope of Article 5(4) rights, with the result that this procedural guarantee now imposes some clear-cut obligations on domestic governments.

---

[87] *Nikolova v. Bulgaria*, Application No. 31195/96, judgment 25 March 1999, (2001) 31 EHRR 3, para. 76.
[88] *H.L. v. the United Kingdom*, Application No. 45508/99, judgment 5 October 2004, para. 149.
[89] See for example, *Curley v. the United Kingdom*, Application No. 32340/96, judgment 28 March 2000, (2001) 31 EHRR 157, paras. 37–8.
[90] *Winterwerp v. the Netherlands, op. cit.*, para. 39.
[91] *Winterwerp v. the Netherlands, op. cit.*, para. 55.

The term 'court' has been given a wide meaning. It does not matter whether the body is called a 'tribunal' as opposed to a 'court' as long as it has three essential attributes: independence from the executive; independence from the parties to the case; and a judicial character. A panel drawn from the hospital's psychiatrists or managers would not have independence from the parties to the case.

In some countries the body which performs the role of a 'court' under Article 5(4) is a specialised administrative tribunal, not necessarily staffed by 'judges' as defined by national constitutions. In England and Wales, for example, the law provides for a 'mental health review tribunal' to decide on such cases. Each of these part-time tribunals has a lawyer as president, sitting with a psychiatrist and lay (meaning non-lawyer and non-medical) member. Such a tribunal is acceptable under the Convention, so long as all those appointed are suitably impartial. In *D.N. v. Switzerland*[92] the ECtHR said that impartiality has both a subjective and objective component. The particular judge must both be and be seen to be impartial. A 'legitimate doubt', viewed objectively, is sufficient to exclude. On the other hand the standpoint of the parties themselves is important but not decisive. What is decisive is whether this fear can be held to be objectively justified;[93] it must be reasonable of the party to think that the judge might be impartial.

If domestic law allows for a psychiatrist as part of the 'court', care must be taken to ensure that his or her impartiality has not been compromised by previous contact with the patient, or settled opinions on the case. The individual should further not be on the staff of the institution in which the detention is to take place. In the system illustrated by the case of *D.N. v. Switzerland*, the psychiatrist, as 'judge rapporteur', had prepared a written report on the patient opposing the application to be discharged, and then sat with a judge as a member of the court. This, the ECtHR said, gave rise to legitimate fears in the applicant that 'he had a preconceived opinion' and would not be impartial. In the United Kingdom, the medical (psychiatric) member of a mental health review tribunal interviews the patient before the hearing on his own, and then sits as a tribunal member for the hearing. But by contrast with the position of a Swiss psychiatrist rapporteur his or her examination is to enable him or her to form a view on the patient's mental condition, as opposed to the merits of the application for discharge. Following the examination the psychiatrist is not expected to have formed a settled view on the case. The psychiatrist does not prepare a written report or communicate views to the parties, although he or she may do so to fellow tribunal members. The psychiatrist is expected to maintain an open mind until all the evidence has been heard. The medical member's role in this respect is controversial.[94] The English court has expressed the view that it does not violate the

---

[92] Application No. 27154/95, judgment 29 March 2001, (2003) 37 EHRR 21.

[93] *D.N. v. Switzerland*, Application No. 27154/95, judgment 29 March 2001, (2003) 37 EHRR 21, para. 46.

[94] See for example, Department of Health Expert Committee, *Review of the Mental Health Act 1983* (the Richardson Report) (London: Department of Health, 1999), para. 5.64, 5.67. Regarding how the tribunal hearings actually function, and the conflicting role of the medical member on the tribunal, see

Convention,[95] but the process has as yet not been subjected to scrutiny by the European Court of Human Rights itself.[96]

Whatever the body is called, it must have court-like attributes. In *Winterwerp* the ECtHR recognised that the Dutch District and Regional Courts which had reviewed and approved continuation of the applicant's detention were 'courts' from an organisational point of view in that they were 'independent both of the executive and the parties to the case'.[97] Nonetheless, citing and adopting the previous decision of the European Commission on Human Rights, the European Court of Human Rights added:

> Nevertheless the intervention of such a body will satisfy Article 5(4) only on condition that 'the procedure followed has a judicial character and gives to the individual concerned guarantees appropriate to the kind of deprivation of liberty in question'.[98]

The reviews of Mr Winterwerp's detention lacked guarantees now regarded as standard. He had often not been notified about the Court proceedings or their outcome, nor been heard in person, nor been given the chance to question the evidence against him. On several occasions the public prosecutor had not even forwarded Mr Winterwerp's requests for discharge to the court, rejecting them as devoid of any prospects of success.

The European Commission of Human Rights in *Winterwerp* had held that for detention of 'persons of unsound mind' the absolute minimum for a judicial procedure was the right of the individual to present his own case and to challenge the medical and social evidence adduced in support of his detention. Before the ECtHR the Applicant contended that a right to be legally assisted should be read into Article 5(4).

By contrast the Dutch Government argued that Article 5(4) did not compel a court to hear in person a patient who had been established, on the basis of objective medical evidence, to be 'incapable of presenting statements of any relevance for the proceedings'.[99] Such was the case, they argued, with Mr Winterwerp.

Rejecting the Government's submission, the ECtHR, in a passage regularly cited in later cases, laid down the broad principles which were to govern cases under Article 5(1)(e):

> The Court does not share the Government's view. The judicial proceedings referred to in Article 5(4) need not, it is true, always be attended by the same guarantees as those required under Article 6(1) for civil and criminal litigation. Nonetheless, it is essential that the person concerned should have access to a court and the opportunity to be heard either in person

---

G. Richardson and D. Machlin, 'Doctors on tribunals: A confusion of roles', 176 *British Journal of Psychiatry* (2000) 110.

[95]   *R. v. MHRT, North and East London Region, ex p. H*, [2001] EWHC Civ 415.

[96]   An identical system in Ontario, Canada has been found to be a breach of the common law duty of fairness, however: see *Re Egglestone and Mousseau and Advisory Review Board* (1983) 150 DLR (3d) 86. The finding of such a breach suggests that a challenge to the English system before the ECtHR would be credible.

[97]   *Winterwerp v. the Netherlands, op. cit.*, para. 56.

[98]   *Winterwerp v. the Netherlands, op. cit.*, para. 57.

[99]   *Winterwerp v. the Netherlands, op. cit.*, para. 59.

or, where necessary, through some form of representation, failing which he will not have been afforded 'the fundamental guarantees of procedure applied in matters of deprivation of liberty'. Mental illness may entail restricting or modifying the manner of exercise of such a right, but it cannot justify impairing the very essence of the right. Indeed, special procedural safeguards may proved called for in order to protect the interests of persons who, on account of their mental disabilities, are not fully capable of acting for themselves.[100]

This implies a fair and disciplined fact-finding process, in which the parties to the case can challenge evidence submitted to the court, all evidence presented to the court is heard by the patient and lawyer, and the patient him or herself has the opportunity to give oral evidence. It is not acceptable for the court to act on information that has not been disclosed to the parties, or worse to just one of the parties. In *Nikolova v. Bulgaria* the ECtHR held:

> A Court examining an appeal against detention must provide guarantees of a judicial procedure. The proceedings must be adversarial and must always ensure "equality of arms" between the parties, the prosecutor and the detained person. . . . Equality of arms is not ensured if counsel is denied access to those documents in the investigation file which are essential in order effectively to challenge the lawfulness of his client's detention.[101]

Although this was a case concerning pre-trial criminal process, the ECtHR expressed its view in general language, and it is therefore suggested that exactly the same principle should hold true for court hearings dealing with detention of people with mental disabilities.

The need for a judicial character almost certainly implies a power of subpoena (a power of the parties of the case to order a third person to give evidence), so that the court can order documents to be submitted, or witnesses to be compelled. However it does not require that hearings be in public, and there is some argument that such court hearings dealing with personal matters should not be heard in public, or at least not without the consent of the person detained.

The judicial character further implies that the court should have the power to ensure compliance with its decisions. This will not be met if the court only advises a separate person who actually makes the decision as to whether detention will be continued.[102] Under some domestic legal systems, the court or tribunal can order an end to detention subject to conditions. In *Johnson v. the United Kingdom*,[103] for example, the tribunal ordered the release of a person detained in a high security psychiatric hospital on condition that he live in hostel accommodation for a time, to allow his gradual re-integration into a non-institutional environment. Such accommodation could not be secured for a number of

---

[100] *Winterwerp v. the Netherlands, op. cit.,* para. 60.
[101] *Nikolova v. Bulgaria, op. cit.,* para. 58.
[102] *X. v. the United Kingdom, op. cit.,* para. 61. In this case, the review tribunal advised the Home Secretary (a politician and cabinet minister), who actually made the decision regarding continued detention. The Home Secretary was not obliged to follow the advice of the tribunal. This system constituted a violation of Article 5(4).
[103] (1997) 27 EHRR 296.

years. The ECtHR held that the imposition of this condition without a corresponding power to require its implementation introduced an indefinite deferral to Mr Johnson's release. This was an unreasonable delay, and constituted a violation of Article 5(1).[104] In *Johnson*, The ECtHR declined to consider Article 5(4) specifically, on the basis that it disclosed no separate issue.

More recently, in *Kolanis v. the United Kingdom*,[105] the ECtHR adopted a somewhat different approach, using Article 5(4). As mentioned above, in that case, a review tribunal ordered the discharge of Ms Kolanis from a psychiatric hospital on condition that she continue to be supervised by a psychiatrist. No psychiatrist was prepared to undertake this responsibility. Rather than find that the continued detention was unreasonable and a violation of Article 5(1), the Court held that it constituted a fresh detention which gave rise to a fresh right under Article 5(4):

> Where, as in the present case, the MHRT [mental health review tribunal] finds that a patient's detention in hospital is no longer necessary and that she is eligible for release on conditions, the Court considers that new issues of lawfulness may arise where detention nonetheless continues, due, for example, to difficulties in fulfilling the conditions. It follows that such patients are entitled under Article 5 § 4 to have the lawfulness of that continued detention determined by a court with requisite promptness.[106]

The fact that no fresh challenge was available for a year constituted unreasonable delay, and was therefore a breach of Article 5(4). *Johnson* was distinguished on the basis that the Applicant in that case no longer had a mental disability at all when the conditions were imposed; Ms Kolanis did remain mentally ill, leaving open the possibility that her continued detention was justified under Article 5(1).

It is not obvious that this solves the problems implied in *Johnson* and *Kolanis*. In both cases, the services required by the tribunal following Article 5(4) hearings were not provided, resulting in the continued detention of the individual. In *Kolanis*, the ECtHR held that 'a failure by the local authority to use 'best efforts' or any breach of duty by a psychiatrist in refusing care in the community would be amenable to judicial review.'[107] That is not the case in England, however, the jurisdiction in question in *Kolanis*. The English court has no jurisdiction to require a medical practitioner to provide services that are against his or her clinical judgment of the individual's best interests,[108] and has steadfastly declined to require that governments make available resources to fund particular medical care.[109] It is therefore not obvious that the failure or refusal to provide services, even

---

[104] *Johnson v. the United Kingdom, op. cit.*, para. 67.
[105] *Kolanis v. the United Kingdom, op. cit.*
[106] *Kolanis v. the United Kingdom, op. cit.*
[107] *Kolanis v. the United Kingdom, op. cit.*, para. 71.
[108] See *Re J* [1992] 4 All ER 614, and, in a psychiatric context, *R v. Ealing District Health Authority, ex p. Fox* [1993] 3 All ER 170 at 183.
[109] See for example, *R v. Secretary of State for Social Services, ex p. Hincks* (1980) 1 BMLR 93; *R v. Central Birmingham Health Authority, ex p. Walker* (1987) 3 BMLR 32; *R v. Cambridge District Health Authority, ex p. B*, [1995] 1 WLR 898.

if those services are available and a condition for discharge laid down by the Article 5(4) tribunal, will be judicially reviewable under English law. Absent this enforcement mechanism, the 'order' of the tribunal becomes little more than a recommendation to the service providers; the 'order' is essentially unenforceable.[110] In *X. v. the United Kingdom*, the ECtHR held that a process where review tribunal orders merely advised a government official were insufficient to meet the safeguards of Article 5(4).[111] There is no reason why orders that cannot be enforced against service providers ought to be any more acceptable.

The timing and frequency of hearings

Two issues of timing arise under Article 5(4). Firstly, how speedily must a decision be reached after a detained person applies to a court, and secondly how frequently can a detained person re-apply to a court?

On the first issue the ECtHR has drawn a distinction between first applications and subsequent applications. For a first application it has declined to lay down a general rule. In *E. v. Norway*,[112] the ECtHR criticised a delay of 55 days (7 weeks and 6 days). In that case it contrasted the speed required under Article 5(4) with the requirement in Article 6(3) to be informed 'promptly' of the nature of a criminal charge. The language of the latter, it concluded, was more pressing. In 2002, however, in *L.R. v. France*,[113] the ECtHR held that a delay of 24 days was insufficiently speedy in a case of involuntary civil (noncriminal) detention that had no unusual features. The ECtHR declined to specify the 'permissible maximum' delay, but it seems unlikely that it would have so emphatically found a violation of Article 5(4) unless it was contemplating a maximum delay of one or two weeks. This period of time is consistent with the United Nations Human Rights Committee, the monitoring body for the International Covenant on Civil and Political Rights, that takes the view that a two-week detention without court review is incompatible with that treaty.[114]

If the longest permissible delay is held to be fourteen or even seven days, it will have implications for the nature of the court hearing and the rights of the parties. There may be no Convention right to have access to an independent psychiatric opinion, but where domestic financial arrangements so allow it can provide a crucial counter-balance to the

---

[110] In *I.H. v. the United Kingdom*, Application No. 17111/04, judgment regarding admissibility 21 June 2005, for example, the local forensic service agency declined to make a psychiatrist available to fulfil the terms of an order on the basis that it viewed the court decision to conditionally discharge the individual as 'premature and dangerous'. [para. 7] This appears to amount to little more than disagreement with the result before the Article 5 tribunal. It is not obvious how referral back for a new hearing will alter that situation, and the new court will be faced with a choice of agreeing with the forensic service agency or continuing the impasse. Either way, the applicant is will not be released. The Fourth Section of the Court nonetheless found the application inadmissible.

[111] *X. v. the United Kingdom, op. cit.*, para. 61.

[112] Application No. 11701/85, judgment 28 August 1990, (1990) 17 EHRR 30.

[113] Application No. 33395/96, judgment 27 June 2002.

[114] See for example, *Concluding observations of the Human Rights Committee: Estonia*, 15 March 2003, CCPR/CO/77/EST, para. 10.

views of a patient's treating psychiatrist, and hence improve the patient's chance of securing release. If the time between application and decision is short, there is unlikely to be sufficient time for a patient to arrange for an independent psychiatric opinion to be provided, particularly since this will usually require obtaining access to a legal aid system to secure the necessary funds.

The solution may lie in treating the requirement of speed as one that the patient may waive if he so wishes. Thus the patient would be entitled to a speedy decision, but could elect for delay in order to, for example, obtain independent medical evidence. In earlier days the ECtHR appeared to have set its face against such a solution. Even when delay had been at a detained person's request, it held that the relevant Government was in violation of its duty. But in later and more recent decisions the line has been softening. In *Cottenham v. the United Kingdom*[115] the ECtHR found that a tribunal could not be criticised for a delay of 10 months caused by a patient's lawyer's request for adjournments in order to obtain an independent psychiatric report.

Less urgency is required with second or subsequent applications. The ECtHR has not yet definitively stated how frequently a patient must be able to exercise the 'periodic' right under Article 5(4) but the case of *Herczegfalvy v. Austria*[116] indicates the ECtHR approach in the early 1990s. It considered three intervals, the first 15 months, the second two years, and the third nine months. It decided that the first two were excessive and the last acceptable. The ECtHR was therefore tolerant of an annual right. However this approach may yield to further challenge. If a newly detained person seeks a court review soon after admission a full year's delay until he or she can present a second application seems a very conservative approach, out of keeping with the time required to treat the acute phase of many mental illnesses.

When exercising a periodic right of access to the court, the same question of speed arises. How quickly must the court give a decision after the application from the patient is received? In *Koendjbiharie v. the Netherlands*[117] the ECtHR found a delay of 4 months between the detainee's application and the actual decision to be excessive, but there are no more recent cases to provide further guidance.

In a number of European jurisdictions, judicial reviews are held periodically without the detainee applying for them. This process is unobjectionable, indeed probably desirable, as it provides a routine opportunity for the reassessment of a detainee's situation, especially if the person is not in a position, through disability or negligence of hospital authorities, to be aware of the right to apply to a court review. Regarding the ECHR, however, two points should be made. First, these court hearings are not a substitute for the ongoing assessment of the detainee's situation by the detaining authority. These hearings often happen annually. If the ECHR grounds for deprivation of liberty cease to apply between court hearings, the detention violates the ECHR from that time.

---

[115] *Cottenham v. the United Kingdom*, Application No. 36509/97, judgment 11 May 1999.
[116] Application No. 10533/83, judgment 31 August 1992, (1992) 15 EHRR 437.
[117] Application No. 11487/85, judgment 28 September 1990, (1991) 13 EHRR 820.

Secondly, however desirable such court hearings are, they do not meet the requirements of Article 5(4). In practice, such court hearings do not necessarily meet the required standard: the detainee is in some countries not told of the hearing, and representation is frequently inadequate or non-existent. More fundamentally, even if these procedural irregularities were corrected, these routine hearings would not satisfy Article 5(4). As the Court makes clear in *Rakevich v. Russia*, control over when to challenge the detention under Article 5(4) must rest with the person detained:

> Article 5 § 4 requires in the first place an independent legal device by which the detainee may appear before a judge who will determine the lawfulness of the detention. When this remedy is available, the detainee's access to the judge should not depend on the good will of the detaining authority. Whilst the legal mechanism contained in sections 33–35 of the Psychiatric Treatment Law, ensuring that a mental patient is brought before a judge automatically, constitutes an important safeguard against arbitrary detention, it would still be deficient if it does not contain the basic guarantee of Article 5 § 4. Surplus guarantees do not eliminate the need for fundamental ones.[118]

The provision of the hearing at a time when the person detained might well not consider himself or herself ready for it cannot be seen as consistent with Article 5(4).

The jurisprudence throughout this area presupposes that the detainee has the capacity to make decisions regarding an Article 5(4) hearing. This is not necessarily the case. As noted above, in some legal systems, 'informal' admissions may be made by the individual's guardian. The court procedure depriving the person of legal capacity and appointing a guardian may or may not consider the ability of the person with mental disability to make decisions regarding admission to and treatment in a psychiatric institution; often, it would seem that these decisions are made on the basis of capacity to manage financial affairs rather than capacity to make personal care decisions. It may thus be quite possible that the individual in fact may have capacity to make the admission decision, and actively object to it. Alternatively, it may be that the individual lacks capacity to make admission decisions. This does not mean that they are not deprived of their liberty, even if they are admitted informally.[119]

These two examples raise different questions. The first is easier to analyse. Rights under the ECHR accrue to individuals, who must themselves be victims in order to apply under the Convention. The fact that a carer or legal guardian rather than the person detained has been involved in the detention decision cannot deprive the detainee of his or her rights under Article 5(4). If the person detained has sufficient understanding to pursue a case under Article 5(4), it is his or her right to do so.

The second example raises the difficulty of what is to be done when the detainee does not have sufficient understanding to pursue his or her Article 5(4) rights. The facts in *H.L. v. the United Kingdom* provide a helpful scenario.[120] As described earlier in this chap-

---

[118] *Rakevich v. Russia*, Application No. 58973/00, judgment 28 October 2003, para. 44.
[119] See *H.L. v. the United Kingdom, op. cit.*, discussed above.
[120] See *H.L. v. the United Kingdom, op. cit.*, discussed above.

ter, in that case, the detained person had severe autism, and was unable to make the decision even to attempt to leave the hospital unit. It would be fantasy to pretend that he could either independently pursue an Article 5(4) court review and participate in a court hearing, or instruct a lawyer to do so on his behalf. The Article 5(4) hearing is an essential safeguard to the deprivation of liberty under Article 5, and the failure to ensure its appropriate provision to detained people who lack capacity such as Mr H.L. would make the *H.L.* case a hollow victory indeed. The question is how to make rights real for people such as Mr H.L. In *H.L.* itself, the problem was solved by the appointment of his cousin to challenge the detention on his behalf. That is fine if a suitable person exists. Even if there are carers and family members, however, they may for whatever reasons not wish to challenge the detention on the detainee's behalf. Unless some form of routine independent advocacy is provided, it is not obvious how far the rights obtained in *H.L.* will in fact be implemented in practice.

Even if the person lacking capacity is able to find a way to challenge the detention, the way in which Article 5 rights have been framed by the ECtHR may severely limit the usefulness of the challenge. For many people who lack capacity, some form of fairly intensive care régime will be necessary. Mr H.L. himself again provides a good example. His disabilities were such that living on his own was simply not an option for him. Instead, he needed care available on a continuous basis. He would not be able to go out on his own, or to make more than the most rudimentary decisions about his personal life. The question for Mr H.L. was not whether a deprivation of liberty would be required, but what form it would take: would it be in a psychiatric hospital, in a care home, or with his private carers? If the care régime in question is such as will constitute a deprivation of liberty, however – and it seems likely that whatever care was chosen for Mr H.L., it would constitute such a deprivation – Article 5 would be unlikely to provide a helpful outcome, since Article 5 concerns itself only with whether the right to liberty should be violated, not with the severity of the deprivation.[121] Yet it is the severity of the deprivation that is most likely to be of primary relevance to people in Mr H.L.'s position.

Representation

The entitlement to an Article 5(4) court hearing is the most tangible right conferred by Article 5, but it only acquires real significance when there is an effective system of legal or other representation. Self-advocacy in a psychiatric setting presents obvious difficulties. The detained person is likely to find the process unsettling and unfamiliar, whereas for those advocating continued detention it is probably a regular feature of their professional work. Hospital life tends to induce compliance from patients.[122] Detainees may therefore find it very difficult to adopt the role of questioner in an adversarial process. Such difficulties in pursuing litigation may be exacerbated in some cases by specific

---

[121] The ECHR contains no express right to be treated in the least restrictive manner possible, although regarding the possible incorporation of this principle by implication, see chapter 3.

[122] For the classic study on this point, see E. Goffman, *Asylums* (London: Penguin, 1961).

types of mental disability that can result in thought-disorder, or the adverse effects of psychiatric medication, which can result in an inability to concentrate. Such difficulties will not affect all psychiatric detainees, and the assumption that such persons are incapable of active involvement in their cases is often an offensive stereotype.[123] Nonetheless, a significant proportion of people who may wish to challenge their detention may be affected by these conditions to a greater or lesser degree.

Further, a successful challenge under Article 5(4) requires practical knowledge that the person detained may not possess. It is not simply a question of knowing the facts of the case, but the person must know the relevant domestic law, and have the specialised professional skills relating to examination of witnesses. Knowledge of the care system may also be of considerable relevance. The staff of the institution may not be prepared to offer helpful advice on what community-based care alternatives might be available to the person detained in the event of release, for example. Without such specialist knowledge, a detainee may be unable to put together a coherent alternative to detention, and that correspondingly decreases the likelihood of success at the Article 5(4) hearing.

Although Article 5 does not have a specific provision referring to representation and legal aid, such as can be found in Article 6(3) for criminal defendants, the ECtHR has strongly endorsed the need for legal representation on several occasions. Remarkably, it has yet to say, in plain terms, that as a matter of invariable principle *every* detained patient should have access to representation, legal or otherwise. Its consistent support for representation has been expressed as individual to the cases before it.

Few countries which have ratified the European Convention on Human Rights have systems of representation that would survive challenge. Most have not considered mental health representation a political or funding priority, and when representation is provided, in some countries it routinely fails to meet any adequate standard.[124] There is therefore a major lack of compliance. The ECtHR's case law is still very limited in this regard, but this may turn out to be an important area of contention in the future.

In its first statement of its expectations for an Article 5(4) court hearing in the field of mental disability in, the ECtHR in *Winterwerp* referred to the issue of representation, although in general terms, as part of the fundamental guarantees of liberty. The Court went on to say that Article 5(4) does not require that persons detained in psychiatric institutions under the head of 'unsound mind' should themselves take the initiative in obtaining legal representation before having recourse to a court.[125]

The question of representation was secondary to the lack of hearings in *Winterwerp*. The ECtHR left open the possibility that representation might not always be required by saying '. . . or, *where necessary*, through some form of representation'.[126] It also left open whether the representative must be legally trained, or could instead be a lay (non legally

---

[123] See further chapters 1 and 4.
[124] See Mental Disability Advocacy Center, *Liberty Denied: Human Rights Violations in Criminal Psychiatric Detention Reviews in Hungary*, (Budapest: MDAC, 2004).
[125] *Winterwerp v. the Netherlands, op. cit.*, para. 66.
[126] *Winterwerp v. the Netherlands, op. cit.*, para. 60.

qualified) advocate. More recent jurisprudence imposes a more robust set of requirements on the provision of legal representation.

In *Megyeri v. Germany* the Applicant had been held not to be criminally responsible
for the offences for which he was charged due to mental illness. The ECtHR put the principle on a stronger basis, and made clear that representation should be legal:

> It follows from the foregoing that where a person is confined in a psychiatric institution on
> the ground of the commission of acts which constituted criminal offences but for which he
> could not be held responsible on account of mental illness, he should – unless there are spe-
> cial circumstances – receive legal assistance in subsequent proceedings relating to the con-
> tinuation, suspension or termination of his detention. The importance of what is at stake for
> him – personal liberty – taken together with the very nature of his affliction – diminished
> mental capacity – compel this conclusion.[127]

In *Pereira v. Portugal* the Applicant was a lawyer who, as in *Megyeri*, had been charged
with a criminal offence for which he was held not to be criminally responsible due to his
disturbed mental state. The ECtHR cited its previous decision in *Megyeri* and continued:

> 58. It is not disputed that the applicant suffered from a mental disability which prevented
> him from conducting Court proceedings satisfactorily despite his legal training. That was,
> moreover, the conclusion of the order of 5 January 2000 by the President of the Criminal
> Division of the Supreme Court, who decided not to take any further account of the appli-
> cations lodged by the applicant, given his mentally disturbed state. . . .
>
> 59. The circumstances of the case therefore required a defence lawyer to be appointed to
> assist the applicant in the proceedings relating to periodic review of the lawfulness of the
> detention.
>
> 60. The Court notes that at the very beginning of the proceedings, in accordance with
> the law, the judge of the Sentence-Supervision Court appointed a trainee barrister as the
> applicant's defence counsel. However, the barrister took no part whatsoever in the pro-
> ceedings. As the Court has held on a number of occasions in respect of Article 6 § 3 (c),
> assigning counsel does not in itself ensure the effectiveness of the assistance he may afford an
> accused. . . .
>
> 61. This lack of effective legal assistance was glaringly apparent at the hearing of 1 July
> 1998. The Government maintained that the judge dispensed with the presence of an
> officially assigned lawyer, given that there were no legal issues to determine. The Court can-
> not accept that argument. It notes, firstly, that the purpose of the hearing in question, under
> Article 504 of the Code of Criminal Procedure, was to enable the judge to decide whether
> the applicant should be kept in detention. It is self-evident that legal issues may arise during
> such a hearing. Secondly, the judge does not appear to have decided that it was unnecessary
> for the applicant to be represented, since he appointed for this purpose an official from the
> prison in which the applicant was detained. Even though that appointment appeared to be
> valid under domestic law and consistent with the case-law of the Constitutional Court, it
> cannot, in the Court's view, be regarded as adequate representation for the applicant.[128]

---

[127] *Megyeri v. Germany*, Application No. 13770/88, judgment 12 May 1992, (1993) 15 EHRR 584, para.
23.

[128] *Pereira v. Portugal*, Application No. 44872/98, judgment 26 February 2002, (2003) 36 EHRR 49,
paras. 58–61.

The ECtHR judgments in *Megyeri* and *Pereira* concerned individuals who had been found to be not criminally responsible on account of mental disorder, suggesting relatively serious mental disabilities in both cases. This leaves theoretically open the possibility that the ECtHR could find it not 'necessary' for a particularly capable patient to have legal representation.

However it now seems extremely unlikely that the ECtHR would wish to engage in the process of classifying people into those with and those without the requisite mental capacity to act for themselves. Significantly, in *Pereira*, the Court pointed out that it was 'self evident that legal issues may arise at a hearing'.[129] This consideration underlines the need for universal representation, and effectively sidelines the question of individual capability. The ECtHR is surely correct to highlight the fact that questions of law do (and should) arise at or in connection with Article 5(4) court hearings. Indeed a detained person needs the benefit of a representative who is knowledgeable of the ECHR case law as well as domestic law. It would be wholly unrealistic to imagine that detained people could acquaint themselves with the relevant law – indeed there is no reason that they should. Moreover even the most capable detained person with mental disabilities is most unlikely to have adequate access to office and communication facilities, like photocopiers or telephone, or for that matter to legal materials which would be necessary to prepare for an effective court hearing.

Any process to determine who requires and who does not require representation would raise practical difficulties arising from the ECtHR's case law on the speed required for Article 5(4) hearings, discussed above. The Court has placed the burden of providing representation on the State, in the sense that people detained are not expected to take the initiative of seeking representation. Any application from a detained person for a court hearing in compliance with Article 5(4) would have to trigger a two-stage process. First, some form of investigation or hearing would be required to assess the person's ability to represent himself or herself. This would have to be conducted prior to the full court hearing, probably with opportunity for an appeal, in order to give the representative the time to take full instructions, obtain and read the case file, investigate post-discharge arrangements and master the case. Now that a delay of twenty-four days has been held to breach the speed requirement, this would set an unfeasibly tight timetable for the detained person, the State and the advocate alike.

The strong probability is therefore that *any* unrepresented detained person can establish a violation of Article 5(4). This prompts the question, why the judicial reticence of the European Court of Human Rights? There would undoubtedly be great advantage if the Court abandoned all its qualifications like 'where necessary', 'where the interests of justice so require' or 'unless there are special circumstances' and made clear that representation must be universal in these court hearings. Compliance by way of the principle of subsidiarity could only be advanced if the ECtHR expressed it as a rule. Indeed there

---

[129] *Pereira v. Portugal, op. cit.*, para. 61.

is an uncomfortable contrast between its insistence that domestic laws should be specific and foreseeable in order to avoid 'arbitrariness' and its own preference for deciding cases as narrowly as possible.

The ECtHR has yet to consider whether representation for detained patients can properly be made subject to a means test, in other words, whether people should pay for legal representation. In criminal proceedings Article 6(3) explicitly contemplates an assessment of means, by use of the formula '. . . or, if he has not sufficient means to pay for legal assistance, to be given it free when the interests of justice so require'. The ECtHR has always stressed that its approach to Article 5 may not always mirror the terms of the guarantees in Article 6. In England and Wales for example, State funding of representation at mental health review tribunals subject to means-testing was introduced in 1983. The overwhelming proportion of people qualified for legal assistance, and means testing was abandoned altogether in 1990. Means assessment may cause delay at precisely the time when a representative needs to work urgently on the case. The Court's timetable for an Article 5(4) hearing may make it difficult or impractical to conduct a means inquiry sufficiently quickly.

The ECtHR has also yet to pronounce in any detail on the standard of legal representation required, although the jurisprudence, such as it is, will be discussed in chapter 9, below. Under-financed systems in which lawyers are assigned by the courts can easily result in representation devoid of almost any value. In 2004 the Mental Disability Advocacy Centre published a report on Article 5(4) hearings for patients detained in a high security institute for patients in Budapest. These people were detained usually for long periods following criminal proceedings. The court hearings take place in public in Budapest's Capital Court. Patients were invariably 'represented' by court-appointed attorneys, but the report showed that the assigned lawyers met their clients for the first time at the courtroom, and had no meaningful chance to familiarise themselves with the case or take proper instructions before the case was called on. The average hearing time for the sixty hearings observed was under eight minutes. Twenty hearings lasted four minutes or less. In none of the court hearings observed did the detained person's lawyer challenge the psychiatric evidence. Prior to January 2003 the lawyers were paid 1,000 HUF (approximately four euros) for the first hour or part of an hour and 500 HUF (two euros) for any subsequent hour. No pre-hearing meetings with patients ever happened, and would have been unpaid. Indeed a representative had to pay for photocopying the psychiatric report out of the fee.[130]

Representation of this type is essentially cosmetic, and would be most unlikely to meet the ECtHR's standards. The purpose of the court hearing is to enable the detained person to examine, test and where appropriate challenge the case for detention. This essentially delineates the representative's task. When applying the concept of 'equality of

---

[130] See Mental Disability Advocacy Center, *Liberty Denied: Human Rights Violations in Criminal Psychiatric Detention Reviews in Hungary, op. cit.*, pp. 20–7. This publication is available electronically at http:// www.mdac.info.

arms' in *Nikolova v. Bulgaria*,[131] in particular confirming that the representative should have access to the 'investigation file', the Court can be taken to have been setting a standard as well as enshrining a right. If such access is essential to achieving 'equality of arms' it surely follows that it must also be the representative's duty to seek it.[132]

---

[131] *Nikolova v. Bulgaria, op. cit.*
[132] The case law regarding standards of representation is discussed below in chapter 9. See also appendix 7, which provides practical advice on the representation of people with mental disabilities.

Chapter 3

Inside Institutions: Institutional Standards and Institutional Controls

This chapter considers a variety of human rights issues that may arise in institutions for people with mental disabilities. Psychiatric hospitals are the most obvious of these institutions, but the issues in the chapter will also arise in other less obviously medical places where people with mental disabilities may be institutionalised, such as social care homes (institutions for people with intellectual disabilities) and homes for the elderly.

The issues that may arise in these facilities are almost infinitely varied. That said, the bulk of the issues fall into three broad categories. First, a number arise because of poor institutional standards. Obvious examples here include overcrowding in facilities, or failure of the facility to purchase sufficient heating oil to maintain the facility at a reasonable temperature over the winter. Often, these will flow from the use of poor or outdated facilities or a lack of resources, but they may also flow from insensitivity of institutional administration. The failure of a facility to make reasonable accommodation of the religious needs of an individual for example may have little to do with resource limitations. A second category of issue relevant in this chapter concerns institutional policies that are over-controlling. Any overuse of seclusion is perhaps the obvious example of this category, but other disciplinary or controlling practices may also be at issue. Finally, cases regarding the privacy of institutionalised persons raise particular issues. This category includes the rights regarding privacy of communications, and also the privacy of medical and other personal information.

These are obviously not exclusive categories. An individual may be placed in seclusion in an inappropriate environment, for example, providing a cross between the first two categories. The failure to provide partitions between toilets may raise issues regarding both poor institutional standards and a lack of privacy, the second and third categories. The inappropriate disclosure of personal information about the individual may raise issues crossing between the second and third categories, over-control and privacy. Notwithstanding the overlaps, the tri-partite division allows for some structural coherence to the subject matter.

There is a certain arbitrariness in separating this chapter from the discussion of treatment in chapter 4. The discussion in that chapter is essentially about ensuring the adequacy of treatment provision and the rights of those who offer competent refusal of that treatment to have that refusal respected. The treatment chapter thus contains specific examples of problems in the first and second categories in the current chapter. Further, the dividing line between 'treatment' and other forms of intervention is porous. The use of medication as a means of restraint for example could be seen as treatment or as institutional control, and, rather surprisingly, the Court in *Herczegfalvy v. Austria* viewed the use of handcuffs on a psychiatric patient as part of his therapeutic treatment.[1] Notwithstanding these overlaps, issues of psychiatric treatment are sufficiently discrete and sufficiently important to warrant their separate chapter.

The Legal Framework

Institutional standards may be established by a number of rights provided by the ECHR. Most obviously, if institutional care is such as would constitute inhuman or degrading treatment or punishment, Article 3 would potentially be infringed. If the rights to private and family life, home or correspondence are threatened, Article 8 may be relevant. Other articles may of course be relevant for specific situations. For example, if the conditions in which a detained patient is kept are positively anti-therapeutic, there may be a violation of Article 5: see chapter 2 above. If an institution refused to allow the detained person to practise his/her own faith, or prevented access to a minister of religion of the individual's faith, or failed to provide culturally appropriate food, the right to freedom of religion in Article 9 might be relevant, or indeed the prohibition on discrimination in Article 14. Nonetheless, Articles 3 and 8 are most obviously and generally relevant to institutional standards, and it is on these two articles that the discussion that follows will primarily focus.

---

[1] *Herczegfalvy v. Austria*, Application No. 10533/83, judgment 24 September 1992, Series A no. 244, (1993) 15 EHRR 437 para. 79–81. The Committee for the Prevention of Torture has by comparison taken the view that such handcuffing is not therapeutic: see Report of visit to Bosnia and Herzegovina, April 2003, CPT/Inf (2004) 40 para. 154; and Report of visit to Germany, December 2000, CPT/Inf (2003) 20 para. 135.

Article 3 provides the right to be free from torture and from inhuman or degrading treatment or punishment. Each of these terms has its own slightly different meaning, in decreasing levels of severity: all torture is inhuman, and all inhuman treatment is degrading. All are prohibited by the article, however, and no derogation is permitted even in time of war.[2]

Torture has generally involved the intentional infliction of pain for a specific purpose such as obtaining a confession or extracting information. In this form it is unlikely to be found in psychiatric facilities. The definition is not fixed, however. The definition of torture, like the remainder of the Convention, is a living tree, and the line between torture and other Article 3 violations is becoming less clear. In *Selmouni v. France*,[3] the Court adopts the definition contained in Article 1 of the United Nations Convention against Torture and Other Cruel, Inhuman or Degrading Treatment or Punishment (1984):

> 1. For the purposes of this Convention, the term 'torture' means any act by which severe pain or suffering, whether physical or mental, is intentionally inflicted on a person for such purposes as obtaining from him or a third person information or a confession, punishing him for an act he or a third person has committed or is suspected of having committed, or intimidating or coercing him or a third person, or for any reason based on discrimination of any kind, when such pain or suffering is inflicted by or at the instigation of or with the consent or acquiescence of a public official or other person acting in an official capacity. . . .

Consistent with this broader approach, some recent case law has acknowledged that particularly egregious cases of inhuman treatment may be considered torture, even absent the collateral purpose of the older definition. In *Aydin v. Turkey*, for example, the rape of a detainee by a state official was considered to be sufficiently severe as to constitute torture.[4] While it is certainly to be hoped that torture under this broader definition would also be rare in psychiatric facilities, it cannot be entirely dismissed. As the Court has noted in Article 3 cases, many institutionalised people with mental disabilities are particularly vulnerable.[5] In the case of an extreme abuse of power, for example severe beatings by institutional staff, this vulnerability could trigger the sense of moral outrage in the Court that could make a finding of torture a possibility.

The thresholds for inhuman or degrading treatment or punishment are less clear. The behaviour complained of must reach a minimum level of severity to engage Article 3. In assessing this minimum, duration of the behaviour may be relevant, as may the sex, age and state of health of the alleged victim.[6] In *Ireland v. the United Kingdom*, for

---

[2] Article 15.

[3] *Selmouni v. France*, Application No. 25803/94, judgment 28 July 1999, (2000) 29 EHRR 403, para. 92–106.

[4] Application No. 23178/94, judgment 25 September 1997, (1997) 25 EHRR 251, para. 86. See also *Salman v. Turkey*, Application No. 21986/93, judgment 27 June 2000, (2002) 34 EHRR 17, paras. 110–116, where severe beatings to the soles of the feet ('falaka') constituted torture.

[5] See, e.g., *Keenan v. the United Kingdom*, Application No. 27229/95, judgment 3 April 2001, (2001) 33 EHRR 38, para. 110; *Herczegfalvy v. Austria, op. cit.*, para. 82.

[6] See, e.g., *Peers v. Greece*, Application No. 28524/95, judgment 19 April 2001, (2001) 33 EHRR 51, para. 74, *Price v. the United Kingdom*, application No. 33394/96, judgment 10 July 2001, (2002) 34 EHRR 53, para. 24.

example, treatment of IRA prisoners was found to violate Article 3 on the basis that the techniques in question 'caused, if not actual bodily injury, at least intense physical and mental suffering to the persons subjected thereto and also led to acute psychiatric disturbances during interrogation.'[7] The effect of the behaviour in question on the individual is thus certainly relevant. Importantly in the mental disability context, intention to degrade is certainly relevant to the threshold, but it is not determinative: ill-treatment may breach Article 3 even if there is no intent to do so.[8]

Whether the threshold for an Article 3 violation is met will therefore depend to a large degree on the facts of the case. That said, any use of force by the authority not strictly necessary will almost always meet the Article 3 threshold.[9] Thus handcuffing a prisoner during chemotherapy,[10] shaving a prisoner's hair,[11] and strip searches conducted in an unduly invasive manner[12] have all been held to be violations of Article 3 in circumstances where the facts did not warrant the behaviour.

A significant restriction on the effect of Article 3 in general has been that the behaviour complained of must exceed that inherent in the nature of judicial punishment itself. The fact of criminal conviction itself may be experienced by some people as humiliating, for example; that does not mean that it meets the Article 3 threshold.[13] In this context it is to be recalled that psychiatric facilities ought not to be understood as punitive institutions. Particularly if the individual is admitted through civil rather than criminal admission procedures, a punitive framework makes no sense. Indeed, a punitive attitude to people with mental disabilities may perhaps be evidence of an Article 3 violation, as such an attitude in itself might be taken to degrade people with mental disabilities. There is nonetheless a possible parallel argument for persons civilly admitted to facilities: most institutions have rules, including set meal times and visiting hours, for example. Some people may well experience those rules as degrading or unpleasant; that does not make them violations of Article 3. That said, people in psychiatric hospitals, social care homes or homes for the elderly are not criminals, and any humiliating or degrading effect

---

[7] *Ireland v. the United Kingdom*, Application No. 5310/71, judgment 18 January 1978, (1978) 2 EHRR 25, para. 167. The IRA was an organised force of armed militants, wishing to unite the provinces of Northern Ireland under British rule to the Republic of Ireland. The treatment in question occurred during interrogation, and included sensory deprivation by placing black hoods on the prisoners, deprivation of sleep and nourishment, subjection to ongoing loud noises, and forcing prisoners to stand spread-eagled against a wall for some hours at a time in a position where most of their body weight was sustained by their fingers. These techniques were held to constitute inhuman and degrading treatment, but not torture.

[8] *Peers v. Greece, op. cit.*, para. 74; *Price v. the United Kingdom, op. cit.*, para. 30.

[9] *Ribitsch v. Austria*, Application No. 18896/91, judgment 21 November 1995, (1995) 21 EHRR 573, para. 38.

[10] *Mouisel v. France*, Application No. 67263/01, judgment 14 November 2002, (2004) 38 EHRR 34, para. 48.

[11] *Yankov v. Bulgaria*, Application No. 39084/97, judgment 11 December 2003, (2005) 40 EHRR 36, para. 120.

[12] *Valasinas v. Lithuania*, Application No. 44558/98, judgment 24 July 2001, 12 B.H.R.C. 2, para. 117 and *Van der Ven v. the Netherlands*, Application No. 50901/99, judgment 4 February 2003, (2004) 38 EHRR 46, para. 62.

[13] See *Tyrer v. the United Kingdom*, Application No. 5856/72, judgment 15 March 1978, (1978) 2 EHRR 1, para. 30.

should be viewed with particular concern. As noted above, they may well be in positions of particular vulnerability, as the court itself points out in *Keenan v. the United Kingdom*:

> In particular, the assessment of whether the treatment or punishment concerned is incompatible with the standards of Article 3 has, in the case of mentally ill persons, to take into consideration their vulnerability and their inability, in some cases, to complain coherently or at all about how they are being affected by any particular treatment.[14]

In this case, Mr Keenan was known to be suffering from depression and a psychotic disorder, and was known to be a suicide risk. He did in fact kill himself whilst in prison, and the Court found that the failure effectively to monitor him, combined with the belated imposition of an inappropriate punishment extending his term of imprisonment just prior to his release date, constituted inhuman and degrading treatment under Article 3.

In *Keenan* the Court was particularly critical of the failure of the institution to keep adequate notes regarding the treatment of Mr Keenan. This is an example of a broader principle under Article 3, that the onus is on the institution to explain any injuries occurring within the institution.[15]

The Court's view that any use of force not strictly necessary offends Article 3 has so far been applied only to institutional policies such as routine strip searches, actions by institutional staff in particular contexts. It is at least arguable that the logic could also apply to the placement of the individual into an institution that had more intrusive policies than the individual required – the placement in a high security facility of an individual who needed only medium security, for example. This line of argument was attempted for placement of a criminal in a particularly intrusive prison régime in *Van der Ven v. the Netherlands*.[16] In that case, the régime was particularly strict, including routine strip searches. Inmates were routinely handcuffed when moved within the prison, surveillance was particularly intrusive and most visits required inmates to be separated from the visitor by a transparent screen and supervised by a member of staff. While there was no doubt that the applicant was appropriately confined in a prison, he argued in that case that the evidence did not justify his confinement in a facility with that level of close regulation.

The ECtHR did not decide on the question of whether admission to a stricter facility than necessary could offend Article 3. Instead, it did not look behind the decision of the prison administration, taken in good faith on evidence reasonably obtained, that Mr Van der Ven's history of escape attempts and danger to the public in the event of escape warranted his admission to that régime, although it did find the routine strip searches to violate his Article 3 rights.[17] The Court's reliance on the domestic assessment of Mr Van

---

[14] *Keenan v. the United Kingdom, op. cit.*, para. 110.
[15] *Aksoy v. Turkey*, Application No. 21987/93, judgment 26 November 1996, (1996) 23 EHRR 553, para. 61.
[16] *Van der Ven v. the Netherlands, op. cit.*
[17] *Van der Ven v. the Netherlands, op. cit.*, para. 55 (concerning accepting the domestic determination of his placement) and 62 (concerning strip searches offending Article 3).

der Ven's appropriate placement is significant. It suggests that the Court will not find a violation of Article 3 based on the severity of regulation in the institution to which an individual is sent, if the domestic authorities following reasonable consideration have determined that the individual's condition warrants that level of severity.

The Court in *Van der Ven* does not close the door however to an argument that Article 3 is offended if an individual is kept in an institution that is more controlling than the state authority's own assessment considers necessary. If the authority's own assessment is that the individual requires only a medium security institution, for example, *Van der Ven* does not rule out a claim that the individual's Article 3 rights might be violated if that individual is instead sent to a high security institution. The higher security in such an institution would result in increased physical control being exerted on the individual. The Court's jurisprudence holds that force that is not strictly necessary violates Article 3. It is not obvious that it should make a difference whether the unnecessary force complained of is an isolated incident or routine individual policy, as in the existing jurisprudence, or implicit in the regimen of the institution as a whole. The relevance of such a holding by the Court would affect not merely initial admissions, where the facility selected would have to be no more intrusive than necessary for the individual, but also the need to move the individual to less-controlling institutions as his or her condition improved over time.

Essentially, such a result would introduce the right to the least restrictive alternative into the ECHR. The principle of least restrictive alternative is contained in most international standards regarding the care and treatment of people with mental disability. The Council of Europe Recommendation concerning the Human Rights and Dignity of Persons with Mental Disorder, for example, phrases it as follows:

> *Article 8 – Principle of least restriction*
> Persons with mental disorder should have the right to be cared for in the least restrictive environment available and with the least restrictive or intrusive treatment available, taking into account their health needs and the need to protect the safety of others.[18]

Such a result would be a limited introduction of this principle into Strasbourg jurisprudence, given the Court's deference to determinations of need at the domestic level, but it would be an appropriate statement of an international norm in the care of people with mental disabilities.

Article 8 of the ECHR protects the right to private and family life, to one's home and one's correspondence. Once again, each of these terms has its own meaning. The right to private life is not capable of exhaustive definition.[19] It protects both the moral and the

---

[18] R(2004)10, Article 8. See also United Nations Principles for the Protection of Persons with Mental Illness, General Assembly Resolution 46/119 (17 December 1991), Principle 9.1; and, using a slightly different wording, Council of Europe Recommendation R(1999)4 on the Principles concerning the Legal Protection of Incapable Adults, Principle 6.2.

[19] *Niemietz v. Germany*, Application No. 13710/88, judgment 16 December 1992, (1993) 16 EHRR 97.

physical integrity of the individual, including rather amorphous rights such as 'self-fulfilment'[20] and the right to identity and personal development.[21] The right to family life under Article 8 protects relationships well beyond the traditional nuclear family, including illegitimate children, unmarried cohabiting partners, and other *de facto* relationships. It does not terminate when a child is taken into care,[22] nor during separation enforced by imprisonment.[23] There can thus be no doubt that it continues following the admission of an individual to a psychiatric facility. The right to correspondence protected by Article 8 includes communications by telephone or letter, and includes both a right to communicate and a right to be free of unreasonable search of those communications.

The Article 8 rights overlap with Article 3 rights. When the Court holds an Article 3 right to have been infringed, it will often not make a determination under Article 8. When behaviour does not meet the threshold for intervention under Article 3, however, it may nonetheless offend Article 8.[24]

Unlike the rights protected by Article 3, the rights under Article 8 are not absolute. A public authority may interfere with these rights when 'in accordance with the law' and 'necessary in a democratic society in the interests of national security, public safety or the economic well-being of the country, for the prevention of disorder or crime, for the protection of health or morals, or for the protection of the rights and freedom of others.'[25]

'In accordance with law' means in accordance with domestic law. That law must be accessible to the citizen. On this point, statutes and statutory instruments or formal regulations that are enforceable and published may suffice. Directives and similar instruments that do not have the force of law will not suffice. The law may allow for discretion – that is inevitable – but it must be sufficiently precise to enable the citizen to regulate his or her conduct.[26]

The restriction must be 'necessary in a democratic society'. 'Necessary' is synonymous neither with 'indispensable' nor with 'desirable'. It must correspond to a pressing social need, and be a proportionate response to that need. While States are accorded a significant margin of appreciation as to how they implement policy in this regard, it is also the case that restrictions to rights are to be narrowly interpreted.[27] The pressing social need must, of course, fall within the specific range of factors listed in Article 8(2).

---

[20] *Niemietz v. Germany, op. cit.*, para. 29.
[21] *Peck v. the United Kingdom*, Application No. 44647/98, judgment 28 January 2003, (2003) 36 EHRR 41.
[22] *W. v. the United Kingdom*, Application No. 9749/82, judgment 8 July 1987, (1987) 10 EHRR 29, para. 59; *Eriksson v. Sweden*, Application No. 11373/85, judgment 23 May 1989, (1989) 12 EHRR 183, para. 58.
[23] *Beldjoudi v. France*, Application No. 12083/86, judgment 26 February 1992, (1992) 14 EHRR 801, para. 76.
[24] *Raninen v. Finland*, Application No. 20972/92, judgment 16 December 1997, (1997) 26 EHRR 563, para. 63.
[25] Article 8(2).
[26] *Silver v. the United Kingdom*, Application No. 5947/72, judgment 25 February 1983, (1983) 5 EHRR 347, paras. 86–9.
[27] *Silver v. the United Kingdom, op. cit.*, para. 97.

This constitutes the broad legal framework. The fact situations that may become an issue within this framework are nearly infinitely varied, and will depend on individual cases. In this regard the jurisprudence regarding Articles 3 and 8 in the context of psychiatric facilities must be viewed with some care. *Herczegfalvy*, for example, was decided in 1992. The CPT had at that time been operational for only two years and only made a few visits to psychiatric establishments.[28] Consequently, it did not publish its standards regarding psychiatric establishments until 1998.[29] Disability rights more generally have similarly advanced by a considerable degree in recent years, with the Council of Europe introducing a new set of recommendations on the rights of people with mental disorders in 2004.[30] The ECHR as a whole is a living tree, and nowhere is this likely to be more true than in the approach to Articles 3 and 8.

Human Rights and Institutional Standards

This section concerns overall standards of care in institutions. It does not discuss issues of restraint or control, or of privacy: those are dealt with later in the chapter. Instead, it concerns minimum standards of institutional provision, including minimum physical standards, programmes and routines, and the creation of a safe environment.

A perusal of some of the case law, CPT reports and international instruments provides an indication of the sorts of issue that may fall to be determined. The most directly relevant guidelines regarding institutional standards for psychiatric and related institutions are those of the CPT. These are broad in scope. The guidance regarding living conditions in psychiatric institutions notes that whatever the economic situation of the member State, adequate food, heating and clothing must be provided.[31] A positive therapeutic environment is to be encouraged, with wards and living spaces as pleasantly appointed as possible, with good lighting and places where personal belongings may be kept. Sanitary facilities should allow residents some privacy, and residents should not be required to remain in pyjamas or nightgowns. Food must be of proper quality and quantity, and should be served to patients at tables, where they can eat with the usual utensils.[32]

The relevant provision of the Council of Europe 2004 Recommendation similarly directs attention to the appropriate standard of facilities:

---

[28] '1st General Report on the CPT's activities covering the period November 1989 to December 1990', CPT/Inf (91) 3 [EN] – Publication Date: 20 February 1991, appendix 3.

[29] '8th General Report on the CPT's activities covering the period 1 January to 31 December 1997', CPT/Inf (98) 12 [EN] – Publication Date: 31 August 1998. Reprinted as part of *CPT Standards*, CPT/Inf/E (2002) 1 – Rev. 2004.

[30] COE Recommendation Rec(2004)10.

[31] CPT/Inf (98) 12, para. 33.

[32] CPT/Inf (98) 12, paras. 34 to 36. The CPT guidelines also refer to minimum standards regarding restraint and seclusion. These are discussed in the next section.

Article 9 – Environment and living conditions
1. Facilities designed for the placement of persons with mental disorder should provide each such person, taking into account his or her state of health and the need to protect the safety of others, with an environment and living conditions as close as possible to those of persons of similar age, gender and culture in the community. Vocational rehabilitation measures to promote the integration of those persons in the community should also be provided.
2. Facilities designed for the involuntary placement of persons with mental disorder should be registered with an appropriate authority.[33]

The United Nations Mental Illness Principles similarly provide that facilities should mirror as closely as possible those of the normal life of the individual, and must in particular include facilities for recreation and leisure, education, and occupational and vocational engagement. Facilities to purchase or receive items for daily living, recreation and communication are to be provided. Forced labour by persons in the facility is expressly prohibited.[34]

The requirement that the facility should provide 'an environment and living conditions as close as possible to those of persons of similar age, gender and culture in the community' serves as a reminder that these are not by their nature punitive facilities. Individuals in these institutions should enjoy, subject to the health and safety concerns identified in the provision, the same rights as people in the community. That of course includes the full panoply of ECHR rights, such as freedom of thought, religion and conscience, freedom of expression, and the right to marry and vote.[35]

These international standards indicate the range of standards to which countries are expected to comply. The failure to comply with such standards is relevant in assessing possible violations of Articles 3 and 8, but it is not determinative.[36] In any event, on questions of physical standards, the published international standards lack specificity. A perusal of the national reports of the CPT provides a better indication of particular fact situations that may arise. While the CPT provides an overall report on their visits to a country, they are also permitted to communicate immediate observations to the government or authority concerned.[37] These immediate observations occur in situations of particular urgency

---

[33] Rec(2004)10.
[34] UN Mental Illness Principles, General Assembly Resolution 46/119, 17 December 1991, Principle 13. Regarding forced labour and the ECHR, see further pages 91 to 93, below.
[35] For a discussion of some of these rights, see chapter 7 on participation in society.
[36] See, for example, *Aerts v. Belgium*, Application No. 25357/94, judgment 30 July 1998, (2000) 29 EHRR 50, paras. 65, and 67; see also *Eggs v. Switzerland*, Application No. 7341/76, decision 11 December 1976, 6 DR 170 at p. 181.
[37] European Convention for the Prevention of Torture and Inhuman or Degrading Treatment or Punishment *(1987)*, Article 8(5). Immediate observations in recent years regarding living conditions in psychiatric hospitals, social care homes and similar facilities have been made concerning Armenia (CPT/Inf (2004) 25, regarding visit of October 2002), Azerbaijan (CPT/Inf (2004) 36, visit of November 2002), Bulgaria (CPT/Inf (2002) 1, visit of April 1999; CPT/Inf (2004) 21, visit of April 2002; CPT/Inf (2004) 23, visit of December 2003), Bosnia and Herzegovina (CPT/Inf (2004) 40, visit of April-May 2003), Estonia (CPT/Inf (2002) 26, visit of July 1997), Germany (CPT/Inf (2003) 20, visit of December 2000), Latvia (CPT/Inf (2001) 27, visit of January 1999), Macedonia (CPT/Inf (2004) 29, visit of November 2002), Romania (CPT/Inf (2004) 10, visit of September 2002/February 2003), and Slovakia (CPT/Inf (2001) 29, visit of October 2000).

or particular concern to the CPT. While relevant comments in its overall country reports are relevant to understanding the CPT's standards, these immediate observations thus warrant particular attention.

The CPT reports of psychiatric hospitals and similar facilities tend to be organised reasonably consistently around set topics: allegations of ill-treatment, living conditions, staffing, treatment, means of restraint and seclusion, and legal safeguards in the context of involuntary placement. Living conditions and staffing will be of particular relevance in this section, and means of restraint and seclusion and allegations of ill-treatment in the next section. Some of the issues regarding legal safeguards will be relevant in the final section of this chapter, although many of those safeguards relate to protections against wrongful admission and are therefore considered in chapter 2. The CPT's views regarding medical treatment are discussed in chapter 4.

The CPT reports refer primarily to the conditions and safeguards of residence in the psychiatric and similar facilities. An exception to this general approach concerns minors. The CPT takes the view that because of their vulnerability and special needs, young people should not reside in facilities for adults. When the CPT has reservations about the care being afforded the minor, an immediate observation appears to be made,[38] but even when the minor is stated by the CPT to be receiving appropriate care, his or her presence in an adult facility is criticised by the CPT.[39]

The CPT also has concerns about the use of people in psychiatric and related institutions for medical research, particularly when that research is carried out on people detained in psychiatric facilities.[40] The CPT has as yet established no fixed guidelines in this regard, although it will presumably have regard to the Council of Europe Convention on Human Rights and Biomedicine[41] and the related Protocol concerning Biomedical Research.[42] The Convention allows research on human subjects only if there is no alternative of competent effectiveness to research on humans, and where risks on the participants are not disproportionate to the potential benefits of the research. Any such research must be approved by an independent body, and all human subjects with capacity must offer full, free and informed consent, which may be withdrawn at any time.[43] For persons who lack capacity to consent, research must in addition be of potentially direct benefit to the participant's health, or, exceptionally, provide significant improvement of the scientific understanding of the participant's condition with no more than minimal risk or burden to the participant. It must further be demonstrated that comparable

---

[38] See, for example, reports on Estonia, CPT/Inf (2002) 26 (visit of July 1997) para. 141; and Latvia, CPT/Inf (2001) 27 (visit of January-February 1999), para. 202.

[39] Germany, CPT/Inf (2003) 20 (visit of December 2000), para. 119.

[40] See report on Czech Republic, CPT/Inf (2004) 4 (visit of April 2002), para. 119; Bulgaria, CPT/Inf (2004) 21 (visit of April 2002), para. 155. In both these cases, no research was actually occurring on involuntary patients at the time of the CPT visits.

[41] Oviedo, 4 April 1997, ETS 164.

[42] Strasbourg, 25 January 2005, ETS 195. This protocol is not yet formally in force, although it may nonetheless serve as a guide for the CPT and for the ECtHR in its interpretation of the ECHR.

[43] Convention on Human Rights and Biomedicine (1997), Article 16.

research cannot be carried out on individuals with capacity to consent to the research. The consent must then be obtained from the participant's legal representative, and even then, the participant may only be involved in the research if he or she does not object.[44]

More frequently, however, the issues of institutional programmes and standards appear to turn on the conditions of the institution. In the context of imprisonment, the Court has articulated the standard to be imposed on States as follows:

> Under this provision [Article 3] the State must ensure that a person is detained in conditions which are compatible with respect for his human dignity, that the manner and method of the execution of the measure do not subject him to distress or hardship of an intensity exceeding the unavoidable level of suffering inherent in detention and that, given the practical demands of imprisonment, his health and well-being are adequately secured.[45]

At a most fundamental level, this must imply that an institution meets minimal standards of health and safety for those housed in it. It is difficult to imagine that the Court would fail to impose at least this standard on psychiatric facilities. In the context of psychiatric and similar establishments, the CPT's approach is as follows:

> The aim in any psychiatric establishment should be to offer material conditions which are conducive to the treatment and welfare of patients: in psychiatric terms, a positive therapeutic environment. Creating such an environment involves, first of all, providing sufficient living space per patient as well as adequate lighting, heating and ventilation, maintaining the establishment in a satisfactory state of repair and meeting hospital hygiene requirements.[46]

In this context, it is unsurprising that the CPT is particularly concerned when the basics of life are not being provided in psychiatric institutions. In a 2002 visit to Karlukovo State Psychiatric Hospital in Bulgaria, for example, the CPT found that meat, fresh vegetables and fruit were only rarely available, and the daily per capita allowance for food was less than half a Euro. In practice, the institution relied on donations of food from relatives of the inmates. The CPT noted a connection between the limited food and the mortality rate in the institution.[47] Similarly, the CPT is critical when there is a failure to provide adequate heating to institutions.[48] In this, the approach of the CPT reflects the ECtHR's case law under Article 3 jurisprudence. In *Cyprus v. Turkey*,[49] for example, the

---

[44] Convention on Human Rights and Biomedicine (1997), Articles 6, 17.
[45] *Valasinas v. Lithuania, op. cit.*, para. 102. See also *Kudła v. Poland*, Application No. 30210/96, judgment 26 October 2000, (2002) 35 EHRR 11, paras. 92–94.
[46] Report on Cyprus, CPT/Inf (2003) 1 (visit of May 2000), para. 56.
[47] CPT/Inf (2004) 21 (visit of April 2002), para. 132–4. See report on Macedonia, CPT/Inf (2004) 29 (Visit of November 2002) para. 79 and, report on Albania CPT/Inf (2003) 6 (visit of December 1997) paras. 21–27.
[48] See, for example, report on Azerbaijan, CPT/Inf (2004) 36 (visit of Nov-Dec 2002) para. 156; Bulgaria, CPT/Inf (2004) 21 (visit of April 2002), para. 133 and CPT/Inf (2004) 23 (visit of December 2003) para. 26, where heating was not provided continuously in the winter and temperatures were recorded as 12°C at midday; and Macedonia CPT/Inf (2004) 29 (visit of November 2002) para. 67, where temperatures in the institution fell to 10°C at night. The absence of adequate clothing in these circumstances is seen by the CPT as an aggravating factor.
[49] Application Nos. 6780/74 and 6950/75, decision 10 July 1976, (1982) 4 EHRR 482 at para. 405.

Commission held that the failure to provide adequate food, water and medical supplies to prisoners constituted inhuman treatment contrary to Article 3.

Issues of basic health and safety extend beyond physical conditions, however. The CPT has also raised concerns over the risk of violence in institutions. Such concerns may refer to the behaviour of staff[50] on residents of the institution, or behaviour between residents, and may include violence or the exploitation of sexual or other vulnerabilities of residents.[51] The CPT tends to articulate this as an institutional failure, caused for example by inadequate staffing, inadequate training of staff, or inadequate institutional controls of staff. This is stated for example in the following comments relating to a visit to institutions in Bosnia-Herzegovina:

> The CPT fully recognises that in times of grave economic difficulties, sacrifices may have to be made, including in health establishments. However, the Committee wishes to stress that the duty of care which is owed by staff to those in their charge includes the responsibility to protect them from other patients who can cause them harm.
>
> It is clearly essential that appropriate procedures be put in place in both establishments, in order to avoid such dramatic incidents recurring and to protect certain patients from other patients who might cause them harm. This requires inter alia an adequate staff presence at *all times* (including at night, weekends and holidays) within the units concerned.
>
> *   *   *
>
> In the CPT's view, such a low level or outright absence of staff can only contribute to the perpetuation of inter-patient violence and will inevitably put the patients – as well as the staff – at risk (in addition to contravening the principle of duty of care). Such a state of affairs is totally unacceptable; no unit should be left without any supervision by staff.[52]

The staff should be professionals.[53] The CPT has been critical of institutional residents being used in a guard or nursing role, presumably because of the risk that residents so employed may be placed in a position to exploit other residents without meaningful check on their behaviour.[54] The CPT further indicates that staff must not merely be sufficient in number, but appropriately trained and motivated to intervene in violent situations:

---

[50]   These will be discussed in the next section.

[51]   See, for example, reports of visits to Bosnia and Herzegovina CPT/Inf (2004) 40 (visit of April-May 2003) para. 120; Bulgaria, CPT/Inf (2004) 23, (visit of December 2003) para. 30; CPT/Inf (2002) 1 (visit of April-May 1999) para. 165; CPT/Inf (2004) 21 (visit of April 2002) para. 125; Estonia, CPT/Inf (2002) 26 (visit of July 1997) paras. 14, 166, 171; CPT/Inf (2005) 6 (visit of September 2003), para. 89; Greece, CPT/Inf (2001) 18 (visit of May-June 1997), para. 197; Macedonia, CPT/Inf (2004) 29 (visit of November 2002), para. 79. A number of these incidents gave rise to the making of immediate observations to the State visited.

[52]   CPT/Inf (2004) 40 (visit of April-May 2002), para. 122. In one unit, approximately 100 persons were cared for by a psychiatrist, two nurses and two police officers. In another, no staff were present for several hours per day.

[53]   See Recommendation R(2004)10, Article 11.

[54]   See, for example, report on visit to Estonia, CPT/Inf (2002) 26 (visit of July 1997), para. 165. In that case, the resident/guard in question was prone to biting other residents. Indeed, the CPT visiting Party itself was warned to stay away from the resident/guard in question because he was prone to biting.

165. A certain number of allegations of ill-treatment between residents themselves were also heard (threats, violence and sexual exploitation) and the delegation itself observed, on two separate occasions, that the level of supervision by staff was inadequate, no action being taken when a fight broke out between residents. Such an attitude is not acceptable; it is essential that appropriate procedures be in place in order to protect more vulnerable residents from other residents who might cause them harm. This requires not only an adequate staff presence at all times, including at night and weekends, but also for the staff to be motivated to exercise their authority and have the necessary skills in this regard.

As regards the latter point, staff should receive training in both non-physical and manual control techniques vis-à-vis violent residents; the possession of such skills will enable staff to choose the most appropriate response when confronted by difficult situations, thereby significantly reducing the risk of injuries to residents and staff.[55]

Issues of basic health and safety may be the clearest examples where Article 3 can be seen to have been breached, but they are not the only ones. The Court has held that conditions of detention short of those creating significant risks to life or safety may violate Article 3. Such violation may not necessarily be the result of a single, egregious factor, but by the overall effects of institutionalisation:

> The Court considers that conditions of detention may sometimes amount to inhuman or degrading treatment. In the "Greek case" . . . the Commission reached this conclusion regarding overcrowding and inadequate facilities for heating, sanitation, sleeping arrangements, food, recreation and contact with the outside world. When assessing conditions of detention, account has to be taken of the cumulative effects of these conditions, as well as of specific allegations made by the applicant.[56]

A brief sample will provide a sense of the sorts of issue of concern to the Court in the prison context. In *Poltoratskiy v. Ukraine*,[57] the factors considered by the Court for persons detained on death row[58] included the size, lighting and heating of the prisoner's cell, the failure to allow him daily access to the outdoors, and restrictions on correspondence and his visits from his relatives. In *Nevmerzhitsky v. Ukraine*,[59] the matters at issue included the overcrowding, lack of proper hygiene, ventilation, sunlight, daily walks, appropriate clean bedding or clothes. In that case, the adverse conditions had a demonstrable effect on the inmate's health, as he contracted skin disorders including scabies and eczema. The failure to provide appropriate medical attention provided a separate

---

[55] Report on visit to Bulgaria, CPT/Inf (2002) 1 (visit of April-May 1999), para. 165.

[56] *Dougoz v. Greece*, (2002) 34 EHRR 61, Application No. 40907/98, judgment 6 March 2001, (2002) 34 EHRR 61, para. 46. The 'Commission' refers to the European Commission on Human Rights. Before 1998, the Commission examined the facts of complaints and issued initial decisions as to admissibility. Only claims considered by the Commission to be admissible went on to be examined by the Court. If, as in the *Greek Case* cited, the Commission considered a claim to pass the threshold of admissibility, it would also issue its views as to the merits of the case, for the information of the Court and the litigants.

[57] Application No. 38812/97, judgment 29 April 2003, (2004) 39 EHRR 43, paras. 136–42.

[58] The death penalty is abolished by Protocol 6 of the ECHR. As of 31 January 2006, Russia was the only State not to have ratified this protocol. The Ukraine did so in 1999, some two years after the application in the *Poltoratskiy* case was made.

[59] Application No. 54825/00, judgment 5 April 2005, paras. 86–7, 106.

violation of Article 3 in that case. In *Kalashnikov v. Russia*,[60] issues included overcrowding to the point where prisoners needed to take turns sleeping, poor ventilation in cells, and infestation by pests causing skin disorders. Toilet facilities were another concern, as they offered no real privacy from other inmates in the cell. In the event that the institutionalised person has a physical disability, the Court has held that minimum standards must take into account that disability. In *Price v. the United Kingdom*, a prisoner in a wheelchair could not easily reach the toilet nor wash herself, in a cold cell. The bed in the cell was hard, and she risked developing sores from it because of her difficulty moving. In these circumstances, the Court found a violation of Article 3.[61]

The CPT reports focus on similar issues regarding psychiatric and related facilities. Generally, the factors giving rise to comment are various, and not easily disentangled. It is in general the cumulative effect that gives rise to an immediate observation, as for example in the following case of the Demir Kapija social care home in Macedonia:

> 79. Living conditions in *Wards C1 and C2* could only be termed execrable. Some of the residents were moving around half or totally naked, their sole activities consisting of hitting fellow residents and protecting themselves from blows. The living/dining rooms were austere and dirty, and the sanitary facilities totally unhygienic. The dormitories offered cramped conditions and the beds and bedding were soiled with urine and faeces. The most distressing moment was when food was brought in the wards: residents were grabbing food with their hands, trying to protect their meagre portion from other residents, and eating on the floor. During those times, one orderly (or at most two) attempted to maintain a semblance of order in the ward; however, the overall impression was that the distribution of food deprived the residents of any dignity.
>
> To sum up, an atmosphere of utter neglect and abandonment prevailed in the C. Wards; the living conditions in those wards could be said to amount to inhuman or degrading treatment.[62]

While the tipping point where substandard conditions become inhuman or degrading will depend on the facts of the individual case, the CPT reports provide some indication of the sorts of factors that may be relevant. Certainly, cleanliness of the facilities is a significant factor.[63] The state and design of basic sanitation facilities including toilets and showers is further of particular concern. The expectation is that such facilities should be of reasonable standard, and provide the user with appropriate privacy.[64] Basic items of hygiene are to be provided, such as soap, toilet paper, washing powder, towels, toothpaste and the like. Residents should be able to shower at least weekly.

---

[60] Application No. 47095/99, judgment 15 July 2002, (2003) 36 EHRR 34, paras. 97–9.
[61] *Price v. the United Kingdom, op. cit.*, para. 30.
[62] CPT/Inf (2004) 29 (visit of November 2002), para. 79.
[63] See for example, reports on Armenia, CPT/Inf (2004) 25 (visit of October 2002) para. 170; Bulgaria, CPT/Inf (2002) 1 (visit of April-May 1999) para. 168 and 169, CPT/Inf (2004) 21 (visit of April 2002) para. 127, CPT/Inf (2004) 23 (visit of December 2003) para. 25; and Macedonia, CPT/Inf (2004) 29 (visit of November 2002), para. 67.
[64] See, for example, reports on Bulgaria, CPT/Inf (2002) 1 (visit of April-May 1999) paras. 169, CPT/Inf (2004) 23 (visit of December 2003) paras. 25, 27; and Macedonia, CPT/Inf (2004) 29 (visit of November 2002), para. 67, and United Kingdom, CPT/Inf (2005) 1 (visit of May 2003), para. 112.

The CPT has an ongoing set of concerns regarding clothing for residents. In part, these concerns flow from health and safety issues: the failure to provide warm clothing on a cold ward increases the vulnerability of the resident to disease and hypothermia.[65] Clothes are also perceived by the CPT as about identity and dignity, however:

> 112. In a number of units (*e.g.* geriatric psychiatric unit, admission unit), the delegation found that patients were continuously dressed in hospital pyjamas/track suits. In this connection, the CPT wishes to stress that for patients to be dressed in uniform hospital clothes at all times is not conducive to strengthening their personal identity and self-esteem; individualisation of clothing should form part of the therapeutic process.[66]

For similar reasons, the use of donated clothing and of former military clothing, and the interchange of clothing between residents is similarly criticised.[67]

Overcrowding is routinely commented on by the CPT, both in terms of the space provided in sleeping rooms[68] and where the facility is accommodating more residents than it was designed for.[69] In the context of prisons and similar institutions, the CPT expects accommodation cells to include a minimum of seven square metres per inmate in individual cells or rooms.[70] Consistent with that, accommodation in psychiatric and related contexts falling significantly short of that standard has been aversely commented on by the CPT.[71]

The design and furnishing of accommodation has been considered by the CPT. All accommodation, including seclusion rooms, should have access to both natural and artificial light, and be well-ventilated.[72] While the CPT has so far stopped short of finding dormitory accommodation per se to warrant an immediate observation (provided of course that it is sufficiently large for the number of residents it contains), it has indicated its reservations about this mode of accommodation:

> 58. Large-capacity dormitories are scarcely compatible with the norms of modern psychiatry. Provision of accommodation structures based on small groups is a crucial factor in preserving/restoring patients' dignity, and also a key requirement of any policy for the

---

[65] See, for example, report on Bulgaria, CPT/Inf (2002) 1 (visit of April-May 1999) para. 172, regarding the absence of socks and shoes combined with poor heating.

[66] Report on Czech Republic, Czech Republic, CPT/Inf (2004) 4 (visit of April 2002), para. 112. See also Bulgaria, CPT/Inf (2002) 1 (visit of April-May 1999) paras. 172, 188; CPT/Inf (2004) 21 (visit of April 2002), para. 130; Estonia, CPT/Inf (2002) 26 (visit of July 1997), para. 151; Macedonia, CPT/Inf (2004) 29 (visit of November 2002), para. 79.

[67] See, for example, report on Bulgaria, CPT/Inf (2004) 23 (visit of December 2003), para. 28.

[68] See, for example, reports on Bulgaria, CPT/Inf (2002) 1 (visit of April-May 1999) para. 168; Czech Republic, CPT/Inf (2004) 4 (visit of April 2002) para. 109.

[69] See, for example, report on Germany, CPT/Inf (2003) 20 (visit of December 2000) para. 121.

[70] CPT 2nd General Report – CPT/Inf (92) 3, para. 43.

[71] See, for example, reports on Bulgaria, CPT/Inf (2002) 1 (visit of April-May 1999) para. 168 (3.5 square metres per resident inadequate); Czech Republic, CPT/Inf (2004) 4 (visit of April 2002) para. 109 (2–2.5 square metres per resident inadequate). See, however, report on Armenia, CPT/Inf (2004) 25 (visit of October 2002) para. 170, where an average of 6 square metres per resident was not criticised.

[72] See, for example, report on Azerbaijan, CPT/Inf (2004) 36 (visit of November-December 2002) para. 156. Regarding lighting and ventilation in seclusion rooms, see report on Bulgaria, CPT/Inf (2004) 21 (visit of April 2002) para. 145.

psychological and social rehabilitation of patients. Such structures also allow patients to be divided into relevant categories for therapeutic purposes.[73]

Facilities are further expected to be reasonably well-maintained, and well-furnished. Furnishings are expected to include lockable spaces for individuals to keep private possessions. Food is expected to be served at tables, with utensils provided for eating. Furnishings are to be replaced as reasonably necessary, and, like the fabric of the facility itself, are to be kept in good repair.[74]

Therapeutic activities and a therapeutic atmosphere are expected to be provided for residents. The CPT requires the provision of appropriate somatic treatment regimes.[75] In particular, in countries affected by tuberculosis, screening programmes for that disorder are expected to be in effect for those in psychiatric and related facilities.[76] It is not restricted to treatment for somatic disorders, however, and 'therapeutic' is not in this context to be read as a narrowly medical term:

> The CPT all too often finds that the fundamental components of effective psycho-social rehabilitative treatment are underdeveloped or even totally lacking, and that the treatment provided to psychiatric patients consists essentially of pharmacotherapy. This situation is generally the result of the absence of suitably qualified staff and appropriate facilities or of an outmoded philosophy based on the custody of patients.[77]

Certainly, this includes psychotherapy and similar psychological treatments.[78] It is not restricted to such programmes, however. In comments regarding a social care home in Bulgaria, for example, the CPT proposed extending the number of residents that were involved in farming and gardening at the facility.[79] Exercise is expected to form a significant part of the resident's daily routine, and the CPT insists that an hour of outdoor exercise be available to all people in psychiatric facilities, unless there is medical reason precluding it.[80] The exercise is to take place in a location sufficient for the resident to

---

[73] Report on Cyprus, CPT/Inf (2003) 1 (visit of May 2000), para. 58. See also criticism of such dormitories in World Health Organization, 'WHO Resource Book on Mental Health, Human Rights and Legislation', (Geneva: WHO, 2005), p. 35.

[74] See, e.g., reports on Armenia, CPT/Inf (2004) 25 (visit of October 2002) para. 181; Azerbaijan, CPT/Inf (2004) 36 (visit of November-December 2002), para. 156; Bulgaria, CPT/Inf (2002) 1 (visit of April-May 1999) paras. 168 and 169, CPT/Inf (2004) 21 (visit of April 2002) para. 127, CPT/Inf (2004) 23 (visit of December 2003) para. 25; Cyprus, CPT/Inf (2003) 1 (visit of May 2000), para. 59; and Macedonia, CPT/Inf (2004) 29 (visit of November 2002), para. 67.

[75] CPT Standards, CPT/Inf/I (2002) 1, Rev. 2004, p. 54, paras. 32–33. This requirement is also present in the Court's jurisprudence: see for example, *McGlinchey v. the United Kingdom*, Application No. 50390/99, judgment 29 July 2003, (2003) 37 EHRR 41, and *Nevmerzhitsky v. Ukraine*, Application No. 54825/00, judgment 5 April 2005.

[76] See report on Armenia, CPT/Inf (2004) 25 (visit of October 2002), para. 179.

[77] Report on Bosnia and Herzegovina, CPT/Inf (2004) 40 (visit of April-May 2003), para. 140.

[78] See, for example, report on Denmark, CPT/Inf (2002) 18 (visit of January-February 2002), para. 85. See also report on Germany, CPT/Inf (2003) 20 (visit of December 2000), para. 143.

[79] CPT/Inf (2002) 1 (visit of April-May 1999) para. 178.

[80] See, for example, reports on Azerbaijan CPT/Inf (2004) 36 (visit of November-December 2002), para. 158; Armenia, CPT/Inf (2004) 25 (visit of October 2002), para. 182; Bulgaria, CPT/Inf (2002) 1 (visit of April-May 1999), para. 188; Czech Republic, CPT/Inf (2004) 4 (visit of April 2002), para. 111;

exert himself or herself physically; the 'exercise' of twenty persons in a yard of thirty square metres was considered unacceptable in this regard.[81] The standards regarding exercise applies both to people on general wards and to those in seclusion.[82] It is further not enough that suitable facilities be provided; they must also be used by the residents.[83]

It would seem that the justification for these standards regarding programmes is in part therapeutic, and in part simply to avoid the tedium of institutional life:

> Apart from the time spent on various medical examinations and interviews, and the meals taken together in the refectory, they remained locked in their rooms with hardly anything to occupy themselves. They were not even offered outdoor exercise. The only activities available to them consisted of listening to the radio and reading books or newspapers brought by their families.[84]

The distinction between therapeutic improvement in the resident's condition and the avoidance of tedium may be relevant in Article 3 litigation. While the jurisprudence certainly provides that States have a duty to provide basic medical and similar care to those it institutionalises,[85] the failure to provide activities to relieve the tedium of a long period of institutionalisation may in itself imply different arguments of inhuman or degrading treatment.

Therapeutic programmes should not, of course, become forced labour. Forced labour is prohibited by Principle 13.3 and 13.4 of the UN Mental Illness Principles:

> 3. In no circumstances shall a patient be subject to forced labour. Within the limits compatible with the needs of the patient and with the requirements of institutional administration, a patient shall be able to choose the type of work he or she wishes to perform.
> 4. The labour of a patient in a mental health facility shall not be exploited. Every such patient shall have the right to receive the same remuneration for any work which he or she does as would, according to domestic law or custom, be paid for such work to a non-patient. Every such patient shall, in any event, have the right to receive a fair share of any remuneration which is paid to the mental health facility for his or her work.[86]

It is also restricted by article 4 of the ECHR, but the general prohibition in that article creates a variety of exceptions, including the following:

> 4.3. (a) any work required to be done in the ordinary course of detention imposed according to the provisions of Article 5 of this Convention or during conditional release from such detention;

Denmark, CPT/Inf (2002) 18 (visit of January-February 2002), para. 84; Sweden, CPT/Inf (2004) 32 (visit of January-February 2003) para. 82.

[81] See report on Armenia, CPT/Inf (2004) 25 (visit of October 2002), para. 177.

[82] See report on Germany, CPT/Inf (2003) 20, (visit of December 2000), para. 143.

[83] See, for example, report on Sweden, CPT/Inf (2004) 32 (visit of January-February 2003) para. 85.

[84] Report on Azerbaijan, CPT/Inf (2004) 36 (visit of November-December 2002), para. 158.

[85] See, e.g., *Nevmerzhitsky v. Ukraine*, Application No. 54825/00, judgment 5 April 2005; *Keenan v. the United Kingdom, op. cit.*, para. 110; *Kudła v. Poland, op. cit.*, para. 96.

[86] UN Resolution 46/119 of 17 December 1991.

On its face, this would appear to permit at least some forced labour for those detained in psychiatric facilities under article 5. The scope of the clause is subject to little jurisprudence and has never been tested in court regarding psychiatric facilities. It may well be that just as the apparent freedom to detain persons of unsound mind under article 5 has become subject to considerable judicial oversight and restriction, so the labour of those under detention may also be so restricted.

Article 4 appears to adopt a wide view of 'labour', including all kinds of work, not merely physical labour.[87] It must however be 'forced': work done voluntarily does not engage the section.[88] It is at least arguable that the force need not be physical in nature. In *Van Droogenbroeck v. Belgium*,[89] the applicant was a prisoner subject to a régime for recidivist offenders. The board that controlled his release from prison noted that he had accumulated no savings during his prison term, and considered that he had no prospects for employment on release. It therefore declined to recommend his release until he had saved 12,000 Belgian francs. The only way to do this was to engage in the employment offered by the prison. He took the view that he was forced to work; the government took the view that he was 'invited' to work. The Court did not find it necessary to make a decision on this point, but did note that 'In practice, once release is conditional on the possession of savings from pay for work done in prison (see paragraphs 13, 16 and 17 above)[. . .], one is not far away from an obligation in the strict sense of the term.'[90]

Any work justified by the clause must be 'in the ordinary course of detention'. In *De Wilde, Ooms and Versyp v. Belgium*, the applicants were required to work under the terms of Belgian vagrancy law. It was held that the work imposed on the applicants had 'not exceeded the "ordinary" limits, within the meaning of Article 4 (3) (a) (art. 4–3–a) [. . .]of the Convention, because it aimed at their rehabilitation and was based on a general standard . . . [contained in Belgian legislation], which finds its equivalent in several member States of the Council of Europe'.[91] The fact that the work in question is legitimately rehabilitative is also mentioned in *Van Droogenbroeck v. Belgium* as a factor the Court is prepared to take into account:

> Moreover, the work which Mr. Van Droogenbroeck was asked to do did not go beyond what is "ordinary" in this context since it was calculated to assist him in reintegrating himself into society and had as its legal basis provisions which find an equivalent in certain other member States of the Council of Europe[.][92]

While the Court appears never to have found a violation of Article 4 in the context of work required in an institution, it does seem at least arguable that work that does not have

---

[87] *Van der Mussele v. Belgium*, Application No. 8919/80, judgment 27 October 1983 (1983) 6 EHRR 163.
[88] See, for example, *Van der Mussele v. Belgium, op. cit.; Dolgov v. Ukraine*, Application No. 72704/01, judgment 19 April 2005, para. 24.
[89] Application No. 7906/77, judgment 27 May 1982, (1982) 4 EHRR 443.
[90] *Op. cit.*, para. 59.
[91] Application No. 2832/66, judgment 18 June 1971, (1979–80) 1 EHRR 373, para. 90.
[92] *Op. cit.*, para. 59.

rehabilitation, reintegration or some other comparable therapeutic purpose as its object may violate that Article. Similarly, there may be some implied requirement that provision be made for the work in domestic legislation, although the legislation in both *De Wilde* and *Van Droogenbroeck* was entirely lacking in specifics. In *De Wilde*, it was that persons detained in vagrancy establishments could be 'required to perform the work prescribed in the institution';[93] in *Van Droogenbroeck* it was that prisoners 'could be required to do prison work'.[94] It is difficult to see such broad wording as creating much of a safeguard.

The ECHR also protects the rights of residents to maintain contact with people outside the institution, and in particular with their families and their lawyers. These rights are clearly protected by the rights to correspondence and to private and family life in Article 8. It is less clear how they apply in an Article 3 claim. The language of the CPT would suggest they may be relevant for both articles:

> The maintenance of patients' *contact with the outside world* is essential, not only for the prevention of ill-treatment but also from a therapeutic standpoint. Patients should be able to send and receive correspondence, to have access to the telephone, and to receive visits from their family and friends. Confidential access to a lawyer should also be guaranteed.[95]

In the view of the CPT, this implies both the right to send and receive letters, and free access to a telephone. The UN Mental Illness principles expect that letters will be uncensored, and that people in mental health institutions will have access to newspapers, radio and television.[96]

The ECHR case law is less clear on the scope of access required to be given to the outside world. In *Wakefield v. the United Kingdom*,[97] the European Commission on Human Rights considered a claim by a prisoner who wished to be moved to a different prison to facilitate visits by his fiancée. The Commission held that the circumstances did not reach the level of severity required to engage Article 3, and that while there was an apparent infringement of Article 8 at first sight, the infringement was in this case justified by security concerns under Article 8(2).

How secure is the *Wakefield* decision; how widely should it be read; and what does it mean for people in psychiatric and similar facilities? The applicant in that case had met his fiancée only once, although they had engaged in a considerable written correspondence, and the limited nature of the relationship was clearly a factor in the Commission's decision. The case does not preclude the fiancée from visiting; it merely restricts the requirement that the State take special measures to facilitate those visits, and the possibility is left open that for a stronger relationship, the result might be different. At its strongest, the case would seem to suggest that if the only issue in a case involves contact with a family member, it should be brought under Article 8 not Article 3. The case law

---

[93] *De Wilde, Ooms and Versyp v. Belgium, op. cit.*, para. 38.
[94] *Van Droogenbroeck v. Belgium, op. cit.*, para. 25.
[95] See CPT Standards, CPT/Inf/E (2002) 1 – Rev. 2004, p. 61, para. 54.
[96] Resolution 46/119, principle 13.
[97] Application No. 15817/89, judgment 1 October 1990.

under Article 8 is stronger in this regard. Prisoners have the right to communicate with close family members,[98] and indeed to attend the funerals of close family members.[99] There is an obligation to provide visiting facilities for prisoners' friends,[100] and particular efforts must be made to give effect to court-ordered rights of access to children.[101] There is no obvious reason these conditions would be different for people detained in psychiatric or other institutions.

While the Court in *Aliev v. Ukraine*[102] noted with approval the movement in some European jurisdictions to allow conjugal visits between prisoners and their spouses, that case stops short of requiring such visits under Article 8.[103] In its view, the failure to provide such visits was justified under Article 8(2) as in the prevention of crime or disorder. It is not entirely clear what the Court means by this. Insofar as the Article 8(2) justification is to be found in the fact that a prison is by its nature a punitive environment, it would not apply to a case involving a psychiatric facility, which is to be therapeutic in nature.

Regarding correspondence, Article 8 provides particular protection for correspondence between lawyers and their clients.[104] It also requires that if an individual is unable to afford postage costs, the facility must make some contribution to the costs of postage so that Article 8 rights to correspondence are realised.[105]

As the Court notes in *Aliev*, the rights under Article 8(1) are subject to restriction under Article 8(2). Such restrictions must be defined in domestic law, and must be 'necessary in a democratic society in the interests of national security, public safety or the economic well-being of the country, for the prevention of disorder or crime, for the protection of health or morals, or for the protection of the rights and freedoms of others'.[106]

Following *Wakefield*, it can be taken that if the sole issue in a human rights concern involves one of these issues of family rights and correspondence, it fits most comfortably under Article 8, although a particularly egregious case might warrant an Article 3 claim

---

[98] *McVeigh, O'Neill and Evans v. the United Kingdom*, Application Nos. 8022/77, 8025/77 and 8027/77, decision 8 December 1979, 25 DR 15, (1983) 5 EHRR 71 paras. 52–3, confirmed by Committee of Ministers, (1983) 5 EHRR CD305.

[99] *Ploski v. Poland*, Application No. 26761/95, judgment 12 November 2002, paras. 32, and 37.

[100] *X. v. the United Kingdom*, Application No. 9054/80, judgment 5 November 1981, 30 DR 113, (1981) 4 EHRR 188.

[101] *Ouinas v. France*, Application No. 13756/88, decision 12 March 1990, 65 DR 265 at p. 277.

[102] Application No. 41220/98, judgment 29 April 2003, (2004) 11 I.H.R.R. 170, para. 188.

[103] *Op. cit.*, para. 188.

[104] *Campbell v. the United Kingdom*, Application No. 13590/88, judgment 25 March 1992, (1993) 15 EHRR 137 at para. 46; *S. v. Switzerland*, Application Nos. 12629/87 and 13965/88, judgment 28 November 1991, (1991) 14 EHRR 670 at paras. 48–50. Regarding searches of correspondence, including correspondence from lawyers, see further below.

[105] *Boyle v. the United Kingdom*, Application No. 9659/82, judgment 24 March 1988, 41 DR 91, (1988) 10 EHRR 425.

[106] See further, p. 81 above.

nonetheless. Further, Article 3 cases are not necessarily based on one factor, but as discussed earlier in this section may be the result of a cumulative burden based on a complex set of facts. If that is the case, there seems to be no reason why the issues based on family rights and correspondence should not form part of that overall collection of facts in an Article 3 case. For example, it would be bizarre for the right to nice furnishings to be more relevant to determination of inhuman treatment than the right to see one's child. It would similarly be inconceivable that the inability to contact a lawyer would be irrelevant in an Article 3 case based for example on a resident's vulnerability to violence in a facility.

All the factors discussed in this section can be understood as building blocks to a claim under Article 3. There is no reason to believe that the preceding list is definitive. In some cases, a single factor may be sufficient to constitute a violation of the ECHR; in other cases, the determination will be based on the cumulative effect of a number of factors. In this regard, the factors discussed in the following sections on restraint and privacy will also be relevant to assessing the cumulative effect of institutionalisation.

Control and Over-Control of Residents

This section concerns the control of people in psychiatric and related institutions, including their restraint and their removal to solitary confinement. The starting point regarding such controls is that 'in respect of a person deprived of his liberty, any recourse to physical force which has not been made strictly necessary by his own conduct diminishes human dignity and is in principle an infringement of the right set forth in Article 3 (art. 3) of the Convention.'[107] Even if the use of force does not in fact breach Article 3, as for example when no adverse effect can been shown on the applicant, the use of force may nonetheless violate Article 8.[108]

This basic law, like most of the Court's cases regarding control of people in institutions, including restraint and the removal of the individual to solitary confinement, comes from a case involving prisons and other similar criminal law facilities. Many of those facilities by their nature include a punitive element. No such role should be assumed in psychiatric contexts, and the above threshold to Article 3 should therefore be read with particular fortitude.

The reports from the CPT from across the Council of Europe generally record the devotion of the staff of psychiatric and related institutions to the individuals in their care. Nonetheless, a smattering of reports do record ill-treatment by staff. The following extract from the report of a CPT visit to Germany is typical:

---

[107] *Ribitsch v. Austria, op. cit.*, para. 38. See also *Sur v. Turkey*, Application No. 21592/93, judgment 3 October 1997, [1997] ECHR 79 para. 43; *Tekin v. Turkey*, Application 21592/93, 3 October 1997, (2001) 31 EHRR 4, para. 53.
[108] See, for example, *Raninen v. Finland, op. cit.*

123. The delegation heard no allegations of ill-treatment of patients by health care staff at the closed psychiatric *Unit 33 of Nordbaden Psychiatric Centre in Wiesloch*. However, at the Forensic Psychiatric Section in Wiesloch, the delegation received allegations from patients in *Units 13 and 16*, claiming that some members of the male nursing staff occasionally treated them brutally (for example, by shoving them to make them enter their rooms more quickly, or punching them). The delegation itself noticed that certain members of the nursing staff did not address patients in an appropriate manner; they shouted orders at patients or answered them in an exasperated manner. **The CPT recommends that the nursing staff of the Forensic Psychiatric Section in Wiesloch be given the clear message that the ill-treatment of patients is unacceptable and will be dealt with severely.**[109]

Usually, domestic law will forbid the use of unnecessary force without reference to the ECHR, and a remedy in domestic courts may well be available by way of criminal charges, for example. There are two difficulties with this. First, prosecutors may be reluctant to initiate a prosecution. Second, even if the case is prosecuted, there may be difficulties in proof: domestic courts may be hesitant at finding witnesses with mental disabilities credible, or may not want to make findings of liability in the face of conflicting testimony. Any reluctance in the court or among the prosecutors to support the rights of people with psychiatric difficulties, or any implied supposition that events in psychiatric or related institutions should be given a 'light touch' by the courts, will compound these difficulties.

Perhaps because the ECtHR does not make findings of liability or guilt against individuals, its approach to evidence is different. Where an individual is injured during a period of confinement, the onus is on the State to provide a plausible explanation for those injuries. When they do not do so, a clear issue arises under Article 3.[110] While the Court normally takes findings of fact of domestic courts as determinative, it is not required to do so, and will substitute its own view of the facts when it finds the domestic view unconvincing or incomplete.[111]

Restraint

Restraint is practised in a variety of ways. At its most basic, it can involve the physical holding by a member of staff of a patient during a period of agitation, aggression or violence. In the longer term, it can involve tying or strapping a person to an object to prevent or restrict bodily movement. Within the Council of Europe Member States there have been recorded uses of leather straps, towels, four-point restraints (i.e., tying the individual's arms and legs to a bed or, occasionally, a chair), metal or netted cage-beds (some-

---

[109] CPT/Inf (2003) 20 (visit of December 2000), para. 123. Emphasis in original. See also reports on Estonia, CPT/Inf (2002) 26 (visit of July 1997) para. 166; Bulgaria, CPT/Inf (2002) 1 (visit of April-May 1999), para. 163; CPT/Inf (2004) 21 (visit of April 2002), para. 124, and Bosnia and Herzegovina, CPT/Inf (2004) 40 (visit of April-May 2003), para. 119. The Bulgarian and Bosnian examples involved not merely punching, but the use of sticks, batons, and the like.

[110] See, for example, *Selmouni v. France*, Application No. 25803/94, judgment 28 July 1999, (2000) 29 EHRR 403, para. 87; *Aksoy v. Turkey*, Application No. 21987/93, judgment 26 November 1996, (1996) 23 EHRR 553, para. 61; *Ribitsch v. Austria, op. cit.*, para. 34.

[111] See, for example, *Ribitsch v. Austria, op. cit.*, para. 33.

times together with leather strapping to a bed),[112] metal cages[113] and handcuffs.[114] Alternatively or in addition, restraint may involve injecting the individual with drugs that have a tranquillising effect.

The CPT acknowledges that restraint of individuals may on occasion be necessary.[115] Indeed, as noted in the previous section, the appropriate use of restraint is viewed by the CPT as a duty of the institution, to ensure the safety of residents from each other or from themselves. That said, the jurisprudence cited above would suggest that such restraint is only justified if it is 'strictly necessary' based on the conduct of the person restrained. Such a view is consistent with the main international instruments. The UN Mental Illness Principles, for example, include the following:

> 11.11   Physical restraint or involuntary seclusion of a patient shall not be employed except in accordance with the officially approved procedures of the mental health facility and only when it is the only means available to prevent immediate or imminent harm to the patient or others. It shall not be prolonged beyond the period which is strictly necessary for this purpose. All instances of physical restraint or involuntary seclusion, the reasons for them and their nature and extent shall be recorded in the patient's medical record. A patient who is restrained or secluded shall be kept under humane conditions and be under the care and close and regular supervision of qualified members of the staff. A personal representative, if any and if relevant, shall be given prompt notice of any physical restraint or involuntary seclusion of the patient.[116]

The CPT has issued the following guidance on the use of restraint:

> 47.   In any psychiatric establishment, the restraint of agitated and/or violent patients may on occasion be necessary. This is an area of particular concern to the CPT, given the potential for abuse and ill-treatment.
>
>   The restraint of patients should be the subject of a clearly-defined policy. That policy should make clear that initial attempts to restrain agitated or violent patients should, as far as possible, be non-physical (e.g. verbal instruction) and that where physical restraint is necessary, it should in principle be limited to manual control.
>
>   Staff in psychiatric establishments should receive training in both non-physical and manual control techniques vis-à-vis agitated or violent patients. The possession of such skills will enable staff to choose the most appropriate response when confronted by difficult situations, thereby significantly reducing the risk of injuries to patients and staff.

---

[112] See Mental Disability Advocacy Center, *Cage Beds: Inhuman and Degrading Treatment in Four EU Accession Countries*, (Budapest: MDAC, 2003). This document is available electronically at http://www.mdac.info.

[113] Amnesty International, *Bulgaria: Arbitrary Detention and Ill-Treatment of People with Mental Disabilities* (London: Amnesty International, 2002), p. 13. This document is available electronically at http://www.amnesty.org.uk/.

[114] See Mental Disability Advocacy Center and Hungarian Helsinki Committee, *Prisoners or Patients: Criminal Psychiatric Detention in Hungary*, (Budapest: MDAC, 2004).

[115] CPT Standards, CPT/Inf/E (2002) 1 – Rev. 2004, p. 59, para. 47.

[116] United Nations General Assembly Resolution 46/119 of 17 December 1991, Principle 11.11. See also Council of Europe Recommendation Rec(2004)10, Article 27. This is substantially similar to the United Nations Principles, except that it does not expressly require the involvement of a personal representative, and it states that it does not apply to 'momentary restraint'.

48. Resort to instruments of physical restraint (straps, straight jackets, etc.) shall only very rarely be justified and must always be either expressly ordered by a doctor or immediately brought to the attention of a doctor with a view to seeking his approval. If, exceptionally, recourse is had to instruments of physical restraint, they should be removed at the earliest opportunity; they should never be applied, or their application prolonged, as a punishment.

The CPT has on occasion encountered psychiatric patients to whom instruments of physical restraint have been applied for a period of days; the Committee must emphasise that such a state of affairs cannot have any therapeutic justification and amounts, in its view, to ill-treatment.[117]

The CPT guidance further requires a register listing instances of restraint to be kept by psychiatric facilities.

This guidance, like the other international instruments, emphasises that restraint should be governed by the principle of least restrictive alternative. It acknowledges that appropriate restraint is a skill in which staff must be trained, but it suggests that such training ought to be provided. Arguably, provision of such training can be seen as a part of the positive obligation on States to ensure compliance with Articles 3 and 8. Consistent with its view that psychiatric facilities are to provide a therapeutic environment, restraint is not to be used as a punishment.

A perusal of the national reports of the CPT again provides some further sense as to how that organisation views its guidance in practice. In its report of its visit to Germany in 2000, the CPT emphasised that restraint could not be used as a matter of routine:

134. In *Straubing Forensic Psychiatric Clinic*, it appeared that patients who had been newly admitted to the Admission Unit (A1) were usually handcuffed during outdoor exercise for the first three days following their arrival. This measure was applied by the security staff. At the *Forensic Psychiatric Section in Wiesloch*, patients who had committed acts of aggression against members of staff, other patients or against themselves (in practice, mainly patients placed in seclusion) were systematically handcuffed during outdoor exercise, or even each time they left their room. In one case, a patient was required to be handcuffed whilst taking a shower. Decisions to apply such measures were taken by the nursing staff and approved by a doctor. In certain cases, the nursing instructions resulted in the patients concerned taking exercise in the security perimeter escorted by two nurses, with hands cuffed behind their backs and legs shackled. Furthermore, a study of the patients' files showed that such measures were also applied for prolonged periods to patients considered to present a risk of escape or a potential threat.

135. The CPT wishes to stress that handcuffing patients can never be part of a therapeutic programme. Therefore, such a measure cannot – and should not – be within the competence of medical or nursing staff.

Routinely handcuffing patients in a secured environment, as practised in Units 13 to 16 of the Forensic Psychiatric Section in Wiesloch, is unacceptable. If the health care staff considers that a given patient or patients require measures of increased attention to guarantee their own security or to protect other patients/staff members, other solutions can and should be found.[118]

---

[117] See CPT Standards, CPT/Inf/E (2002) 1, Rev. 2004, p. 59, para. 48.
[118] Report on Germany, CPT/Inf (2003) 20 (visit of December 2000), paras. 134–5.

The CPT reports further emphasise that the use of restraints must be for a short period of time only, even when the initial restraint may have been justifiable:

> The CPT must emphasise that applying instruments of physical restraint to patients for a period of days at a time cannot have any therapeutic justification and, in its view, amounts to ill-treatment.[119]

The reports also indicate that when restraint occurs, it should be done outside the sight of other residents.[120]

Two specific forms of restraint warrant particular attention. The first involves the use of psychiatric medication for its sedative properties. The CPT discusses this in its report on its 2002 visit to Latvia:

> 153. At the *Vīķi Psychiatric Centre Children's Section*, means of physical restraint (such as fixation) were rarely applied and only upon the decision of the psychiatrist. However, the CPT is very concerned about the manner in which psychotropic drugs were used at the establishment, in order to manage/control children who were agitated and/or displayed behavioural disorders.
>
> In the light of the information gathered by medical members of the delegation (including the examination of medical files), it appeared that 50 of the 63 children were receiving neuroleptics on a regular basis. Many eight to twelve-year old children were receiving (on a daily basis) sedating drugs with dosages that would even sedate adults; in some cases, the dosages given would be even extremely sedating for an adult. By way of example, a bedridden boy (15 years old), who was diagnosed to be auto-aggressive and profoundly retarded, was receiving four different psychotropic drugs with sedative potential, including chlorpromazine 200 mg × 4, every day.
>
> Even though many of the children at the Centre had psychiatric diagnoses, the main reason for the medication seemed to be to control behavioural disturbance. The disturbance described in some cases was behaviour that is typical for the mentally retarded, and not behavioural disturbance connected with psychosis. In the CPT's view, the indications for prescription seemed to be questionable; the dosages used were certainly too high in many cases and detrimental to the well-being of the children concerned.[121]

Although the CPT did in this case recommend a review of the practice by Latvian authorities,[122] it is nonetheless a peculiarly indecisive report. As the CPT report makes clear, the nature and degree of medication in this regard provides cause for concern. Although the CPT acknowledges that the drugs were prescribed to manage behaviour, it does not appear to analyse the situation as a problem of restraint. Yet what the delegation is describing is clearly restraint; it is not obvious that restraint by medications should be subject to a lower threshold of acceptance or different safeguards than physical

---

[119] Report on Germany, CPT/Inf (2003) 20 (visit of December 2000), para. 132. An earlier case, where an individual had been in restraints for an almost uninterrupted period of four months, warranted an immediate observation by the CPT: see report on Norway, CPT/Inf (2000) 15 (visit of September 1999), para. 55.

[120] See report on Denmark, CPT/Inf (2002) 18 (visit of January-February 2002), para. 75.

[121] CPT/Inf (2005) 8 (visit of September-October 2002), para. 153.

[122] At para. 155.

restraint. The CPT report offers no explanation for what must be viewed in this sense as a surprisingly irresolute approach. It is difficult to believe that such medication is the only way to deal with behavioural problems in a children's psychiatric facility; as such, it is difficult to consider the practice to be in conformity with Article 3.

The CPT shows no such reticence in its condemnation of restraint beds. These are beds with either metal cages ('cage beds') or net cages ('net beds') attached onto the sides and top of them. Typically, the restrictions are such that the occupant of the bed is unable fully to stand up in the bed, making prolonged containment in the beds very uncomfortable. Such beds are in use in countries such as Austria[123] and are still widely used in psychiatric hospitals in Hungary, Slovakia and the Czech Republic,[124] the latter of which is the only country within the EU which permits their use in social care institutions. In its report on its 2002 visit to the Czech Republic, the CPT makes clear its opposition to these methods of restraint:

> 127. Particular mention should be made of the frequent use of *net- and cage-beds* at the two establishments visited (26 net-beds at Opava; 11 net-beds and two cage-beds at Ostravice). Staff in both establishments indicated that, apart from their use to restrain agitated or aggressive patients/residents, the net-beds were being used to prevent falls/injuries or nocturnal disorientation/sleepwalking (in some cases for years on end). At Ostravice, heavily agitated residents were placed in a cage-bed, usually until the injected sedative medication became effective. One resident, who suffered from a contagious mouth-infection, had been placed in a cage-bed for one week, due to the lack of alternative facilities to segregate him temporarily from other residents. At both establishments, the delegation was told that it would often be possible to avoid the use of net/cage-beds if there were more staff present (especially during night shifts).
>
> Patients/residents placed in net/cage-beds were usually accommodated in rooms together with other patients/residents. As a consequence, they were exposed to the view not only of their roommates but also of outside visitors. Such a situation could be described as degrading for the person concerned and could also affect the psychological state of the other residents/patients.
>
> 128. The CPT is of the opinion that net- and cage-beds are not an appropriate means of dealing with patients/residents in a state of agitation. **It recommends that cage-beds be immediately withdrawn from service and that net-beds cease to be used as a tool for managing such persons as soon as possible.**
>
> For as long as net-beds remain in use, **the CPT recommends that measures be taken to ensure that persons placed in such facilities are not exposed to the view of other patients/residents and are subject to appropriate supervision by staff; this recommendation applies *mutatis mutandis* to other means of restraint, such as straight-jackets or fixation. This should not preclude persons subject to means of restraint being visited by fellow patients/residents, if this is advisable from a medical standpoint.**

---

[123] See response of Austrian government to CPT report of visit of 14–23 April 2004, published as CPT/Inf (2005) 14, p. 40. It would seem that in the near future, such beds will no longer be in use in Austria.

[124] See Mental Disability Advocacy Center, *Cage Beds: Inhuman and Degrading Treatment in Four EU Accession Countries, op. cit.*

> Similarly, **more suitable means than net-beds can also be found to ensure the safety of persons with impaired mobility or nocturnal disorders (*e.g.* disorientation/sleep-walking).**[125]

Notwithstanding these views, it would appear that net and cage beds remain in use in some parts of central Europe.

Seclusion

Seclusion generally means involuntary placement in locked room generally designed for that purpose. Depending on the situation, the room may have padded walls and soft furnishings so that the person in the room cannot hurt him or herself. Typically seclusion rooms contain either no or minimal furniture. Staff are to monitor a person in seclusion room, and this is done via a small window in the locked door, or via closed-circuit television. Sometimes the person placed into seclusion is forcibly undressed and then dressed with special garments which cannot be torn, in order to prevent suicide attempts.

In the prison context, the placement of a prisoner into solitary confinement does not of itself constitute a violation of Article 3. Instead, such a violation may flow from the reasons, duration and condition of such confinement, with repeated short confinements having a potentially cumulative effect. The same rules apply to seclusion in a psychiatric context.[126] One permitted justification for placement of a prisoner in solitary confinement is his dangerousness to other prisoners.[127] That is the obvious justification for placing a person into seclusion in a psychiatric context.

The Council of Europe Recommendation R(2004)10 and the UN Mental Illness Principles do not distinguish between restraint and seclusion in the safeguards which should be applied. Thus under both regimes persons may only be secluded if it is the least restrictive alternative to prevent harm to the individual concerned or other residents, if the seclusion is under medical supervision and properly documented, and if regular monitoring occurs. The Mental Illness Principles further require the involvement of a personal representative.

The CPT Standards do have specific provisions related to seclusion:

> 49. Reference should also be made in this context to the seclusion (i.e. confinement alone in a room) of violent or otherwise "unmanageable" patients, a procedure which has a long history in psychiatry.
>
> There is a clear trend in modern psychiatric practice in favour of avoiding seclusion of patients, and the CPT is pleased to note that it is being phased out in many countries. For so long as seclusion remains in use, it should be the subject of a detailed policy spelling out,

---

[125] CPT/Inf (2004) 4 (visit of April 2002), paras. 127–8. Emphasis in original.
[126] *Dhoest v. Belgium*, Application No. 10448/83, judgment 14 May 1987 (1990) 12 EHRR paras. 117, 121.
[127] *M. v. the United Kingdom*, Application No. 9907/82, decision 12 December 1983, 35 DR 130, (1984) 6 EHRR CD576.

in particular: the types of cases in which it may be used; the objectives sought; its duration and the need for regular reviews; the existence of appropriate human contact; the need for staff to be especially attentive.

Seclusion should never be used as a punishment.[128]

The CPT Standards further requires that any instances of seclusion be recorded in the institution's register of restraint.

The conditions of seclusion must meet the standards discussed earlier in this chapter. In particular, seclusion rooms must be of appropriate physical standard, including appropriate furnishings and access to natural light, and be appropriately clean and well-maintained. During the seclusion, the resident must be appropriately dressed, have appropriate access to sanitary facilities, and have at least an hour of outdoor exercise per day.[129]

Privacy

Rights to privacy in psychiatric and similar facilities raise two different sorts of issue. The first involves privacy within the facility. People in institutions are entitled to correspond and interact with people outside the institution. The issue is how far those relationships are private, and how far the facility is permitted to intrude into them by way of search or surveillance. How far is there an obligation on the institution not to intrude into private behaviours, including smoking, enjoying alcohol or sexual activity? People are similarly entitled to keep a reasonable range of personal possessions; how far are these possessions protected from searches and seizures by the institution? The second set of issues involve disclosures by the institution. Information about the resident will be possessed by the institution, and there is a corresponding duty to keep that information private. The issue is how far that duty extends to preclude disclosures to staff, other residents in the facility, and the rest of the community. Information regarding the individual's psychiatric history is the obvious example of such information, but it is not necessarily the only example. The institution may become aware of a wide array of details of the individual's private life that he or she would wish to remain confidential.

Private Life

Regarding privacy within an institution, the starting point is relatively simple. 'Private life' has been read widely by the Court, and virtually any search, surveillance or seizure of a resident's person or personal belongings will engage the right to privacy under Article 8(1).[130]

---

[128] See CPT Standards, CPT/Inf/E (2002) 1, Rev. 2004, p. 59, para. 49.
[129] See, for example, report on Germany, CPT/Inf (2003) 20 (visit of December 2000), para. 128.
[130] Regarding the breadth of 'private life', and its application to searches, see e.g., *Funke v. France*, Application No. 10828/84, judgment 25 February 1993, (1993) 16 EHRR 297, *Cremieux v. France*, Application No. 11470/85, judgment 25 February 1993, (1993) 16 EHRR 357, *Niemietz v. Germany*, Application No. 13710/88, judgment 16 December 1992, (1993) 16 EHRR 97, *Camerzind v. Switzerland*, Application

Surreptitious listening devices will also raise an Article 8 issue,[131] and by extension similar closed circuit visual surveillance would also raise such an issue.[132] Similarly, any monitoring of correspondence will engage Article 8(1). That includes both written correspondence and telephone conversations.[133]

The significant issues regarding search and surveillance are likely therefore not to lie in the engagement of Article 8(1), but in the potential justifications contained in Article 8(2).[134] The acceptability of a justification will no doubt depend on the facts of the situation, and in particular the nature of the institution in question. Issues of public safety or the rights of others, for example, may be of considerably more relevance in a high security forensic facility than in a local care home for adults with dementia. Certainly, facilities have the right (and indeed the duty – see page 86 to 87 above) to ensure that all residents are able to enjoy a reasonable level of safety within the institution. That may require some limitations on the rights to privacy of other residents.

A considerable margin of appreciation is left to States as to how to form policy within these parameters, but they must be formulated in domestic law, and sufficiently clear that the individual is protected from arbitrary applications. As an example, in *Herczegfalvy v. Austria*, the psychiatric facility sent all a resident's outgoing letters (except those addressed to his lawyer or to the guardianship court) to the resident's guardian, who would then decide which should be sent on to the addressee. This policy was held not to have adequate protections against arbitrary interference with the person's rights.[135]

Particular protections are offered for correspondence to and from lawyers. The ECHR jurisdiction regarding prisons provides that clients have the right to speak with their lawyer outside the hearing of institutional staff, and for any instructions to the lawyer to remain confidential.[136] Letters from a lawyer to a prisoner may be opened by prison staff only if there is reasonable reason to believe that the letter contains illicit enclosures. Such letters may then be opened, but not read, and suitable guarantees to this effect should be provided to the prisoner. The search of the letter could, for example, be conducted in the prisoner's presence. Reading correspondence between a lawyer and a client is allowed only

---

No. 21353/93, judgment 16 December 1997, (1999) 28 EHRR 458. Regarding searches in particular and Articles 8 and 3, see *Valasinas v. Lithuania, op. cit.; Van der Ven v. the Netherlands, op. cit.*

[131] *Khan v. the United Kingdom*, Application No. 35394/97, judgment 12 May 2000, (2001) 31 EHRR 45, para. 25.

[132] See in particular *Peck v. the United Kingdom*, Application No. 44647/98, judgment 28 January 2003, (2003) 36 EHRR 41, where closed circuit surveillance of a street did not of itself raise an Article 8 issue, as (unlike life in a psychiatric facility) activities in the street were already public. Nonetheless, the subsequent release of the tapes for public broadcast did raise an Article 8 issue.

[133] *Halford v. the United Kingdom*, Application No. 20605/92, judgment 27 May 1997, (1997) 24 EHRR 523.

[134] See further discussion of Article 8(2) at page 81 above.

[135] *Herczegfalvy v. Austria* Application No. 10533/83, judgment 24 September 1992, (1993) 15 EHRR 437, paras. 87–92.

[136] *Campbell v. the United Kingdom*, Application No. 13590/88, judgment 25 March 1992, (1993) 15 EHRR 137, para. 46.

if there is reasonable reason to believe that the solicitor-client privilege is being abused.[137] There is certainly no reason for a stricter régime to be employed in psychiatric and similar facilities, and depending on the facility, a much less intrusive approach might well be more appropriate.

How far Article 8 rights extend beyond this narrow relatively interpretation of privacy has not been litigated. Article 8(1) also protects the right to respect for an individual's 'home', defined by the Court in the following terms:

> 'Home' is an autonomous concept that does not depend on classification under domestic law. Whether or not a particular habitation constitutes a home which attracts the protection of Article 8(1) will depend on the factual circumstances, namely, the existence of sufficient and continuous links.[138]

On this basis, it would seem that institutions in which an individual resides for only a short period of time (such as a few days for psychiatric assessment) may not constitute a 'home' for the purposes of Article 8, but institutions in which an individual lives or is expected to live for months or years almost certainly will. It is at least arguable that rights to respect for private life are particularly relevant to the home environment, and the State's restrictions of conduct in the home environment therefore subject to particular scrutiny. That said, the institutional context places practical pressures on the rights to respect for home. The most obvious of these flow from the fact that individuals live closely together. The provision in Article 8(2), that Article 8(1) rights may be restricted in the interests of 'the protection of the rights and freedom of others', gives Convention acknowledgement of these pressures.

Tobacco smoking provides a concrete example of these rather abstract competing provisions. A number of European countries have moved to ban smoking from hospitals, or indeed from public buildings entirely. Any move to do so in a long-stay institution for people with mental disabilities would however be open to the objection that it fails to acknowledge the individual's right to respect for private life, a right which should be read with particular robustness regarding an individual's conduct in his or her home. Such a non-smoking policy would make smoking virtually illegal for persons detained in facilities, unlike the remainder of the population who can still smoke in their homes, outside the scope of the anti-smoking laws. This would raise questions of discrimination under Article 14. At the same time, the Court would have to consider the rights of non-smoking residents and staff in the institution, and in particular their rights to the health benefits that flow from a smoke-free environment. It is by no means clear how the Court would resolve these complexities.

---

[137] *Campbell v. the United Kingdom, op. cit.*, para. 48.
[138] *Buckley v. the United Kingdom*, Application No. 20348/92, judgment 26 August 1996, (1996) 23 EHRR 101, para. 63

Disclosure of private information

Medical records and similar personal data attract a right to confidentiality as part of the right to privacy under Article 8.[139] This right is buttressed in a psychiatric context by the provisions of the Council of Europe Recommendation No. R(2004)10:

> *Article 13 – Confidentiality and record-keeping*
> 1. All personal data relating to a person with mental disorder should be considered to be confidential. Such data may only be collected, processed and communicated according to the rules relating to professional confidentiality and personal data protection.
> 2. Clear and comprehensive medical and, where appropriate, administrative records should be maintained for all persons with mental disorder placed or treated for such a disorder. The conditions governing access to that information should be clearly specified by law.[140]

In the general course of things, this information therefore should not be disclosed without the consent of the resident. Any other disclosure must be consistent with the terms of Article 8(2). While the individual is resident in the facility, the need for disclosure outside the institution would therefore be rare indeed, although disclosure of some aspects may be necessary for discharge planning, for example. Even in that case, it would be an unusual case where disclosure would not be contingent on the consent of the resident. The Article 8(1) rights apply equally within an institution, however, and disclosure to staff members of the institution would similarly require justification under Article 8(2). The most obvious justifications would be for the safety of the resident or others on the ward, or on a need-to-know basis of medical professionals engaged in the health care of the resident. This provides a different sort of argument as to why the use of residents as ward staff, an approach criticised by the CPT,[141] is inappropriate. The confusion of roles might mean that the resident would need to be told personal information about other residents. It is difficult to see that this would be acceptable.

Article 8(1) also provides a right to the resident to view the records held by an institution.[142] This raises the difficulty that some of the information in the records may have been provided in confidence, on the express or implied expectation and understanding that the person in question would not have access to it. The problem here is how to balance the rights of the provider of the information with the rights of the individual to whom it refers.

---

[139] *M.S. v. Sweden*, Application No. 20837/92, judgment 27 August 1997, (1999) 28 EHRR 313; *Z. v. Finland*, Application No. 22009/93, judgment 25 February 1997, (1998) 25 EHRR 371.
[140] Council of Europe Recommendation Rec(2004)10, Article 13.
[141] See further page 86 above.
[142] See also UN Mental Illness Principles, Principle 19. This principle allows information disclosure to the patient to be restricted only when domestic legislation allows it, with a view to preventing 'serious harm' to the patient, or to avoiding risk to the health and safety of others. Notification and an explanation of such withholding are to be given to the patient or the patient's counsel. The principle further requires the comments of the patient or his or her personal representative to be included in the file, if the patient so requests.

The case law in this area tends to involve files created well in advance of the application, with the applicants motivated by a desire to know about their childhood or adolescence.[143] The classic statement balancing the rights of those involved is contained in *Gaskin v. the the United Kingdom*:

> Confidentiality of public records is of importance for receiving objective and reliable information, and . . . such confidentiality can also be necessary for the protection of third persons. Under the latter aspect, a system like the British one, which makes access to records dependent on the consent of the contributor, can in principle be considered to be compatible with the obligations under Article 8, taking into account the State's margin of appreciation. The Court considers, however, that under such a system the interests of the individual seeking access to records relating to his private and family life must be secured when a contributor to the records either is not available or improperly refuses consent. Such a system is only in conformity with the principle of proportionality if it provides that an independent authority finally decides whether access has to be granted in cases where a contributor fails to answer or withholds consent.[144]

The facility need not show confidential information, therefore, but it cannot ultimately decide to withhold information on its own. An independent authority must determine whether access ought to be granted.[145] The right to access further includes a right to correction of incorrect or misleading information.[146]

As noted, the leading case law tends to deal with situations where the applicant is seeking information to understand his or her past. Information to allow an applicant to make sense of an immediate decision might well be viewed as a more pressing need on the part of the applicant. The right of an applicant to view a record might for example be perceived by the Court to be particularly compelling if it were in the context of a desire to decide whether or not to consent to treatment. Similarly, as discussed in chapter 2, Article 5 provides a separate right to information regarding the justification for confinement of the individual.

The Duty of the State

The State is responsible for the actions of its servants and agents, and will therefore be responsible for any ECHR breaches committed by those individuals. Ignorance of such

---

[143] See, for example, *Gaskin v. the United Kingdom*, Application No. 10454/83, judgment 7 July 1989, (1990) 12 EHRR 36, *Martin v. the United Kingdom*, Application No. 27533/95, judgment 28 February 1996, (1996) 21 EHRR CD 112, *Odièvre v. France*, Application No. 42326/98, judgment 13 February 2003, (2004) 38 EHRR 43. But see *McGinley and Egan v. the United Kingdom*, Application No. 21825/93, judgment 9 June 1998, (1998) 27 EHRR 1, *M.G. v. the United Kingdom*, Application No. 39393/98, judgment 24 September 2002, (2003) 36 EHRR 3, and *Rotaru v. Romania*, Application No. 28341/95, judgment 4 May 2000, 8 BHRC 449.

[144] *Gaskin v. the United Kingdom, op. cit.*, para. 49.

[145] For an application of this approach in a psychiatric context, see *Martin v. the United Kingdom, op. cit.*

[146] *Rotaru v. Romania, op. cit.*, para. 46.

violations is not an excuse.[147] The duties of the State regarding ECHR rights is not limited to its own institutions, servants and agents, however. The State must take measures to ensure ECHR compliance throughout society, as the following statement from *A. v. the United Kingdom* makes clear:

> The Court considers that the obligations on the High Contracting Parties under Article I of the Convention to secure to everyone within their jurisdiction the rights and freedoms defined in the Convention, taken together with Article 3, requires States to take measures designed to ensure that individuals within their jurisdiction are not subjected to torture or inhuman or degrading treatment or punishment, including such ill-treatment administered by private individuals. . . . Children and other vulnerable individuals, in particular, are entitled to State protection, in the form of effective deterrence against serious breaches of personal integrity. . . .[148]

The reference to 'other vulnerable individuals', a phrase that would include people with mental disabilities, emphasises a particular duty of the State to ensure appropriate protection of this group from ECHR violations.[149]

The fact that an institution is privately run, therefore, does not mean the standards implied by the ECHR are necessarily inapplicable. Article 13 requires the State to provide an effective domestic remedy for ECHR violations. Criminal sanctions are an obvious way to fulfil this requirement, so long as they do indeed govern the conduct in question.[150] Criminal law has further been held to be an inadequate remedy when it proceeds too slowly to provide a meaningful remedy, as when a fourteen-month period elapsed between the complaint of an alleged beating in a prison and the complainant being asked to identify the perpetrators.[151]

The individual making a complaint under Article 3 is entitled to have that complaint investigated:

> The Court considers that where an individual makes a credible assertion that he has suffered treatment infringing Article 3 at the hands of the police or other similar agents of the State, that provision, read in conjunction with the State's general duty under Article 1 of the Convention to "secure to everyone within their jurisdiction the rights and freedoms defined in . . . [the] Convention", requires by implication that there should be an effective official investigation. As with an investigation under Article 2, such investigation should be capable of leading to the identification and punishment of those responsible. . . . Otherwise, the general legal prohibition of torture and inhuman and degrading treatment and punishment

---

[147] *Cyprus v. Turkey*, Application No. 25781/94, judgment 10 May 2001, (1976) 4 EHRR 482 at para 37; *Ireland v. the United Kingdom*, Application No. 5310/71, judgment 18 January 1978, (1978) 2 EHRR 25, para.159.

[148] *A. v. the United Kingdom*, Application No. 25599/94, judgment 23 September 1998, (1998) 27 EHRR 611, para. 22.

[149] On an analogous point relating to Article 5, see *Storck v. Germany*, Application. No. 61603/00, judgment 16 June 2005, para. 103–6.

[150] See *A. v. the United Kingdom, op. cit.*, paras. 23–4, a case involving corporal punishment of a child, where the English law allowing 'reasonable chastisement' of children did not adequately protect the applicant's rights under Article 3.

[151] *Labita v. Italy*, Application No. 26772/95, judgment 6 April 2000, para. 133.

would, despite its fundamental importance . . ., be ineffective in practice and it would be possible in some cases for agents of the State to abuse the rights of those within their control with virtual impunity. . . .[152]

The failure to provide such an investigative structure into complaints itself constituted a violation of Article 3. While this statement is made with reference to a state-owned facility, a prison, there is no reason that a different standard would be applied for alleged Article 3 violations occurring in the private sector.

At this time, the Court has not moved beyond these procedural protections in its insistence under Article 1 that States secure the Convention's rights and freedoms to their citizens. Particularly for vulnerable populations such as people in psychiatric facilities, such an approach may not be sufficient, as it presupposes an applicant with the intellectual and emotional resources to pursue a case. The Court has noted on numerous occasions the particular vulnerability of people in psychiatric institutions;[153] it is at least arguable that the Court should use Article 1 to require a broader array of rights safeguards in psychiatric facilities. In this context, appropriate staffing and appropriate inspections raise potential Article 1 issues.

The Council of Europe Recommendations concerning the Rights and Dignity of Persons with Mental Disorder contain the following provision regarding staffing of mental health services:

> *Article 11 – Professional standards*
> 1. Professional staff involved in mental health services should have appropriate qualifications and training to enable them to perform their role within the services according to professional obligations and standards.
> 2. In particular, staff should receive appropriate training on:
>   i. protecting the dignity, human rights and fundamental freedoms of persons with mental disorder;
>   ii. understanding, prevention and control of violence;
>   iii. measures to avoid the use of restraint or seclusion;
>   iv. the limited circumstances in which different methods of restraint or seclusion may be justified, taking into account the benefits and risks entailed, and the correct application of such measures.[154]

As noted above, the CPT similarly expects sufficient levels of staffing to ensure appropriate and professional running of psychiatric institutions. In its view, such staffing levels are necessary to prevent persons in facilities from harming each other, and also to ensure provision of appropriate programmes.[155] The failure to meet the substantive standards

---

[152] *Labita v. Italy, op. cit.,* para. 131.
[153] See, for example, *Herczegfalvy v. Austria, op. cit.,* para. 82; *Keenan v. the United Kingdom, op. cit.,* para. 110.
[154] Rec(2004)10, Article 11.
[155] See CPT Standards, CPT/Inf/E (2002) 1, Rev. 2004, p. 54 para. 30; p. 58, paras. 42–46; p. 50 para. 47. The requirement that staff be appropriately trained extends throughout the range of staff employed, and in that regard the CPT particularly includes orderlies and similar staff within the class of those requiring appropriate training: para. 28.

required by the ECHR is arguably predictable from the failure to provide adequate staff. If the Court is serious about protecting these substantive rights for people with mental disabilities, therefore, it may well be that it should impose a duty on States under Articles 1 and 13 to ensure adequate staffing of institutions.

Similarly, the CPT actively encourages duplicating itself on the national scale, that is, it encourages States to fund inspectorates independent of the institution to visit such establishments as a matter of routine:

> 55. The CPT also attaches considerable importance to psychiatric establishments being vis-ited on a regular basis by an independent outside body (e.g. a judge or supervisory commit-tee) which is responsible for the inspection of patients' care. This body should be authorised, in particular, to talk privately with patients, receive directly any complaints which they might have and make any necessary recommendations.[156]

The logic here is that the staff who would be found to be infringing ECHR standards can-not be relied upon to police those standards. The inspection body should therefore be independent of the institution, and contain people knowledgeable in the care of people with mental difficulties. The provision of independent investigation is particularly important for people with mental disabilities, who cannot be assumed to have the intel-lectual, emotional, or knowledge resources to press justifiable complaints of ill-treatment. While the Court has not yet held it to be required by the ECHR, it is at least arguable that it forms part of the particular duty of States cited in *A.*. above to protect particularly vulnerable people.

---

[156] CPT Standards, CPT/Inf/E (2002) 1, Rev 2004, p. 61, para. 55.

Chapter 4

Medical Treatment

Introduction

For purposes of this book, the medical treatment of people by mental health services raises two sorts of problem. The first arises when treatment is unavailable, or at least, unavailable at a standard desired by the person seeking treatment or his or her carers. In many Member States of the Council of Europe, need surpasses resources, and compromises are made in provision of medical services. Too frequently, marginalisation of people with mental health difficulties means that they are particularly susceptible to limited services. The question arising in the current context is whether the ECHR can require the provision of treatment at all, and if so, whether it can impose standards on the treatment provided. The second concerns the rights of people to refuse psychiatric or related medical treatment. The availability of treatment does not imply that a non-consenting person should be required to accept it. People may have coherent and cogent objections for refusing treatment, or for preferring one plan of treatment over another. The introduction of neuroleptic medications or electro-convulsive therapy to the body over the objection of a competent patient raise important human rights concerns. These two sets of problem overlap. It is rare that a patient will wish to refuse all treatment, so the question of refusal often becomes a question of availability of a choice of treatments.

Analysis of treatment rights under the ECHR is problematic, as here more than ever, the relevant issues were almost certainly not in the minds of the authors of the treaty. Nonetheless, the issues are of fundamental importance. Psychiatric treatment affects who the person is in an extraordinarily direct and personal way. This is not necessarily a bad thing: making disembodied voices go away or lifting an individual from a depressed emotional state may well be perceived by that individual as exceptionally beneficial. These, more than any other decisions in mental health law and perhaps in law as a whole, are decisions about altering the self. Fundamental questions of human rights are thus at issue.

A Right to Minimal Treatment?

As discussed in Chapter 1, mental disorders are very common in society. Globally, roughly 450 million people suffer from mental or neurological disorders, or other forms of mental disability. While mental disability constitutes roughly 12 per cent of the burden of disease internationally, for a majority of countries, it accounts for less than one per cent of health expenditures.[1] Only a minority of people affected receives treatment. This is so, not merely in relatively poor countries, but also in wealthy ones.[2] In recent years, the right to health has been gaining increasing prominence in international law,[3] but such a right applied to mental disability has been slow to be applied.

A variety of 'soft' international law does import a duty on the part of States to provide a reasonable standard of health care to persons with mental disabilities. For example, Article 10 of the 2004 Council of Europe Recommendations regarding the Rights of Persons with Mental Disorder advises:

> Member states should, taking into account available resources, take measures:
> i. to provide a range of services of appropriate quality to meet the mental health needs of persons with mental disorder, taking into account the differing needs of different groups of such persons, and to ensure equitable access to such services;[4]

All countries which have ratified the ECHR are Member States of the Council of Europe, so it is a reasonable expectation that they will comply with this Recommendation.

---

[1]   United Nations Commission on Human Rights, Report of the Special Rapporteur on the right of everyone to the enjoyment of the highest attainable standard of physical and mental health, E/CN.4/2005/51 (11 February 2005), para 6.

[2]   See for example, R. Kessler, O. Demler, et al., 'Prevalence and treatment of mental disorders, 1990 to 2003' 352(24) *New England Journal of Medicine* (2005), 2515.

[3]   The right to health is contained in a variety of United Nations human rights instruments, including the Universal Declaration of Human Rights (1948), Article 25(1); the International Covenant on Economic, Social and Cultural Rights (1966), Article 12; the Convention on the Elimination of All Forms of Discrimination Against Women (1979), Article 12; the United Nations Convention on the Rights of the Child (1989), Article 24. With the appointment by the General Assembly of a Special Rapporteur on the Right to Health, Professor Paul Hunt, in 2002, the United Nations provisions have acquired a renewed impetus. Within the Council of Europe, the right is recognised in the European Social Charter (1961), Principle 11 and Article 13; Convention on Human Rights and Biomedicine (1997), Article 3.

[4]   Recommendation Rec(2004)10 of the Committee of Ministers (adopted 22 September 2004). See also UN Principles for the Protection of Persons with Mental Illness, General Assembly Resolution 46/119 (17 December 1991), principles 1.1 (right to best available mental health care), 8 (standards of care), 14 (resources for mental health facilities). Principle 14 of the UN Principles emphasises that mental health facilities must be resourced comparably to other comparable non-mental health facilities.

It is not entirely clear how far these aspirational values translate into hard rights under the ECHR. For people outside psychiatric and social care institutions, the case law is currently silent. In the long term, arguments may be able to be made by analogy to the State's responsibilities to people in institutions. Why, after all, should people in State institutions have better rights to health care than people living in the community, particularly in the context of mental disability, where government policies are increasingly moving towards community-based care? The case law regarding rights to health care in institutions focuses primarily on Articles 3 and 8 of the ECHR. Neither of these refers directly to an institutional context as its trigger for its engagement, so it may be that parallel arguments could apply to people living in the community. The Court has been prepared in some circumstances to impose positive obligations onto the State under Articles 3[5] and 8,[6] although it has expressly not as yet moved into the realm of requiring provision of financial assistance.[7] It seems unlikely that the Court will find a general right to health in the immediate future.

The obvious risk of imposing positive obligations to provide mental health care generally is that the State will respond by detaining the individual in a psychiatric facility rather than offering good community treatment. This response may not prove as easy for the State as might at first appear. In *Kolanis v. the United Kingdom* the applicant claimed that his release from detention in a psychiatric institution would have been possible if an appropriate range of services were made available in the community. On the facts, the ECtHR declined to rule on the level of services that the State must provide to enable such releases from detention, but it did not rule out the possibility that it would establish such duties in the future.[8] If a duty is found that a standard of services must be provided such as would allow release from detention, it is difficult to see that a comparable standard must not be provided to allow prevention of detention in the first place.

Arguments for standards of treatment in the community are speculative at this time. The case law is considerably stronger regarding the provision of medical services to people in institutions. Article 3 requires the State to provide appropriate medical services for prisoners,[9] including psychiatric treatment.[10] A similar requirement would presumably

---

[5]   *A. v. the United Kingdom*, Application No. 25599/94, judgment 23 September 1998, (1998) 27 EHRR 611, para. 22; *Costello-Roberts v. the United Kingdom*, Application No. 13134/87, judgment 25 March 1993, A.247-C (1993) 19 EHRR 112.

[6]   See, e.g., *X. and Y. v. the Netherlands*, Application No. 8978/80, judgment 27 February 1985, A91 (1985) 8 EHRR 235, *Gaskin v. the United Kingdom*, Application No. 10454/83, judgment 23 June 1989 (1990) 12 EHRR 36.

[7]   *Petrovic v. Austria*, Application No. 20458/92, judgment 27 March 1998, 1998–II 579. See also *Botta v. Italy*, Application No. 21439/93, judgment 24 February 1998, (1998) 26 EHRR 241, where the applicant was unsuccessful in claiming a breach of Article 8 based on the failure of the state to enforce laws requiring private business to provide facilities for persons with disabilities.

[8]   *Kolanis v. the United Kingdom*, Application No. 517/02, judgment 21 June 2005, (2006) 42 EHRR 12, para. 71. See further pp. 45–6, above.

[9]   *Nevmerzhitsky v. Ukraine*, Application No. 54825/00, judgment 5 April 2005, paras. 100–106; *McGlinchey v. the United Kingdom*, Application No. 50390/99, judgment 29 July 2003, (2003) 37 EHRR 41, paras. 46, 57.

[10] *Keenan v. the United Kingdom*, Application No 27229/95, judgment 3 April 2001, (2001) 33 EHRR 38, para. 108–115.

apply for people detained in psychiatric facilities. The existing jurisprudence concerns cases where needs were overlooked in individual situations, and there is therefore little discussion of what standard of provision applies. The issues in the cases did not concern the overall provision of services in an equitable fashion, as for example between different categories of people with mental health problems, or between people with mental health problems versus somatic (physical) illnesses or disorders. Nonetheless, the jurisprudence does provide a right to medical services.

The case law under Article 5 of the ECHR may provide a better sense of the approach of the Court to substantive standards in this area. For people whose liberty is deprived under Article 5, the ECHR provides a right to be held in an institution that is not destructive of the individual's mental health. The classic statement of this right is contained in *Aerts v. Belgium*:

> [T]here must be some relationship between the ground of permitted deprivation of liberty relied on and the place and conditions of detention. In principle, the "detention" of a person as a mental health patient will only be "lawful" for the purposes of sub-paragraph (e) of paragraph 1 if effected in a hospital, clinic or other appropriate institution.[11]

In that case, the facility in question was a medical wing of a prison that had only a part-time psychiatrist, who had time to see patients only at their request. Other carers, without medical qualifications, were administering medical interventions such as intramuscular injections. The standards of the institution itself were inadequate, with few programmes for people to occupy themselves. The Court found a violation of Article 5:

> [T]he Lantin psychiatric wing could not be regarded as an institution appropriate for the detention of persons of unsound mind, the latter not receiving either regular medical attention or a therapeutic environment. On 2 August 1993, in response to an application for leave lodged by Mr Aerts, the Mental Health Board expressed the view that the situation was harmful to the applicant, who was not receiving the treatment required by the condition that had given rise to his detention. Moreover, the Government did not deny that the applicant's treatment in Lantin had been unsatisfactory from a therapeutic point of view. The proper relationship between the aim of the detention and the conditions in which it took place was therefore deficient.[12]

The *Aerts* judgment does not provide a right to a particularly high standard of treatment. A somewhat higher standard may be implied in Article 5 when the justification for the deprivation of liberty under domestic law includes the requirement that the person suffers from a mental disability that is amenable to treatment. In *Hutchinson Reid v. the United Kingdom*, the applicant had an untreatable personality disorder. He alleged that his continued detention in a psychiatric hospital was inappropriate and thus in violation of Article 5 because treatment for his disorder was not available. His claim was not suc-

---

[11] Application No. 25357/94, judgment 29 June 1998, (1998) 29 EHRR 50, para. 46, citing *Ashingdane v. the United Kingdom*, Application No. 8225/78, judgment 28 May 1985, A/93 (1985) 7 EHRR 528, para. 44.
[12] Para. 49.

cessful, as the threat he posed to himself and others was itself sufficient under domestic law to confine him notwithstanding the medical consensus that he could not be 'treated', and the proper application of this domestic law did not constitute a violation of Article 5. The Court did not however close the door on a parallel argument where domestic law uses treatability as part of the justification for detention.[13] This might provide a right to treatment in the least restrictive environment possible, a standard also contained in the Council of Europe Recommendations of 2004,[14] or at least a right to treatment for the disorder for which the individual was detained.

It is less obvious that the Court would be prepared to use Article 5 to insist on one treatment rather than another for the person's mental disability – the question of standards or choice as distinct from basic availability of treatment. As will be discussed shortly, Article 3 has the potential to give some protection to restrict the use of some forms of particularly intrusive treatment. At issue now is whether Article 5 brings anything additional to that standard. At least in theory, it ought to. These Article 3 issues apply to all patients; Article 5 applies only to patients deprived of their liberty. If, as quoted above, the Court is serious in its view that there must be 'some relationship between the ground of permitted deprivation of liberty relied on and the place and conditions of detention'[15] and the ground of detention is based on treatment for a mental disorder, this must surely mean more than not being treated in an inhuman or degrading way. At the same time, determining such standards leads the Court into territory it traditionally avoids for both doctrinal and practical reasons. Traditionally, Article 5 jurisprudence focuses on the fact of detention, not the conditions of detention.[16] The approach in *Aerts* and similar cases may suggest a certain permeability of this distinction, but it is likely that a considerable margin of appreciation will be permitted on treatments offered. There are also practical issues of which the Court is likely to be concerned. Better treatments may be more expensive. In theory, that should not necessarily deter the Court: human rights often have financial implications, and the provision of superior medical treatment may be less financially significant than the requirement, for example, to provide judicial processes for the determination of rights. Further, any hesitancy by the Court based on expense suggests putting a price tag on rights, an approach that ought to cause concern in determining human rights. Nonetheless, courts are generally hesitant to pass into fiscal territory. Courts are also hesitant to trespass into the expertise of non-legal professionals. An applicant wishing to make a challenge in this area would thus be well-advised to include compelling medical evidence in support of his or her application.

---

[13] *Hutchison Reid v. the United Kingdom*, Application No. 50272/99, judgment 20 May 2003, (2003) 37 EHRR 9, paras. 51–2.
[14] See Article 8 of the 2004 Recommendations (2004)10.
[15] *Aerts v. Belgium*, Application No. 25357/94, judgment 29 June 1998,. 29 EHRR 50, para. 46.
[16] *Ashingdane v. the United Kingdom, op. cit.*, para. (1985) 7 EHRR 528, para. 44.

Controls on Overly Intrusive Treatment

To this point, the argument has focused primarily on how far the ECHR can be used to enforce the provision of a range of medical services for mental disabilities. Substantive issues also arise, however, regarding some forms of particularly invasive treatment and the need to restrict or regulate their use. Electro-convulsive therapy (ECT) and mandatory sterilisation are perhaps obvious examples, but they are not necessarily the only ones.

Article 3, which provides for the right to be free from inhuman or degrading treatment or punishment, has not yet been found to have been violated by psychiatric treatment. However, in theory at least, mental health treatment may engage Article 3. The treatment complained of must reach a 'minimum level of severity' in order to engage the Article. The determination of the level depends on the circumstances of the individual case, the nature of the treatment and the manner in which it is imposed, and duration and effects.[17] The most directly relevant case from the ECHR on this threshold as applied to psychiatric treatment is *Herczegfalvy v. Austria*.[18] This case will be discussed at length below, regarding consent to psychiatric treatment. Certainly when issues of consent are absent, however, it adopts the standards of the medical profession as pivotal in determining Article 3 compliance:

> The established principles of medicine are admittedly in principle decisive in such cases; as a general rule, a measure which is a therapeutic necessity cannot be regarded as inhuman or degrading. The Court must nevertheless satisfy itself that the medical necessity has been convincingly shown to exist.[19]

In a sense, this merely pushed the question a step back, for what are the 'established principles of medicine'? There is no ECHR jurisprudence on point to assist the analysis. Certainly, it seems likely that the domestic practice will be relevant to the standard, but will the Court look more broadly to standards of practice across the countries of the Council of Europe?

Electro-convulsive therapy (ECT) provides an illustration here. In most of the Council of Europe's Member States, ECT is performed only after the administration of anaesthetics and muscle relaxants (so-called 'modified' ECT). Failure to do so both renders the procedure considerably more unpleasant to the patient, and also exposes him or her to significantly increased risks of injury, particularly bone fractures. In some countries within the Council of Europe, 'unmodified' ECT, that is, ECT without administration of the above medication, is still performed.[20] If the Court looks to the broader Euro-

---

[17] See, eg, *Kudła v. Poland*, Application No. 30210/96, judgment 26 October 2000, (2002) 35 EHRR 11, para. 91.

[18] Application No. 10533/83, judgment of 24 September 1992, (1993) 15 EHRR 437.

[19] *Herczegfalvy v. Austria, op. cit.*, at para. 82.

[20] Unmodified ECT has recently been documented in Turkey for example: Mental Disability Rights International (MDRI), *Behind Closed Doors: Human Rights Abuses in the Psychiatric Facilities, Orphanages and Rehabilitation Centers of Turkey* (Washington: 2005), pp. 1–2.

pean standard, it seems considerably more likely that the Court will find a violation of Article 3 in a case of unmodified ECT.

Unmodified ECT provides a particularly compelling example where the broader European practice ought to be determinative. The European Committee for the Prevention of Torture and Inhuman or Degrading Treatment or Punishment (CPT) has raised particular concerns about this form of the treatment, stating that 'this method can no longer be considered as acceptable in modern psychiatric practice'.[21] There would be a particular irony if the CPT's views in this regard were ignored by the Court in deference to medical expertise, as the CPT, unlike the Court, has both legal and medical expertise among its membership.

While the Court refers to the 'established principles of medicine', it is arguable that these must be read in the light of other human rights instruments. One reason for the continuation of unmodified ECT, for example, might be the expense of the additional medications and, perhaps more significant, of an anaesthetist qualified to administer them. In that event, the 'established principles of medicine' are not insulated from broader social, political, economic, and psychiatric-cultural factors. In that context, it seems reasonable for the Court to look to other human rights documents such as the UN Mental Illness Principles, which require States to provide the same level of resources to psychiatric facilities as is provided to other health facilities, and in particular sufficient resources to employ appropriate professional staff.[22] Indeed, if the evidence in a given case supported a funding disparity, there might even be a question of discrimination under Article 14 of the ECHR, which protects against a discriminatory approach in the application of Convention rights.

Unmodified ECT provides an important example of a potential violation of Article 3, but it is by no means the only one. 'Mega-dosing' – the provision of medication well in excess of the dosage recommended by the drug's manufacturer – is not uncommon. The concurrent prescription of a wide array of psychiatric medications is also common. Both these practices are controversial, as they may expose the person to excessive adverse effects. The efficacy of mega-dosing is further subject to question by the recent medical literature. For example haloperidol, a common antipsychotic, is prescribed by some psychiatrists in excess of 35 mg per day, although the relevant Cochrane study finds that doses of 7.5 mg per day may be equally effective, with far fewer adverse effects.[23] While it would seem that neither such excessive prescription nor prescription of several psychiatric medications can yet be said as a general rule to violate the standards of the medical profession, there may well be individual cases where such a case could be made.

The UN Mental Illness Principles state that psychosurgery, which involves surgical intervention on the brain, should never be carried out on people who are involuntarily

---

[21] *The CPT Standards*, CPT/Inf/E (2002) 1 – Rev. 2004, para. 39.
[22] Principle 14.
[23] P.S. Waraich, C.E. Adams, et al., 'Haloperidol dose for the acute phase of schizophrenia' 4 *Cochrane Library* (2005), available at http://www.thecochranelibrary.com. Cochrane studies are meta-analyses that compare published clinical trials and assess them according to their statistical merit.

detained and, when domestic law allows it for other persons, only with the patient's full and informed consent.[24] Failure to comply with these provisions would raise issues of Article 3 compliance.

Sterilisation raises slightly different issues. The UN Mental Illness Principles preclude sterilisation as a treatment for mental disorder,[25] and the Council of Europe 2004 Recommendations state that 'the mere fact that a person has a mental disorder should not constitute a justification for permanent infringement of his or her capacity to procreate.'[26] These provisions raise arguments under Article 3 analogous to the ones described above. Sterilisation also raises a separate set of issues under Article 12 of the ECHR, which provides the right to marry and 'found a family'.[27] While there has been no case law on the question, it is difficult to see that a procedure intended to terminate an individual's physical ability to become a natural parent can be consistent with the right to found a family.

Treatment with sedatives raises potentially different issues. In many cases, people with mental disabilities receive sedatives as part of their overall treatment package. Further, many drugs (particularly antipsychotic, but also some antidepressants) have sedative properties in addition to their psychiatric properties. Indeed, drugs such as promazine have a history of being used not merely for their antipsychotic effects, but also to control 'agitation and restlessness', particularly in the elderly.[28] The use of such drugs may raise issues under Article 5. The deprivation of liberty under that Article does not extend merely to individuals who are formally confined, but may also extend to informal patients (meaning those not detained in law), depending on the type, duration, effects and manner of implementation of the measures in question which are intended to dissuade them from leaving.[29] The use of sedation to control people and to dissuade informal patients from leaving the institution may contribute significantly to this overall factual situation, and may lead to a finding that Article 5 engages. Whether such sedation, either alone or as part of a range of other factors, violates Article 5 will depend on whether the particular country has sufficiently robust substantive and procedural protections against abuse, and whether they have been correctly applied to the individual.[30] The Court's articulation of minimum standards in the context of incapacity is in its infancy, but the *Winterwerp* criteria under Article 5 require the individual to be suffering from a disorder warranting detention. It is difficult to see that such a standard would be reached if sedation deprived an informal patient of liberty for reasons of convenience rather than necessity.

---

[24] UN Mental Illness Principles, principle 11.15.
[25] UN Mental Illness Principles, principle 11.13.
[26] Council of Europe Recommendations, Article 30.
[27] For a discussion of the right to found a family, see chapter 7 below, on participation in society.
[28] Joint Formulary Committee [United Kingdom], *British National Formulary*, 49th ed. London: British Medical Association, 2005, section 4.2.1.
[29] *H.L. v. the United Kingdom*, Application No. 45508/99, judgment 5 October 2004, (2005) 40 EHRR 32, para. 89. See further chapter 2, above.
[30] See further chapter 3, above.

Whether or not an individual is legally detained, sedation would sometimes not be necessary if appropriate staffing arrangements were in place in the institution. This, normally, comes to a question of resources. So far, the Court has refused to rule on whether and to what extent States are obliged to make specific levels of staffing available, although levels of staffing are of concern to the CPT in their visits.[31] Insofar as it could be shown that the sedative property of a drug was the motivation for its use, it could be argued to constitute restraint, raising issues under Article 3.[32] When drugs with sedative properties are used for their other, therapeutic, properties, medical advice is likely to be pivotal to determining whether the drugs constitute an appropriate medical option, given their sedative effects.

The *Herczegfalvy* case suggests that the standard of medical evidence provided to the Court may be particularly significant in determining whether there is an Article 3 violation flowing from psychiatric practice. In the *Herczegfalvy* case itself, the applicant had been placed in handcuffs and his feet belted together for a period of over two weeks. While the Court considered this 'worrying', it held nonetheless that the evidence before the Court was 'not sufficient to disprove the Government's argument that, according to the psychiatric principles generally accepted at the time, medical necessity justified the treatment in issue.'[33] Applicants bringing an Article 3 challenge would thus be well-advised to include strong evidence relating to the applicable medical standards in support of their application. If the analysis earlier in this chapter is correct, then the established principles of medicine are to be determined not solely with regard to medical practice in the respondent State, but with regard to Europe-wide norms and international human rights standards. Advocates will therefore wish to look outside the country in question for evidence of these broader practices, and in appropriate cases lead evidence of these practices from medical experts outside the respondent State. To this end, it may be useful to consult either the European Pharmacopoeia or the British National Formulary. Either may be very helpful in providing a sense of basic properties, uses, dosages and adverse effects of medications.[34]

Involuntary Treatment and the Right to Consent and Refuse

The fact that a treatment for mental disability is made available does not mean that the patient is necessarily obliged to accept the treatment. Reasons for refusal are many. Adverse effects are certainly one. In much of Europe, the treatments of choice for psychotic

---

[31] See *The CPT Standards*, CPT/Inf/E (2002) 1 – Rev. 2004, p. 58, paras. 42–6.
[32] See chapter 3, above.
[33] *Herczegfalvy v. Austria, op. cit.*, para. 83. As to whether the Court would find the same way today, see chapter 3 above.
[34] The European Pharmacopoeia is published by the European Directorate for the Quality of Medicines, and is currently in its fifth edition: see http://www.pheur.org. The British National Formulary is available both in printed form and free online at http://www.bnf.org.

disorders such as schizophrenia are the so-called 'atypical' antipsychotics, such as risperi-done and olanzapine. The most frequent adverse effects of these drugs include obesity, diabetes, and dizziness. While less common and less severe than in older neuroleptic med-ication, 'extrapyramidal symptoms' remain identified as significant adverse effects of these newer medications. These extrapyramidal symptoms include parkinsonian symp-toms (including tremors), dystonia (abnormal face and body movements), akathesia (restlessness), and tardive dyskinesia (rhythmic involuntary movements particularly of the tongue, lips, face, hands and feet). In some parts of Europe, the older medications are still used, and for those patients the extrapyramidal effects are more frequent and more severe.

Depression is most frequently treated with either tricyclic medication or selective sero-tonin re-uptake inhibitors (SSRIs). The former can cause heart problems, particularly in patients with other heart disorders, and resulting death from heart attacks is not unknown. They have also been associated with convulsions. These are some of the significant clinical adverse effects. SSRIs can cause nausea, vomiting and other gastro-intestinal problems, and, less frequently, anorexia, and skin rashes associated with vascular problems.

Other effects, while less apparently dangerous to health, may nonetheless cause con-siderable problems for the individual person. Some medications may have sedative prop-erties, and may leave the patient feeling nauseous, drowsy, apathetic or feeling that he or she is under-performing intellectually and socially. Some psychiatric medication leaves the person with an intolerance of sunlight, making it difficult to go outdoors.[35]

ECT is an accepted treatment for severe forms of depression,[36] and it would appear sometimes to be an effective treatment in situations where other therapies fail. None-theless, it can have adverse effects. One of these can be loss of parts of the memory. Such loss is usually temporary, but users have also reported permanent loss.[37] It is certainly an intrusive procedure, where electricity induces a grand mal seizure. The application of elec-trodes to the head is unlike other forms of treatment, and is often represented in the media and in fiction as frightening in a way that injection by psychiatric medications is not, notwithstanding the correspondingly severe adverse effects of those medications.

---

[35] These examples are drawn from a more extensive list of adverse effects of psychiatric medications found in Joint Formulary Committee [United Kingdom], *British National Formulary*, 49th ed. London: British Medical Association, 2005, sections 4.2 and 4.3. The *British National Formulary* is available online free of charge at http://www.bnf.org.

[36] See for example, *The CPT Standards*, CPT/Inf/E (2002) 1 – Rev. 2004, para. 39; [United Kingdom] National Institute for Clinical Excellence, *Guidance on the Use of Electroconvulsive Therapy* (London: NICE, 2003); American Psychiatric Association, *The Practice of Electroconvulsive Therapy: Recommenda-tions for Treatment, Training, Privileging* (Arlington: APPI, 2000), pp. 66–9.

[37] American Psychiatric Association, *The Practice of Electroconvulsive Therapy: Recommendations for Treatment, Training, Privileging* (Arlington: APPI, 2000), pp. 66–9. See also the systematic review of research by D. Rose, T. Wykes, et al., 'Patients' perspectives on electroconvulsive therapy: systematic review', 326 *British Medical Journal* (2003) 1363, which reported that between twenty-nine and fifty per cent of persons undergoing ECT reported persistent memory loss.

ECT has also been politically controversial. All these factors combine to make some people particularly reluctant to consent to it.

It is appropriate to emphasise that the mental health conditions these therapies treat can be exceptionally unpleasant. A reasonable person with mental health problems might in many cases choose treatment over the continuation of the disorder – indeed, they do, in large numbers. Few people with serious mental health difficulties would argue that medicine has no role in the care of their disorders. The point is instead that the treatments should not be viewed simplistically, uncritically, or as a panacea. A person with mental health problems may be facing a variety of possible courses of action, each with its own advantages and disadvantages. Different drugs have different adverse effects, and the person may well have views on which drugs, with their implied combination of good and bad effects, he or she wishes. Viewed in this light, the selection of a treatment programme for mental disabilities closely resembles the comparable choices for physical illnesses. Ethically, it is difficult to see why individuals with mental health problems should be marginalised from choices over their treatment any more than people with physical illnesses are.

Some people with mental health problems, like some people with physical problems, do stop taking their medication against medical advice. Sometimes, this has very unfortunate effects, with the individual harming or killing himself or herself, or, much more rarely, subjecting another person to serious violence. It should be emphasised that people with mental disabilities are violent only very rarely.[38] It must also be acknowledged that for some people, the decision to live with their disorder may be preferred to intrusive treatment, and the results are not necessarily bad. The Hearing Voices Network in the United Kingdom, for example, is composed of individuals who have chosen to coexist with their voices.[39] Some people with a diagnosis of a mental disability, it would seem, are happy the way they are, or at least, not so unhappy that they wish to engage in intrusive treatment.

Such engagement with the views of the person living with the mental health problem coincides with good medical practice. Indeed, insofar as the pattern of care in the Council of Europe countries continues to shift from long-term institutionalisation to care provided in community settings, engagement with the patient's views is likely to prove a necessity. As individuals move from the intrusive surveillance of institutions to the relative freedom of non-institutional care, it is often difficult routinely to enforce treatment: if the person does not want the treatment, it is often practically easier for him or her to stop it once they are outside the institution. Longer-term continuation of treatment therefore is likely to depend, for many people, on the establishment of trust between

---

[38] For a summer of the literature on dangerousness, see J. Monahan, H. Steadman, et al., *Rethinking Risk Assessment: The MacArthur Study of Mental Disorder and Violence* (Oxford: Oxford University Press, 2001), chapter 1.

[39] See A. James, *Raising our Voices: An Account of the Hearing Voices Movement* (London: Handsell Publications, 2001).

patient and doctor, and the person receiving the treatment deciding that the treatment plan is actually one he or she wishes to continue.

In legal terms, this suggests that people with mental disabilities should enjoy the same rights regarding their treatment as people affected by physical illnesses or disorders. Persons with physical illnesses have the right to consent to or to refuse treatments if they have the mental capacity to make those decisions. In theory, that ought to be a right enjoyed by people diagnosed with mental disabilities as well.

Such a right is meaningful only if the person with mental disability is provided with proper information about the treatment proposed. These requirements for appropriate consent are stated most clearly in the UN Mental Illness Principles. Principle 11 requires that the person giving consent must be competent[40] to do so, and competence is assumed unless there is evidence to the contrary. The consent must be obtained freely, without threats or improper inducements. There must be appropriate and adequate disclosure of information as to the purpose, method, likely duration and expected benefits of the proposed treatment, including the diagnosis for which the treatment is offered. Possible pain or discomfort and risks of the proposed treatment, and likely adverse effects, must be adequately discussed with the patient, as must the consequences of refusing treatment. Treatment choices should be offered, if available, in accordance with good clinical practice, and less-intrusive alternatives should be given particular consideration. Information should be provided in a language and form that is understandable by the patient. The right to consent does not cease with the commencement of treatment: if the individual withdraws consent during a course of treatment, the treatment must cease. Principle 11 further requires that consent be documented in the patient's medical records. It is also clear that the right to consent cannot be waived by a patient, and if a patient wishes to do so, he or she should be informed that treatment cannot proceed without informed consent.[41] Council of Europe documents are less specific than the UN Principles regarding the detail required for valid consent, but in their insistence on 'informed, written consent' for intrusive treatments for mental disorder, they are consistent with the overall approach.[42]

The patient is required to consent only if he or she has capacity to make the treatment decision in question; otherwise, consent is to be provided by a legal representative or tribunal.[43] Guardianship arrangements in general will be discussed in chapter 6 below; suffice it here to say that the appointment of a guardian does not necessarily mean that the individual lacks the actual or functional capacity to consent to medical treatment.

---

[40]   The fact that an individual is under a guardianship régime does not mean that the individual should be treated without consent, if that individual is able to make the treatment decision in question: see chapter 6 on guardianship for a further discussion.

[41]   Mental Illness Principles, UN General Assembly Resolution 46/119 (17 December 1991), Principle 11.

[42]   Rec(2004)10, Article 28(1); see also Convention on Human Rights and Biomedicine, ETS 164, Article 5 for similar language.

[43]   See Council of Europe Rec(2004)10, Article 12(2); Council of Europe Recommendation Rec. (1999) 4, Principle 22(2); Convention on Human Rights and Biomedicine, ETS 164, Article 6; UN Mental Illness Principles, Principle 11.7.

The appointment process for such guardians often flows from financial concerns, for example, and does not necessarily focus expressly on the question of whether the subject of the guardianship application can make treatment decisions. If the person who is the subject of the guardianship order is in fact capable of making the treatment decision in question, he or she ought to be allowed to make it. This is made explicit in the two alternative articles relating to interventions in the health field in the 2004 Council of Europe Recommendation on Principles concerning the Legal Protection of Incapable Adults. Article 22(1) of that recommendation states:

> Where an adult, even if subject to a measure of protection, is in fact capable of giving free and informed consent to a given intervention in the health field, the intervention may only be carried out with his or her consent. The consent should be solicited by the person empowered to intervene.[44]

Article 23(1) states:

> Where an adult is subject to a measure of protection under which a given intervention in the health field can be carried out only with the authorisation of a body or a person provided for by law, the consent of the adult should nonetheless be sought if he or she has the capacity to give it.[45]

It should be emphasised that the presence of mental disorder cannot be equated with incapacity to consent to treatment. Incapacity in this context means an inability to understand and appreciate the information relevant to consenting to or refusing the treatment proposed.[46] The fact that an individual has a mental disability, even if it is a psychotic disorder, does not necessarily mean that he or she is unable to meet that standard. The leading study of incapacity among people with psychiatric difficulties is the MacArthur study of newly admitted in-patients to American psychiatric wards.[47] This survey uses a variety of indicators of impairment relevant to determination of capacity to consent to treatment. Only about half of newly admitted people with a diagnosis of schizophrenia, and less than a quarter of people admitted with a diagnosis of major depression, showed impairment on at least one of these measures. The proportion of people who would have lacked capacity to consent may well have been less than this. Impairment needs to reach a certain degree, and affect the individual's understanding or ability to appreciate information in ways relevant to the treatment decision in order for a finding

---

[44] Council of Europe Recommendation R (99) 4, Principle 22(1). The recommendation that people should retain the right to consent to treatment even if under broad legal guardianship is discussed in the explanatory notes to the Recommendation: Explanatory Memorandum Rec(1999)4, paras. 73, 80.

[45] Council of Europe Recommendation R (99) 4, Principle 23(1).

[46] Regarding the definition of capacity, see for example World Health Organization, *WHO Resource Book on Mental Health, Human Rights and Legislation* (Geneva: WHO, 2005), pp. 39–41; L. Roth, A. Meisel, C. Lidz, 'Tests of Competency to Consent to Treatment', 134:3 *American Journal of Psychiatry* (1977) 279; P. Bartlett and R. Sandland, *Mental Health Law: Policy and Practice*, 2nd ed., (Oxford: Oxford University Press, 2003), chapters 10 and 11.

[47] T. Grisso and P. Appelbaum, 'The MacArthur Treatment Competency Study III. Abilities of Patients to Consent to Psychiatric and Medical Treatments'. 19(2) *Law and Human Behavior* (1995) 149.

of incapacity to be made. People lacking capacity will thus be only a subset of the impaired group identified by the MacArthur study.[48] In most legal systems, there is a presumption of capacity for adults asked to consent to treatment. There is no reason not to continue that presumption for persons asked to consent to treatment for mental disorder.

Incapacity is not to be equated to disagreement with the doctor. There are a wide variety of reasons why an individual may choose not to follow the advice of his or her doctor. For example, as noted above, medications have powerful effects, both beneficial and non-beneficial. Those effects will be relevant to different people in different ways, and not all patients will balance the risks and benefits in the same way. By further example, disagreement with the doctor may flow from a failure to establish or a breakdown in trust between patient and doctor. In this circumstance, the question may be why the breakdown in trust has occurred. If, for example, the doctor figures in the patient's psychotic delusions, it may well be that the patient lacks capacity. On the other hand, if it were to flow for example from an accurate realisation that the doctor is only newly qualified as a professional, the breakdown in trust might be entirely consistent with the patient having full capacity.

Similarly, a failure to believe the doctor's diagnosis or analysis of the psychiatric problem does not necessarily imply incapacity. Here again, the reason *why* the person does not believe the doctor's analysis may be significant to assessing capacity. A patient who is diagnosed with depression, for example, might dispute the medical label, preferring instead to understand his or her situation in terms of unhappy things in his or her life such as relationship breakdown, bereavement or loss of employment. Such a view could be entirely consistent with the patient continuing to have capacity. If a person's failure to believe himself or herself to be ill flowed instead from a psychotic delusional structure (e.g., 'I am not crazy; my mind *is* being controlled by the government'), that fact might well be relevant to determining his or her capacity, but only if that delusion were actually relevant to the decision being made: as noted above, people with psychotic disorders do not necessarily lack capacity.[49] Alternatively, a change in diagnosis may result in a breakdown in trust. Such a change is not necessarily a mark of poor practice – indeed, it is good practice for the doctors to revisit the question of diagnosis on a reasonably regular basis. Nonetheless, these changes can be perceived by patients as extremely frustrating, and can result in a loss of trust between patient and doctor. That is not necessarily a mark of incapacity.

For all this, it is to be emphasised that the assessment of capacity is to determine whether the person is *able* to understand the relevant information for a treatment

---

[48] The authors of the MacArthur study themselves make this distinction between incapacity and impairment at p. 170.

[49] See, for example, the English case of *Re C (Adult: Refusal of Medical Treatment)* [1994] 1 All ER 819. In that case, a man with schizophrenia refused consent to the amputation of his gangrenous leg. He believed among other things that he had previously had a career as a world-famous surgeon who had never lost a patient. This was entirely false. He nonetheless was held by the English High Court to have capacity to refuse the amputation, because the delusional beliefs were not held to be sufficiently related to the amputation decision to justify a finding of incapacity.

decision, appreciate the consequences of that decision, and make that decision unaffected by a psychotic delusion directly related to that decision. It does not matter that his or her choice is unwise, ill-considered or eccentric if the information is understood and appreciated, free of delusion. The reasons given by the individual for that choice may be good or bad, but they are relevant to the capacity assessment only if they demonstrate an *inability* to understand or appreciate, or the presence of a relevant delusion. Absent such inability, the basic rule in law is that he or she may decide whether or not to accept treatment.

An exception that allows involuntary psychiatric treatment of a competent patient is provided by the Council of Europe documents and United Nations Mental Illness Principles recommendations, but only in limited circumstances. The 2004 Council of Europe Recommendations restrict such interventions to situations where a mental disorder poses a significant risk of serious harm to the patient or another person, *and* no less intrusive means of providing appropriate care is available. Even in those circumstances, the involuntary treatment is only to be performed if the patient's opinion has been taken into consideration.[50] This is broadly consistent with the views of the standards of the European Committee for the Prevention of Torture (CPT) on the subject:

> Patients should, as a matter of principle, be placed in a position to give their free and informed consent to treatment. The admission of a person to a psychiatric establishment on an involuntary basis should not be construed as authorising treatment without his consent. It follows that every competent patient, whether voluntary or involuntary, should be given the opportunity to refuse treatment or other medical intervention. Any derogation from this fundamental principle should be based upon law and only relate to clearly and strictly defined exceptional circumstances.[51]

The CPT Standards, like the other Council of Europe documents and the UN Mental Illness Principles, stop just short of saying that involuntary treatment of competent people is never justified. Nonetheless, the unanimous view of these documents is that the general rule is that people who have capacity to make treatment decisions should be allowed to make decisions about their treatment, and any departure from that norm is to be exceptional.

---

[50] Rec(2004)10, Article 18. Involuntary treatment in the short-term in emergency situations is also envisaged by Article 21, and treatment of those convicted of offences by Article 34(1). Principle 11 of the UN Mental Illness principles is broadly to the same effect as the Council of Europe Recommendations. The Convention on Human Rights and Biomedicine and Council of Europe Recommendation R(1999)4 on Principles Concerning the Protection of Incapable Adults are of similar effect, although they allow involuntary treatment only in cases of serious risk to the health of the patient himself or herself, not for the benefit or safety of others. The UN approach has recently come under criticism in the Report of the Secretary-General concerning Progress of Efforts to Ensure the Full Recognition and Enjoyment of the Human Rights of Persons with Disabilities, A/58/181 (24 July 2003), which states that the 'generous exceptions' to the principle of consent in Principle 11 'deprive it of real meaning'. It goes on to state:
> Psychiatric detention should not mean giving up a person's right to choose his or her medical treatment. This right is firmly established under international human rights law. Limitation of rights concerning treatment decisions should always be subject to judicial review. [para. 45]

[51] CPT Standards, CPT/Inf/E (2002) 1, Rev 2004, p. 57, para. 41.

The international instruments and the CPT are clear that involuntary admission to a psychiatric facility should not, subject to clearly defined exceptions, result in a loss of the right to consent to treatment. International law is less clear whether involuntary admission is a precondition to the loss of that right. While there are moves internationally to allow mandatory treatment in community settings, the UN Mental Illness Principles would instead require non-consensual treatment to occur only if the individual is detained involuntarily.[52] The ECHR has the potential to give life to these rights through the application of Articles 3 and 8, perhaps with Article 14 in aid.

Article 3

For Article 3, the question is whether the absence of consent of a competent person adds anything to the nature of the treatment more generally, allowing that Article to be engaged when it otherwise would not. The *Herczegfalvy* case has been cited as authority for the proposition that the absence of consent adds nothing, and that treatment meeting the clinical standards of medical practice will not violate Article 3.[53] The relevant paragraphs of the case are therefore worth quoting in full:

> The Court considers that the position of inferiority and powerlessness which is typical of patients confined in psychiatric hospitals calls for increased vigilance in reviewing whether the Convention has been complied with. While it is for the medical authorities to decide, on the basis of the recognisable rules of medical science, on the therapeutic methods to be used, if necessary by force, to preserve the physical and mental health of patients who are entirely incapable of deciding for themselves and for whom they are responsible, such patients nevertheless remain under the protection of Article 3, the requirements of which permit no derogation.
>
> The established principles of medicine are admittedly in principle decisive in such cases; as a general rule, a method which is a therapeutic necessity cannot be regarded as inhuman or degrading.[54]

These paragraphs do not support the broad interpretation sometimes placed on them. They are restricted to cases 'of patients who are entirely incapable of deciding for themselves'. That is not the case for a patient who is capable of consenting to treatment. This distinction is entirely consistent with the facts of that case: the Court accepted that the applicant in that case was affected by paranoia that in turn affected his understanding of

---

[52] UN Mental Illness Principles, principle 11.6. This paragraph does not apply if a personal representative has been appointed for a patient under the terms of domestic law: principle 11.7. The Council of Europe Mental Disorder Recommendations R(2004)10 would allow a doctor to make the decision regarding people detained in psychiatric facilities, but would require an independent tribunal or court to make decisions for other inpatients or those in the community: see Rec(2004)10, Article 20(2). The other Council of Europe documents are silent on whether involuntary treatment must occur in a facility, and if so, whether the individual must be detained in the facility.

[53] See, for example, the English case of *R (PS) v. G (RMO) and W (SOAD)* [2003] EWHC 2335 (Admin) para. 99.

[54] *Herczegfalvy v. Austria, op. cit.,* para. 82.

his situation.[55] He had been declared legally incapable and a guardian had been appointed to make decisions for him.[56] The guardian had consented to the treatment that was the basis of the Article 3 challenge.[57] The paragraph therefore cannot reasonably be taken to govern the situation where the patient has capacity and refuses treatment.

Capacity in this context is a pragmatic assessment of the individual's ability to make the treatment decision. Some legal systems view consent as an all-or-nothing concept: either one has capacity to make decisions with legal effect, or one does not: see discussion of guardianship, chapter 6 herein. The language of *Herczegfalvy*, 'patients who are entirely incapable of deciding for themselves', suggests instead that the issue under the ECHR is whether the patient is capable of making the treatment decision, not whether they have been deemed incompetent as a result of a general guardianship statute.

Not all treatments administered without consent will engage Article 3. As noted above, ill-treatment will only violate Article 3 if it reaches a 'minimum level of severity', based on a variety of circumstances. In *Kudła v. Poland*, the Court provided the following guidance as to the meaning of inhuman or degrading treatment:

> The Court has considered treatment to be "inhuman" because, *inter alia*, it was premeditated, was applied for hours at a stretch and caused either actual bodily injury or intense physical or mental suffering. It has deemed treatment to be "degrading" because it was such as to arouse in the victims feelings of fear, anguish and inferiority capable of humiliating and debasing them. On the other hand, the Court has consistently stressed that the suffering and humiliation involved must in any event go beyond that inevitable element of suffering or humiliation connected with a given form of legitimate treatment or punishment.[58]

In order to succeed under Article 3, it would be necessary therefore to show that the involuntary intervention complained of was beyond 'legitimate treatment', at least an arguable view given the significance of consent in health care law and the international instruments noted above. Involuntary treatments involving relatively minor interventions may nonetheless fall at this hurdle. While there has not yet been a case, however, it does seem compelling that involuntarily injecting a chemical designed to alter the individual's mental state over that individual's competent objection would be a sufficiently serious intervention to trigger Article 3.

There is however a difficulty. As noted above, the international 'soft law' instruments do allow for enforced psychiatric treatment of patients with capacity in some circumstances, most significantly 'emergencies' and where treatment is necessary when a person is dangerous to himself or herself or, in some instruments, to others. If the essence of the apparent violation is intrusive treatment over the objection of the competent person, it is at best questionable whether these exceptions would be allowed under Article 3.

---

[55] *Herczegfalvy v. Austria, op. cit.*, paras. 13, 61, 64.
[56] *Herzcegfalvy v. Austria, op. cit.*, paras. 10–11.
[57] *Herczegfalvy v. Austria, op. cit.*, para. 81.
[58] Application No. 30210/96, judgment 26 October 2000; (2002) 35 EHRR 11, para. 92.

At least three possible responses can be made. First, it is open to the Court to take a view more protective of human rights than the international instruments. In some jurisdictions, the exception for mental disorders does not exist: treatment of the competent patient is never permitted without the informed consent of that person. In Ontario, Canada, for example, treatment decisions are separated entirely from decisions to detain individuals. A person with capacity can make treatment decisions for mental conditions whether he or she is in a psychiatric facility or in the community, and if in a psychiatric facility, whether he or she is detained or an informal[59] patient in that facility. The Ontario law thus treats without distinction decisions regarding treatment for psychiatric and physical illnesses or disorders.[60] This has not caused major difficulties in practice. In theory, it is possible that people with capacity will be detained in a psychiatric institution but decline all effective treatment; in practice this seems to happen only in exceptionally rare cases.[61] It represents the strongest option in human rights terms, in that it allows the competent individual to make decisions about himself or herself.

It is difficult to see that the Court could view the Article 3 violation as a simple balancing act between the severity of the disorder and the protection of autonomy, where the violation of the patient's right of consent would be justified in cases of particularly severe disorders. The difficulty is that it does not take account of the reason the individual may be refusing the treatment. By definition, the individual is not unduly influenced by psychosis, nor is he or she unable to make a considered decision regarding treatment. If either of those were the case, the patient would lack capacity. The reasons for a person to refuse treatment are more likely to involve a desire to avoid adverse effects, or a lack of trust in the medical staff. If it is the former, a human rights analysis would suggest that the decision should be respected: the patient is in the best position to balance adverse effects and benefits. If it is the latter, the case is stronger still. If the import of the question is the imposition of non-consensual treatment by an agent on the authority of the State, the argument against imposition of treatment would appear stronger when it is an agent that the competent patient does not trust.

The Court could instead view the scope of Article 3 as modified by conflicts with other Convention rights. The most obvious example would be the right to life in Article 2, as discussed in chapter 5 of this volume. This is a more promising approach, as it is reflected in the Court's broader case law: the Court has for example held that the force-feeding of prisoners does not necessarily contravene Article 3, when the life of the prisoner was at risk.[62] Insofar as the safety of the competent patient is compromised by his or her treatment refusal, such a conflict could be seen to exist, and grounds could be

---

59 That is, a person admitted without the use of legal compulsion, whether or not that person consents to the admission in any meaningful sense: see discussion at p. 33.
60 See *Health Care Consent Act 1996*, SO 1996, c. 2, sch. A. The Ontario legislation is discussed in P. Bartlett, 'English Mental Health Reform: Lessons from Ontario?', [2001] *Journal of Mental Health Law* 27–43.
61 P. Bartlett, 'English Mental Health Reform: Lessons from Ontario?', *op. cit.*, p. 42.
62 *Nevmerzhitsky v. Ukraine*, Application No. 54825/00, judgment 5 April 2005, para. 93.

found to restrict the scope of Article 3. This approach has the attraction that it fits with the terms of the override provisions in the Council of Europe documents. Article 2 concerns the right to life, however. If this approach were adopted, it would therefore require a notably strict reading of the 'safety' standard in the soft law.

Finally, it might be possible to adopt an approach analogous to *Herczegfalvy*. In that approach, the test of the Article 3 violation would remain based on the 'established principles of medicine', but those would be read in the light of the international human rights instruments restricting the use of involuntary treatment. Those instruments, after all, were developed with the involvement of the medical profession, and therefore can be taken to represent appropriate medical standards. Such an approach would allow consideration to be given to autonomy and right to consent, while taking into account the international standards. This approach would further allow the Court to give some deference to the views of other professionals. The difficulty with this argument is that it turns a question of fundamental human rights into a question of clinical practice. The scope of Article 3 becomes what doctors say it ought to be, based not simply on clinical science but also on their subjective view of the appropriate balance between autonomy and other interests. On a question of human rights, that latter determination ought really to lie with the Court.

Article 8

Article 8 is the provision of the ECHR most clearly relevant to involuntary treatment. The Court has held that all enforced medical treatment *prima facie* engages Article 8. This initial engagement is made clear by *Y.F. v. Turkey*, a case concerning an allegedly involuntary gynaecological examination:

> The Court observes that Article 8 is clearly applicable to these complaints, which concern a matter of "private life", a concept which covers the physical and psychological integrity of a person. . . . It reiterates in this connection that a person's body concerns the most intimate aspect of private life. Thus, a compulsory medical intervention, even if it is of minor importance, constitutes an interference with this right. . . .[63]

This language clearly covers involuntary psychiatric treatment. Importantly, this statement is not limited to persons with capacity. *Any* involuntary psychiatric treatment would appear to be a violation of a person's private life, and therefore engage Article 8.

That moves the analysis to the question of whether such a violation is justified under Article 8(2):

> 8(2) There shall be no interference by a public authority with the exercise of this right except such as is in accordance with the law and is necessary in a democratic society in the interests of national security, public safety or the economic well-being of the country, for the prevention of disorder or crime, for the protection of health or morals, or for the protection of the rights and freedoms of others.

---

[63] *Y.F. v. Turkey*, Application No. 24209/94, judgment 22 July 2003, (2004) 39 EHRR 34, para. 33.

This raises two broad hurdles for those defending compulsory treatment: the compulsory treatment must be in accordance with domestic law, and it must be necessary in a democratic society for one of the enumerated purposes.

Any involuntary treatment must first have some basis in domestic law. A statutory justification most clearly meets this standard, although in common law countries,[64] sufficiently clear judicial pronouncements may also suffice. Whether expressed in the domestic law or instead merely implemented in practice, safeguards must exist to ensure effective control of those interfering with the individual's rights, and the safeguards are particularly important when wide discretion is accorded by domestic law.[65] The law must also be accessible to those affected by it, and sufficiently precise as to allow an individual to regulate his or her conduct. Domestic law that gives discretion in its implementation must indicate the scope of that discretion.[66]

There must therefore be some form of domestic legal framework if the involuntary treatment of persons with mental disabilities is to be justified. The fact that there may be a long informal tradition of compulsory treatment of people with mental disabilities will not be sufficiently in accord with domestic law unless is buttressed by the formal legal structure, providing sufficient clarity and safeguards.

Y.F. v. Turkey seems to go somewhat further than that in the context of medical treatment. The case itself involved a gynaecological investigation of a woman prisoner allegedly without her consent, to determine whether she had been subjected to sexual assault during the period of her incarceration:

> Finally, while the Court accepts the Government's submission that the medical examination of detainees by a forensic doctor can prove to be a significant safeguard against false accusations of sexual molestation or ill-treatment, it considers that any interference with a person's physical integrity must be prescribed by law and requires the consent of that person. Otherwise, a person in a vulnerable situation, such as a detainee, would be deprived of legal guarantees against arbitrary acts. In the light of the foregoing, the Court finds that the interference in issue was not "in accordance with law".[67]

While the facts do not involve an individual with mental disabilities, there are also similarities. The involuntary treatment of people with mental disabilities also often occurs when that individual is detained. The Court in *Y.F.* acknowledges that being detained places the individual in an exceptionally vulnerable position:

> The Court notes that the applicant's wife complained to the authorities that she had been forced to undergo a gynaecological examination against her will. . . . For their part, the Government contended that it would not have been possible to perform such an examination without the consent of Mrs F., who could have objected to it when she was taken to the

---

[64] Only two out of the 46 Member States of the Council of Europe are common law countries: the United Kingdom and the Republic of Ireland.

[65] *Silver v. the United Kingdom*, Application No. 5947/72, judgment 25 February 1983, (1983) 5 EHRR 347 para. 90.

[66] *Silver v. the United Kingdom, op. cit.*, at paras. 67–88.

[67] *Y.F. v. Turkey, op. cit.*, para. 43.

doctor's consulting room. However, the Court considers that, in the circumstances, the applicant's wife could not have been expected to resist submitting to such an examination in view of her vulnerability at the hands of the authorities who exercised complete control over her throughout her detention.[68]

Similar concerns arise regarding treatment in psychiatric facilities, where the Court has also noted the vulnerability of people with mental health difficulties.[69] The Court's concern in *Y.F.* to ensure appropriate standards applies with equal force in a psychiatric or social care setting.

Quite what those safeguards ought to be is not clearly defined in the case law under Article 8, although the international instruments provide clear guidance. The 2004 Council of Europe Mental Disorder Recommendation R(2004)10 provides both substantive and procedural conditions upon the imposition of involuntary treatment. According to those Recommendations, the individual must have a mental disorder creating a significant risk of serious harm to his or her health or to other persons. The proposed treatment must be the least intrusive possible, and the views of the individual must have been taken into account. The treatment must address specific clinical signs and symptoms, and must be proportionate to the person's state of health. It must be documented and form part of a formal treatment plan, agreed with the patient or his or her representative and routinely reviewed on a periodic basis. A suitably qualified doctor may make decisions regarding people detained in psychiatric facilities, but if the individual is not detained, the decision to impose treatment is to be taken by a court or similar body. In any event, the individual affected or his or her representative should have the right to appeal to court a decision regarding involuntary treatment, and to be represented by a lawyer at that appeal. Emergency exceptions to these safeguards should be as limited in duration as possible.[70]

Article 8(2) of the Convention further requires that rights infringed under 8(1) will further be justified only if the infringement is necessary in a democratic society, with reference to one of the enumerated purposes. For involuntary treatment, this question of necessity is likely to relate primarily to the protection of health, but may also extend into debates about public safety or the prevention of crime. Certainly, it is difficult to see that an unfettered involuntary treatment of people with psychiatric difficulties or mental disabilities would be justified. As noted above, that is inconsistent with the UN Mental Illness Principles, the Council of Europe Recommendation Rec(2004)10 and the CPT Standards. Whether any involuntary psychiatric treatment of people with capacity to

---

[68] *Y.F. v. Turkey, op. cit.*, para. 34.
[69] See for example *Herczegfalvy v. Austria, op. cit.*, para. 82, quoted above.
[70] See Council of Europe Recommendations, Rec(2004)10, Articles 18 to 25. See also UN Mental Illness Principles, principles 9 to 11. The UN principles are in some ways more restrictive than those of the Council of Europe. They would allow involuntary treatment only on individuals who are involuntarily admitted to psychiatric facilities, for example, not on individuals in the community or informally admitted to psychiatric facilities. It would require that any decisions regarding such treatment be taken by an independent body rather than the patient's doctor: see principle 11.6.

make treatment decisions is necessary in a democratic society is further an open point. Certainly, as noted above, there are democratic societies that survive perfectly well without it. The Court's statement in *Y.F.* that 'any interference with a person's physical integrity . . . requires the consent of that person',[71] although made in the context of a gynaecological examination rather than treatment for mental disability, provides some support for this strong position against involuntary treatment of people with capacity.

The Person without Capacity, The Personal Representative and Surrogate Decision-Making

The Court's statement in *Y.F.* that 'any interference with a person's physical integrity must be prescribed by law and requires the consent of that person'[72] must presupposes that the person has capacity to consent. What is the legal situation if the individual lacks the capacity to consent?

Both the United Nations Mental Illness Principles and the Council of Europe Recommendation Rec(2004)10 envisage the appointment of a legal representative as one way to make decisions on behalf of the person lacking capacity.[73] Alternatively, such representatives may be required to be consulted prior to the imposition of compulsory treatment. Whether the appointment of such a representative is a right under the ECHR, and if so, what the scope of the relevant requirement is, raise rather different questions under Article 8.

It is when the representative would be a close family member such as a parent, child, or spouse that the rights under Article 8 appear most clearly. Care of such close relations is perceived by the other family members as part of their role. When the person cared for is a dependent child who has not reached the age of majority, this is acknowledged explicitly in the ECtHR's case law.[74] When all the family members are adults, there is no obvious jurisprudence on point. They clearly remain family members; it is at least arguable that the right to make decisions on behalf of such family members as lose capacity is part of the right to family life under Article 8, potentially both of the carer and the person being cared for.

From this relatively simple scenario, a variety of complications flow. The first relates to the balance between the right to respect for family life and the right to respect for privacy. It may well be that the individual lacking capacity would not want his or her fam-

---

[71] Para. 43.

[72] Para. 43.

[73] Council of Europe Recommendations, Article 12(2); UN Principles, principle 11.7. The instruments also envisage such decisions being made by independent bodies such as courts or tribunals.

[74] For a somewhat extreme case, see *Nielsen v. Denmark*, Application No. 10929/84, judgment 28 November 1988, (A/144) (1989) 11 EHRR 175, paras. 72–3. See also *Glass v. the United Kingdom*, Application No. 61827/00, judgment 9 March 2004, (2004) 39 EHRR 15. See also an extensive jurisprudence regarding the rights of parents over children who are proposed to be taken into care, including *W v. the United Kingdom*, Application No. 9749/82, judgment 8 July 1987, A.121.A (1987) 10 EHRR 29; *B. v. the United Kingdom, R. v. United Kingdom*, Application No. 10496/83, judgment 8 July 1987, A.121–C (1988) 10 EHRR 74.

ily members to be making the decisions in question. In *J.T. v. the United Kingdom*,[75] for example, Ms. J.T., an adult with a history of mental disability, had a difficult relationship with her mother. These difficulties in part related to alleged sexual abuse by Ms. J.T.'s stepfather. Under English law, the mother as the 'nearest relative' had a variety of rights related to the detention and treatment in hospital. Ms. J.T. did not wish her mother to be given any information about her whereabouts, nor to be involved in any subsequent decisions relating to her confinement or care. The case reached a friendly settlement on the undertaking that the English law would be amended,[76] but the problem raised by the case remains relevant. If an adult patient has capacity, as Ms. J.T. did, and wishes to determine that a given individual will not be involved in decision-making in the future, a cogent argument can be made that such an exclusion is a part of the person's right to privacy.

Some domestic legislation allows individuals, while they have capacity to do so, to appoint representatives to make treatment decisions for them in the event of subsequent incapacity.[77] The Court has adopted a relatively open-ended view of who constitutes a 'family',[78] and if the person named as the representative is in a close personal relationship outside marriage or traditional family ties, it is at least possible that he or she might be brought into the realm of Article 8.

The rights under Article 8 are however not absolute. Quite appropriately, for example, the State could restrict the right of family members to make decisions about each other in the event that an adult incapacitated person would be subject to abuse.[79] What is significant here is that for family relationships in which Article 8 is engaged, such an exclusion would be by reference to Article 8(2), and would therefore require an express basis in domestic law. Medical discretion without such a structure would not appear to be sufficient. It is of course necessary for the substitute decision maker to be appointed via a procedure which is itself in accordance with domestic and ECHR law – for a discussion of these procedures, see chapter 8 below.

Article 8 appears to import conflicting rights relevant to the appointment of representatives. Without clear indications to the contrary, family members may have rights to make decisions about their incapacitated loved ones, but that situation continuing in an unrefined manner may violate the privacy rights of the incapacitated person. This suggests that legislative intervention may be the only practical option for States party to the ECHR.

---

[75] Application No. 26494/95, judgment 30 March 2000, 30 EHRR CD77, [2000] 1 FLR 909. For the view of the European Commission on Human Rights, see (1997) 23 EHRR CD81. See also a discussion of this case in the chapter on legal incapacity, guardianship and substituted decision making, chapter 6, below.

[76] For a discussion of friendly settlements, see chapter 8 on applying to the European Court of Human Rights, below. In Ms. J.T.'s case, the English law was not amended with reasonable dispatch, and the English courts ruled the relevant provision in violation of Article 8: *R (M) v. Secretary of State for Health* [2003] E.W.H.C. 1094.

[77] See, for example, *Mental Capacity Act 2005* [United Kingdom], s. 4(7)(a) and 9.

[78] See *X., Y. and Z. v. the United Kingdom*, Application No. 21830/93, judgment 22 April 1997, 1997–II 619 (1997) 24 EHRR 143, para 36.

[79] Authority for this proposition, if it is needed, can be gleaned by analogy from the child custody cases noted above.

Article 6: A Different Right to Procedural Safeguards?

Article 6(1) of the ECHR provides:

> In the determination of his civil rights and obligations or of any criminal charge against him, everyone is entitled to a fair and public hearing within a reasonable time by an independent and impartial tribunal established by law.

Article 6 further requires that judgment shall be pronounced publicly, subject to certain exceptions.[80]

In order for Article 6 to be engaged, the issue in question must be in the 'determination of his civil rights': there must be a genuine and serious dispute over a civil right that is, on at least arguable grounds, recognised under domestic law.[81] Article 6 is not about the establishment of new substantive rights, therefore: such matters must be argued under other Convention Articles, many of which also import procedural safeguards. Article 6 ensures that disputes over the existence, scope or application of civil rights in domestic law may be heard and determined in an appropriate judicial forum.

The right to consent to or refuse medical treatment is a right recognised across the Council of Europe territory. As noted above, compulsory treatment will violate Article 8 unless the conditions of Article 8(2) are satisfied. That requires domestic legal systems to provide a basis for any compulsory treatment. Further, as noted above, the conflicting rights relating to privacy and family life will mean that in practice, rights relating to consent and incapable adults will require formal legal articulation in domestic law. In the event that domestic law is substantively compliant with the ECHR, therefore, it will also provide a considerable regulatory structure in which genuine and serious disputes may arise. Within this substantive realm, Article 6 will require that recourse be available to an independent and impartial tribunal for determination of these resulting domestic law disputes.

There are several caveats and complexities to that basic position. First, issues of detention have been held to fall within Article 5 rather than Article 6.[82] For many issues of detention, the difference will be minimal, since *Winterwerp* and subsequent jurisprudence under Article 5 also provide a right to an independent court or tribunal. In jurisdictions where the statutory detention criteria in law are based in whole or in part upon the need to provide involuntary treatment, and where those criteria meet the ECHR standards regarding involuntary treatment, it may be that the issues relevant to treatment provision may be appropriately dealt with in that context.

For statutes that distinguish treatment rights from detention issues however, Article 6 would require that a fair trial by an impartial and independent court be available

---

[80] The article provides that the hearing need not be public when the privacy rights of one of the parties is at stake, for example. That exception could reasonably taken to apply to people with mental disabilities.

[81] *Z. v. the United Kingdom*, Application No. 29392/95, judgment 10 May 2001, para. 87.

[82] *A.R. v. the United Kingdom*, Application No. 25527/94, decision 29 November 1995, EHRLR 1996, 3, 324.

prior to the enforcement of treatment. Article 6 would further be relevant, for example, regarding involuntary treatment in the community, where there is no issue of detention.

Article 6 will also be relevant for people who are denied the right to consent because of alleged incapacity. Such people would have the right to a formal court hearing to challenge that allegation. Similarly, in the event that a statute allowed compulsory treatment of a competent person, Article 6 would clearly require the threshold criteria for that compulsion to be challenged in a formal court hearing. It is less clear whether, once the criteria for compulsory treatment were shown to be met or incapacity demonstrated, Article 6 would allow the person or his or her representative the right formally to challenge the treatment plan to be imposed. Much may depend on the wording of the specific statute: is the patient given a right to specific involvement, or is a mere duty imposed on the treating physician to consult the patient or representative? If the former, the likelihood of its constituting a 'right' within the terms of the Article is greater than if it is the latter.

In general, Article 6 provides the *right* to a hearing; it does not provide an automatic hearing. There may be some scope to question the appropriateness of this limitation as regards people of borderline capacity and people confined in psychiatric facilities. As the Court notes in the *Y.F.* case discussed above, detainees may be in circumstances where they could not be expected to resist the proposals put to them, and may be very unlikely to request a hearing for these reasons. If the point of Article 6 is to ensure appropriate procedural independence in determination of fundamental civil rights, it may be the case that it should provide the automatic provision of a hearing in questions concerning violations of human rights in these circumstances.[83]

The court or tribunal is required to be independent and impartial. When looking to the independence of the tribunal, the European Court of Human Rights will consider the manner of appointment of its members, their security of tenure, their freedom from control of the government and the institution they are meant to regulate, the scope of guarantees of independence, and their appearance of independence.[84] In the current context, that suggests independence both from the government and from the immediate treatment context of the patient.

---

[83] For a comparable argument in a domestic context, see *R (MH) v. Secretary of State for Department of Health* [2004] EWCA 1609. Under English law, people detained under mental health law had the right to a tribunal(court) tribunal of the lawfulness of their detention, but no early automatic review. The English Court of Appeal held that people lacking capacity should be deemed to apply for such court hearings routinely upon detention, effectively providing such hearings automatically. The House of Lords, the final appellate court within the United Kingdom, disagreed, holding instead that Article 5 offered no automatic right to a hearing: see [2005] UKHL 60.

[84] *Campbell and Fell v. the United Kingdom*, Application No. 7819/77, judgment 3 May 1984, A.80 (1984), (1985) 7 EHRR 165, para. 78.

Chapter 5

Life and Death

Introduction

Including a chapter on death in a book about the rights of people with mental disabilities may seem unnecessarily morbid. Unfortunately, the intersections between mental disability and death are numerous. Suicidal behaviour is considered to be a symptom of a mental health problem, and suicides can reportedly be reduced if depression and anxiety are treated.[1] Mental disability and death are further related by grossly elevated mortality rates in some psychiatric or social care institutions, with people dying from hypothermia and malnutrition. Deaths sometimes occur during or after incidents of over/mis-medication and the use of physical restraints. The ECHR's provision on 'right to life' is engaged if a State takes inadequate measures to prevent a death in a psychiatric or social care institution. It is also engaged when a State fails adequately to investigate deaths within institutions. These two major topics are the focus of this chapter.

Suicide

European health ministers have recently pledged to address suicide prevention and the causes of harmful stress, violence, depression, anxiety and alcohol and other substance use

---

[1]   See WHO Euro Region Briefing on Suicide Prevention, accessed at http://www.euro.who.int/mental-health.

disorders.[2] The statistics are alarming: from 1950 to 1995 the global rate of suicide increased by 60%[3] and among young and middle-aged people, especially men, suicide is currently a leading cause of death even in developed countries.[4] According to the latest available data, an estimated 873,000 people around the world kill themselves every year, suicide being the thirteenth leading cause of death globally and seventh in the WHO's European region. The highest rates in the European region are also the highest in the world. Suicide rates vary across Europe, with 5.9 suicides per 100,000 population in Italy, rising to 36.4 in Russia.[5]

The causes of suicidal behaviour are a complex interaction of a number of interrelating factors including psychiatric such as major depression, schizophrenia, alcohol and other drug use, and anxiety disorders; biological factors or genetic traits (family history of suicide); life events (loss of a loved one, loss of a job); psychological factors such as interpersonal conflict, violence or a history of physical and sexual abuse in childhood, and feelings of hopelessness; social and environmental factors, including availability of the means of suicide (firearms, toxic gases, medicines, herbicides and pesticides), social isolation and economic hardship.[6]

Although suicide has been de-criminalized in most European States and therefore people with capacity are free to take their own life, suicide is relevant to the ECHR when a person in a State-run institution such as a prison or psychiatric hospital takes her own life, raising questions of adequate supervision by the State.[7]

Deaths in institutions

Sadly, deaths do sometimes occur in psychiatric institutions. First, people lose their lives in institutions as a result of suicide or homicide. A 2003 Amnesty International report documented one psychiatric hospital in Romania where at least four patients had died following assaults by other patients. These psychiatric incidents reportedly occurred in circumstances in which patients had not been adequately supervised by staff of appropriate number and with appropriate training.[8]

---

[2] *Mental Health Declaration for Europe*, WHO European Ministerial Declaration (Helsinki: January 2005), EUR/04/5047810/6, Article 10ix.

[3] J. Bertolote and S. Fleischmann, 'Suicide and psychiatric diagnosis: a worldwide perspective', 1(3) *World Psychiatry* (2002) 181.

[4] The United Kingdom's Mental Health Foundation reports that in the United Kingdom suicides are the second highest cause of death after accidents.

[5] European Health for All database – mortality indicators (HFA-MDB) [online database]. Copenhagen, WHO Regional Office for Europe, 2004.

[6] WHO Euro Region Briefing on Suicide Prevention, accessed at http://www.euro.who.int/mentalhealth.

[7] A suicide attempt, or suicidal ideation are factors which are sometimes taken into account in the decision to detain someone under mental health legislation.

[8] Amnesty International: Romania Memorandum to the government concerning inpatient psychiatric treatment. AI Index: EUR 39/003/2004. See also CPT report on its 2003 visit to Bosnia and Herzegovina Report (2003 visit) CPT/Inf (2004) 40, para. 120.

Second, people in psychiatric institutions sometimes die because of high doses of medications and/or the use of restraints, such as being tied with leather straps to a hospital bed, or rough handling by security guards.

The third group of deaths in psychiatric institutions are perhaps the most horrific. These deaths are due to the lack of basic needs, such as food, warmth, shelter and medications, which has been exposed recently in the eastern parts of the Council of Europe region.[9] During a visit to the Karlukovo State Psychiatric Hospital in Bulgaria in 2002 the European Committee for the Prevention of Torture (CPT) commented on the mortality levels of the previous year, out of which half were less than 50 years old (25% less than 40 years). Nearly 60% of all deceased patients had a recorded weight of less than 60 kg (almost 20% weighed less than 50 kg). The CPT went on to comment on the inadequate procedures following death:

> The hospital's records did not mention the cause of death of all patients. However, diagnoses frequently found in the files of deceased patients, such as anaemia (sideropenia), tuberculosis, pneumonia and other respiratory diseases, suggest a link between mortality and the conditions of deprivation (including in terms of nutrition) from which the vast majority of patients were suffering.[10]

The CPT has found large numbers of people dying in psychiatric hospitals from tuberculosis, such as in Ukraine.[11] In February 2004 Amnesty International reported that in the 500-bed psychiatric hospital in Poiana Mare in southern Romania 17 patients had died in 2004, 'apparently from malnutrition and hypothermia, and that 84 patients had died, many from similar causes, in 2003.' The report went on to explain these deaths:

> Some hospital staff expressed concern about the lack of funds to adequately care for the patients, who were hungry, poorly clothed, infested with lice and had inadequate bedding. The heating system does not appear to be used at the hospital, a former army barracks, in a region where temperatures frequently fall below freezing for days, sometimes weeks at a time between November and March.[12]

As discussed in chapter 3 above, such conditions can themselves constitute violations of the ECHR, in particular the right under Article 3 to be free from inhuman or degrading treatment or punishment. The discussion in this chapter focuses instead on the requirements imposed by the ECHR when a death occurs.

---

[9] In 1997 the CPT visited Elbasan Hospital in Albania (CPT/Inf (2003) 6 (visit of December 1997), paras. 20 to 26). When the CPT visited during 1998 they noted a reduction of the number of deaths by two thirds in a year.

[10] Report to the Bulgarian Government on the visit to Bulgaria carried out by the CPT from 17 to 26 April 2002CPT/Inf (2004) 21, para. 33. The same situation prevailed at Terter Social Welfare Home in Bulgaria: see CPT report on its 1999 visit to Bulgaria CPT/Inf (2002) 1, para. 174.

[11] Report to the Ukrainian Government on the visit to Ukraine carried out by the CPT from 10 to 26 September 2000, CPT/Inf (2002) 23, para. 151

[12] Amnesty International, AI Index: EUR 39/002/2004 UA 71/04 Denial of medical care/health concern 20 February 2004.

ECHR duty to prevent deaths

The ECHR specifies the State obligation to prevent deaths. Article 2 of the Convention reads:

1) Everyone's right to life shall be protected by law. No one shall be deprived of his life intentionally save in the execution of a sentence of a court following his conviction of a crime for which this penalty is provided for by law.
2) Deprivation of life shall not be regarded as inflicted in contravention of this Article when it results from the use of force which is no more than absolutely necessary:
   (a) in defence of any person from unlawful violence
   (b) in order to effect a lawful arrest or to prevent the escape of a person lawfully detained;
   (c) in action lawfully taken for the purposes of quelling a riot or insurrection

Article 2 mirrors provisions in the UN's human rights treaties.[13] The ECtHR has held that '[t]he convergence of the above-mentioned [UN] instruments is significant: it indicates that the right to life is an inalienable attribute of human beings and forms the supreme value in the hierarchy of human rights'.[14]

During the 1990s numerous cases involving counter-terrorism activity, particularly by the United Kingdom and Turkey, began to reach the ECtHR. These cases led to extensive analysis of the implications of lethal action by State agents, and the circumstances in which killing can claim to be justified under the second paragraph of Article 2, topics which fall outside the scope of this book. The reference in Article 2 to the death penalty has now been superseded by Protocol 6 to the Convention, which reads that: '[t]he death penalty shall be abolished. No-one shall be condemned to such penalty or be executed'.

The Court's case law under Article 2 has identified both substantive and procedural obligations. Substantively, the State has a 'negative obligation' to refrain from taking life. The State also has a 'positive obligation' to take reasonable measures to safeguard the lives of those within its jurisdiction, to establish a functioning legal framework which properly protects life and investigates deaths.[15] The Court has repeatedly Stated that 'Article 2 enshrines one of the basic values of the democratic societies making up the Council of Europe',[16] and so its interpretation and application must ensure that its safeguards are

---

[13] See Article 3 of the Universal Declaration of Human Rights of 10 December 1948 and Article 6 of the International Covenant on Civil and Political Rights of 16 December 1966.

[14] *Streletz, Kessler and Krenz v. Germany*, Application Nos. 34044/96, 35532/97 and 44801/98, judgment 22 March 2001, (2001) 33 EHRR 31, para. 94.

[15] *Osman v. the United Kingdom*, Application No. 87/1997/871/1083, judgment 28 October 1998, *Reports of Judgments and Decisions* 1998–VIII, p. 3159, (2000) 29 EHRR 245, para. 115; see also *Tanribilir v. Turkey*, Application No. 21422/93, judgment 16 November 2000, para. 70, and *L.C.B. v. the United Kingdom*, judgment 9 June 1998, *Reports* 1998–III, p. 1403, (1999) 27 EHRR 212, para. 36.

[16] *McCann and Others v. the United Kingdom*, judgment 22 September 1995, Series A no. 324, p. 45, (1996) 21 EHRR 97, para. 147.

practical and effective. For an issue as fundamental as the right to life, it is surprisingly that it was only from the 1990s onwards that the Court had occasion to interpret this Article.

In fulfilling its positive obligation, the State is obliged to secure the right to life by establishing effective criminal law provisions to deter the commission of offences, backed up by law-enforcement machinery for the prevention, suppression and punishment of such crimes.[17] Article 2 implies in some circumstances an additional positive obligation on the authorities to take preventive operational measures to protect an individual whose life is at risk from the criminal acts of another individual. The ECtHR has recognised that this duty is subject to practical limitation:

> [B]earing in mind the difficulties involved in policing modern societies, the unpredictability of human conduct and the operational choices which must be made in terms of priorities and resources, such an obligation [to take operational measures] must be interpreted in a way which does not impose an impossible or disproportionate burden on the authorities.[18]

Where a real and immediate risk to the life of one or more identified individuals exists, the State is duty-bound to take reasonable measures to prevent the risk from materialising.[19] In a case which was declared inadmissible by the ECtHR, a prisoner had been released for a period of home leave towards the end of his prison sentence. Whilst on leave he killed a woman. The woman's mother brought the case to the ECtHR alleging that her daughter's life had not been adequately protected, contrary to Article 2 of the ECHR. The Court observed that there was no evidence indicating that the authorities knew, or ought to have known, that the prisoner was likely to commit a crime of violence if he was released for a period of home leave, noting the absence of any medical diagnosis of mental illness and indicating that he posed a risk to life and the fact that he had previously returned from two periods of home leave without incident. The ECtHR found no evidence that the applicant's daughter in particular was at foreseeable risk, and that in the circumstances of this case, the release of the prisoner on home leave shortly before the end of his sentence disclosed by itself no failure to protect the life of the applicant's daughter.[20]

In the hospital context the Article 2 obligation to prevent deaths includes the requirement for hospitals to have regulations for the protection of their patients' lives.[21] Authorities are obliged to protect people in institutions (prisons, psychiatric institutions etc.) from taking their own life. In assessing whether authorities have fulfilled their obligations, the Convention requires an examination into whether the authorities knew or ought to have known that the person posed a real and immediate risk of suicide and, if so, whether they did all that could reasonably have been expected of them to prevent that risk.[22]

---

[17]   *Makaratzis v. Greece*, Application No. 50385/99, judgment 20 December 2004, (2005) 41 EHRR 49, para. 57.
[18]   *Osman v. the United Kingdom, op. cit.*, para. 116.
[19]   *Mastromatteo v. Italy*, Application No. 37703/97, judgment 24 October 2002, para. 68.
[20]   *Dawn Bromiley v. the United Kingdom*, Application No. 33747/96, decision 23 November 1999.
[21]   *Erikson v. Italy*, Application No. 37900/97, decision 26 October 1999.
[22]   *Keenan v. the United Kingdom*, Application No. 27229/95, judgment 3 April 2001, (2001) 33 EHRR 38.

Investigations of death – ECHR requirements

Procedural obligations are not set out in the terms of Article 2, but have evolved in the ECtHR's case-law in order to make real the substantive obligations to prevent deaths, discussed above. In its early decisions on the right to life, the Court established that the State's obligation to protect the right to life, read in conjunction with the State's general duty under Article 1 to 'secure to everyone within [its] jurisdiction the rights and freedoms defined in [the] Convention', requires by implication that there should be some form of effective official investigation when individuals have been killed as a result of the use of force.[23] The Court has further held that 'where agents of the State potentially bear responsibility for loss of life, the events in question should be subject to an effective investigation or scrutiny which enables the facts to become known to the public and in particular to the relatives of any victims'.[24]

The Court has explained that '[t]he essential purpose of such investigation is to secure the effective implementation of the domestic laws which protect the right to life and, in those cases involving State agents or bodies, to ensure their accountability for deaths occurring under their responsibility'.[25] Further, a thorough and public investigation of deaths theoretically at least will ensure that such fatal incidents are not repeated. When deaths are hidden and not investigated complacency becomes the norm.

It is clear that the Article 2 obligation to investigate deaths is not limited to killing by State agents, nor even to cases of violent deaths, or deaths which were intentional. The ECtHR has established that effective judicial system required by Article 2 may, and under certain circumstances must, include recourse to the criminal law.[26]

If a person with mental disabilities dies in a psychiatric or social care institution – whether from suicide, over-medication, restraints, malnutrition or hypothermia – there might well have been no crime committed, and no intention on the part of the authorities for the death to have occurred. Article 2 compliant investigations must take place, because the obligations 'apply in the public-health sphere too'.[27] Deaths occurring whilst a person is receiving medical care must also be fully investigated:

---

[23] *McCann and Others v. the United Kingdom*, Application No. 18984/91, judgment 27 September 1995, (A/324) (1996) 21 EHRR 97, para. 161, and *Kaya v. Turkey*, Application No. 22729/93, judgment 19 February 1998, (1999) 28 EHRR 1, para. 86.

[24] *Nelina Sieminska v. Poland*, Application No. 37602/97, decision 29 March 2001. *Ergi v. Turkey*, Application No. 23818/94, judgment 18 July 1998, (2001) 32 EHRR 18, para. 82, and *Yasa v. Turkey*, Application No. 22495/93, judgment 2 September 1998, (1999) 28 EHRR 408, paras. 98–100); *Erikson v. Italy* Application No. 37900/97, decision 26 October 1999.

[25] *Paul and Audrey Edwards v. the United Kingdom*, Application No. 46477/99, judgment 14 March 2002, (2002) 35 EHRR 19, para. 69.

[26] See among other authorities, *Kılıç v. Turkey*, Application No. 22492/93, 28 March 2000, (2001) 33 EHRR 58, and *Kaya v. Turkey, op. cit.*

[27] *Calvelli and Ciglio v. Italy*, Application No. 32967/96, Grand Chamber judgment 17 January 2002, para. 49.

The Court considers that the procedural obligation as described cannot be confined to circumstances in which an individual has lost his life as a result of an act of violence. In its opinion, [. . .] the obligation at issue extends to the need for an effective independent system for establishing the cause of death of an individual under the care and responsibility of health professionals and any liability on the part of the latter.[28]

It was acknowledged at the start of this chapter that suicide represents one of the intersections between the right to life and people with mental disabilities. Although taking one's own life has now been legalized in most jurisdictions, the ECtHR has had to balance autonomy and paternalism in determining whether a State has the duty to prevent suicides within institutions. In the case of *Keenan v. the United Kingdom*, the applicants' son Mark Keenan, a man who had been diagnosed with a mental illness, killed himself in a prison. At the ECtHR, the British government argued that special considerations arise where the State prevents a suicide from being carried out due to the principles of dignity and autonomy. Responding to this argument, the ECtHR held:

[R]estraints will inevitably be placed on the preventive measures taken by the authorities, for example in the context of police action, by the guarantees of Articles 5 and 8 of the Convention [. . .]. The prison authorities, similarly, must discharge their duties in a manner compatible with the rights and freedoms of the individual concerned. There are general measures and precautions which will be available to diminish the opportunities for self-harm, without infringing on personal autonomy. Whether any more stringent measures are necessary in respect of a prisoner and whether it is reasonable to apply them will depend on the circumstances of the case.[29]

The circumstances of the *Keenan* case were that Mark Keenan, since entering the prison, had engaged in behaviour such as making a noose that, the Court held, was sufficient to put the institution on notice that he was at risk of suicide.[30] The risk was not a constant one, however, and the institution's response had been to place him under watch when risk appeared high. That was sufficient to meet its obligations, under the particular circumstances of that case.[31]

The State is also obliged to ensure that legal machinery is in place to protect lives in institutions which are not in direct control of the State. In a case concerning a baby who died in an Italian hospital, the ECtHR held that there must be regulations for public and private hospitals to adopt appropriate measures for the protection of their patients' lives. In the same case, the Court held that an effective independent judicial system must be established so that the cause of death of patients in the care of the medical profession can be determined and those responsible made accountable.[32] The Court went on to say that those deaths in psychiatric hospitals where the infringement on the right to life may not

---

[28] *William and Anita Powell v. the United Kingdom*, Application no. 45305/99, decision 4 May 2000.
[29] *Keenan v. the United Kingdom, op. cit.*, para. 91.
[30] *Keenan v. the United Kingdom, op. cit.*, paras. 94–5.
[31] *Keenan v. the United Kingdom, op. cit.*, para. 98.
[32] *Calvelli and Ciglio v. Italy, op. cit.*, para. 49.

caused intentionally, the positive obligation imposed by Article 2 to set up an effective judicial system does not necessarily require the provision of a criminal-law remedy in every case. In medical negligence cases the obligation may also be satisfied if the legal system provides a remedy in the civil courts (either alone or with a remedy in the criminal courts), which would enable possible liability of the doctors concerned to be established and any appropriate civil redress (eg. damages or a declaration), to be obtained. Disciplinary measures may also be an option. The Court went on to say that such measures – civil, criminal, disciplinary – must be not merely theoretical, 'but operate effectively in practice'.[33]

The form of investigation required

Exactly how the State must investigate deaths – the form of the investigatory machinery, the extent of the obligation for the investigation to be conducted in public, and the extent to which next-of-kin must be involved – is still being developed by the ECtHR. The Court recognises that certain categories of cases require higher degrees of rigour and openness than others, particular cases where agents of the State are involved, and where deaths have occurred in custodial institutions like prisons and mental health facilities. In many States and institutions, dedicated staff work exceptionally hard to ensure the best available quality of life for residents, and government provision is adequate to ensure conditions well in excess of ECHR minimum requirements. Where this does not occur, however, this aspect of the Court's jurisprudence provides a powerful tool to assist some of the most vulnerable people in society.

There is no doubt that State compliance with Article 2 requires systems of investigation after deaths. The form of investigation which will achieve those purposes may vary in different circumstances. However, whichever mode is employed, the authorities must act if the issue comes to their attention. They cannot leave it to the initiative of the next-of-kin either to lodge a formal complaint or to take responsibility for the conduct of any investigative procedures.[34] This touches on issues of what happens when there is no family member and when a State refuses to investigate – a topic to which we return later in the chapter when we address the issue of victim status.

The ECtHR has stressed the importance of the investigating body being independent from those implicated in the events.[35] This means not only a lack of hierarchical or institutional connection but also a practical independence.[36] In the mental disability context

---

[33] *Calvelli and Ciglio v. Italy, op. cit.*, para. 51.
[34] *İlhan v. Turkey*, Application No. 22277/93, Grand Chamber judgment 27 June 2000, (2002) 34 EHRR 36, para. 63.
[35] *Güleç v. Turkey*, Application No. 21593/93, judgment 27 July 1998, (1999) 28 EHRR 121, paras. 81–82, and *Oğur v. Turkey* Application No. 21954/93, Grand Chamber judgment 20 June 1999, paras. 91–92.
[36] *Hugh Jordan v. the United Kingdom*, Application No. 24746/94, judgment 4 May 2001, (2003) 37 EHRR 2, para. 120, and *Kelly and Others v. the United Kingdom*, Application No. 30054/96, judgment 4 May 2001, para. 114.

this would rule out, for example, the investigation into a death in psychiatric hospital from being carried out by a panel of medical professionals from the hospital in which the person died, or medical professionals who know the doctors involved. This is especially a concern in smaller European countries where the medical profession is collegiate to the point where the appearance of independence could be said to be compromised.

The investigation must also be effective in the sense that it is capable of leading to a determination of whether the force used was or was not justified in the circumstances and to the identification and punishment of those responsible. The Court has emphasised that the investigation is not an obligation of result, but of means. That is to say, the investigating authorities must take reasonable steps to secure the evidence concerning the incident, including eyewitness testimony (including other patients/residents from the institution being called as witnesses), forensic evidence and, where appropriate, an autopsy providing a complete and accurate record of injury and an objective analysis of clinical findings,[37] including the cause of death. Any deficiency in the investigation which undermines its ability to establish the cause of death or the person or persons responsible will risk falling foul of this standard.[38]

Implicit in the obligation to investigate deaths is the requirement of promptness and reasonable expedition.[39] The ECtHR has accepted that there may be obstacles when investigating deaths, but that a prompt response maintains public confidence in their adherence to the rule of law and in preventing any appearance of collusion in or tolerance of unlawful acts.[40] Further, any delay risks witnesses forgetting what happened.

In order to comply with the requirements of Article 2, an investigation into a death must have powers to compel witnesses to give evidence. In the case of *Paul and Audrey Edwards v. the United Kingdom*, the inquiry panel which had been set up had no power to compel witnesses. As a result two prison officers – people who could potentially give crucial information about the death of the Applicants' son whilst detained in a prison – declined to attend. Although the prison officers had submitted two written Statements and that there was no indication that they had anything different or additional to add to those Statements, the ECtHR noted that the officers was not available for questions to be put to him which might have required further detail or clarification or for any inconsistency or omissions in their accounts to be tested. The ECtHR found that:

> the lack of compulsion of witnesses who are either eye-witnesses or have material evidence related to the circumstances of a death must be regarded as diminishing the effectiveness of the Inquiry as an investigative mechanism. In this case [. . .] it detracted from its capacity to establish the facts relevant to the death, and thereby to achieve one of the purposes required by Article 2 of the Convention.[41]

---

[37] For an example of how an inadequately-performed autopsy was criticized by the ECtHR, see *Salman v. Turkey* Application No. 21986/93, judgment 27 June 2000, para. 106.
[38] *Paul and Audrey Edwards v. the United Kingdom, op. cit.*, para. 71.
[39] *Paul and Audrey Edwards v. the United Kingdom, op. cit.*, para. 71.
[40] See, for example, *Hugh Jordan, Hugh Jordan v. the United Kingdom, op. cit.*, paras. 108 and 136–40.
[41] *Paul and Audrey Edwards v. the United Kingdom, op. cit.*, para. 79.

In all cases the next-of-kin of the victim must be involved in the procedure to the extent necessary to safeguard his or her legitimate interests.[42] The involvement of the next-of-kin in the investigation allows the grieving family to ask questions to witnesses, either by themselves, or through legal representation. The inclusion of next-of-kin in the investigation goes some way to help with psychological closure, and to ensure a sufficient element of public scrutiny of the investigation. To emphasise a point already made, the relatives have rights within the process of the investigation, but they need not instigate the investigation once it has come to the attention of the authorities, and they need not take responsibility for the conduct of the investigatory procedures.[43]

Burden and Standard of Proof

When it examines whether there has been a violation of Article 2 of the Convention, the ECtHR has generally applied the standard of proof of 'beyond reasonable doubt',[44] adding in later cases that such proof may follow from the coexistence of sufficiently strong, clear and concordant inferences or of similar unrebutted presumptions of fact. Where concern is raised about the manner of the death of a person with mental disabilities, the likelihood is that the person died in an institution. The ECtHR has held that owing to the importance of the protection afforded by Article 2, deprivations of life must be subjected to the most careful scrutiny, taking into consideration not only the actions of State agents but also all the surrounding circumstances.[45]

In situations where someone dies in custody and it is therefore likely that only the authorities have access to evidence of how the person died, the onus is on the authorities to provide that evidence. As was discussed in chapter 3 on inside institutions, the Court has said:

> Where the events in issue lie wholly, or in large part, within the exclusive knowledge of the authorities, as in the case of persons within their control in custody, strong presumptions of fact will arise in respect of injuries and death occurring during such detention. Indeed, the burden of proof may be regarded as resting on the authorities to provide a satisfactory and convincing explanation.[46]

The Court in this Turkish case emphasised that '[t]he obligation on the authorities to account for the treatment of an individual in custody is particularly stringent where that individual dies'.[47] In the *Edwards* case discussed above, the ECtHR added that 'persons in custody are in a vulnerable position and that the authorities are under a duty to protect them'.[48]

---

[42] *Paul and Audrey Edwards v. the United Kingdom, op. cit.*, para. 71.
[43] *Paul and Audrey Edwards v. the United Kingdom, op. cit.*, para. 69.
[44] *Ireland v. the United Kingdom*, judgment 18 January 1978, Series A no. 25, pp. 64–65, (1979–80) 2 EHRR 25, para. 161.
[45] *Hugh Jordan v. the United Kingdom, op. cit.*, para. 103.
[46] *Salman v. Turkey, op. cit.*
[47] *Salman v. Turkey, op. cit.*, para. 99.
[48] *Paul and Audrey Edwards v. the United Kingdom, op. cit.*, para. 56.

Who can apply to the Court under Article 2?

A person can apply to the European Court of Human Rights only if he/she can claim to be a 'victim' within the meaning of Article 34 of the Convention (see chapter 8, below). This normally means that the applicant must have been directly affected by the violation in issue. An application alleging a violation of Article 2 cannot be brought in the name of the deceased person. Instead a next-of-kin or other relative, or an heir to an State can apply on behalf of the deceased, and in the person's own name. In cases where the relative has accepted compensation in domestic proceedings based on medical negligence, the relative can in principle no longer claim to be a victim for the purposes of lodging an application with the ECtHR.[49]

An applicant to apply under Article 2 as a potential victim, the cases decided so far to apply under the Court have concerned deportations where the applicant risks death. Expulsion by a country of an alien may give rise to an issue under Article 2 of the Convention, and hence engage the responsibility of that State under the Convention, where substantial grounds have been shown for believing that the person in question, if expelled, would face a real risk of being killed.[50]

In mental disability cases, a person could be said to be a potential victim of Article 2 if that person is confined in an institution with a high mortality rate, or one in which investigations are not investigated. However, it is suggested that in such a case, notwithstanding the possibility of the Court to order interim measures,[51] litigation before the European Court of Human Rights may not be the most appropriate strategy, and in any event the Court is more likely to address the issue under Article 3.[52]

In a case where a deceased person's substantive or procedural rights under Article 2 may have been violated, an application will depend on the existence and willingness of a family member or guardian willing to bring a case to the ECtHR. Without such a person, it is difficult to see how the deceased person's rights to have a proper investigation are respected.[53] The ECtHR has said that, '[t]he mere knowledge of the killing on the part of the authorities gives rise *ipso facto* to an obligation under Article 2 of the Convention to carry out an effective investigation into the circumstances surrounding the death'.[54] Relatives do not need to instigate such investigations, yet the Court insists on Article 2 cases being brought by relatives who could be classified as a 'victim' under Article 34.[55]

---

[49] *Calvelli and Ciglio v. Italy, op. cit.*, para. 55.
[50] *Headley v. the United Kingdom*, Application No. 39642/03, decision 1 March 2005. See also *Osman v. the United Kingdom, op. cit.*, where the Court accepted the second applicant's life was put at serious risk and was therefore eligible to claim victim status under Article 34.
[51] See chapter 9 on procedure before the ECtHR.
[52] See chapter 3 on inside institutions.
[53] O. Lewis, 'Right to life: European Convention on Human Rights, Case Commentary on *Paul and Audrey Edwards v. the United Kingdom*' (2003) *Journal of Mental Health Law*, 75–84.
[54] *Ergi v. Turkey*, Application No. 23818/94, judgment 28 July 1998, (2001) 32 EHRR 18, para. 82.
[55] See Article 34 of the Convention and *Yasa v. Turkey* (1999) 28 EHRR 408 (nephew of deceased as victim); *H v. the United Kingdom*, Application No. 9833/82; 42 D.R. 53 (mother of murdered person as

What happens in cases where there are no family members, as there are so often in large institutions where abuses are more likely to occur in central and east of the Council of Europe region? When residents die (for example of malnutrition or hypothermia) there are no investigations of any sort beyond a death certificate and perhaps an autopsy examination. For people facing early and un-investigated deaths there is often no-one to bring such failures of the State to the ECtHR's attention. If the Convention is 'intended to guarantee not rights that are theoretical or illusory but rights that are practical and effective',[56] the Court needs to become more flexible in its approach to victim status when cases come before it brought on behalf of people without family members. Alternatively, the political organs of the Council of Europe may consider proposing a Protocol to the Convention which would amend Article 34 to allow, for example, those international non-governmental organizations with participatory status with the Council to bring cases on behalf of people who have died and who have no family members to bring the case on their behalf.[57]

It is arguable that where a State fails to carry out proper investigations into cause of death – for example where high mortality is occurring in a social care institution without an effective inquiry into the death – a resident of the social care institution may be able to claim to be a potential victims of Article 2.[58] Such a person who fears premature death in such circumstances will also be able to claim a violation of Article 3.

---

victim); *Wolfgram v. Germany*, Application No. 11257/84; 49 D.R. 213, (1987) 9 EHRR CD548 (parents of deceased as victims).

[56] *Airey v. Ireland*, Application No. 6289/73, judgment of 9 October 1979, Series A no. 32, (1979–80) 2 EHRR 305, para 24.

[57] This could be akin to the European Social Charter's system whereby specified international non-governmental organizations from a list maintained by the Charter's secretariat are entitled to bring a 'collective complaint' against a Member State which has ratified the Revised European Social Charter, and the Optional Protocol to the Charter establishing the collective complaints mechanism.

[58] See *Osman v. the United Kingdom, op. cit.*, where the Court accepted the second applicant's life was put at serious risk and was therefore eligible to claim victim status under Article 34.

Chapter 6

Legal Capacity, Guardianship and Supported Decision-Making

Introduction

Most countries have legal mechanisms to respond to situations where an individual needs assistance with making particular decisions. Such assistance may be required when a person has a difficulty with cognitive functioning caused, for example, by intellectual disabilities, some forms of "mental illness", brain damage or degenerative diseases such as Alzheimer's disease. This chapter deals mainly with safeguards required during the process of depriving someone of legal capacity, appointing a guardian, contesting decisions made by a guardian, displacing a guardian and reviewing the need for being deprived of decision-making powers. People who have been deprived of their legal capacity are, by definition, deprived of the ability to decide upon certain aspects of their life. These other aspects are considered in different chapters of the book: consenting to or refusing treatment (chapter 4), deciding where to live (chapter 2), having the right to participate in various aspects of community living (chapter 7).

Five examples illustrate different scenarios:
1. Andras, aged 40, has Down's syndrome and lives with his family. His relatives are getting old and are worried about where Andras will live when they cannot care for him, and concerned about how he will manage the money which one day he will inherit.

2. Beata, a woman in her 20s, has been diagnosed with 'bi-polar affective disorder'. Every few months for the past two years her behaviour becomes manic or 'high', during which time she goes out to shops and spends all her money on things which, later, she realises she does not need at all.

3. Charles had a motorcycle accident and sustained a head injury. He is currently in a coma but doctors say he may well regain consciousness in a few weeks.

4. Dora is in her 70s and lives alone without any social support. She has been diagnosed with Alzheimer's disease, and is starting to forget things and is finding it difficult to cook.

5. Edgar has mild learning difficulties. He has a part time job, but cannot do arithmetic, so finds it difficult to manage his personal finances, such as monthly budgeting and arranging bank transactions.

Different legal responses would be appropriate for each of these people. Edgar's difficulties could be solved if someone provided him with occasional assistance in his mathematics. There may be no need to recognise this relationship in law, because Edgar is able to make choices about every aspect of his life – he just needs assistance with sums. Andras is capable of taking many decisions, but does need someone to live with him to look after him. He requires plans to be put into place in the event that his parents can no longer look after him. For Andras perhaps a person could be assigned to have the legal responsibility and authority to make decisions in conjunction with Andras in the event of him being left without carers.

Beata, Charles and Dora had or have the capacity to make all decisions. Beata has a fluctuating mental illness which means that for those periods she may well feel that she needs someone to temporarily have the authority to make financial decisions for her (pay the bills, limit her credit card, allow her some spending money). She could assign these rights to someone by signing a legal document which is sometimes called an enduring power of attorney or lasting power of attorney. Beata could also consider making a decision about treatment which may detail for example the sorts of treatment options which she likes and does not like when she is in a manic state. Such advance planning of medical treatment in some countries is valid even if the person – at the time of the manic behaviour – refuses treatment.

Dora has a degenerative disease which, unfortunately, will probably get worse with time. She may well want to plan ahead, so she could also appoint a trusted person to make legal decisions for her in the event that she cannot make them herself. She could also think about making a 'living will'; that is an advance decision about treatment, meaning that a person can make a decision now, about treatment which he or she would not want in future when that person has lost capacity.

Lastly, Charles does not currently have capacity to make any decisions as he is in a coma. For him a different legal mechanism would be appropriate, perhaps one in which a trusted family member or friend who can be appointed to take decisions on his behalf. However Charles may at some point recover, so the legal arrangement would need to be regularly reviewed to ensure that his autonomy is respected when he regains the capacity to express his wishes.

The issue of capacity then, is a complex one. One-size-fits-all legal frameworks are inappropriate, for two main reasons: (1) capacity often fluctuates throughout a person's life, sometimes in a remarkably short space of time such as days or, sometimes, hours, and (2) capacity is specific to a particular decision. Andras, for example, probably has the capacity to decide on personal welfare issues such as clothes and food, but may not have capacity to understand complex medical procedures or financial transactions.

Capacity issues are dealt with differently by different countries. Some legal systems are designed to ensure that alternative decision-making processes are available for only those decisions an individual is actually incapable of making.[1] Others are less subtle, and some do not allow for partial capacity at all: if the individual is given a guardian, the guardian acquires authority over all the decisions relating to that person. This latter approach is often based on Roman law,[2] which deprives such persons of 'legal personhood'. In law, the person effectively loses all rights: in the eyes of the law, the person becomes a non-person. As the above examples show, such persons may in fact have capacity to make many decisions that affect them, but these legal systems preclude them from doing so. Of particular relevance, these legal systems do not allow people under guardianship to instruct their own lawyer, and commence proceedings (even if they are in fact capable of doing so). In some countries, people under guardianship are not even legally entitled to lodge a case at a domestic court to challenge their guardianship.[3] As discussed elsewhere in this volume,[4] that restriction does not apply for applications to the European Court of Human Rights: the ECHR provides rights to *all* people within countries which have ratified the Convention, whether or not they have capacity, and anyone in fact (even if not in law) capable of doing so can apply for the enforcement of those rights.

Definitions, and the Meaning of Functional Incapacity

The terms most often used in the context of legal incapacity and guardianship issues are 'capacity;' and 'competence'. The World Health Organization's definition is that capacity refers specifically to the presence of mental abilities to make decisions or to engage in a course of action, while competence refers to the legal consequences of not having the mental capacity.[5] In the view of the WHO, the former is determined by (health) professionals, the latter by judges (albeit on the basis of the expert opinions of health and other

---

[1]   See, for example, the English and Welsh *Mental Capacity Act 2005*.
[2]   See in particular the cura furiosi in the Twelve Tables of Justinian, especially I.1.23.3.4.
[3]   For example, Russia.
[4]   See below in this chapter, but also chapters 2 (detention) and 9 (representation).
[5]   World Health Organization (2005), *Resource Book on Mental Health, Human Rights and Legislation*, page 39, section 7.1.

professionals). That said, it must be admitted that the terms are sometimes used interchangeably.

As noted above, individuals may be able to make some decisions and not others. The question of the individual's actual ability actually to make a given decision refers to 'functional' capacity, as distinct from whether he or she is precluded by law from making a decision, which may be termed 'legal' capacity.

Functional incapacity is not the same thing as having a mental disability. Some mental disabilities, be they mental illnesses or intellectual disabilities, will cause such incapacity; others will not. Indeed, empirical studies show that a significant majority of people, even with serious mental illnesses such as schizophrenia and clinical depression, are nonetheless no less competent than the general public to make decisions regarding medical treatment.[6] Functional capacity instead is about the individual being able to understand the information relevant to the decision, possessing the reasoning ability to reach a decision, and to appreciating both the relevance of the information at issue and the likely results of the various choices that may be made.[7] How these criteria are to be applied will of course depend on the decision in question. Nonetheless, a few comments are appropriate.

As noted, the fact that an individual has a serious mental disability does not necessarily mean that he or she lacks functional capacity to make a decision. The question is how that disability affects their view of the information. If an individual is experiencing an episode of psychosis, for example, he or she may still have functional capacity, as long as the psychosis does not affect the decision in question. The fact that an individual has psychotic beliefs about one medication, for example, does not mean he or she lacks capacity to make treatment decisions regarding medications not affected by the psychosis.

Reaching a decision that professional people or family members believe is not in the individual's best interests is not in itself evidence of incapacity. The fact that an individual may spend a lot of money may have serious impact on the family budget, but it does not of itself make the person functionally incapacitous of handling money. Beata's case, above, provides a helpful guide. The fact that she buys things she later decides she did not need does not mean that she lacks functional capacity to make those purchases. The fact that the purchases occur at specific times in her experience of her disability makes it much more likely that she lacks such capacity, however. The question is, at the time she is making the purchases, whether she appreciates what she is doing, or whether the mania she is experiencing has the effect of removing her appreciation of the decisions she is making at the time she is making them.

The need to separate best interests from capacity flows throughout the determination of functional capacity. People with mental disabilities frequently complain that they are

---

[6]   T. Grisso and P. Appelbaum, 'The MacArthur Treatment Competence Study III: Abilities of Patients to Consent to Psychiatric and Medical Treatments' (1995), 19:2 *Law and Human Behavior* 149.

[7]   The classic paper on standards of capacity is L. Roth, A. Meisel and C. Lidz, 'Tests of Competency to Consent to Treatment' (1977) 134:3 *American Journal of Psychiatry* 279.

found to lack capacity for treatment only when they disagree with the doctor's assessment of their best interests. Disagreeing with a doctor does not in itself imply incapacity, so long as it does not flow directly as a symptom of the disorder or disability with which the individual is affected. Similarly, in decisions regarding institutionalisation, individuals do not lack capacity merely because they are unduly optimistic about whether they can survive outside the institution.

Functional capacity refers to the *ability* of the individual to understand the information relevant to a decision. This is not the same as requiring the individual to believe the information without question. If an individual does not believe the information the professional or family member believes to be relevant to a decision, the reasons for the non-belief should be examined. In some cases, it may be the direct result of psychosis: an individual may believe, for example, that medication has been poisoned by nurses who have been brainwashed by foreign spies. Such a delusion would obviously be relevant to the individual's functional capacity to consent to the treatment. An individual does not necessarily lack functional capacity just because he or she refuses medication because he or she thinks it does not help, or because he or she has (sometimes for understandable reasons) lost trust in the doctor prescribing it.

Positive duty to protect

It could be argued that Article 8 of the ECHR establishes a positive obligation on the State to ensure that the law adequately protects the rights of people who lack the capacity to make decisions. If a person with intellectual disabilities for example, inherits a large sum of money, she may require assistance to manage that money. If the law does not provide for the person to be assisted in such decision making she may not be able to take advantage of what is rightfully hers. The person may have a claim under the Convention that her Article 8 right to a private life (to manage her own affairs) remains merely 'theoretical and illusory'[8] without such assistance. The argument is particularly strong when one considers the overarching duty under Article 1 of the Convention to secure to everyone the rights and freedoms set out in the Convention. If the ECtHR finds that such a positive obligation exists, the sorts of mechanisms which a State would have to ensure are in place would include a mechanism so that people who are thought to lack capacity can have access to speedy, accurate and independent incapacity evaluations. It would also include provisions that a person judged to lack capacity is able to enjoy the maximum possible respect for private and family life, which may necessitate appointing someone to act on that person's behalf. To date, there has been no such case on such positive obligations relating to incapacity at the European Court of Human Rights. Indeed there is little case law brought by adults who lack capacity in an area of their life. Similarly there have been

---

[8]   *Airey v. Ireland*, Application No. 6289/73, judgment 9 October 1979, (A/32) (1979–80) 2 EHRR 305, para. 24.

few cases brought by children, especially children with disabilities who face dual discrimination of being both a child and a disabled person. The lack of cases may have more to do with access to justice (see conclusion, chapter 10) than providing us with an indication of numbers of people affected.

Guardianship as a human rights issue

As noted above, some legal systems are organised to ensure that the person with mental disabilities can continue to make those decisions for which he or she has functional capacity. In other countries, instead of the law providing tailor-made options to fit an individual's needs, people are subject to a one-size-fits-all legal approach, in which they are subjected to restrictions (or complete deprivation) of their legal authority to make decisions. Such an approach is disproportionate to functional incapacity. There is growing evidence that in some countries judges routinely deprive people with mental disabilities of their legal capacity in procedures which do not meet fair trial guarantees.[9] Once the person is legally incapacitated, their right to decide on many important issues is taken away and handed over to another person, sometimes called a 'guardian'. The adult who has been legally incapacitated (hereinafter 'the adult')[10] may be subject to total guardianship[11] in which the individual retains almost none of the areas of decision making capacity. Or, the adult may be placed under 'partial guardianship' where the individual retains the legal ability to make some decisions (e.g. small financial transactions) but not others.

Guardianship issues are therefore human rights issues. The Secretary General of the United Nations has observed:

> The function of guardianship is to protect the individual from any danger which his or her mental conditions may cause. International human rights law requires the adoption of substantial and procedural guarantees to prevent improper recourse to, and use of, guardianship arrangements.[12]

Much of this chapter necessarily focuses on problematic aspects of guardianship systems and offers some insights through the lens of the ECHR. There are of course legitimate reasons for establishing systems in which the decision-making powers of a person who lacks capacity to make such decisions is given to someone else. Indeed if there were no sys-

---

[9] See Mental Disability Advocacy Center (2006) *Human Rights and Guardianship in Bulgaria*. See similar reports on Hungary, Russia and Serbia. Available from www.mdac.info.

[10] The adult to whom guardianship applies is sometimes referred to as a 'ward', but this term is avoided in this book as unduly condescending. The simple word 'adult' is used to denote the 'person under guardianship'.

[11] Sometimes referred to as 'plenary guardianship'.

[12] Report of the United Nations Secretary-General presented to the Fifty-eighth session of the General Assembly, 24 July 2003, Ref: A/58/181, 'Progress of efforts to ensure the full recognition and enjoyment of the human rights of persons with disabilities'. Report of the United Nations Secretary-General presented to the Fifty-eighth session of the General Assembly, 24 July 2003, Ref: A/58/181.

tems established to protect the well-being and support decision-making of people who, temporarily or otherwise, lack functional capacity, the State may violate people's right to a private life under Article 8 of the ECHR. This view is supported by a United Nations instrument, the 'Declaration on the Rights of Mentally Retarded Persons', which points out that a person with intellectual disabilities 'has a right to a qualified guardian when this is required to protect his personal well-being and interests'.[13]

The issue, which we estimate to affect several hundreds of thousands of people within the Council of Europe region[14] is the opposite hypothesis, that 'human rights abuses pervade guardianship: from judicial enquiry into incapacity, appointment of the guardian, the guardian's powers, oversight of the guardian and review of necessity of guardianship'.[15] There is growing concern that guardianship systems which are established with benevolent intentions, are now used intentionally to deprive people of their civil and political as well as economic, social and cultural rights. Guardianship has only recently been considered at the highest political levels. In the report already cited, the UN Secretary General explains:

> The right to recognition as a person before the law is often neglected in the context of mental health. The concept of guardianship is frequently used improperly to deprive individuals with an intellectual or psychiatric disability of their legal capacity without any form of procedural safeguards. Thus, persons are deprived of their right to make some of the most important and basic decisions about their life on account of an actual or perceived disability without a fair hearing and/or periodical review by competent judicial authorities. The lack of due process guarantees may expose the individual whose capacity is at stake to several possible forms of abuse. An individual with a limited disability may be considered completely unable to make life choices independently and placed under "plenary guardianship". Furthermore, guardianship may be improperly used to circumvent laws governing admission in mental health institutions, and the lack of a procedure for appealing or automatically reviewing decisions concerning legal incapacity could then determine the commitment of a person to an institution for life on the basis of an actual or perceived disability.[16]

Professor Paul Hunt, the UN Special Rapporteur on the Right to the Highest Attainable Standard of Physical and Mental Health highlighted this concern in his thematic report on the interface between mental disabilities and the right to health. Commenting in a section discussing the concerns of people with intellectual disabilities, Professor Hunt states:

---

[13] 'Declaration on the Rights of Mentally Retarded Persons', Proclaimed by General Assembly resolution 2856 (XXVI) of 20 December 1971.

[14] Figures based on Mental Disability Advocacy Center research on legal incapacity in seven Council of Europe Member States: Bulgaria, Croatia, Czech Republic, Georgia, Hungary, Russia and Serbia and Montenegro. Reports on legislation and practice are forthcoming.

[15] O. Lewis, 'Mental Disability Law in Central and Eastern Europe: Paper, Practice, Promise', 8 *Journal of Mental Health Law* (2002) 293.

[16] See para. 15 of the UN Secretary-General's report, cited at note 12.

Guardianship has been overused and abused in the medical, as well as other, contexts, including at the most extreme level to place persons with intellectual disabilities in psychiatric institutions. This is inappropriate medically and socially, and is inconsistent with the rights of persons with intellectual disabilities to health, autonomy, participation, non-discrimination and social inclusion.[17]

The same words could equally be used in relation to people with mental illness. The stigma and discrimination experienced by people with such disabilities can only be perpetuated by guardianship systems which do not comply with international law and standards.

Recommendation R(99)4: Principles Concerning the Legal Protection of Incapable Adults

In 1999 the Council of Europe focused its attention on decision making of people who lack capacity by issuing 'Recommendation No. R(99)4 of the Committee of Ministers to Member States on Principles Concerning the Legal Protection of Incapable Adults'.[18] Recommendation No. R(99)4 is the only Council of Europe instrument which sets detailed standards in this area.

The Commissioner of Human Rights of the Council of Europe has urged States to implement Recommendation No. R(99)4:

> Legislation and practises in several countries relating to the judicial finding of incapacity and the placement under guardianship give rise to concern. The transfer of civil, political and welfare rights with inadequate or only formal judicial control obviously opens up the possibility of abuse by unscrupulous family members, "professional guardians" and directors of institutions. The implementation of Recommendation No. R(99)4 of the Committee of Ministers of the Council of Europe on Principles concerning the legal protection of incapable adults would greatly reduce such abuses, whilst enabling people to act appropriately on behalf of others in need of assistance.[19]

As a human rights document, Recommendation No. R(99)4 is authoritative and useful because it helps to put flesh on the bones of the ECHR in relation to legal incapacity and guardianship law. The ECtHR has already cited Recommendation No. R(99)4 with authority in one guardianship case.[20] This section of the chapter will offer guidance on

---

[17] Report of the UN Special Rapporteur on the right of everyone to the enjoyment of the highest attainable standard of physical and mental health, Paul Hunt, Report to the Sixty-first session of the Commission on Human Rights, 11 February 2005, Ref: E/CN.4/2005/51. Para. 79.

[18] Adopted by the Committee of Ministers on 23 February 1999 at the 660th meeting of the Ministers' Deputies.

[19] Conclusions of the Commissioner, Seminar organized by the Council of Europe Commissioner for Human Rights and hosted by the World Health Organization Regional Office for Europe, Copenhagen, Denmark 5–7 February 2003, paragraph 11.

[20] *H.F. v. Slovakia*, Application No. 54797/00, judgment 8 November 2005.

how the Recommendation can be used by litigants, lawyers and judges to support Convention arguments in future cases in domestic courts and at the Strasbourg Court.

Recommendation No. R(99)4 concerns 'the protection of adults who, by reason of an impairment or insufficiency of their personal faculties, are incapable of making, in an autonomous way, decisions concerning any or all of their personal or economic affairs, or understanding, expressing or acting upon such decisions, and who consequently cannot protect their interests'.[21] The Explanatory Memorandum to Recommendation No. R(99)4 explains that the concept of autonomy 'is used in a wide sense – based on the idea of the authenticity of decisions in the light of a person's character, values and life history. An autonomous decision must be free from external coercion and internal compulsion due, for example to such factors as schizophrenic delusions or severe depressive episodes. It should also be based on a sufficient understanding of the importance and consequences of the decision'. The Explanatory Memorandum makes it clear that the concept of rationality has no part in Recommendation No. R(99)4, as it could be easily misinterpreted. As discussed above in this chapter and in chapter 4, capacity must not be allowed to boil down to whether the patient agrees with the doctor. A similar argument can be made in relation to other areas where there is a substitute decision maker. The Explanatory Memorandum goes on to explain that '[t]he incapacity may be due to a mental disability, a disease or a similar reason,' the latter category of which may include accidents or states of coma in which the person is unable to formulate his or her wishes or to communicate them.[22]

The Need for a Flexible Approach

One of the main criticisms of guardianship systems is that they allow for solutions which are not tailor-made to the individual's needs. In many countries only total (or 'plenary') guardianship is available. That is to say, in law the person retains either all or no rights. This makes no logical or legal sense considering that many people can make some but not all decisions on their own or with appropriate support, and given the general principles underlying the Recommendation of maximising autonomy, self-determination and social inclusion, and the fundamental principle running through the Convention of proportionality.

People with mental health problems raise different sorts of practical problems for systems of guardianship, because their capacity can vary over time. Sometimes such variation will be unpredictable; in other circumstances there may be some warning that changes are occurring. Sometimes the incapacity will be a single occurrence, if caused for example by some forms of psychosis; sometimes it may be recurrent, if caused by bipolar disorder ('manic depression'), for example. In many cases, recurrence may depend on the

---

[21] Part 1, para. 1.
[22] Explanatory Memorandum to Recommendation No. R(99)4, para. 20.

medical régime prescribed, and whether the individual chooses to continue on the medication. The difficulty from a guardianship perspective is how to create a system that will have sufficient human rights protections, but at the same time will be flexible and sensitive enough that the individual has control over decisions at the time when they have capacity, and have appropriate protection in the form of a guardian when they lose that capacity. The processes taken as standard in determination of a person's rights can be too cumbersome to react swiftly to these situations, and, if repeated for periodic incapacity, can prove expensive.

Recognising the need for a flexible legal approach, Recommendation R(99)4 advises that measures to protect the personal and economic interests of the person in question 'should be sufficient, in scope or flexibility, to enable a suitable legal response to be made to different degrees of incapacity and various situations'.[23] Further, the Recommendation goes on to say that laws should preserve legal capacity as far as possible:

> The legislative framework should, so far as possible, recognise that different degrees of incapacity may exist and that incapacity may vary from time to time. Accordingly, a measure of protection should not result automatically in a complete removal of legal capacity. However, a restriction of legal capacity should be possible where it is shown to be necessary for the protection of the person concerned.[24]

The legal measure should be 'proportional to the degree of capacity of the person concerned and tailored to the individual circumstances and needs of the person concerned',[25] and the 'measure of protection should interfere with the legal capacity, rights and freedoms of the person concerned to the minimum extent which is consistent with achieving the purpose of the intervention'.[26]

The Recommendation uses ECHR language of 'necessity', warning that a Recommendation warns that a measure of protection should not be pursued 'unless the measure is necessary, taking into account the individual circumstances and the needs of the person concerned'.[27] Anticipating that the national legislation allows for alternatives to guardianship (which in many countries it does not) the Recommendation suggests that 'account should be taken of any less formal arrangements which might be made, and of any assistance which might be provided by family members or by others.'[28] Later, it emphasises this point by elaborating that it is for 'national law to determine which juridical acts are of such a highly personal nature that they can not be done by a representative'.[29]

---

[23]   Recommendation No. R(99)4, Principle 2(1).
[24]   Recommendation No. R(99)4, Principle 3(1).
[25]   Recommendation No. R(99)4, Principle 6(1).
[26]   Recommendation No. R(99)4, Principle 6(2). The World Health Organization emphasises that 'legislation should contain provisions and procedures for discharge from guardianship when the affected person regains competence in the future'. World Health Organization, *Resource Book on Mental Health, Human Rights and Legislation*, (Geneva: WHO, 2005), p. 42.
[27]   Recommendation No. R(99)4, Principle 5(1). See also ECHR 'necessity' language in Article 8 of the Convention and related case law.
[28]   Recommendation No. R(99)4, Principle 5(2).
[29]   Recommendation No. R(99)4, Principle 19(1).

The Explanatory Memorandum to the Recommendation makes clear that there are some matters which almost everyone would agree are so personal that a guardian should never undertake on behalf of the person under guardianship – these include voting, marrying, and recognising and adopting a child.[30]

Conversely, national law must 'determine whether decisions by a representative on certain serious matters should require the specific approval of a court or other body'.[31] The Explanatory Memorandum explains that such a technique can be used to require a court to give specific approval before decisions of a certain nature are made, such as consent to a certain serious or controversial health decision, disposal of certain capital, or incurring a certain type of obligation.[32]

Recommendation No. R(99)4 makes a series of points urging States to consider reforming their laws so as to reflect the following legal arrangements. Laws could include the legal recognition of advance directives, which are decisions made by a person who has capacity to provide for any subsequent incapacity.[33] Laws could regulate measures under which the appointed person acts jointly with the adult concerned, and of measures involving the appointment of more than one representative.[34] Finally, laws need 'to provide expressly that certain decisions, particularly those of a minor or routine nature relating to health or personal welfare, may be taken for an incapable adult by those deriving their powers from the law rather than from a judicial or administrative measure'.[35]

Procedural Aspects of Legal Incapacity and Guardianship

It has been emphasised in chapter 2 on detentions for reason of mental disability that the vast majority of mental disability cases brought to the European Court on Human Rights have been about process rather than substance. A similar observation may be made regarding capacity, where the Court has been more forthcoming on matters of process than substance, even in interpreting Articles that on their face appear to be primarily about substance. Thus in a case brought by people with mild intellectual disabilities, the Court held that, 'whilst Article 8 contains no explicit procedural requirements, the decision-making process leading to measures of interference must be fair and such as to afford due respect to the interests safeguarded by Article 8'.[36]

---

[30] Explanatory Memorandum to Recommendation No. R(99)4, para. 67.
[31] Recommendation No. R(99)4, Principle 19(2).
[32] Explanatory Memorandum to Recommendation No. R(99)4, para. 67. For a further discussion of right to property in chapter 7 on "participation in society".
[33] Recommendation No. R(99)4, Principle 2(7).
[34] Recommendation No. R(99)4, Principle 2(6).
[35] Recommendation No. R(99)4, Principle 2(8).
[36] *Kutzner v. Germany*, Application No. 46544/99, judgment 26 February 2002, (2002) 35 EHRR 25., para. 56.

The ECHR Article most relevant in procedural matters is Article 6, the right to a fair trial. Article 6(1) states:

> In the determination of his civil rights and obligations or of any criminal charge against him, everyone is entitled to a fair and public hearing within a reasonable time by an independent and impartial tribunal established by law. Judgment shall be pronounced publicly but the press and public may be excluded from all or part of the trial in the interests of morals, public order or national security in a democratic society, where the interests of juveniles or the protection of the private life of the parties so require, or to the extent strictly necessary in the opinion of the court in special circumstances where publicity would prejudice the interests of justice.

Guardianship that affects someone's property rights falls within 'civil rights' and is thus afforded the protection of Article 6. In the earliest mental health case, *Winterwerp v. the Netherlands*,[37] Mr Winterwerp was detained in a psychiatric hospital. As a result of the detention, he was automatically deprived of his legal capacity to administer property. The European Court of Human Rights examined this aspect of the case under Article 6, stating:

> The capacity to deal personally with one's property involves the exercise of private rights and hence affects "civil rights and obligations" within the meaning of Article 6 para. 1 [. . .]. Divesting Mr. Winterwerp of that capacity amounted to a "determination" of such rights and obligations.[38]

The Court went on to point out that '[w]hatever the justification for depriving a person of unsound mind of the capacity to administer his property, the guarantees laid down in Article 6 para. 1 (art. 6-1) must nevertheless be respected'.[39] In the case of *Matter v. Slovakia*, decided twenty years after *Winterwerp*, the Court re-stated its position:

> The purpose of the proceedings is to determine whether or not legal capacity can be restored to the applicant, i.e. whether or not he is entitled, through his own acts, to acquire rights and undertake obligations set out, *inter alia*, in the Civil Code. Their outcome is therefore directly decisive for the determination of the applicant's "civil rights and obligations". Accordingly, Article 6 § 1 is applicable.[40]

The scope of Article 6 is not restricted to decisions regarding property, however, but applies to the determination of civil rights generally. The right to sick pay at work,[41] the right to receive disability living allowance,[42] and the right to register an association,[43] for example, have been found by the Court to be 'civil rights' and therefore to engage Arti-

---

[37] *Winterwerp v. the Netherlands*, Application No. 6301/73, judgment 24 October 1979, (A/33) (1979) 2 EHRR 387. *Winterwerp* is discussed in detail in chapter 2, above.

[38] *Winterwerp v. the Netherlands, op. cit.*, para. 73.

[39] *Winterwerp v. the Netherlands, op. cit.*, para. 75.

[40] *Matter v. Slovakia*, Application No. 31534/96, judgment 5 July 1999, (2001) 31 EHRR 32, para. 51.

[41] *Feldbrugge v. the Netherlands*, Application No. 8562/79, judgment 29 May 1986, (A/99) (1986) 8 EHRR 425.

[42] *Salesi v. Italy*, Application No. 13023/87, judgment 26 February 1993, (A/257–E) (1998) 26 EHRR 187.

cle 6. The right to liberty has also been held by the ECtHR to be a 'civil right' under Article 6,[44] suggesting that the Court may be prepared to ensure a wide reading of the term. In that event, it is likely that the right to consent to treatment and the right to make other personal decisions may well be within the scope of Article 6, and a court hearing would be available to challenge the restriction of any restriction on those rights.

Recommendation No. R(99)4 states that there should be 'fair and efficient procedures for the taking of measures for the protection of incapable adults'.[45] The Recommendation continues that there 'should be adequate procedural safeguards to protect the human rights of the persons concerned and to prevent possible abuses,'[46] with the Explanatory Memorandum warning that:

> It is necessary to be on guard against the danger that a change to welfare terminology will conceal the essential nature of what is being done. A measure which is called a measure of protection or assistance may in reality be an infringement of rights and freedoms from the point of view of the adult concerned.[47]

The Court has echoed this approach, although not yet in a guardianship context. In cases concerning paternity, for example, the Court has been careful to articulate that 'particular diligence is required in cases concerning civil status and capacity'.[48]

In this chapter typical guardianship proceedings will be examined in as near chronological order as is possible, and some suggestions will be made as to how the Court may deal with these issues in future cases. During domestic court proceedings at which a person's legal capacity is in question, a number of issues may arise, namely: notification about the hearing, expert evidence, right to be heard in person, entitlement to test the evidence, legal representation and its quality, access to court and medical file, and appeal rights. These issues will be taken in turn.

Sufficient notice

The person whose capacity is in question must obviously be informed of the proceedings, and be given a reasonable time to prepare a case. Recommendation No. R(99)4 specifies:

> The person concerned should be informed promptly in a language, or by other means, which he or she understands of the institution of proceedings which could affect his or her legal capacity, the exercise of his or her rights or his or her interests unless such information would be manifestly without meaning to the person concerned or would present a severe danger to the health of the person concerned.[49]

---

[43] *APEH Üldözötteinek Szövetsége and others v. Hungary*, Application No. 32367/96, judgment 5 October 2000, (2002) 34 EHRR 34.
[44] *Aerts v. Belgium*, Application No. 25357/94, judgment 29 June 1998, (1998) 29 EHRR 50, para. 59.
[45] Recommendation No. R(99)4, Principle 5(1).
[46] Recommendation No. R(99)4, Principle 7(2).
[47] Explanatory Memorandum to Recommendation No. R(99)4, para. 48.
[48] *Szarapo v. Poland*, Application No. 40835/98, judgment 23 May 2002, para. 40.
[49] Recommendation No. R(99)4, Principle 11(2).

It is not clear why the 'manifestly without meaning' provision was included, as there appears to be no disadvantage to anyone to provide information in *all* situations. It is difficult to imagine a situation where someone's health would be put in 'severe danger' on being told about an incapacity procedure.

Any procedure in which civil rights are determined without hearing the parties is plainly in violation of Article 6(1). In the criminal law context, the Court has held that a person can waive his or her rights to be present at the court hearing only if sufficient notice has been served, and such a desire not to be present has unequivocally been made.[50] Such safeguards are not always provided in guardianship proceedings. In some countries it sometimes happens that the entire proceedings in which a person is deprived of their legal capacity without notifying or involving the person in question.[51]

Incapacity assessment

If the State is under a positive obligation to provide assistance in decision making where a person lacks capacity to make that particular decision, then it would seem logical that the package of positive obligations should contain a right to have one's capacity assessed. There has been no case law on this point. Recommendation No. R(99)4 advises that the list of those entitled to institute guardianship proceedings (or other measures) should be sufficiently wide to ensure that measures of protection can be considered in all cases where they are necessary.[52] Carers (such as family members) may be in good position to apply for an incapacity assessment in order to instigate legal protection. However, as ECHR cases have illustrated, family members may sometimes have ulterior motives for instigating guardianship proceedings.[53] A court therefore needs to carry out a rigorous assessment as to the need for an adult's decision-making rights to be limited or removed altogether, and not make assumptions based on diagnoses. There is an argument that the adult's lawyer or at least an independent person, should be present during the incapacity assessment itself, as an extra safeguard against abuse.

The more common issue is that during the course of incapacity/guardianship the adult's capacity is assessed without that person's consent. In such circumstances there is a tension between respecting the person's right to privacy (and therefore right to assistance *if* the person lacks capacity), and another aspect of the person's right to privacy (in terms of unnecessary psychiatric and other examinations).

---

[50] See *Poitrimol v. France*, Application No. 14032/88, judgment 26 October 1993, (1993) 6 EHRR 516, (para. 31).
[51] The Mental Disability Advocacy Center, to which the authors are connected, is currently litigating cases from Bulgaria, Czech Republic, Estonia and Russia at the European Court of Human Rights where the applicant has been placed under guardianship without having been notified of the proceedings.
[52] Recommendation No. R(99)4, Principle 11(1).
[53] See, for example, *Bock v. Germany*, Application No. 11118/84, judgment 21 February 1989, (1987) 9 EHRR CD562 [*sub nom A. v. Germany*].

Various aspects of the incapacity assessment may engage the Convention. For example, the expert's independence from the parties could be brought into question if there is any collusion, or if the family member pays for the assessment. The expert must be, in the words of Recommendation No. R(99)4, 'suitably qualified',[54] which probably means a psychiatrist or psychologist.[55] Interestingly, a UN document from 1971 specifies that the incapacity assessment should include an evaluation of the 'social capability' of the person in question.[56] The expert must provide a report within a reasonable period of time.[57]

In the case of *Bock v. Germany*,[58] on the face of it a length of time case, the applicant's wife insisted during protracted divorce proceedings, that he lacked the capacity to conduct legal proceedings. Over a period of six years the applicant underwent a total of five psychiatric examinations resulting in two failed attempts by the wife to have the husband placed under guardianship. In examining length of time issues under Article 6 of the Convention, the Court said that, 'there was not so much a lack of judicial activity as an excessive amount of activity which focused on the petitioner's mental state.' The Court went on to say that despite the protracted legal proceedings, 'doubts still persisted in the national courts as to his soundness of mind, although, by the time of the final divorce judgment, there was a total of five reports attesting Mr Bock's soundness of mind [. . .] Finally, the Court cannot disregard the personal situation of the applicant who, for some nine years, suffered by reason of the doubts cast on the state of his mental health which subsequently proved unfounded. This represented a serious encroachment on human dignity'.[59] The Court (perhaps because it was not raised by the parties) did not consider whether this encroachment constituted a violation of Article 8.

Two Polish cases illustrate the Court's approach to forced psychiatric evaluations. In the first case, decided in 2002, *Nowicka v. Poland*,[60] the applicant had been detained on several occasions for a total period of eighty-three days and was imposed in the context of a private prosecution arising out of a neighbours' dispute. The Court found that even though the detention was 'lawful' under Article 5(1)(b) following a court order, any deprivation of liberty should be consistent with the purpose of Article 5, namely to protect individuals from arbitrariness. It went on to hold that a balance must be struck between the fulfilment of a court order and a person's right to liberty. The Court found that the balance had not been struck and found a violation of Article 5.

---

[54] Recommendation No. R(99)4, Principle 12(2).
[55] This could itself be an area of challenge by a lawyer or the adult him/herself. In some countries there are questions to be asked as to the training which psychiatrists receive in assessing incapacity.
[56] 'Declaration on the Rights of Mentally Retarded Persons', Proclaimed by General Assembly resolution 2856 (XXVI) of 20 December 1971, para. 7.
[57] *Martins Moreira v. Portugal*, Application No. 11371/85, judgment 7 October 1988, (1991) EHRR 517.
[58] Application No. 11118/84, judgment 21 February 1989. See also the Commission Report, 13 November 1987.
[59] *Bock v. Germany, op. cit.*, para. 48.
[60] Application No. 30218/96, judgment 3 December 2002, [2003] 1 FLR 417.

The case of *Worwa v. Poland*, decided in 2003, was again not a guardianship case, but one in which the district court had, at very short intervals, ordered medical reports on the applicant's mental state in connection with a number of similar criminal cases pending before it. The ECtHR found that these constituted interference by a public authority in her private life, within the meaning of Article 8(1) of the Convention, and that that interference was in accordance with the law. The Court went on to find a violation of Article 8, because the domestic court did not strike a fair balance between the rights of the individual's right to respect for private life, and the concern to ensure the proper administration of justice, and therefore that interference with the applicant's private life was unjustified.[61]

The Court has recently for the first time referred authoritatively to Recommendation R(99)4 in the case of *H.F. v. Slovakia*.[62] In this case the applicant had been deprived of her legal capacity in November 1997 by the Bratislava District Court based on a psychiatric report of July 1996 and statements from the applicant's former husband and witnesses he had called. The applicant was given no opportunity to give evidence to the district court. The European Court of Human Rights considered that the psychiatric report could not be regarded as 'up-to-date' as per Recommendation No. R(99)4, which speaks of 'at least' one qualified expert.[63] The Court noted that a second psychiatric expert should have been instructed to report. This was not only in the interests of the applicant, whose mental condition was liable to evolve with treatment, but also in the interests of the truth, which the district court had an obligation to establish. In finding a violation of Article 6 of the Convention, the Court stated that a further report would have enabled the district court to establish more effectively whether the psychiatrist's recommendation in 1996 that it should not hear evidence from the applicant remained valid at the date of its decision.

In summary, forced psychiatric examinations have been found by the Court in different cases to violate Articles 5, 6 and 8 of the Convention. State authorities must carefully balance external interests with the fundamental rights guaranteed in the Convention.

Right to be heard in person

Recommendation No. R(99)4 states that '[t]he person concerned should have the right to be heard in person in any proceedings which could affect his or her legal capacity'.[64] Phrased in this way, the person is entitled to be heard not just in the trial itself, but in administrative proceedings leading up to the trial, as well as case management hearings. The Recommendation also advises that the judge should personally see the adult or be satisfied as to the adult's condition.[65] It sometimes happens that that the person whose

---

[61] Application No. 26624/95, judgment 23 November 2003.
[62] Application No. 54797/00, judgment 8 November 2005.
[63] Recommendation No. R(99)4, Principle 12(2).
[64] Recommendation No. R(99)4, Principle 13.
[65] Recommendation No. R(99)4, Principle 12(2).

capacity is in question does not attend court because the psychiatrist author of the report on capacity has additionally recommended that the person is 'too mentally ill' to attend court. This situation creates a conflict of interests because the person supporting the application for deprivation of legal capacity is also asking the court not to see the person in question. It is a Convention right under Article 6 to attend proceedings concerning one's civil rights, and the judge is put in the impossible position of relying only on one side of the story, without hearing from the very person whose rights are in question. In these circumstances, it is our view that the judge should hold the court procedure at the hospital or institution in which the person whose capacity in question is being cared for. The judge should insist on seeing and speaking with the person, however 'mentally ill' the person is reported to be.

Adequacy of evidence

Related to the question about the adult attending the court hearing is the quality of evidence of the application. In the *H.F. v. Slovakia* case referred to above,[66] the district court deprived Mrs H.F. from her legal capacity in a court hearing at which she did not give evidence. Instead, the district court relied on a psychiatric report written one and a half years previous, and on statements by the applicant's former husband and witnesses he had called. These and other procedural defects led the European Court of Human Rights to find a violation of Article 6(1) of the Convention. It is to be expected that future cases will challenge flimsy evidence supporting incapacity applications. In such cases the Court may import guarantees now well established under Article 5 into the Article 6 guardianship arena. Such basic safeguards may include fresh medical evidence,[67] written by a qualified person,[68] and the basic fair trial guarantee that evidence should be served on the person enough in advance of the court hearing for that person to instruct alternative experts, if required. It bears repeating that these guarantees are so low to make the 'rights' almost meaningless: as was discussed in chapter 2 on detention, the Court must be prepared to set some standards in substantive issues.[69]

Experts' reports should be in written form,[70] and the expert should give oral evidence at the incapacity hearing so that the adult in question and his/her lawyer as well as the judge can cross-examine the expert and challenge the opinions put forward. Any reports from experts instructed by or on behalf of the person whose capacity is in question should be considered by the court in the same way as other expert reports.[71]

---

[66] *H.F. v. Slovakia*, Application No. 54797/00, judgment 8 November 2005.
[67] See *Varbanov v. Bulgaria*, Application No. 31365/96, judgment 5 October 2000, (1998) 25 EHRR CD154 [*sub nom D.V. v. Bulgaria*].
[68] *Winterwerp .v the Netherlands, op. cit.*
[69] The World Health Organization's *International Classification of Functioning, Disability and Health* moves away from a reliance on diagnosis and provides a helpful guide to psychologists, psychiatrists, lawyers and judges involved in guardianship proceedings.
[70] Explanatory Memorandum to Recommendation No. R(99)4, para. 54.
[71] In an analogous case of *Kutzner v. Germany* (see right to family life section in chapter 7 on participation

Disclosure of documents

The person whose capacity is in question and that person's lawyer must have access to documents held by the other party and by the court, such as the application by the family member or local government, expert psychiatric or psychological opinions and medical records. In civil proceedings a party is entitled to documentation in the possession of the State if this is relevant to the civil claim. This requirement is consistent with the Article 6(1) case-law in which the Court has stated:

> [T]he principle of equality of arms is only one feature of the wider concept of a fair trial, which also includes the fundamental right that proceedings should be adversarial. [. . .] The right to an adversarial trial means the opportunity for the parties to have knowledge of and comment on the observations filed or evidence adduced by the other party.[72]

Courts which hear incapacity and guardianship cases must therefore ensure that the adults in question and their lawyers are given full disclosure of all documentation upon which the application is based.

Legal representation

There have been no cases directly concerning legal representation during incapacity procedures, but as was discussed in chapter 2 above, in the context of detention hearings the Court has stated that '[s]pecial procedural safeguards may prove called for in order to protect the interests of persons who, on account of their mental disabilities, are not fully capable of acting for themselves'.[73] The same must be true of incapacity and guardianship procedures.

During incapacity court hearings, if the very allegation made by the opposing party is that the adult in question cannot manage his or her affairs to the extent that the adult's very legal capacity is in doubt, then it follows, given the gravity of issues to be decided, that such a person be represented by a qualified lawyer. The necessity of good quality legal representation is even more strong when one considers (a) that in every such case there are expert witnesses, (b) that such a case will often have serious consequences for the person affecting many aspects of the person's civil, political, economic, social and cultural rights, and (c) that the person's mental health will undoubtedly be centre stage. It would be difficult for a government to muster arguments to suggest that Article 6 does not mandate legal representation in court proceedings concerning legal capacity. The arguments discussed regarding representation in challenges to deprivation of liberty under Article 5(4) apply *mutatis mutandis*.[74]

---

in society), the Court said that reports could not be disregarded simply because the experts were acting privately.

[72] *Ruiz-Mateos v. Spain*, Application No. 12952/87, judgment 23 June 1993, (A/262) (1993) 16 EHRR 505, para. 63.

[73] *Megyeri v. Germany*, Application No. 13770/88, judgment 10 November 1992, (1992) 15 EHRR 584, para. 22.

[74] See further chapters 2 and 9.

This position is enshrined in international law via Principle 6 of the UN Resolution 46/119 on the Protection of Persons with Mental Illness and the Improvement of Mental Health Care:

> The person whose capacity is at issue shall be entitled to be represented by a counsel. If the person whose capacity is at issue does not himself or herself secure such representation, it shall be made available without payment by that person to the extent that he or she does not have sufficient means to pay for it. The counsel shall not in the same proceedings represent a mental health facility or its personnel and shall not also represent a member of the family of the person whose capacity is at issue unless the tribunal is satisfied that there is no conflict of interest.[75]

The one ECHR case which touches on legal representation is again *H.F. v. Slovakia*, in which the European Court of Human Rights noted that the Slovak Code of Civil Procedure required the courts to appoint a guardian to act on behalf of those whose legal capacity was at issue, even if the person was assisted by a lawyer. In this case it appeared that the applicant had not been represented by a guardian in the district court and had only been represented in a formal way on appeal. Referring to Recommendation R(99)4, the ECtHR accepted the applicant's submission that the purpose of the appointment of a guardian had not been fulfilled in her case.[76]

Where legal representation *is* provided, where does the State's responsibility end? In general, where the State provides for legal representation, it must of course be adequate because the Convention is intended to guarantee not rights that are theoretical or illusory but rights that are practical and effective.[77] In the chapter on detention (chapter 2 above), we discussed adequacy of counsel issues and made the point that Article 6 guarantees have been drawn by the Court into Article 5(4) jurisprudence. In the context of incapacity hearings of course, Article 6 is directly applicable.

---

[75] See Principle 6 of the MI Principles, adopted by the General Assembly on 17 December 1991. Similarly, the World Health Organization adopts this position: '[i]deally, a legal counsel should routinely be made available to a person whose competence is in question. Where a person is unable to afford a counsel, legislation may require that counsel be provided to the beneficiary free of charge'. The WHO adds that '[l]egislation should ensure there is no conflict of interest for the counsel. That is, the counsel representing the concerned person should not also be representing other interested parties, such as the clinical services involved in the care of the concerned person and/or the family members of the concerned person.'

[76] See also a curious admissibility decision by the (now defunct) European Commission of Human Rights in the case of *Bocsi v. Hungary*, Application No. 24240/94, admissibility decision 21 May 1998. In this case the Commission considered an application by a woman who was deprived of her legal capacity and who complained about the lack of legal representation at the Supreme Court relating to her incapacity case. Recalling the general right to legal representation for people who do not have the capacity to conduct litigation themselves, the Commission stated that 'a refusal to appoint a guardian to a person not able to litigate in connection with a case which has no prospect of success does not interfere with the right, in civil cases, of access to court'. In its decision the Commission went on to explain that the applicant, 'whose action had been based on the very claim that her mental state no longer required her to be placed under guardianship, could reasonably be expected to arrange for her representation before the Supreme Court. Her submissions do not, therefore, disclose any appearance of a breach of her right of access to court, as enshrined in Article 6 para. 1 [. . .] of the Convention'.

[77] *Belgian Linguistic case*, Application Nos. 1474/62, 1677/62, 1691/62, 1769/63, 1994/63 and 2126/64, judgment 23 July 1968, para. 31.

In criminal cases, the Court has said in the context of Article 6 that the State has an ongoing duty to ensure adequate representation:

> Mere nomination does not ensure effective assistance since the lawyer appointed for legal aid purposes may die, fall seriously ill, be prevented for a protracted period from acting or shirk his duties. If they are notified of the situation, the authorities must either replace him or cause him to fulfil his obligations.[78]

As a matter of logic, if the State could meet Article 6 guarantees merely by nominating or appointing a lawyer, in many instances free legal assistance would prove to be worthless.[79] For a practical guide to representing people with mental disabilities, including in guardianship proceedings, see appendix 7 of this volume.

Appeal rights

Article 6(1) does not guarantee appeals from a court of first instance. However, where domestic law allows for an appeal, the appeal process is subject to the guarantees of Article 6. Recommendation No. R(99)4 states that there should be a right to an adequate appeal.[80] The UN Resolution on the Protection of Persons with Mental Illness and the Improvement of Mental Health Care goes further by specifying who should have the standing to appeal: 'The person whose capacity is at issue, his or her personal representative, if any, and any other interested person shall have the right to appeal to a higher court against any such decision.'[81]

The fact that there may be no appeals available in domestic law should not prevent a thorough examination of the proceedings for any aspects that may not comply with the Convention. In these circumstances of course, the person affected has a right to remedies under Article 13 of the European Convention on Human Rights, and such complaints should be lodged with the relevant domestic authorities and courts and a case lodged at the European Court of Human Rights (see chapter 8 below on applying to the ECtHR). In the case of *Delcourt v. Belgium* the Court re-stated that Article 6(1) of the Convention does not compel countries to set up courts of appeal, but went on to say that '[n]evertheless, a State which does institute such courts is required to ensure that persons amenable to the law shall enjoy before these courts the fundamental guarantees contained in Article 6'.[82]

---

[78] *Artico v. Italy*, Application No. 6694/74, judgment 13 May 1980, (A/37) (1981) 3 EHRR 1, para. 33.

[79] See chapter 2 above on detention, and chapter 9 on legal representation, as well as appendix 7 of this volume. See also Mental Disability Advocacy Centre, *Liberty Denied: Human Rights Violations in Criminal Psychiatric Detention Reviews in Hungary*, (Budapest: MDAC, 2004).

[80] Recommendation No. R(99)4, Principle 14(3). See also 'Declaration on the Rights of Mentally Retarded Persons, Proclaimed by the UN General Assembly resolution 2856 (XXVI) of 20 December 1971, para. 7.

[81] Principle 1(6) UN Resolution 46/119 on the Protection of Persons with Mental Illness and the Improvement of Mental Health Care, adopted by the General Assembly on 17 December 1991.

[82] *Delcourt v. Belgium*, Application No. 2689/65, judgment 17 January 1970, (1979–80) 1 EHRR 355 para. 25.

Such guarantees are important because in some countries the person under guardianship lacks legal standing (legal ability) to appeal the court decision depriving him or her of legal capacity. It would not meet the spirit of *Delcourt v. Belgium* if an individual was denied access to legal remedies, precisely because they had been deprived of their rights by the judgment he or she wished to appeal.

It is similarly important that other people are entitled under domestic legislation to challenge a decision to deprive a person of legal capacity, because the adult may not have the capacity to know that there have been procedural or other violations or how to go about challenging the decision.

Length of proceedings

The Court examined length of guardianship proceedings in *Matter v. Slovakia*. The proceedings relating to the decision to deprive the applicant of his legal capacity began in 1987 and were still pending at the time of the Court's judgment, over seven years since the former Czech and Slovak Federal Republic ratified the Convention and recognised the right of individual petition in March 1992. The Court noted that the case's complexity did not justify its length, and went on to identify periods of inactivity for which no satisfactory explanation had been provided by the Government. The Court found that the domestic courts had failed to act with the special diligence required by Article 6(1) in cases of this nature. This, 'and having regard to what was at stake for the applicant',[83] the Court found a violation of Article 6 of the Convention.

Choosing a guardian

Recommendation No. R(99)4 suggests that the paramount consideration when choosing a guardian should be the suitability of that person to safeguard and promote the 'interests and welfare' of the adult lacking capacity.[84] The Recommendation says that 'the wishes of the adult as to the choice of any person to represent or assist him or her should be taken into account and, as far as possible, given due respect'[85] The Explanatory Memorandum to the Recommendation warns wisely, that whilst the invaluable and irreplaceable role of relatives must be recognised and valued, the law must watch out for unscrupulous family members.[86]

It follows that the law needs to have mechanisms for such issues to be dealt with in a manner compliant with the ECHR. It could be argued that there is a right under Article 8 of the Convention that the person whose personal decisions are being made by someone else should have an opportunity in deciding who that person should be. The

---

[83] *Matter v. Slovakia*, Application No. 31534/96, judgment 5 July 1999, (2001) 31 EHRR 32, para. 61.
[84] Recommendation No. R(99)4, Principle 8(2).
[85] Recommendation No. R(99)4, Principle 9(2).
[86] Explanatory Memorandum to Recommendation No. R(99)4, para. 44.

case of *J.T. v. the United Kingdom*,[87] illustrates a similar point. In the case, the applicant had a history of mental disability and had a difficult relationship with her mother, her closest relative. The difficult relationship arose in part to alleged sexual abuse by the applicant's stepfather. Under English law, the mother as the nearest relative had a variety of rights related to her detention in a psychiatric hospital, and the applicant did not want her mother to be given any information about her whereabouts, nor did she want her mother to be involved in any subsequent decisions relating to her care and treatment in hospital. At the level of the European Court of Human Rights the case reached a friendly settlement under Articles 37–39 of the Convention on an undertaking by the British government that the relevant law would be amended to allow a more flexible approach to appointing the nearest relative.[88]

Alternatively, a family member may have an argument that they should be the guardian, because of their rights under Article 8 of the Convention (right to private and family life). This remains untested at the European Court of Human Rights, but a coherent argument could be made that family members should be allowed to care for each other, unless there is a strong reason to the contrary. However, rights under Article 8 are not absolute and evidence that guardianship by a specific family member would put the health or rights of the person with mental disability at risk, for example, would justify the refusal to appoint that person as guardian.

Contesting decisions made by a guardian

Recommendation No. R(99)4 advises that 'in implementing a measure of protection for an incapable adult the interests and welfare of that person should be the paramount consideration'.[89] The Recommendation goes on to say that '[i]n establishing or implementing a measure of protection for an incapable adult the past and present wishes and feelings of the adult should be ascertained so far as possible, and should be taken into account and given due respect'.[90] Similar to standards of proxy or supported decision making in the treatment context (see chapter 4), the person representing or assisting an adult should give that person adequate information, whenever this is possible and appropriate so that he or she may express a view.[91] If the adult is unable to give his or her views about the proposed decision,[92] the guardian is obliged 'so far as reasonable and practicable' to consult with people who have a close interest in the welfare of the adult concerned.[93]

---

[87]   Application 26494/95, judgment 30 March 2000, (2000) 30 EHRR CD77, [2000] 1 FLR 909. See also the more detailed decision of the European Commission on Human Rights, (1997) 23 EHRR CD81.

[88]   In fact, the English law was not amended with reasonable dispatch, and the English courts ruled the relevant provision in violation of Article 8: *R (M) v. Secretary of State for Health* [2003] E.W.H.C. 1094.

[89]   Recommendation No. R(99)4, Principle 8(1).

[90]   Recommendation No. R(99)4, Principle 9(1).

[91]   Recommendation No. R(99)4, Principle 9(3).

[92]   Naturally, whether someone is or is not able to give views about a particular situation may in many cases depend on the skill of the person explaining the different options.

[93]   Recommendation No. R(99)4, Principle 10.

The Explanatory Memorandum to Recommendation No. R(99)4 explains the background debate around these issues. When a person makes a decision on behalf of someone who does not have capacity to make that decision, the decision-maker can either act on the basis of the person's pre-expressed withes (if the person had them and they are known) or make a substituted judgment based on knowledge of the person's wishes, values and beliefs, or as a last resort, make a decision based on the person's 'best interests'.

When the decision-maker wants to make a decision which runs contrary to the adult's known prior wishes, the question arises as to whose opinion should be respected: the person lacking legal capacity or the person with the legal authority to decide. The Explanatory Memorandum advises that when the choice is between the interests of the adult and the interests of other people and when the adult has no known wishes on the matter, it is reasonable to regard the interests of the adult as the paramount consideration. However, when the choice is between the current interests of the adult and the prior wishes of the adult, the Explanatory Memorandum suggests that it would be acceptable not necessarily to respect the prior wishes of the adult, but rather for the decision-maker to pay 'due respect' to the past and present wishes and feelings of the adult, insofar as they can be ascertained. In human rights terms, this probably means that the decision-maker (guardian) when making these difficult decisions should document the method of how a decision was made, with reasons why a particular option has been preferred.

If any of these recommended procedures have not been followed, the adult may have reason to complain using European Convention on Human Rights arguments. Each case will turn on its own facts, and issues such as the seriousness of the decision in question, or the length of time a person has been legally incapacitated, will have a bearing on the case. In some countries, the greatest hurdle for a person who would like to challenge bad performance by a guardian may be how to get the case to court in the first place – again access to justice issues to which we return in the Conclusion chapter. The situation is complicated even more where clear conflict of interest issues arise from the fact that the guardian is also the director of the residential institution where the person is living. The lack of standing is an issue to which we will return in appendix 7 on representing people with mental disabilities.

A crucial issue relevant in litigating against a guardian's poor performance is whether there are adequate control mechanisms monitoring the acts and omissions of guardians.[94] An active guardianship office at the local government may have such a responsibility of supervising and controlling guardians, and will be responsive to letters by (or on behalf of) the person under guardianship. Such a body may well displace (remove) the guardian and appoint a more suitable person. However, experience in many countries is that such guardianship offices are in some cases unwilling to intervene, and remain content with a guardian neglecting and abusing the adult in question. Alternatively the guardianship office may have no adequate procedures in place to ensure that a person under guardian-

---

[94]   Recommendation No. R(99)4, Principle 16.

ship has the means to lodge a complaint. Further, the guardianship office may have established no effective procedure for regular oversight of a guardian's performance.

If the guardianship office becomes aware that the guardian is not doing the job adequately, a new guardian must be appointed. Recommendation No. R(99)4 specifies that there should be a pool of 'suitably qualified persons for the representation and assistance of incapable adults'[95] who should be adequately trained.[96] The guardianship office should also have powers to challenge guardians in court where there are serious allegations of abuse or malpractice. Recommendation No. R(99)4 states that guardians 'should be liable, in accordance with national law, for any loss or damage caused by them to incapable adults while exercising their functions. [. . .] In particular, the laws on liability for wrongful acts, negligence or maltreatment should apply to representatives and others involved in the affairs of incapable adults'.[97] Under the Convention it is still questionable whether such abuse by private guardians can be litigated at the ECtHR because the Convention protects against abuses by State agents. However, the wording of the Recommendation supports an argument that there is a positive duty on the State under Articles 1 and 13 of the Convention to create accessible mechanisms for people to seek remedies for loss or damage caused by guardians.

Delay in appointing guardian

In some countries a person is deprived by a court of his or her legal capacity but there is a delay of several months before a guardian is appointed.[98] This situation could be challenged under Article 8 of the ECHR, because a court has found that a person needs to be assisted in order to protect the person's rights, but the State (normally a local authority) has not fulfilled its obligations to secure that person such assistance. It could be argued that this constitutes an interference with the person's private life.

Periodic Review of Guardianship

A problematic feature of many guardianship systems in Member States of the Council of Europe is that determinations of legal incapacity are not subject to periodic review. Recommendation No. R(99)4 states in Principle 14:

1. Measures of protection should, whenever possible and appropriate, be of limited duration. Consideration should be given to the institution of periodical reviews.

---

[95]   Recommendation No. R(99)4, Principle 17(1).
[96]   Recommendation No. R(99)4, Principle 17(2).
[97]   Recommendation No. R(99)4, Principle 20.
[98]   Mental Disability Advocacy Centre, report on Bulgaria, (Budapest: MDAC, forthcoming, 2006).

2. Measures of protection should be reviewed on a change of circumstances and, in particular, on a change in the adult's condition. They should be terminated if the conditions for them are no longer fulfilled.[99]

The Explanatory Memorandum to Recommendation No. R(99)4 emphasises that an indefinite incapacity order should be the exception, and this should happen only in cases where the individual has a condition, such as senile dementia or Alzheimer's disease, for which currently there is no cure and, save small periods of lucidity, the person's condition will unfortunately worsen. The wording of Recommendation No. R(99)4 on periodic review is surprisingly weak given other parts of the Recommendation such as Principle 6(2) which speaks of minimal measures of protection consistent with achieving the purpose of the intervention. Given that many people's capacity fluctuates throughout the person's lifetime, the logical legal response is one which is proportionate, and therefore the necessity of the legal measure must be regularly reviewed. The Explanatory Memorandum states that the person whose legal capacity has been deprived 'should be entitled to demand a review'.[100]

The Court agreed with this approach in the case of *Matter v. Slovakia*,[101] discussed above, in which the applicant had been deprived of his legal capacity for over seven years, notably described by the Court as 'a serious interference with his rights under Article 8 § 1'.[102] In the Court's view, 'it may be appropriate in cases of this kind that the domestic authorities establish after a certain lapse of time whether such a measure continues to be justified. Such a re-examination is particularly justified if the person concerned so requests'.[103]

Having found that forced examination in a psychiatric hospital engaged Article 8(1) of the Convention in the *Matter* case, the Court examined whether this interference with private life was justified under Article 8(2). In the domestic proceedings the district court – as it had been instructed by the Supreme Court – had sought to obtain an expert opinion on the applicant's mental health. The medical expert tried to examine the applicant on a voluntary basis which the applicant refused. The district court invited the applicant twice to submit to the examination in the psychiatric hospital and warned him that if he did not comply he could be forcibly brought there. The applicant failed to comply again and the district court ordered that the applicant be brought to the hospital. The

---

[99] Recommendation No. R(99)4, Principle 14. See also Principle 1(6) of the UN Resolution 46/119 on the Protection of Persons with Mental Illness and the Improvement of Mental Health Care, adopted by the General Assembly on 17 December 1991: 'Decisions regarding capacity and the need for a personal representative shall be reviewed at reasonable intervals prescribed by domestic law.' See also the World Health Organization (2005), *Resource Book on Mental Health, Human Rights and Legislation* which states at page 41, section 7.3 that '[l]egislation should contain a provision for automatic review, at specified periodic intervals, of the finding of lack of competence'.

[100] Explanatory Memorandum to Recommendation No. R(99)4, para. 56.

[101] *Matter v. Slovakia*, Application No. 31534/96, judgment 5 July 1999, (2001) 31 EHRR 32.

[102] *Matter v. Slovakia, op. cit.*, para. 68.

[103] *Matter v. Slovakia, op. cit.*, para. 68.

applicant was indeed brought to the hospital on 19 August 1993 and he was discharged on 2 September 1993, when the examination was concluded. The European Court of Human Rights decided that the interference in question was not disproportionate to the legitimate aims pursued. It was therefore 'necessary in a democratic society' within the meaning of Article 8(2) of the Convention and therefore found no violation of Article 8.[104]

This is a strange reasoning. Although the applicant himself had instigated a review of guardianship which probably requires some sort of expert evaluation, the Court could have found an Article 8 violation for at least two reasons. First, the ECtHR could have noted that the domestic court could have better balanced competing rights. The Court could have decided that protecting the applicant's right to liberty (he did not want to be detained in a psychiatric hospital for an evaluation) plus right to privacy (he did not want to undergo an evaluation at all) trumped the restriction of rights which would have resulted from forcing the applicant to go through with his request of reviewing the incapacity. There seems to be no evidence that the domestic authorities explained these options to the applicant. Second, the European Court of Human Rights did not specify any of the grounds under Article 8(2) on which it relied when finding that the interference with the applicant's private life was 'necessary in a democratic society'. Probably the Court had in mind that the interference was justified for the prevention of disorder or crime, for the protection of health or morals or for the protection of the rights and freedoms or others. It is difficult to see any plausible argument under any of these heads. Of additional curiosity is why this case was not examined under Article 5, where the Court could have found that the detention for forced incapacity examination did not meet the standards of detention of Article 5 (see the case of *Nowicka v. Poland*, discussed above in this chapter).

Concluding remarks

Legal incapacity and guardianship proceedings in many countries of the Council of Europe are problematic as they do not afford the adult in question procedural safeguards. Issues under Article 6 ECHR include imprecise legal definitions of incapacity, the appropriateness of a one-size-fits-all legal approach to capacity, and the availability of a range of legal (and non-legal) measures to protect people who lack capacity to make certain decisions at some points in the lives. Further procedural issues involve notice of guardianship proceedings, adequate incapacity examinations which do not equate diagnosis with incapacity, the appropriateness of forced psychiatric evaluations, the right to be heard in person during incapacity proceedings, the right to be represented by a lawyer who takes an active part in representing the adult, the adequacy of evidence presented to

---

[104] *Matter v. Slovakia, op. cit.*, paras. 71–2.

the court and the disclosure of documents to the adult and that person's lawyer in order to guarantee a fair trial. The right to appeal findings of incapacity, the right to have an opinion about who will exercise decision-making, and the right to effectively challenge the decisions a substitute decision-maker are also relevant. Further, a regular review of the necessity of the legal measure will also be increasingly relevant, especially for people with fluctuating mental disabilities. The Council of Europe Recommendation No. R(99)4 has started to assist the Court to give relevance to fair trial and privacy rights in the context of substitute decision-making and it is hoped that the Court will continue to cite the Recommendation and other international instruments with authority.

Some countries' civil codes and civil procedural codes will require significant re-writing to bring them in line with the basic guarantees set forth in the to Recommendation No. R(99)4 and given legal force by an increasing number of cases to the ECtHR. Ironically, given the extraordinarily huge numbers of people affected across Europe, the Court will not be flooded with applications. This has more to do with practical and legal difficulties by people under guardianship to bring cases in domestic courts and to the European Court. The Court is encouraged to use its pilot judgment procedure in appropriate guardianship cases in order to send clear signals to domestic authorities that legislative revisions are necessary in order to secure Convention compliance.

Chapter 7

Participation in Society

Introduction

To this point, this book has focussed on the classic Convention rights, such as the right to be free from detention, the right to protection from abuse and the right to standards of process in the determination of civil rights. It is these sorts of rights that were predominant in the minds of the framers of the ECHR, even if their application to people with mental disabilities was not. In this chapter, we turn instead to a diverse range of rights which are essential for a people to be recognised as members of and participants in broader civil society. The barriers to these rights stem from the same stereotypes about people with mental health problems or intellectual disabilities: that such people cannot make rational choices (and neither should they be allowed to exercise choices); that they are dangerous and unpredictable; that as children they are uneducable; that they should not reproduce; that they cannot be adequate parents; that they cannot and should not participate in political life; and that they need to be looked after, rather than being allowed to make decisions for themselves. Certainly, many people with mental disabilities have special and distinct needs – indeed, the recognition and meeting of those needs is often a prerequisite to the attainment of their rights – but the uncritical application of these stereotypes creates pervasive barriers to the participation in society of people with mental disabilities .

This chapter differs from others because it contains a series of diverse issues, each probably deserving its own chapter in future editions. In other chapters there has been a body of ECtHR jurisprudence upon which we have been able to argue by analogy; this chapter is more speculative and merely suggests the range of human rights consequences of being diagnosed with an intellectual disability or a mental health problem. The areas which are covered in this chapter are the right to community integration, right to education, right to property, right to vote, right to marry and found a family, right to associate and right to work.

Right to community integration

A basic element of human rights protection for persons with disabilities is the right to community integration. Indeed, a number of the rights which will be discussed later in the chapter, such as rights to education and to work, can be seen as integrally related to the broader right to community integration. A right to community integration encompasses the right to live in the community, rather than in a large, regimented and impersonal institution. Considerable progress has been made in much of Europe in introducing these community alternatives, but the progress is not universal. In Poland, for example, there are around 50,000 people with mental health problems and intellectual disabilities living in around 400 institutions.[1] Similar figures exist for a number of other countries, illustrating that a significant proportion of European citizens are socially excluded on the basis of their disabilities or perceived disabilities. Such institutionalisation can start from childhood and continue for the remainder of the individual's life. Challenging the most severe of the human rights violations that occur within these institutions has already been discussed, mainly in chapter 3. This section instead examines the degree to which the right to be free of such institutions may be recognised under the ECHR.

Certainly, there is ample evidence that the right to community integration is now perceived in human rights terms by the bodies of the United Nations, Council of Europe and European Union. The ECtHR is increasingly deciding cases by examining the respondent Government's international undertakings and interpreting the ECHR in the light of public international law, especially when the issue before the Court is new and contextual.[2] We therefore outline the international instruments and statements of intergovernmental bodies which are firmly embedding the right to community integration into public international law, and on which the Court may in future cases rely to aid its interpretation of Articles of the Convention.

The United Nations Mental Illness Principles provide that '[e]very person with a mental illness shall have the right to live and work, to the extent possible, in the com-

---

[1]   G. Freyhoff, et al., eds, *Included in Society, Results and Recommendations of the European Research Initiative on Community-Based Residential Alternatives for Disabled People* (Brussels: Inclusion Europe, Autism Europe, Mental Health Europe and the Open Society Mental Health Initiative, 2005).

[2]   See O. De Schutter, 'Reasonable Accommodations and Positive Obligations in the European Convention on Human Rights', in A. Lawson and C. Gooding (eds), *Disability Rights in Europe: from Theory to Practice*, (Oxford: Hart, 2005).

munity'.[3] Each person further has 'the right to be treated and cared for, as far as possible, in the community in which he or she lives'[4] and 'the right to be treated in the least restrictive environment and with the least restrictive or intrusive treatment appropriate to the patient's health needs and the need to protect the physical safety of others'.[5]

In a succinct description of the right to community integration, the UN Special Rapporteur on the Right to Health explains further:

> Deriving from the right to health and other human rights, the right to community integration has general application to all persons with mental disabilities. Community integration better supports their dignity, autonomy, equality and participation in society. It helps prevent institutionalization, which can render persons with mental disabilities vulnerable to human rights abuses and damage their health on account of the mental burdens of segregation and isolation. Community integration is also an important strategy in breaking down stigma and discrimination against persons with mental disabilities.[6]

The Special Rapporteur goes on to make the sometimes overly intimate link between legal incapacity (discussed in Chapter 6 above) and detention in institutions, namely that people in some countries are placed into institutions using the convenient system of legal incapacitation where the guardian is legally empowered to make all decisions, including those regarding housing.[7]

Within the Council of Europe itself, Recommendation Rec(2004)10 of the Committee of Ministers to member states concerning the protection of the human rights and dignity of persons with mental disorder states that people with mental disabilities 'should have the right to be cared for in the least restrictive environment available and with the least restrictive or intrusive treatment available, taking into account their health needs and the need to protect the safety of others'.[8] In 2005 all Council of Europe member States further pledged to 'develop community-based services to replace care in large institutions for those with severe mental health problems'.[9]

The Council of Europe's Commissioner for Human Rights has added that 'the development of effective support and community care services is to be encouraged as a

---

[3] UN Resolution 46/119 on the Protection of Persons with Mental Illness and the Improvement of Mental Health Care, adopted by the General Assembly on 17 December 1991, Principle 4, Life in the community, hereinafter 'UN Mental Illness Principles'.

[4] UN Mental Illness Principles, *op. cit.*, Principle 7, Role of community and culture.

[5] UN Mental Illness Principles, *op. cit.*, Principle 9, Treatment.

[6] Report of the UN Special Rapporteur on the right of everyone to the enjoyment of the highest attainable standard of physical and mental health, Paul Hunt, Report to the sixty-first session of the Commission for Human Rights, para. 85: 'Guardianship has been overused and abused in the medical, as well as other, contexts, including at the most extreme level to place persons with intellectual disabilities in psychiatric institutions. This is inappropriate medically and socially, and is inconsistent with the rights of persons with intellectual disabilities to health, autonomy, participation, non-discrimination and social inclusion.'

[7] Report of the UN Special Rapporteur on the right of everyone to the enjoyment of the highest attainable standard of physical and mental health, Paul Hunt, Report to the sixty-first session of the Commission for Human Rights, para. 79.

[8] Article 8 – Principle of least restriction.

[9] *Mental Health Declaration for Europe*, World Health Organization Ministerial Conference on Mental Health, Helsinki, January 2005, para. 10(xi).

preferable alternative to unnecessary prolonged institutionalisation'.[10] Similarly, the CPT Standards actively encourage the provision of community-based services and the reduction of institutional settings for people with mental disabilities.[11]

The Revised European Social Charter, the major Council of Europe treaty covering economic, social and cultural rights, contains the right for people with disabilities to 'the effective exercise of the right to independence, social integration and participation in the life of the community'.[12]

In 2006 the landmark Disability Action Plan was adopted by the political arm of the Council of Europe, the Committee of Ministers. The plan seeks to translate the aims of the Council of Europe with regard to human rights, non-discrimination, equal opportunities, full citizenship and participation of people with disabilities into a European policy framework on disability for the next decade. In this document, the Committee of Ministers calls on member States 'to ensure community-based quality service provision and alternative housing models, which enable a move from institution-based care to community living'.[13]

---

[10]   Conclusions of the Commissioner, Seminar organized by the Council of Europe Commissioner for Human Rights and hosted by the World Health Organization Regional Office for Europe, Copenhagen, Denmark 5–7 February 2003, para. 8.

[11]   CPT Standards, para. 58: 'The organisational structure of health-care services for persons with psychiatric disorders varies from country to country, and is certainly a matter for each State to determine. Nevertheless, the CPT wishes to draw attention to the tendency in a number of countries to reduce the number of beds in large psychiatric establishments and to develop community-based mental health units. The Committee considers this is a very favourable development, on condition that such units provide a satisfactory quality of care.

It is now widely accepted that large psychiatric establishments pose a significant risk of institutionalisation for both patients and staff, the more so if they are situated in isolated locations. This can have a detrimental effect on patient treatment. Care programmes drawing on the full range of psychiatric treatment are much easier to implement in small units located close to the main urban centres.'

[12]   European Social Charter (Revised), Strasbourg, 3 May 1996: Article 15 – The right of persons with disabilities to independence, social integration and participation in the life of the community: 'With a view to ensuring to persons with disabilities, irrespective of age and the nature and origin of their disabilities, the effective exercise of the right to independence, social integration and participation in the life of the community, the Parties undertake, in particular:

1.   to take the necessary measures to provide persons with disabilities with guidance, education and vocational training in the framework of general schemes wherever possible or, where this is not possible, through specialised bodies, public or private;
2.   to promote their access to employment through all measures tending to encourage employers to hire and keep in employment persons with disabilities in the ordinary working environment and to adjust the working conditions to the needs of the disabled or, where this is not possible by reason of the disability, by arranging for or creating sheltered employment according to the level of disability. In certain cases, such measures may require recourse to specialised placement and support services;
3.   to promote their full social integration and participation in the life of the community in particular through measures, including technical aids, aiming to overcome barriers to communication and mobility and enabling access to transport, housing, cultural activities and leisure.'

[13]   Recommendation R(2006)5 of the Council of Europe to member States on the Council of Europe Action Plan to promote the rights and full participation of people with disabilities in society: improving the quality of life of people with disabilities in Europe 2006–2015 (Adopted by the Committee of Ministers on 5 April 2006 at the 961st meeting of the Ministers' Deputies), para. 3.8.3(vi).

This is a substantial array of policy documents by intergovernmental bodies, unanimous in their position that the right to community integration is a human right. The question for the ECtHR will be whether to locate this right within the Convention, and if so, where. Convention jurisprudence is not developed in this area, and any analysis must to some degree be speculative.

As discussed in chapter 2, there have been attempts to argue that detention under Article 5 is arbitrary if it could be avoided by appropriate provision of community services.[14] The Court so far has declined to address that argument directly, but we noted in chapter 2 that the Court has not ruled out doing so in the future. The existing attempts to press for community services as an alternative to detention have concerned people who are already detained and seeking their release, but it is difficult to see that the Court could adopt a different standard of provision for people in the community wishing to avoid institutionalisation. Particularly when it is recalled that persons who lack capacity to decide whether or not to be admitted to an institution may still be deprived of their liberty under Article 5,[15] any ruling made by the Court might go a long way to establishing a right to community integration.

An attempt might also be made to read into the ECHR the principle that the individual has a right to be cared for in the least restrictive setting appropriate to his needs. This right to the 'least restrictive alternative' as it applies to people with mental disabilities is also well-established in international law. It was argued in chapter 3 that this principle might, possibly, be implied in Article 3. If this possibility is realised, it might go some way towards establishing a right to community integration, at least in cases where institutionalisation was not demonstrably necessary.

Alternatively, there might be some possibility in the rights contained in Article 2(1) of Protocol 4 to the ECHR, subject to the qualifications in Articles 2(3) and 2(4):

> 2(1) Everyone lawfully within the territory of a State shall, within that territory, have the right to liberty of movement and freedom to choose his own residence.
>
> [*   *   *]
>
> 2(3) No restriction shall be placed on the exercise of these rights other than such as are in accordance with law and are necessary in a democratic society in the interests of national security or public safety, for the maintenance of ordre public, for the prevention of crime, for the protection of health or morals, or for the protection of the rights and freedoms of others.
>
> 2(4) The rights set forth in paragraph 1 may also be subject, in particular areas, to restrictions imposed in accordance with law and justified by the public interest in a democratic society.

---

[14] See *Kolanis v. the United Kingdom*, Application No. 517/02, judgment 21 June 2005, (2006) 42 EHRR 12, and *Johnson v. the United Kingdom*, Application No. 22520/93, judgment 24 October 1997, (1997) 27 EHRR 296, both discussed in chapter 2.

[15] See *H.L. v. the United Kingdom*, Application No. 45508/99, judgment 5 October 2004, (2005) 40 EHRR 32, discussed in chapter 2.

Article 2(1) of Protocol 4 has attracted few cases of the ECtHR, decided on grounds not relevant for current purposes. The Court has held that 'liberty of movement prohibits any measure liable to infringe that right or to restrict the exercise thereof which does not satisfy the requirement of a measure which can be considered as "necessary in a democratic society" in the pursuit of the legitimate aims referred to in the third paragraph of the above-mentioned Article'.[16]

In the mental disability context, the Article would certainly seem to suggest that, subject to the qualifications in Paragraphs (3) and (4), an individual has a right to choose to live in the community rather than in an institution. That would not necessarily impose an obligation on the part of the State to provide funding or support services to make that choice practical. Nonetheless, this Article is subject to the positive obligations on the State contained in Article 1 of the Convention, to 'secure to everyone within their jurisdiction the rights and freedoms' of the ECHR. Such positive obligations are bound to imply costs, so the fact that the provision of community services would imply costs is not necessarily an objection (although the Court might find the scale of costs a matter of concern). Whether the ECtHR would, following the American case of *Olmstead v. L.C.*,[17] look at funding of institutional as compared to community services as a discrimination argument under Article 14 is likewise a matter of speculation to which we return below.

There may alternatively be a right to live in the community which is protected by the Convention under Article 8. As we have seen, Article 8 of the Convention protects against unjustified interferences with a person's private and family life, home and correspondence. It is now uncontroversial that there is a positive obligation on the State flowing from Article 8 to take reasonable and appropriate measures to secure and protect individuals' rights to respect for their private life.[18]

The case law under the right to respect for 'home' has mainly included the protection of a person's home and their belongings, for example, against police entering homes, and security forces deliberately destroying houses. However, beyond these cases there is nothing directly on point. If it is uncontroversial that the State has positive obligations under Article 8, in the appropriate factual scenario it is at least arguable that Article 8 is violated when the State fails to provide a person with mental disabilities with an adequate 'home'. The case may be stronger in cases where the current 'home' of the person is a State-run institution with many of the violative features described in chapter 3. Analogous to cases where security forces have destroyed homes are those cases where the homes (apartments or houses in the community) of people with mental disabilities are taken away through guardianship and sold by family members, and the person is placed into an institution. Further, there is some support for the proposition that accommodation provided to people with disabilities must be appropriate for their needs. However, this focus on 'home'

---

[16] *Baumann v. France*, Application No. 33592/96, judgment 22 May 2001, (2002) 34 EHRR 44, para. 61.
[17] *Olmstead v. L.C.* (1999) 527 US 581. This case is discussed below.
[18] See *Hatton and Others v. the United Kingdom* Application No. 36022/97, Grand Chamber judgment 8 July 2003, (2003) 37 EHRR 28.

may lead the Court towards recognising the right to housing, a social and economic right which the Court may be reluctant to import into its interpretation of the Convention.

Perhaps a more palatable argument for the Court would be to base such a case on the applicant's right to privacy as protected under Article 8, focussing on the positive State obligations to protect people's right to private life. The obvious argument is that a person has the respect to private life. Institutions commonly violate this right cumulatively by way of overcrowding, invasive treatment, lack of activities, etc. The State would argue that it is providing services to the individual with mental disabilities and may cite one of the grounds in Article 8(2) as justification for its actions. However, the respondent Government in such a case may find it difficult to persuade the Court that the services provided meet the proportionality test. The applicant could argue that it is only community-based services which provide services in the least restrictive setting, with the least possible invasion of privacy rights. This line of argumentation may be more appealing for the Court because it uses Convention concepts of positive obligations, proportionality and reasonable accommodation of people with disabilities.

In chapter 3 we discussed the case of *Price v. the United Kingdom*, a case which used concepts of reasonable accommodation of people with disability. In this case the Court found a violation of Article 3 for detention of merely a few days in conditions which were not conducive to a person who did not have the use of her limbs. In the case of *Marzari v. Italy*, the applicant argued that the Italian authorities' refusal to provide him with an apartment suited to his needs constituted a violation of Article 8, arguing also that he was 'deprived of liberty for lack of alternatives'.[19] Mr Marzari had a condition called metabolic myopathy which left him susceptible to extreme temperatures. The Court noted the authorities' willingness to take measures to adapt his apartment, and found that therefore the authorities had discharged their positive obligations to the applicant. The Court declared the case inadmissible as manifestly ill founded. However, the Court established an important principle that

> although Article 8 does not guarantee the right to have one's housing problem solved by the authorities, a refusal of the authorities to provide assistance in this respect to an individual suffering from a severe disease might in certain circumstances raise an issue under Article 8 of the Convention because of the impact of such refusal on the private life of the individual.[20]

The Court reiterated its statement in the case of *Botta v. Italy* (in which the Court declared that private life 'includes a person's physical and psychological integrity'),[21] namely that Article 8 contains a positive obligation where it can be established that there exists a direct link between the appropriate accommodation requested and a person's everyday life. This line of reasoning clearly sets the groundwork for future cases in which applicants with mental disabilities argue that the State has positive obligations to provide housing and other services in a community setting.

---

[19] *Marzari v. Italy*, Application No. 36448/97, decision 4 May 1999, (1999) 28 EHRR CD175.
[20] *Ibid.*, at CD179–180.
[21] *Botta v. Italy*, Application No. 21439/93, judgment 24 February 1998, (1998) 26 EHRR 241.

It could further be argued that Article 8 implies a positive obligation on States to ensure that when a person with disabilities is institutionalised there is a thorough assessment by a range of qualified and independent professionals who would review the person's needs and recommend options to that person and his or her family members where that is appropriate. Such assessments should be regularly carried out to ensure that the services provided do actually meet the person's individual needs. As Professor Olivier De Schutter points out, these procedural aspects have wider policy concerns. In the case of *Hatton v. the United Kingdom*, a case about whether night flights at Heathrow Airport affected the neighbours' right to respect for their private lives because of the noise, the Court said that it itself was under an obligation to consider:

> all the procedural aspects, including the type of policy or decision involved, the extent to which the views of individuals (including the applicants) were taken into account throughout the decision-making procedure, and the procedural safeguards available.[22]

By analogy, this obligation would extend to the Court's examining the legal and policy framework affecting people with mental disabilities, including the extent to which the authorities had consulted stakeholders including groups of people with mental disabilities,[23] to carry out impact assessments which would examine the proportionality of the proposed policies and viability of alternatives. The procedural aspect also imports an individualised assessment to ensure that the services which are offered (and sometimes imposed) do actually meet the person's needs. When rights are being considered, these individual assessments must of course be judicial in character.[24]

Finally, it could be argued that the institutionalisation of people with disabilities constitutes discrimination, in violation of Article 14 of the Convention, which states that:

> The enjoyment of the rights and freedoms set forth in this Convention shall be secured without discrimination on any ground such as sex, race, colour, language, religion, political or other opinion, national or social origin, association with a national minority, property, birth or other status.

Few people would suggest that disability does not fall within the 'other status' provision of this Article, yet to date there have been no cases in which the Court has found a violation of Article 14 on grounds of disability – indeed, few cases have argued this point.

---

[22] *Hatton and others v. the United Kingdom*, Application No. 36022/97, judgment 8 July 2003 (2003) 37 EHRR 28, para. 104.

[23] See the comments of the European Committee for Social Rights commenting on Article 15(3) of the Revised Social Charter (reproduced in footnote 12), Conclusion 2003–1 at p. 168 (France), p. 507 (Slovenia), that 'persons with disabilities and their representative organisations should be consulted in the design, and ongoing review of such positive action measures and that an appropriate forum should exist to enable this to happen.' The United Nations Standard Rules on the Equalization of Opportunities for Persons with Disabilities similarly recommends that 'States should establish ongoing communication with organizations of persons with disabilities and ensure their participation in the development of government policies.' (Rule 18).

[24] For further discussions, see chapter 2 on Article 5(4) court hearings, and in relation to Article 6 and 8 of the Convention, see chapter 4 on treatment and chapter 6 on guardianship.

Article 14 complements other substantive rights, and therefore needs to be argued along-side another Article (e.g., Article 8) in claiming that a Convention right has been implemented in a discriminatory manner. There are further possibilities which are created by Protocol 12 to the Convention, which is now in force, but only for the handful of countries which have ratified it. Article 1 of this Protocol uses Article 14 language but begins with 'The enjoyment of any right set forth by law shall be secured without discrimination on any ground such as . . .' and employs the same list as Article 14. Protocol 12 therefore creates the opportunity to argue that a law – for example on social security payments, or on allowances provided by the state – are discriminatory, without having to make reference to another Convention right. It will be interesting to see what sort of cases will be argued under Protocol 12.

Whether Article 14 or Protocol 12 will have an impact on a case about the right to community integration is at this stage a matter of speculation. Such future cases in which the individual or group of individual applicants allege that their institutionalisation in a social care or psychiatric institution is discriminatory could be supported by looking across the Atlantic. In the 1999 *Olmstead v. L.C.* case, the United States Supreme Court held that institutionalisation of people with mental disabilities amounted to discrimination, contrary to the Americans with Disabilities Act.[25]

In the *Olmstead* case the two applicants with intellectual disabilities alleged that the funding arrangements in the State of Georgia to support people with disabilities were biased towards institutions, and failed adequately to fund community-based alternatives. The Supreme Court held that that the unnecessary segregation of individuals with disabilities in institutions constitutes discrimination based on disability. Justice Ginsburg delivered the opinion of the Court, finding a violation of the anti-discrimination legislation. She said:

> Unjustified isolation, we hold, is properly regarded as discrimination based on disability. But we recognize, as well, the States' need to maintain a range of facilities for the care and treatment of persons with diverse mental disabilities, and the States' obligation to administer services with an even hand.

Justice Ginsburg went on to say,

> Recognition that unjustified institutional isolation of persons with disabilities is a form of discrimination reflects two evident judgments. First, institutional placement of persons who can handle and benefit from community settings perpetuates unwarranted assumptions that persons so isolated are incapable or unworthy of participating in community life. [. . .] Second, confinement in an institution severely diminishes the everyday life activities of individuals, including family relations, social contacts, work options, economic independence, educational advancement, and cultural enrichment.

The Supreme Court ordered community-based treatment for persons with mental disabilities when the State's treatment professionals determine that such placement is

---

[25] *Olmstead v. L.C.* (1999) 527 US 581.

appropriate, the affected persons do not oppose such treatment, and the placement can be reasonably accommodated, taking into account the resources available to the State and the needs of others with mental disabilities.

The UN Special Rapporteur for the Right to Health supports the view that institutionalisation can amount to discrimination:

> Decisions to isolate or segregate persons with mental disabilities, including through unnecessary institutionalization, are inherently discriminatory and contrary to the right of community integration enshrined in international standards. Segregation and isolation in itself can also entrench stigma surrounding mental disability.[26]

In European Union law, Article 13 of the EC Treaty sets out a legal basis for action at Community level for combating discrimination *inter alia* based on disability. The EU has recognised that institutionalisation perpetuates stigma and discrimination against people with mental disabilities, which 'increases personal suffering, social exclusion and can impede access to housing and employment. It may even prevent people from seeking help for fear of being labelled'.[27]

It remains to be seen whether, given a particular factual matrix, the ECtHR will be prepared to find that life-long institutionalisation and social exclusion itself constitutes a violation of any of the substantive provisions of the Convention, and whether such isolation constitutes discrimination.

Right to education

The UN human rights treaty system formally and specifically acknowledged in 1966 one aim of education as enabling 'all persons to participate effectively in a free society'. The text and subsequent interpretation of the 1989 Convention on the Rights of the Child, which enjoys near-universal ratification,[28] develops this acknowledgment further in two principal ways: by emphasising a general right of all children to participate in society (Articles 12 to 17); and secondly by insisting that the right to education applies to all children and, vitally, is based on and is dependent upon 'equal opportunity' (Articles 28 and 29).[29]

---

[26] Report of the UN Special Rapporteur on the right of everyone to the enjoyment of the highest attainable standard of physical and mental health, Paul Hunt, Report to the sixty-first session of the Commission for Human Rights, para. 54.

[27] Commission of the European Communities, Brussels, 14 October 2005, COM(2005) 484 final, Green Paper: Improving the mental health of the population. Towards a strategy on mental health for the European Union, para. 6.2.

[28] International Covenant on Economic, Social and Cultural Rights, Article 13(1). At the time of going to print (September 2006), the Convention on the Rights of the Child had been ratified by all States except Somalia and the United States of America.

[29] Article 28(1). States Parties recognize the right of the child to education, and with a view to achieving this right progressively and on the basis of equal opportunity, they shall, in particular:

This emphasis, in UN human rights treaty texts, on education and participation in society through inclusive education is complemented by the work of the UN's education body, UNESCO. The focus of UNESCO has, virtually since inception, been on inclusive education, illustrated by its adoption in 1960 of both a Convention and Recommendations against Discrimination in Education.[30] It continues to encourage governments to move from segregated schooling towards education systems which are inclusive. The concept of inclusive education requires all States to provide appropriate responses to a broad spectrum of leaning needs in both formal and informal settings: 'inclusive education is an approach that looks into how to transform education systems in order to respond to the diversity of learners'.[31]

Despite such binding instruments and institutional guidance, genuine 'inclusive education' is out of reach for many children, particularly those frequently identified as vulnerable (such as those belonging to racial minorities and those with disabilities) and consequentially requiring enhanced protections. Numerous examples can be found in NGO reports and comments by treaty-monitoring bodies. In some countries a 'professional' decision about a child's education may result in the child' leading a life going from

    (a) Make primary education compulsory and available free to all;
    (b) Encourage the development of different forms of secondary education, including general and vocational education, make them available and accessible to every child, and take appropriate measures such as the introduction of free education and offering financial assistance in case of need;
    (c) Make higher education accessible to all on the basis of capacity by every appropriate means;
    (d) Make educational and vocational information and guidance available and accessible to all children;
    (e) Take measures to encourage regular attendance at schools and the reduction of drop-out rates.

  2. States Parties shall take all appropriate measures to ensure that school discipline is administered in a manner consistent with the child's human dignity and in conformity with the present Convention.
  3. States Parties shall promote and encourage international cooperation in matters relating to education, in particular with a view to contributing to the elimination of ignorance and illiteracy throughout the world and facilitating access to scientific and technical knowledge and modern teaching methods. In this regard, particular account shall be taken of the needs of developing countries.

Article 29: 1. States Parties agree that the education of the child shall be directed to:

    (a) The development of the child's personality, talents and mental and physical abilities to their fullest potential;
    (b) The development of respect for human rights and fundamental freedoms, and for the principles enshrined in the Charter of the United Nations;
    (c) The development of respect for the child's parents, his or her own cultural identity, language and values, for the national values of the country in which the child is living, the country from which he or she may originate, and for civilizations different from his or her own;
    (d) The preparation of the child for responsible life in a free society, in the spirit of understanding, peace, tolerance, equality of sexes, and friendship among all peoples, ethnic, national and religious groups and persons of indigenous origin;
    (e) The development of respect for the natural environment.

  2. No part of the present article or article 28 shall be construed so as to interfere with the liberty of individuals and bodies to establish and direct educational institutions, subject always to the observance of the principle set forth in paragraph 1 of the present article and to the requirements that the education given in such institutions shall conform to such minimum standards as may be laid down by the State.

[30] Adopted by the General Conference of UNESCO on 14 December 1960.
[31] UNESCO, Towards Inclusion, Defining Inclusive Education, UNESCO website.

one institution to another, vulnerable to human rights abuses throughout. Discrimination against children with disabilities is pervasive in many educational systems,[32] in countries where the concept of inclusive education seems far off. In some countries parents of children who have a recognisable mental disability at birth receive medical recommendations to give up their child to State care shortly after the child is born. If the parents agree, they sign a document assigning their legal rights as parents to the State. In some countries, a child is assessed at birth or at a young age and can be certified as 'uneducable' (in some countries such as Russia the term 'imbecile' and 'idiot' are used),[33] and then placed in a boarding 'school' or other residential institution where the education may be of substandard quality or non-existent.

A right to education is also found in European texts and guidance. The Council of Europe's recently adopted Disability Action Plan,[34] a major policy document setting out a continent-wide disability strategy for a ten-year period, emphasises the existing right to education for people with disabilities. The document calls for mainstream education for all children, noting that '[t]he creation of opportunities for disabled people to participate in mainstream education is not only important for disabled people but will also benefit non-disabled people's understanding of human diversity'.[35] Further, the Council of Europe's Revised Social Charter, the sister document of the European Convention on Human Rights, contains an obligation on States to provide children and young persons with free primary and secondary education.[36]

Unfortunately, it is far from clear that bringing cases under the European Convention on Human Rights will assist with the reform which is needed towards respecting the right to education. The right to education is dealt with in Article 2 of Protocol 1 to the Convention, which reads:

> No person shall be denied the right to education. In the exercise of any functions which it assumes in relation to education and to teaching, the State shall respect the right of parents to ensure such education and teaching in conformity with their own religious and philosophical convictions.

Interestingly this provision, in contrast to education provisions in other treaties, both is drafted in broad non-descriptive terms and is negatively formulated.[37] Despite potential

---

[32] See also Committee of the Rights of the Child, General Comment 1 on the Aims of Education, CRC/GC/2001/1, para. 10.

[33] See Amnesty International, 'A life sentence: Children with mental disability in the Russian Federation', 14 October 2003, Index No: EUR 46/078/2003.

[34] Recommendation Rec(2006)5 of the Council of Europe to member States on the Council of Europe Action Plan to promote the rights and full participation of people with disabilities in society: improving the quality of life of people with disabilities in Europe 2006–2015 (Recommendation R (2006) 5, op. cit., note 13).

[35] Recommendation Rec(2006)5 of the Council of Europe to member States on the Council of Europe Action Plan to promote the rights and full participation of people with disabilities in society: improving the quality of life of people with disabilities in Europe 2006–2015 (Recommendation R (2006) 5, op. cit.), para. 3.4.1.

[36] European Social Charter (revised), Strasbourg, 3 May 1996, Article 17(2).

[37] See U. Kilkelly, *The Child and the European Convention on Human Rights*, (Aldershot: Ashgate, 1999), pp. 62–63.

confusion as to its scope and meaning, however, the European Court of Human Rights has now established that the Article does contain a right to education which must be secured to all children. The right to education refers to primary, secondary and tertiary (higher) education. In the *Belgian Linguistic Case*, decided in 1968, the Court described the right to education as a right which 'by its very nature calls for regulation by the State, regulation which may vary in time and place according to the needs and resources of the community and of individuals'.[38] There have been few other cases brought under this Article, although some cases have touched on peripheral issues related to education such as corporal punishment,[39] compulsory sex education in schools,[40] and military aspects of schooling.[41]

The ECtHR has only recently been asked to deal with a core aspect of education, namely the discriminatory approach of an entire education system. In the case of *D.H. and others v. Czech Republic*,[42] the ECtHR was asked to rule on whether the eighteen applicants of Roma origin were discriminated against when they were educated in special schools for children with mental disabilities. The applicants argued that they were *de facto* subjected to racial segregation and discrimination that was reflected in the existence of two independent educational systems for members of different racial groups, namely special schools for the Roma and 'ordinary' primary schools for the majority of the population. It was argued that the difference in treatment was not based on any objective and reasonable justification. Specifically it had deprived them of the right to education because the curriculum followed in special schools was inferior and pupils in special schools were unable to return to primary school or to obtain a secondary education other than in a vocational training centre because of the inadequate education which they had received.

The applicants argued that the right to education had been denied in a way which violated the prohibition on discrimination under Article 14 of the ECHR.[43] In a passage which illustrates the ECtHR's deferential approach to a State to arrange its educational system, couched in the 'margin of appreciation' terms, the Court said:

> With regard to pupils with special needs, the Court accepts that the choice between having a single type of school for everyone, highly specialised structures or unified structures with specialist sections is not an easy one and there does not appear to be an ideal solution. It involves a difficult exercise in balancing the various competing interests. The Court wishes to reiterate with regard to the States' margin of appreciation in the education sphere that the

---

[38] *Belgian Linguistic Case*, judgment 23 July 1968, A/6.
[39] *Campbell and Cosans v. the United Kingdom*, Application Nos. 7511/76 and 7743/76, judgment 25 February 1982, (A/48) (1982) 4 EHRR 293.
[40] *Kjeldsen, Busk, Madsen and Pedersen v. Denmark*, Application Nos. 5095/71; 5920/72 and 5926/72, judgment 7 December 1976, (1979–80) 1 EHRR 711.
[41] *Efstratiou v. Greece*, Application No. 24095/94, judgment 27 November 1996.
[42] Application No. 57325/00, judgment 7 February 2006.
[43] 'The enjoyment of the rights and freedoms set forth in [the] Convention shall be secured without discrimination on any ground such as sex, race, colour, language, religion, political or other opinion, national or social origin, association with a national minority, property, birth or other status.'

States cannot be prohibited from setting up different types of school for children with difficulties or implementing special educational programmes to respond to special needs.[44]

Although the *D.H.* applicants had argued that there were no uniform rules governing the choice of tests used by the educational experts or the interpretation of the results, the ECtHR noted that the parties did not dispute that the tests were administered by qualified professionals. These professionals were expected to follow the rules of their profession and to be able to select suitable methods. The applicants relied on the statistically disproportionate number of Roma children placed in special schools and that the educational tests were adapted to the Czech language and cultural environment. Thus, they argued, Roma children were disadvantaged because the tests contained errors that distorted the findings, since the majority of the children concerned were not suffering from any learning or intellectual disability. The applicants further argued that there were no uniform rules governing the manner in which the tests were administered and the results interpreted, so that much was left to the discretion of the psychologists which allowed considerable scope for racial prejudice and cultural insensitivity. The Court's surprising deference to 'professionals' may be one of the issues which the Grand Chamber will address, the case having recently been referred to that body.

The *D.H.* case merely exposed at the European level what had already been identified by a number of active NGOs: discrimination towards racial minorities and children with disabilities in education systems remains despite concerted international and regional efforts. In some countries a child is diagnosed using outmoded tests and placed into a residential 'education' institution, where little actual education is provided. In other countries such institutions are managed by, for instance, a ministry of social affairs, rather than a ministry of education. Often a child institutionalised this way reaches the age of eighteen and is transferred to an adult social welfare institution where he or she will remain for life.[45] Whether it is appropriate to institutionalise children with disabilities has yet to be challenged before the ECtHR. Most probably the reason for this is the children's inability to access justice, a topic which will be addressed in the book's conclusion.

Right to property

The proposition that all people diagnosed with a mental health problem or an intellectual disability are unable to manage financial affairs is an offensive and inaccurate gener-

---

[44] *D.H. and others v. the Czech Republic, op. cit.*, para. 47.

[45] See Amnesty International report 'Children of Dzhurkovo denied life of dignity and respect', 18 November 2004, in which it is reported that in this institution of 69 children, 'practically all 43 "bedridden" children were in bed and not engaged in any activity. It is evident that they spend most of their time in this way. A girl with Down's syndrome who is eight years old and had been observed two and a half years earlier chewing the sides of her wooden cot was found still chewing on the cot, driven to this activity from lack of attention and means to occupy herself. Her situation was described in our 2002 report yet nothing had changed in the way she was being treated.'

alisation. However, some legal systems assume this to be an obvious truth, arbitrarily depriving a person of the right to manage his or her own finances through legal incapacity, handing over to another person the right to decide on, for example, the person's apartment and giving the person full access to their bank account (the procedure of depriving a person of his or her legal capacity was dealt with in chapter 6). In some other countries there are flexible systems whereby financial decision-making is dealt with in an individualised way.[46]

The right to manage property is protected by the Convention in Article 1 of Protocol No. 1 to the Convention:

> Every natural or legal person is entitled to the peaceful enjoyment of his possessions. No one shall be deprived of his possessions except in the public interest and subject to the conditions provided for by law and by the general principles of international law.
> The preceding provisions shall not, however, in any way impair the right of a State to enforce such laws as it deems necessary to control the use of property in accordance with the general interest or to secure the payment of taxes or other contributions or penalties.[47]

Article 1 of Protocol No. 1 protects against the arbitrary deprivation of a person's existing possessions. Any deprivation of a person's property must be reasoned and must be in accordance with the law. Whatever the justification for depriving a person with mental disabilities of the capacity to administer property, the fair trial guarantees of Article 6 of the Convention must be respected.[48]

The right to own property is clearly articulated in the wording of the Article 1 of Protocol 1, and in the 1979 case of *Marckx v. Belgium*, the Court confirmed that 'the right to dispose of one's property constitutes a traditional and fundamental aspect of the right to property'.[49] This right probably means that owner of the property can enter into a legal relationship with another person whatever the form of the transaction, for example, a sale or rent of an apartment.[50]

Article 1 of Protocol No. 1 also has 'horizontal' applicability. That is to say, the State must protect against arbitrary removal of a person's property by another person (in mental disability cases, for example, a guardian). Applying to the European Court of Human Rights for a remedy against a private person acting as guardian may be found inadmissible under Article 34 of the Convention unless the State has some responsibility in supervising the actions of a private guardian (see chapter 10 on applying to the ECtHR for a discussion of procedure). It will be relatively easy to establish such State

---

[46] See, for example, the English and Welsh Mental Capacity Act 2005, which allows a person to make a lasting power of attorney in financial (or other) matters, as well as a possibility of a court-appointed deputy to make such decisions.
[47] This Protocol opened for signature on 20 March 1952, and has equal legal force as articles in the Convention itself.
[48] *Winterwerp v. the Netherlands*, Application No. 6301/73, judgment 24 October 1979, (1979–80) 2 EHRR 387, para. 75.
[49] *Marckx v. Belgium*, Application No. 6833/74, judgment 13 June 1979, (1979) 2 EHRR 330, para. 63.
[50] A.R. Çoban, *Protection of Property Rights within the European Convention on Human Rights*, (Aldershot: Ashgate, 2004), p. 146.

responsibility because of the clear duties of local authorities in many countries to regulate the decisions of and generally supervise guardians. The case will be stronger where the court which deprived the individual of legal capacity did not properly examine the person's actual/functional capacity to manage property, but based the decision on a psychiatric or other diagnosis. A disagreement by a person under guardianship of a guardian's decision to dispose of property may itself be evidence that the person has some capacity to understand the consequences of disposing of the property. In such circumstances, if the situation is not rectified by domestic authorities, the European Court of Human Rights may find that the interference with property rights was such as to violate Article 1 of Protocol No. 1 to the Convention. A claim by a person with disabilities alleging a violation to the right to property may be strengthened by citing the Council of Europe's ten-year Disability Action Plan, in which the member States have been asked 'to take effective measures to ensure the equal right of persons with disabilities to own and inherit property, providing legal protection to manage their assets on an equal basis to others'.[51]

In order for the Court to find a violation of Article 1 of Protocol No. 1 it is important to prove that the property is in the applicant's possession. In guardianship cases this should not be an obstacle, since the legal entitlement to the property usually remains with the person under guardianship. Supporting this proposition, Committee of Ministers Recommendation No. R(99)4, which was referred to extensively in Chapter 6 above, stipulates that 'the property of the incapable adult should be managed and used for the benefit of the person concerned and to secure his or her welfare'.[52]

Right to marry, to found a family, and to respect of family life

This section deals with issues of sexuality, relationships and child bearing by people with mental health problems or intellectual disabilities, topics which have been the focus of intense cross-disciplinary discussions for some years. Sadly, notwithstanding that rights are provided on paper, the rights to marry and found a family are, according to the UN Committee on Economic, Social and Cultural Rights, 'frequently ignored or denied, especially in the case of persons with mental disabilities'.[53] Similarly, the UN Standard Rules on Equalization of Opportunities for Persons with Disabilities state, 'persons with disabilities must not be denied the opportunity to experience their sexuality, have sexual

---

[51] Recommendation Rec(2006)5 of the Council of Europe to member States on the Council of Europe Action Plan to promote the rights and full participation of people with disabilities in society: improving the quality of life of people with disabilities in Europe 2006–2015 (Recommendation R (2006) 5, op. cit., note 13), section 3.12.3.xiii.

[52] Recommendation No. R(99)4, Principle 8(3). For a discussion of this Recommendation, see chapter 6 on legal capacity, guardianship and supported decision-making, above.

[53] Committee for Economic, Social and Cultural Rights, General Comment No. 5: Persons with disabilities, 9 December 1994, para. 30.

relationships and experience parenthood'.[54] People with mental health problems face prejudices that a diagnosis of a mental illness automatically equates bad parenting skills, and that any children of a person with a mental disability will itself be more prone to developing a mental illnesses. In the past, women with intellectual disabilities many of whom have the capacity to decide on medical treatment, were sterilized against their will through eugenic policies which, for example in Sweden, continued until the mid 1970s.[55] In some countries today women with mental disabilities are still sterilised, albeit in the woman's 'best interests'.[56]

In some jurisdictions people deprived of legal capacity (see chapter 6) have no right to marry without the permission of the guardian. This situation is somewhat analogous to the situation in some jurisdictions of minors age 16 and 17 who have the right to marry, provided that the parents agree. Further, a person deprived of legal capacity may have no legal rights to bring up their own children or adopt. Even if a person with mental disabilities has full legal capacity he or she may face extra hurdles in keeping a child or being able to adopt.

The ECHR imposes on States a negative obligation not to interfere with, but also positive obligations to respect a person's private and family life (Article 8). Similarly, there are negative obligations not to interfere with, and positive duties to respect, a person's right to marry and found a family (Article 12).[57]

Article 12 of the ECHR reads, 'Men and women of marriageable age have the right to marry and found a family, according to the national laws governing the exercise of this right.' For the purposes of securing the right to marry, it does not matter if the person has no particular person in mind. The only important consideration is whether the person is able to marry in law. The right to marry is similarly not contingent on the couple's ability or desire to have children. As the Court has explained, this Article 'secures the fundamental right of a man and a woman to marry and found a family. The second aspect is not however a condition of the first and the inability of any couple to conceive or parent a child cannot be regarded as *per se* removing their right to enjoy the first limb of this pro-

---

[54] Standard Rules on the Equalization of Opportunities for Persons with Disabilities, A/RES/48/96, 85th Plenary Meeting 20 December 1993, Rule 9(2).

[55] Commission Report, 2000:20 Steriliseringsfrågan i Sverige 1935–1975: Historisk belysing – Kartlåggning, Intervjuer, SOU 2000:22. 'Från politik till praktik. De svenska steriliseringslagarna, 1935–1975'.

[56] See, for example, cases decided by courts in the United Kingdom: *F v. West Berkshire Health Authority* [1989] 2 All ER 545, [1990] 2 AC 1, [1989] 2 WLR 938; *Re W (Mental Patient)* [1993] 1 FLR 381. Court procedures to be followed prior to such operations are contained in *Practice Note (Official Solicitor: Declaratory Proceedings: Medical and Welfare Decisions for Adults who Lack Capacity)* [2001] 2 FLR 158, appendix I.

[57] Rule 9 of the UN Standard Rules on the Equalization of Opportunities for Persons with Disabilities contains strong wording on the rights of people with disabilities to family life and personal integrity, saying that 'States should promote the full participation of persons with disabilities in family life. They should promote their right to personal integrity and ensure that laws do not discriminate against persons with disabilities with respect to sexual relationships, marriage and parenthood' and that 'Persons with disabilities must not be denied the opportunity to experience their sexuality, have sexual relationships and experience parenthood.'

vision.'[58] In terms of the right to found a family, the difference between Article 12 and Article 8 is that Article 12 protects the right to create or form a family whereas Article 8 protects family life itself.[59] Article 8 of the Convention reads:

> 1. Everyone has the right to respect for his private and family life, his home and his correspondence.
> 2. There shall be no interference by a public authority with the exercise of this right except such as is in accordance with the law and is necessary in a democratic society in the interests of national security, public safety or the economic well-being of the country, for the prevention of disorder or crime, for the protection of health or morals, or for the protection of the rights and freedoms of others.

The positive duty on the state to respect family life was confirmed by the European Court of Human Rights in the case of *Kutzner v. Germany*,[60] which will be examined in detail below, where the Court stated that '[w]here existence of a family tie has been established, the State must in principle act in a manner calculated to enable that tie to be developed and take measures that will enable parent and child to be reunited.'

The Court has defined 'family life' as embracing the tie between parent and child, even where the parents are not married or do not live together.[61] Further, the mutual enjoyment by a parent and child of each other's company constitutes a fundamental element of family life, and it is 'an interference of a very serious order to split up a family'.[62]

In assessing whether the denial of the right to respect for family life is 'in accordance with the law' under Article 8(2), the law or regulation has to be clear and accessible in order to enable those likely to be affected by it to understand it and to regulate their conduct so as to avoid breaking the law.[63] The interference must be in pursuit of a legitimate aim, listed in paragraph 2 of Article 8. In family law proceedings the obvious justification is 'to protect the rights and freedoms of others' namely, the child. The Court would then examine to what extent the interference is 'necessary in a democratic society'. This was the crucial question which the Court addressed in the case of *Kutzner v. Germany*, a case concerning applicants with intellectual disabilities and which is worth examining in some detail.

In *Kutzner*, the applicants were married, had themselves attended a special school for people with learning difficulties, and had two daughters. Owing to their late physical and mental development, the children were examined on a number of occasions by doctors

---

[58] *Goodwin v. the United Kingdom*, Application No. 28957/95, judgment 11 July 2002, (2002) 35 EHRR 18, para. 98.
[59] *Cossey v. the United Kingdom*, Application No. 10843/84, judgment 27 September 1990, (1991) 13 EHRR 622.
[60] *Kutzner v. Germany*, Application No. 46544/99, judgment 26 February 2002, (2002) 35 EHRR 25.
[61] *Kroon v. the Netherlands*, Application No. 18535/91, judgment 27 October 1994, (1995) 19 EHRR 263.
[62] *Olsson v. Sweden*, Application No. 10465/83, judgment 24 March 1988, (1989) 11 EHRR 259.
[63] See *Sunday Times v. the United Kingdom*, A/30, judgment 26 April 1979, (1979–80) 2 EHRR 245.

and had received educational assistance and support from an early age. However, parental rights were withdrawn and the children were placed in foster care on the grounds that the applicants did not have the intellectual capacity required to bring up their children, and that the girls were late in their mental and physical development. The girls were placed in separate, unidentified, foster homes, and restrictions were imposed on the applicants' visiting rights: they were not permitted to see their children during the first six months; and thereafter allowed to visit only in the presence of third parties, initially for one hour monthly, subsequently increased to two hours monthly.

The applicants successfully argued that the removal of their children from their care constituted a violation of their right to family life as protected by Article 8 ECHR. The Court noted that some psychologists retained as expert witnesses by national NGOs as well as family doctors urged that the children be returned to their family of origin. The experts commented in particular on the lack of danger for the children's welfare and on the applicants' ability to bring up their children. The Court was concerned with the 'most extreme measure, namely separating the children from their parents', and reiterated that removal of the child from the family must in principle be regarded as a temporary measure, to be discontinued as soon as circumstances permitted. Although the domestic authorities had a margin of appreciation, the European Court of Human Rights found that the interference had not been proportionate to the legitimate aims pursued and therefore there had been a violation of Article 8.

This is the first family law case to be brought by parents with intellectual disabilities. Indeed it is one of the few cases brought by people with intellectual disabilities under any Article of the Convention. Its significance is that the Court sharply criticised the national authorities for acting as they did merely because the parents had disabilities. In arguing future cases which raise similar points, lawyers for the applicants may seek to refer to Recommendation (2005)5 of the Committee of Ministers to member States on the rights of children living in residential institutions.[64] This Recommendation states that the family is the 'natural environment for the growth and well-being of the child and the parents have the primary responsibility for the upbringing and development of the child'. Significantly, the Recommendation advises that the decision taken about the placement of a child and the placement itself 'should not be subject to discrimination on the basis of gender, race, colour, social, ethnic or national origin, expressed opinions, language, property, religion, *disability*, birth or *any other status* of the child and/or his or her parents (emphases added).

---

[64] Adopted by the Committee of Ministers on 16 March 2005 at the 919th meeting of the Ministers' Deputies on 16 March 2005.

Right to vote

In many jurisdictions in the Council of Europe region, people who have been deprived of legal capacity are automatically denied the right to vote.[65] Recommendation R(99)4 advises against arbitrary removal of the right to vote.[66] People who have legal capacity sometimes face legal obstacles or other difficulties in exercising their right to suffrage.[67] The Council of Europe's Disability Action Plan foresees that people with disabilities shall exercise the right to vote on an equal basis with others. The document commits Member States of the Council of Europe:

> i. To ensure that voting procedures and facilities are appropriate and accessible to people with disabilities so that they are able to exercise their democratic rights, and allow, where necessary, the provision of assistance in voting;
> ii. to protect the right of people with disabilities to vote by secret ballot and, where necessary, upon their request, allow assistance in voting by a person of their choice;
> iii. to ensure that no person with a disability is excluded from the right to vote or to stand for election on the basis of her/his disability.[68]

A restriction of a person's the right to vote engages Article 3 of Protocol 1 to the ECHR, which sets out the following provisions:

> The High Contracting Parties undertake to hold free elections at reasonable intervals by secret ballot, under conditions which will ensure the free expression of the opinion of the people in the choice of the legislature.

Curiously, the right to vote is not directly articulated on the face of the Article. Although a State has a margin of appreciation to limit voting rights, the Court has held that this must be done so as not to impair the very essence of the rights or deprive them of their effectiveness.[69] The provision applies to national and some local elections as well as elections for the European Parliament.[70]

---

[65] In some countries, this amounts to a constitutional bar. See, for example, Hungary's Constitution, Article 70(3) of which states: 'The right to vote shall not be granted to persons who are under guardianship limiting or excluding their capacity, to persons who are subject to a final legal judgment forbidding them to participate in public affairs, nor to persons who are incarcerated on the basis of a final legal judgment or who are under compulsory institutional care on the basis of a final legal judgment rendered in criminal proceedings.'

[66] Recommendation No. R(99)4, Principle 3(2).

[67] See Mental Disability Advocacy Center and Bulgarian Helsinki Committee: The right to vote at risk in Bulgaria (Press Release) 24 June 2005, available on www.mdac.info.

[68] Recommendation Rec(2006)5 of the Council of Europe to member States on the Council of Europe Action Plan to promote the rights and full participation of people with disabilities in society: improving the quality of life of people with disabilities in Europe 2006–2015 (Recommendation R (2006) 5, op. cit., note 13), para. 3.1.3.

[69] *Mathieu-Mohin and Clerfayt v. Belgium*, Application No. 9267/81, judgment 2 March 1987, (A/113) (1988) 10 EHRR 1, para. 52.

[70] *Matthews v. the United Kingdom*, Application No. 24833/94, judgment 18 February 1999, (1999) 28 EHRR 361.

There have not yet been any cases brought by a person claiming that voting rights have been restricted because of their mental disabilities or legal incapacity. The Court has, however, dealt with a right-to-vote case brought by a British prisoner serving life imprisonment.[71] As a convicted prisoner, Mr Hirst, like all other prisoners in the United Kingdom, was prohibited by statute from voting in elections. Mr Hirst tried unsuccessfully to challenge the legislation using ECHR arguments in British courts. He then sought a remedy at the ECtHR, which eventually heard the case as a Grand Chamber of 17 judges.

The Court held that voting rights were crucial to establishing and maintaining the foundations of an effective and meaningful democracy governed by the rule of law. The right to vote was a *right* and not a privilege, so any departure from the principle of universal suffrage risked undermining the democratic validity of the legislature elected and its laws and that an exclusion of categories of people had to be reconcilable with the underlying purposes of Article 3 of Protocol No. 1.

The Court emphasised that prisoners generally continued to enjoy all Convention rights, except for the right to liberty, where lawfully imposed detention is permitted by Article 5. There was no question that prisoners give up their Convention rights merely because of their status as detainees following conviction. Nor was there any place in the Convention system, where tolerance and broadmindedness were the acknowledged hallmarks of democratic society, for automatic disenfranchisement based purely on what might offend public opinion. The principle of proportionality required a discernible and sufficient link between the sanction and the conduct and circumstances of the individual concerned.

In an analogous argument which could be made in future mental disability cases, the Court recalled that Article 3 of Protocol No. 1, unlike Article 8 of the Convention for example, did not specify or limit the aims which a measure pursues. The Court accepted that the British law aimed at preventing crime by way of sanctioning prisoners, but did not accept that denying the right to vote was proportionate. The Court noted that the denial of the right to vote affected an estimated 48,000 prisoners, including those who had committed a wide range of offences and were serving sentences from one day to life. In finding a violation of Article 3 of Protocol No. 1 the Court found that the United Kingdom's approach of disenfranchising all serving prisoners was a general, automatic and indiscriminate restriction on a vitally important Convention right. It fell outside any acceptable margin of appreciation.[72]

The importance of the *Hirst* case is that it is illustrative if a case were taken to challenge the lack of voting rights of people with mental disability or those who have been deprived

---

[71] *Hirst v. the United Kingdom*, Application No. 74025/01, judgment 6 October 2005, 19 BHRC 546.

[72] An interesting issue in *Hirst* – and one which may be important in mental disability cases – was the extent to which a lack of consensus among countries which have ratified the Convention was an important factor for the Court to take into consideration. The Court noted that, although there was some disagreement about the state of the law in certain countries, it was undisputed that the United Kingdom was not alone among Convention countries in depriving all convicted prisoners of the right to vote. The lack of a common European approach to the problem was not of itself determinative of the issue.

of their legal capacity. The Court emphatically recognised the importance to a democratic society of marginalized groups being given a voting voice. The *Hirst* judgment also makes the point that the denial of voting is not something which is considered at trial by the judge. Similarly in mental disability law, incapacity or guardianship court hearings usually consider a test only of whether someone can manage their own affairs, not whether the person has or does not have the capacity to vote.

Right to associate

A Convention right which is sometimes compromised when a person is deprived of legal capacity and/or detained in a psychiatric or social care institution is the right to associate. In some jurisdictions within the Council of Europe territory, people who have been deprived of their legal capacity cannot join associations, or cannot be governing members of such organisations.[73] This prohibition itself may partly explain the lack of activity to promote the rights of people under guardianship: there is, to the best of the authors' knowledge, no national association for protecting the rights of people under guardianship.[74] It could be argued that such a prohibition on associating with others to pursue a common aim engages Article 11 of the ECHR, which states:

---

[73] See, for example, Mental Disability Advocacy Center, and Guardianship and Human Rights in Bulgaria (2006, Mental Disability Advocacy Center, Budapest), available from www.mdac.info.

[74] Principle 17(2) of the Recommendation No. R(99)4 states that 'Consideration should be given, in particular, to the establishment or support of associations or other bodies with the function of providing and training such people.' The UN Standard Rules on the Equalization of Opportunities for Persons with Disabilities provides a basis for pursuing such arguments under the Convention. Rule 18 of the Standard Rules reads:
Organizations of persons with disabilities
States should recognize the right of the organizations of persons with disabilities to represent persons with disabilities at national, regional and local levels. States should also recognize the advisory role of organizations of persons with disabilities in decision-making on disability matters.
1. States should encourage and support economically and in other ways the formation and strengthening of organizations of persons with disabilities, family members and/or advocates. States should recognize that those organizations have a role to play in the development of disability policy.
2. States should establish ongoing communication with organizations of persons with disabilities and ensure their participation in the development of government policies.
3. The role of organizations of persons with disabilities could be to identify needs and priorities, to participate in the planning, implementation and evaluation of services and measures concerning the lives of persons with disabilities, and to contribute to public awareness and to advocate change.
4. As instruments of self-help, organizations of persons with disabilities provide and promote opportunities for the development of skills in various fields, mutual support among members and information sharing.
5. Organizations of persons with disabilities could perform their advisory role in many different ways such as having permanent representation on boards of government-funded agencies, serving on public commissions and providing expert knowledge on different projects.
6. The advisory role of organizations of persons with disabilities should be ongoing in order to develop and deepen the exchange of views and information between the State and the organizations.

1. Everyone has the right to freedom of peaceful assembly and to freedom of association with others, including the right to form and to join trade unions for the protection of his interests.
2. No restrictions shall be placed on the exercise of these rights other than such as are prescribed by law and are necessary in a democratic society in the interests of national security or public safety, for the prevention of disorder or crime, for the protection of health or morals or for the protection of the rights and freedoms of others. [. . .]

Article 11 provides for people to gather together formally and associate with each other in order to pursue a common goal, including the right to establish or join associations, organisations or political parties which have a particular aim.[75] Although the wording of Article 11 does not expressly refer to it, the Court has confirmed that 'an inherent part of the right set forth in Article 11' is the right to form associations.[76] The Court has emphasised the importance to democratic societies of associations whose aims are 'essential role played by political parties in ensuring pluralism and democracy, associations formed for other purposes, including those protecting cultural or spiritual heritage, pursuing various socio-economic aims, proclaiming or teaching religion, seeking an ethnic identity or asserting a minority consciousness, are also important to the proper functioning of democracy'.[77]

Right to work

The mental distress experienced by people with mental health problems may result in their having to take time off work, or leaving their employment altogether. For people with intellectual disabilities, a job may seem like a dream especially in regions where there is high unemployment and where laws are ineffective in preventing discrimination in recruiting a person with disabilities, and providing reasonable accommodation during employment. Commenting on the situation of people with disabilities worldwide, a UN body has said that '[i]n most countries the unemployment rate among persons with disabilities is two to three times higher than the unemployment rate for persons without disabilities. Where persons with disabilities are employed, they are mostly engaged in low-paid jobs with little social and legal security and are often segregated from the mainstream of the labour market'.[78]

---

7. Organizations should be permanently represented on the national coordinating committee or similar bodies.
8. The role of local organizations of persons with disabilities should be developed and strengthened to ensure that they influence matters at the community level.

[75] *X. v. Sweden*, Application No. 6094/73, decision 6 July 1977; 9 DR 5.
[76] *Sidiropoulos v. Greece*, Application No. 26695/95, judgment 10 July 1998, (1998) EHRR 633.
[77] *Gorzelik and Others v. Poland*, Application No. 44158/98, judgment 19 February 2004, (2005) 40 EHRR 4, para. 92.
[78] Committee for Economic, Social and Cultural Rights, General Comment No. 5: Persons with disabilities, 09 December 1994, para. 20.

Many people with mental disabilities are offered 'work' in sheltered employment, where pay and conditions are substandard. Similarly, for people in psychiatric and social welfare institutions, the reality is that either no employment is possible, or people are forced to carry out mundane tasks on the pretext that these tasks constitute 'therapy'.[79]

People who have been deprived of their legal capacity are often unable in law to sign employment contracts, therefore barring a fundamental aspect of belonging to a community, of mental well-being, and – as is the case for most employed and unemployed people alike – of striving for a greater income. The prohibition on work, along with the misplaced and offensive assumption that people with mental health problems or intellectual disabilities are not capable of working, is another reason why the one-size-fits-all approach to assisted decision making, as discussed in chapter 6 above, does not accord with real life.

The 'right to work' has been historically viewed as an economic and social right. It is located, for example, in the European Social Charter, a Council of Europe treaty dealing with , economic, social and cultural rights, which is traditionally seen as the (toothless) sister treaty to the ECHR.[80] However, the ECtHR has for many years held that human rights are indivisible and interrelated and therefore in Articles of the ECHR which allow for some flexibility (such as Article 8), the Court is beginning to loosen the traditionally tight boundaries between economic and social rights on the one hand, and civil and political rights on the other. This section will explore the extent to which the 'right to work' is becoming justiciable under the ECHR.

United Nations soft law instruments promote the right to work for people with intellectual disabilities[81] and people with mental health problems.[82] The cross-disability UN Standard Rules on the Equalization of Opportunities for Persons with Disabilities man-

---

[79] Principle 13(3) and (4) of the UN Resolution 46/119 on the Protection of Persons with Mental Illness and the Improvement of Mental Health Care, adopted by the General Assembly on 17 December 1991 states:

> 3. In no circumstances shall a patient be subject to forced labour. Within the limits compatible with the needs of the patient and with the requirements of institutional administration, a patient shall be able to choose the type of work he or she wishes to perform.
> 4. The labour of a patient in a mental health facility shall not be exploited. Every such patient shall have the right to receive the same remuneration for any work which he or she does as would, according to domestic law or custom, be paid for such work to a non-patient. Every such patient shall, in any event, have the right to receive a fair share of any remuneration which is paid to the mental health facility for his or her work.

[80] Article 15(2) of the European Social Charter (revised), Strasbourg, 3 May 1996, provides for States: 'to promote their access to employment through all measures tending to encourage employers to hire and keep in employment persons with disabilities in the ordinary working environment and to adjust the working conditions to the needs of the disabled or, where this is not possible by reason of the disability, by arranging for or creating sheltered employment according to the level of disability. In certain cases, such measures may require recourse to specialised placement and support services.'

[81] See paragraph 3 of the Declaration on the Rights of Mentally Retarded Persons, Proclaimed by General Assembly resolution 2856 (XXVI) of 20 December 1971: 'The mentally retarded person has a right to economic security and to a decent standard of living. He has a right to perform productive work or to engage in any other meaningful occupation to the fullest possible extent of his capabilities.'

[82] See Principle 3 of the UN Resolution 46/119 on the Protection of Persons with Mental Illness and the Improvement of Mental Health Care, adopted by the General Assembly on 17 December 1991: 'Every person with a mental illness shall have the right to live and work, to the extent possible, in the community.'

dates governments to take positive action to include people with disabilities into the workplace.[83] These actions include promulgating laws and regulations in the employment field which do not discriminate against persons with disabilities nor which put in place barriers to employment. Further, States should actively support the integration of persons with disabilities into open employment. For those countries which are also members of the European Union, the EU's Employment Framework Directive is binding and opens up litigation possibilities.[84]

Under the ECHR, the right to work can be argued under Article 8 (right to private life). As the ECtHR has acknowledged,

> it is, after all, in the course of their working lives that the majority of people have a significant, if not the greatest, opportunity of developing relationships with the outside world.[85]

The ECtHR had occasion to address the right to work in the case of *Sidabras and Džiautas v. Lithuania*.[86] The Court examined whether restrictions on the 'right to work' engaged Article 8 of the Convention. As KGB officers in the former Soviet régime, the applicants were prohibited by a Lithuanian law from working as 'lawyers and notaries, in banks and other credit institutions, strategic economic projects, security companies (structures), other companies (structures) providing detective services, communications system, educational system as teachers, educators or heads of those institutions, and [also jobs] requiring a weapon'.[87] The applicants complained that being banned from finding employment in the private sector for ten years on the ground that they had been former KGB officers violated Articles 8 and 14 of the Convention.

In examining the applicants' claim under Article 14 of the Convention (non-discrimination) taken together with Article 8 (right to private life), the ECtHR referred to the European Social Charter and commented on several issues, which could be similarly argued in cases challenging the legal ban on work by people who have been deprived of their legal capacity. The Court observed that the applicants were treated differently from other people in Lithuania who had not worked for the KGB, and who as a result had no restrictions imposed on them in their choice of professional activities or in relation to their employment prospects. The ban had affected the ability of the applicants to develop relationships with the outside world to a very significant degree, which had created serious difficulties for them in relation to earning their living, with repercussions on their enjoyment of their private lives. The ECtHR accepted that the applicants continued to labour under the status of 'former KGB officers' and that fact might of itself be considered an impediment to the establishment of contacts with the outside world.

---

[83] Rule 7, 'Right to work', of the UN Standard Rules. Ref: A/RES/48/96, 85th Plenary Meeting 20 December 1993.

[84] Council Directive 2000/78/EC of 27 November 2000, establishing a general framework for equal treatment in employment and occupation

[85] *Niemietz v. Germany*, Application No. 13710/88, judgment 16 December 1992, (A/251–B) (1993) 16 EHRR 97, para. 29.

[86] Application Nos. 55480/00 and 59330/00, judgment 27 July 2004.

[87] *Ibid.*, paras. 36 and 47.

The Court therefore considered that the impugned ban affected, to a significant degree, the possibility for the applicants to pursue various professional activities and that there were consequential effects on the enjoyment of their right to respect for their 'private life' within the meaning of Article 8. It followed that Article 14 was applicable in the circumstances of this case taken in conjunction with Article 8.

The ECtHR commented on the ambiguous manner in which the Lithuanian law dealt with, on the one hand, the question of the applicants' lack of loyalty to the State and, on the other hand, the need to apply the restrictions to employment in certain private-sector jobs. With the exception of references to lawyers and notaries, the law contained no definition of the specific jobs, functions or tasks which the applicants were barred from holding and therefore the Court found that it was impossible to ascertain any reasonable link between the positions concerned and the legitimate aims sought by the ban on holding those positions. Such a legislative scheme lacked the necessary safeguards for avoiding discrimination and for guaranteeing an adequate and appropriate judicial control of the imposition of such restrictions. The Court also found that the restrictions on the applicants' professional activities were imposed on them 13 years (Sidabras) and 9 years (Džiautas) after their departure from the KGB constituted a disproportionate measure, even having regard to the legitimacy of the aims pursued by that ban. The Court therefore held that there had been a violation of Article 14 taken in conjunction with Article 8.

The ECtHR has not yet had the opportunity to examine a case where the applicant is a person deprived of legal capacity who challenges the ban on taking up employment. Lawyers representing such a person may want to think about making an Article 14 claim, arguing that the legal status of 'legal incapacity' should be recognised by the Court as an 'other status' for the purposes of Article 14, which reads: 'The enjoyment of the rights and freedoms set forth in this Convention shall be secured without discrimination on any ground such as sex, race, colour, language, religion, political or other opinion, national or social origin, association with a national minority, property, birth or other status.'

The Lithuanian case concerns barriers to getting a job. Once a person has a job, does the ECHR protect against an employer's discriminating against a person with disabilities? The duty to provide 'reasonable accommodation' to people with disabilities in the employment context is a new issue for the ECtHR.[88] The concept of reasonable

---

[88] The term 'reasonable accommodation' appears in the European Union's Employment Framework Directive, Article 5 of which states:

In order to guarantee compliance with the principle of equal treatment in relation to persons with disabilities, reasonable accommodation shall be provided. This means that employers shall take appropriate measures, where needed in a particular case, to enable a person with a disability to have access to, participate in, or advance in employment, or to provide training for such a person, unless such measures would impose a disproportionate burden on the employer. When this burden is, to a sufficient extent, remedied by existing measures as an element of disability policy in the Member State, it should not be considered disproportionate.

The preamble to the Employment Framework Directive explains this further:

Appropriate measures should be provided, i.e. effective and practical measures to adapt the workplace to the disability, for example adapting premises and equipment, patterns of working time, the distribution of tasks or the provision of training or integration resources.

accommodation in the workplace of people with disabilities has generally been framed in terms of accommodating people with physical disabilities. Reasonable accommodation means that the employer should take adequate steps to accommodate the person's differences.[89] For people with mental health problems, reasonable accommodation in the workplace may include such adjustments as flexible working hours, the provision of quiet areas, availability of leave at short notice in order to seek mental health treatment, mentoring schemes, education of other workers about the affects of mental distress, and specific policies detailing harassment against people with psychosocial problems. For people with intellectual disabilities, reasonable accommodation in the workplace may include an extended induction period, mentoring schemes, shorter working hours; more regular supervisory meetings; education of other employees about the nature of intellectual disabilities; and policies detailing harassment against people with intellectual disabilities. It remains to be seen, however, if the ECHR will assist with applications by people with disabilities who claim to have been dismissed because of their disability, or whose employers fail to provide reasonable accommodation.

Discussion

The other substantive chapters in this book deal mostly with controlling the excess of the State's interference in the lives of people with mental disabilities. Certainly, rights to be free of arbitrary detention, rights to be free from institutional abuse or neglect, rights to appropriate medical treatment and to the control of that treatment, rights to appropriate process in guardianship hearings and – of course – the right to life are vital for the protection of rights and dignity of people with mental disabilities; but these rights merely pick at the edges of the traditional social structures that have kept people with mental disabilities on the margins of European, and other, societies.

This chapter has instead raised the possibility of fundamental and long-lasting social change. The issue confronting policymakers and the Court is whether we understand people with mental disabilities as an integral part of our society. Are we content to leave 'those people' on the fringes of society, ensuring merely that they are not actively hurt by the State; or is our objective to develop a society in which they belong? If we are satisfied with the former, we will not have moved far from nineteenth-century attitudes. The attainment of the latter requires a sea change in attitude, however, and while law cannot bring this about on its own, it can certainly play a part.

The division between this chapter and those that precede it is of course not absolute. Provision of adequate treatment, for example, discussed in chapter 4, may be an essential component of a life integrated into the community. It is in the current chapter, however, that the larger policy issue is brought to a head. Some of the rights discussed in this

---

[89] For more on reasonable accommodation and people with mental disabilities under the Convention, see O. De Schutter, *op. cit.*

chapter have been practical. The right to community integration, for example, would require provision of services in communities. This is of course not an impossibility: many of the countries within the Council of Europe are successfully implementing community integration approaches; but others are not. Such local provision of community-based services is vital if individuals are not to lose the relationships they have formed with others, the relationships that are vital if 'community' is to have meaning. The right to education does not merely provide a sense of self-worth. It also provides a skills base from which an individual can seek employment, connecting obviously with the right to work, a right that acknowledges the importance of work in establishing both self-respect and the respect of ones peers, and providing the financial means to enjoy the benefits of social membership.

Other rights discussed in this chapter seem more symbolic. It is probably unlikely, for example, that the results of many elections will be altered by the votes of people with mental disabilities, even with the knowledge that one in four of us at some time in our lives will have a mental health problem. The right to vote is in democratic societies the fundamental badge of membership, important not merely to the voter, although certainly the right to vote provides self-respect. It is also important to the rest of society, in that it acknowledges that people with mental health problems and those with intellectual disabilities have a right equal to the rest of the population to decide who will govern. Disenfranchising a whole segment of the population dislocates that 'group' from political activism. Similarly, the right to associate with others to voice group concerns is a hallmark of democratic societies, and one which the Court has held democratic societies ought to be encouraging.

As noted in the first chapter of this volume, one in four of all of us will have a mental health problem at some time in our lives. In political terms, it is not possible to pretend that 'they' can be quietly left on the margins. 'They' are we. Many of the issues in this chapter the ECHR was not designed to deal with, yet the Convention is viewed as a living instrument. The question in the current chapter is whether it can expand to take into account this new generation of human rights.

Chapter 8

Procedure of the European Court of Human Rights

This chapter elaborates on issues pertinent to applicants with mental disabilities. Its aim is not to be a comprehensive analysis of the intricacies of taking a case to the ECtHR, because there are excellent resources already available.[1] A legal advisor without ECHR experience would be well advised to consult with general ECHR textbooks, and to contact an organization regularly which deals with these issues.

Domestic proceedings

The ECHR can be invoked in domestic proceedings in countries that have ratified it. As this chapter will explain, a case needs to have exhausted effective remedies available in the domestic legal system before applying to Strasbourg. The large backlog of the European Court of Human Rights (by December 2005 there were 82,100 pending cases)[2] means

---

[1] See, among others, C. Ovey and R.C.A. White, *Jacobs and White: The European Convention on Human Rights*, 4th ed., (Oxford: Oxford University Press, 2005); P. Leach, *Taking a Case to the European Court of Human Rights*, (Oxford: Oxford University Press, 2005); K. Reid, *A Practitioner's Guide to the European Convention on Human Rights*, (London: Sweet & Maxwell, 2004).

[2] See Review of the *Working Methods of the European Court of Human Rights*, Lord Woolf et al., December 2005, p. 7, accessible from www.echr.coe.int. The number of cases is expected to rise to 250,000 pending cases by 2010.

that victims of human rights violations are advised to seek justice in domestic courts. The necessary reform of the procedure of the European Court of Human Rights over the next few years will see the Court finding ways to accept fewer cases, and diverting cases away from the Court.[3]

Victim status

In order to apply to the European Court of Human Rights the applicant must be a 'victim' as set out by Article 34 of the ECHR:

> The Court may receive applications from any person, non-governmental organisation or group of individuals claiming to be the victim of a violation by one of the High Contracting Parties of the rights set forth in the Convention or the protocols thereto. The High Contracting Parties undertake not to hinder in any way the effective exercise of this right.

This Article sets out that not only individuals, but non-governmental organizations (NGOs) and groups of individuals can bring a case to the ECtHR. Therefore companies, trade unions, professional organizations, political parties and the like can submit applications. The company or NGO itself needs to have suffered a violation of its 'human' rights in order to bring a case in its own name. This would be the case, for example, if the group were not allowed to be registered contrary to Article 11; if the NGO suffered from a ban on demonstrations contrary to Article 10,[4] or a ban on advertising contrary to Article 10,[5]; or if, contrary to Article 10,[6] the NGO were prevented from providing information which was within its mandate.

The situation differs where an NGO would like to bring a case where the NGO *represents* the victim. The Court has held that the persons entitled to lodge a case on behalf of someone else are restricted to cases where the victim has severe intellectual disabilities,[7] or is a child, irrespective of whether that person has standing to bring cases under national law. Legal representation of people who lack legal capacity is dealt with in chapter 9 of this volume.

Groups of individuals can also bring cases to the European Court of Human Rights.[8] The Court has not yet dealt with an application brought by a group of individuals with

---

[3]   See Lord Woolf's report, *op. cit.* The report recommends, for example, a greater use of national ombudsman mechanisms, setting up a "friendly settlement" unit at the Registry to more vigorously pursue negotiations, the use of "pilot cases".

[4]   See *Christians Against Racism and Fascism v. the United Kingdom*, Application No. 8440/78, decision 16 July 1980, (1980) 21 DR 138.

[5]   See *Vgt Verein gegen Tierfabriken v. Switzerland*, Application No. 24699/94, judgment 29 January 2001, (2002) 34 EHRR 4.

[6]   *Open Door and Dublin Well Woman Clinic v. Ireland*, Application Nos. 14234/99 and 14253/99, judgment 29 October 1992, (A/246) (1993) 15 EHRR 244.

[7]   *H.L. v. the United Kingdom*, Application No. 45508/99, judgment 5 October 2004, (2005) 40 EHRR 32.

[8]   See for example, *Guerra and others v. Italy*, Application No. 14967/89, judgment 19 February 1998, (1988) 57 DR 81, (1998) 26 EHRR 357, in which 40 people villagers brought a case on pollution.

mental disabilities claiming human rights violations, but this could be a useful technique when targeting particularly egregious mental health institutions. This differs from the Anglo-Saxon model of 'class actions' (meaning a representative action in which one or more plaintiffs are named in the complaint, pursue a case for themselves and the defined class against one or more defendants), a type of action which is not provided for within the Convention.

Legal capacity

Lack of legal capacity does not prevent a person from being an applicant him/herself at the European Court of Human Rights.[9] This is important for mental disability litigators to bear in mind, even in cases where domestic law prohibits the person from having legal standing to bring cases in domestic courts. Things get more complex when considering people who have been deprived of legal capacity and who lack actual/functional capacity to instruct a lawyer. In these circumstances, the Court may well allow applications to be brought by family members or carers.[10] Chapter 9 on representation discusses these predicaments in more detail.

Children

Children may bring cases directly to the ECtHR, either together with a parent,[11] or by being represented by a parent.[12] There must also be scope for a child to be represented by someone else other than a parent, especially in cases where there is evidence or allegations of parents abusing the child. The Court has been flexible in its approach to allowing parents who have been deprived from parental rights to bring a case to the Court on behalf of their child.[13] The (now defunct) European Commission of Human Rights took the view that it would not take a restrictive or technical approach to victim questions, as children generally relied on others to represent their interests and required specific protection of their interests which had to be both practical and effective.[14]

Death

The issue of victim status in relation to Article 2 (right to life) cases has been covered above in Chapter 5. In cases where someone has died, the Court has allowed the deceased

---

[9] See *Winterwerp v. the Netherlands*, Application No. 6301/73, judgment 24 October 1979, (A/33) (1979) 2 EHRR 387 and *Matter v. Slovakia*, Application No. 31534/96, judgment 5 July 1999, (2001) 31 EHRR 32. See also chapter 6 on legal capacity, guardianship and supported decision-making.

[10] See *H.L. v. the United Kingdom*, Application No. 45508/99, judgment 5 October 2004, (2005) 40 EHRR 32.

[11] *Marckx v. Belgium*, Application No. 6833/74, judgment 13 June 1979, (1979) 2 EHRR 330, para. 63.

[12] See *Campbell and Cosans v. the United Kingdom*, Application Nos. 7511/76 and 7743/76, judgment 16 May 2980, (1981) 3 EHRR 531.

[13] See *Scozzari and Giunta v. Italy*, Application No. 39221/98, Judgment 13 August 2000, (2002) 35 EHRR 12.

[14] *S.D., D.P. and T. v. the United Kingdom*, Application No. 23715/94, 5.96 (1996) 22 EHRR CD 148.

person's next of kin to bring the application on the deceased person's behalf.[15] However, as is noted in the chapter 5, if a person dies without a family, there seems no way for anyone to litigate any State failure not to investigate the circumstances surrounding the death, despite evidence that there others may be at risk of dying.

If the victim dies during the course of proceedings before the European Court of Human Rights, the Court may allow a relative to continue with the application. However, the Court has refused to allow the continuation of a case by an executor of the original applicant's estate for purely monetary motives, as there was no legitimate interest or prevailing public policy reasons for the Court to continue with the application.[16]

Potential victims

A person who is adversely affected by a law that does not comply with the Convention could claim to be a victim for the purposes of Article 34 of the Convention even where there has been no specific measure taken against the person. The Court has found a potential future violation only in a handful of cases. In one, a gay man claimed to be a potential victim in a country where homosexual acts were at that time criminalized.[17] The Court has found that there is a legitimate psychological distress suffered by the person because of the existence of laws that could persecute that person because of his sexuality.

The other set of cases concern people who are planned to be deported to countries where they may suffer rights violations, such as the case of *D. v. the United Kingdom*, in which a man who was HIV-positive claimed that his imminent deportation to St. Kitts, where there is a lack of adequate medical treatment for Aids, would risk him to suffer inhuman and degrading treatment contrary to Article 3 of the Convention.[18] There are some cases where applicants have argued that a lack of mental health treatment in the receiving country would violate their Convention rights, but the Court has yet to find such a violation in such cases.[19]

Many legal incapacity/guardianship cases, in which a person is prohibited by legislation from marrying, voting, joining associations, etc., could be said to contain dormant violations of the Convention. For example, such a person is prohibited from marrying whether or not he/she would actually like to get married. In such cases the person

---

[15]   See for example *Paul and Audrey Edwards v. the United Kingdom*, Application No. 46477/99, (2002) 35 EHRR 19, para. 55, ECHR 2002–III.

[16]   *Scherer v. Switzerland*, Application No. 17116/90, judgment 25 March 1995, (1994) 19 EHRR 276 and *Karner v. Austria*, Application No. 40016/98, judgment 24 July 2003, (2004) 38 EHRR 24. For a discussion of these issues, see P. Leach, *Taking a Case to the European Court of Human Rights, op. cit.*, pp. 120–3.

[17]   *Dudgeon v. the United Kingdom*, Application No. 7525/76, judgment 23 September 1981, Series A, No. 45, (1982) 4 EHRR 149 (see particularly para. 41), *Norris v. Ireland*, Application No. 10581/83, judgment 26 October 1998, Series A, No. 142, (1991) 13 EHRR 186, *Modinos v. Cyprus*, Application No. 15070/98, judgment 22 April 1993, Series A, No. 259, (1993) 16 EHRR 485.

[18]   *D. v. the United Kingdom*, Application No. 30240/96, judgment 2 May 1997, (1997) 24 EHRR 423.

[19]   See *Bensaid v. the United Kingdom*, Application No. 44599/98, judgment 6 February 2001, (2001) 33 EHRR 10, and *Salkic v. Sweden*, Application No. 7702/04, admissibility decision 29 June 2004.

affected could in theory be classed as a potential victim. However, it is questionable whether the Court would find such a case admissible unless there were evidence that the person had made attempts to vote, marry, join an association, etc. If that were the case, the person would be able to claim an actual violation.

Access to victims, access to justice

Some people with disabilities face insurmountable obstacles to accessing justice. The European Court of Human Rights does not make it easy for people with disabilities to benefit from the protection of the Convention and the mechanism of its enforcement. The authors of this text have visited mental health institutions in countries which have ratified the Convention where there are obvious abuses taking place against people with mental health problems or intellectual disabilities. A benevolent human rights lawyer visiting such institutions may be in the frustrating position of not being able to do anything if the person with disabilities lacks the legal capacity to instruct a lawyer.[20] Put another way, a guardian of a person with intellectual disabilities will take an active interest in the well-being of that person. Such a guardian will make complaints to the relevant authorities and will pursue other remedies, including legal remedies, if matters remain unresolved. However, a guardian who performs in a negligent way will perpetuate the abuse of the person under guardianship by failing to carry out duties even when alerted to a problem. Such behaviour can block a person's access to justice, and in these situations Convention rights remain no more than merely fanciful. In some countries the director or staff member of the institution is also the legal guardian, a situation which creates an obvious conflict of interests.

A person with an intellectual disability who has no guardian will find it enormously difficult to access justice, both in domestic proceedings and at the European Court of Human Rights. In the case of *Skjoldager v. Sweden* the applicant was a psychologist who visited an institution for people with intellectual disabilities in Sweden and found that some of the residents were unlawfully detained.[21] The psychologist was denied access to speak with these people, who would, in any event, probably have lacked capacity to 'instruct' him to represent them. The nursing home refused to give him the names of these residents and therefore he applied to the (then) European Commission of Human Rights in his own name. He argued that the three residents referred to by him were unable to lodge an application on their own and that the authorities had refused to disclose information enabling him to fully identify all of them and to procure powers of attorney either from the patients themselves or from their possible guardians, showing that he was entitled to represent them before the Commission. The Commission noted that the psychologist could not claim to be an 'indirect victim' for example, having a personal interest in the case, because there was no close connection between him and the direct victims.

---

[20] See chapter 9 of this volume for a further discussion.
[21] *Skjoldager v. Sweden*, Application No. 22504/93, decision 17 May 1995.

Further the Commission commented that no evidence had been adduced to the effect that the direct victims were functionally unable to lodge an application in their own names, and found the case inadmissible. Although possibly unintended, the message that the Convention organs send out in deciding declaring such cases inadmissible is that the Convention does not apply to people with mental disabilities in institutions where agents of the state control access, and who, it could be argued, require even more protection than other individuals.

Grounds for declaring a case inadmissible

In order to understand how to apply to the European Court of Human Rights, we must examine first the prerequisites which an applicant must fulfil in order for the case to be declared admissible, which essentially asks the question 'have all the criteria been fulfilled in order for the Court to look at this case?'[22] In this section, the main grounds for declaring a case inadmissible will be discussed. These are contained within Article 35 of the Convention, which reads:

> Article 35 – Admissibility criteria
> 1. The Court may only deal with the matter after all domestic remedies have been exhausted, according to the generally recognised rules of international law, and within a period of six months from the date on which the final decision was taken.
> 2. The Court shall not deal with any application submitted under Article 34 that:
>   a. is anonymous; or
>   b. is substantially the same as a matter that has already been examined by the Court or has already been submitted to another procedure of international investigation or settlement and contains no relevant new information.
> 3. The Court shall declare inadmissible any individual application submitted under Article 34 which it considers incompatible with the provisions of the Convention or the protocols thereto, manifestly ill-founded, or an abuse of the right of application.
> 4. The Court shall reject any application which it considers inadmissible under this Article. It may do so at any stage of the proceedings.

We will examine the major components of Article 35 in turn: exhaustion of domestic remedies, six months rule, anonymous applications, previously similar applications and then incompatibility with the Convention.

Exhaustion of domestic remedies

Probably the most difficult part of taking a case to the European Court of Human Rights is decide whether or not the case has exhausted effective domestic remedies. Mental disability cases are sometimes complicated by factors which raise issues of exhaustion of

---

[22] The admissibility stage results in a 'decision'. The second stage is where the Court examines the merits and produces a 'judgment'.

domestic remedies. Such issues range from the applicant having no legal standing in domestic courts because of legal incapacity (does the applicant have to pursue a remedy which the domestic court is bound to reject because the applicant cannot instruct a lawyer and has no standing?), inadequacy of lawyers during court proceedings (in which case does the applicant have to bring a civil suit against the under-performing attorney?), and lack of clarity of domestic laws and procedures (for example, to challenge bad decisions by the guardian, what remedies does a person under guardianship have?). Further, few cases have been brought that challenge abusive systems and practices, so there remain many unanswered questions on exhaustion of domestic remedies. Given the lack of mental disability jurisprudence, it may be all too easy for respondent Governments to raise arguments that the applicant has failed to exhaust domestic remedies and ask the Court to declare the case inadmissible.

In exhausting domestic remedies, the applicant must have substantively raised in domestic courts those Convention points on which he or she wishes to rely at Strasbourg proceedings. The applicant need not specify the exact ECHR Articles in domestic proceedings, but, as the Court says, the applicant should 'ventilate', or outline the grievances before the domestic courts which will later be submitted to the European Court.[23]

The applicant must comply with domestic law and procedure, including time limits. In some cases it will be impossible to know if and when domestic proceedings have been exhausted, because there is no case law on the specific point being raised. Such issues could be, for example, whether an application to the Constitutional Court is considered to be an effective remedy in a particular type of case. Another example of a lack of clarity in domestic law may be where an applicant who has just found out about guardianship proceedings in which she took no part must apply to a court to open time limits long passed where it is obvious that the court has no power to re-open such time limits or where the applicant because of his or her legal incapacity has no standing to bring such a case to a domestic court. Another example of a difficulty in complying with domestic law and procedure is that it may not be easy to locate ECHR rights domestically. For example, how does a family member litigate against a lack of investigation into a death when there is no such procedure for carrying out the investigation, or how does a person in a hospital litigate a lack of investigation into allegations of abuse when there are no such procedures in place to investigate?

Given these complexities it is somewhat reassuring that the European Court of Human Rights has indicated that it takes a flexible approach to the question of exhaustion of domestic remedies, recognising that each case turns on its facts, and that the applicant might have special circumstances which should be taken into account. In *Yaşa v. Turkey*, for example, the Court raised this point:

---

23 *Glassenap v. Germany*, Application No. 9228/80, judgment 28 August 1986, (A/104) (1987) 9 EHRR 25, para. 44.

The Court emphasises that the application of the exhaustion of domestic remedies rule must make due allowance for the fact that it is being applied in the context of machinery for the protection of human rights that the Contracting Parties have agreed to set up. Accordingly, it has recognised that [the Convention] must be applied with some degree of flexibility and without excessive formalism. It has further recognised that the rule of exhaustion is neither absolute nor capable of being applied automatically; for the purposes of reviewing whether it has been observed, it is essential to have regard to the circumstances of the individual case. This means in particular that the Court must take realistic account, not only of the existence of formal remedies in the legal system of the Contracting Party concerned, but also of the general context in which they operate, as well as the personal circumstances of the applicant. It must then examine whether, in all the circumstances of the case, the applicant did everything that could reasonably be expected of him to exhaust domestic remedies. . . .[24]

The Court has explained that 'the obligation to exhaust domestic remedies requires that an applicant make normal use of remedies which are effective, sufficient and accessible in respect of his Convention grievances.'[25]

Separating out the terms *effective and sufficient and accessible* is complex because the Court has not been clear on what each of these words means. What is clear is that a remedy is one which is able to provide a remedy for the alleged violation of the Convention, and which does not rely on the discretion of the body in question. For example, applicants generally need not complain to an Ombudsman's office if the Ombudsman can offer only remedies which are non-binding. Similarly, the applicant need not apply to a body (such as an authority, ministry or court) if such a body has a wide discretion to provide a binding remedy.[26] An applicant need not pursue more than one remedy if it would not achieve anything. Lawyers are advised to be cautious about pursuing a remedy which they think is not effective: the Court may rule otherwise and declare the case inadmissible. In order to persuade the Court of the likely effectiveness of a remedy it may be helpful to lodge alongside the application an opinion on remedies by a senior lawyer or law professor.

The applicant must be able to directly initiate proceedings to pursue the remedy. A person under guardianship, for example, who is prohibited in law from applying to a court without the permission of the guardian, does not have direct access to instigate proceedings, and therefore is likely not to have an effective remedy especially in a case where the case is about the negligent performance of the guardian. In such a case it is likely that the ECtHR would find that there are no domestic remedies, and the individual could apply without further ado to the ECtHR.[27] Another example would be that in many

---

[24] *Yaşa v. Turkey*, Application No. 22495/93, judgment 2 September 1998, (1999) 28 EHRR 408, para. 77.
[25] *Balogh v. Hungary*, Application no. 47940/99, judgment 20 July 2004.
[26] For example, in the United Kingdom certain higher courts may issue a 'declaration of incompatibility' if a law does not comply with the *Human Rights Act 1998* (the legislation which incorporates the ECHR into domestic law). The declaration of incompatibility is not binding on the parties, but is sent to the relevant government minister for consideration. The European Court of Human Rights has said that such a declaration cannot considered to be an effective domestic remedy: see *Hobbs v. the United Kingdom*, Application No. 63684/91, decision 18 June 2002.
[27] Legal representatives are advised to be cautious. A proceeding which may obviously be non-effective may

countries individuals cannot initiate proceedings before Constitutional Courts. The European Court of Human Rights has ruled that in such instances the Constitutional Court proceedings cannot be considered as constituting an effective remedy.[28] In deciding whether a remedy is accessible, the Court has taken into account factors such as whether the person is able to defend themselves, whether legal representation is compulsory and how complex the proceedings are.[29]

Where is a choice of remedies available to the applicant to obtain redress for an alleged violation of the Convention, the Court applies Article 35 of the Convention in a manner corresponding to the reality of the applicant's situation in order to guarantee effective protection of the rights and freedoms in the Convention.[30]

We advise legal representatives to err on the side of caution. In many cases one can never be sure that the Court will rule that a remedy not pursued was ineffective and therefore declare the case inadmissible. Legal representatives should advise clients to pursue all possible remedies that could potentially be effective, even if the legal advisor (perhaps correctly) believes that the particular remedy has little chance of success. The Court has emphasised that the existence of mere doubts as to the prospects of success of a particular remedy which is not obviously futile is not a valid reason for failing to exhaust domestic remedies.[31] Lawyers are advised to send a pre-application letter in order to protect the client's position in relation to the six months rule, explaining to the Court that domestic remedies are being pursued, but that these are thought to be ineffective (see section below on pre-application letters). It should be noted that domestic remedies can be exhausted after submitting the ECHR application form, but all domestic remedies must have been completed by the time the Court decides on admissibility.[32]

Only one of a possible number of remedies must be pursued. If the person, for example, has lodged a case in a civil court and it is thought that there is a reasonable chance of success at that court, there is no obligation on the victim to lodge parallel applications with (for example) an administrative court which offers similar chances of success.

The burden of proof is on the Government claiming non-exhaustion to satisfy the Court that an effective remedy was available in theory and in practice at the relevant time. That is to say, it is for the respondent Government to prove that the remedy was accessible, was capable of providing redress in respect of the applicant's complaint and offered

---

be viewed differently by the Court. Therefore it is advised that every effort be made to battle through domestic legal proceedings in order to demonstrate that the client has taken every opportunity to have the violation remedied domestically. Representatives should of course keep an eye on the clock to ensure that the client is not disadvantaged by a future ruling that the remedy was actually *not* effective, and therefore the relevant date is more than six month ago – see later in this chapter for a discussion.

[28] *Zvolsky and Zvolská v. The Czech Republic*, Application no. 46129/99, judgment 12 November 2002.

[29] See *Airey v. Ireland*, Application No. 6289/73, judgment 9 October 1979, Series A, No. 32, (1979–80) 2 EHRR 305.

[30] *Airey v. Ireland, op. cit.*, para. 23, and *Hilal v. the United Kingdom*, Application no. 45276/99, decision 8 February 2000.

[31] *Van Oosterwijck v. Belgium*, Application No. 7654/76, judgment 6 November 1980, Series A no. 40, p. 18, (1981) 3 EHRR 557 para. 37.

[32] *Luberti v. Italy*, Application No. 9019/80, decision 7 July 1981, 27 DR 181.

reasonable prospects of success.[33] Once this burden of proof has been satisfied, it falls to the applicant to establish that the remedy advanced by the Government was in fact exhausted, or was for some reason inadequate or ineffective in the particular circumstances of the case, or that there existed 'special circumstances' absolving the applicant from the requirement.

The Court may find 'special circumstances' if it takes the view that national authorities' remained totally passive in the face of serious allegations of misconduct or infliction of harm by State agents, for example, where they have failed execute a court order. In such a case, it is for the respondent Government to show what it has done in response to the scale and seriousness of the matters complained of. In one case, the Court, having regard to findings in a CPT report, held that the national authorities had remained totally passive for more than a year in complying with six injunctions to repair rather serious structural shortcomings of an elementary hygienic and humanitarian nature in prison facilities. The Court concluded that, in the absence of convincing explanations from the Government for their failure to take the necessary measures within a reasonable time to repair the structural problems, and to observe the court orders, there were special circumstances at the material time which dispensed the applicant from the obligation to exhaust the remedy suggested by the Government.[34]

A lawyer representing a client with mental disabilities in a human rights case may consider arguing special circumstances, but should tread carefully. If in any doubt, the lawyer would be well advised to try all possible effective remedies in parallel with sending a pre-application letter to the Court in order to protect the client's time limits (see six months rule, below).

Article 13

There is no natural place in a book on the ECHR to discuss Article 13 of the Convention. Article 13 is a substantive article of the Convention which can be argued separately from all other allegations, unlike Article 14, which must apply to another right protected by the Convention. Article 13 is intimately linked with procedure and domestic remedies and is therefore dealt with here:

> Article 13 – Right to an effective remedy
> Everyone whose rights and freedoms as set forth in this Convention are violated shall have an effective remedy before a national authority notwithstanding that the violation has been committed by persons acting in an official capacity.

Article 13 places a positive obligation on States to establish mechanisms whereby a victim can seek remedies for alleged violations of the Convention. The logical purpose of

---

[33] *V. v. the United Kingdom* Application No. 24888/94, judgment 16 December 1999, (2000) 30 EHRR 121, ECHR 1999-IX, para. 57.
[34] *A.B. v. the Netherlands*, Application no. 37328/97, judgment 29 January 2002, (2003) 37 EHRR 48, para. 69.

the Article is to allow national authorities (including but not exclusively courts) to deal with substantive complaints of the Convention, and in appropriate cases provide be provided with remedies, without recourse to international justice system. The Article has been interpreted to include those who *claim* that a Convention right has been violated.[35]

Article 13 can be invoked alongside any arguable claim of a violation of another Article of the Convention. The Court has refused to provide an abstract definition of the notion of 'arguability', leaving the issue to be decided in the light of the particular facts and the nature of the legal issue or issues raised.[36] Notwithstanding the terms of Article 13 read literally, the existence of an actual breach of another provision is not a prerequisite for the application of the Article.[37] However, where an arguable breach of one or more Convention rights is made out, there should be available to the victim a mechanism for establishing liability of State officials or bodies for that breach. States are afforded some discretion as to the manner in which they conform to their Convention obligations under this provision. As a general rule, if a single remedy does not by itself entirely satisfy the requirements of Article 13, the aggregate of remedies provided for under domestic law may do so.[38]

It is noteworthy that in the context of Article 13 the Court has said that where there are violations of either Article 2 or 3, 'compensation for the non-pecuniary damage flowing from the breach should in principle be available as part of the range of possible remedies'.[39]

Article 13 will be relevant for many cases brought by people with mental disabilities – especially guardianship cases, where the individual is prohibited in law from taking cases to court – including those in which they seek to argue violations of their Convention rights. Lawyers are advised to think about adding an Article 13 claim in cases where there has been a difficulty or impossibility in bringing such a case domestically.

Six months rule

In accordance with Article 35(1) of the Convention, the Court may only examine complaints in respect of which domestic remedies have been exhausted and which have been submitted within six months from the date of the 'final' domestic decision. The Court has stated:

---

[35] *Klass and others v. Germany*, Application no. 5029/71, judgment 6 September 1998, Series A, No. 28, (1979–80) 2 EHRR 214, para. 64.

[36] *Boyle and Rice v. the United Kingdom*, Application Nos. 9659/82 and 9658/82, judgment 27 April 1988, Series A. No. 131, (1988) 10 EHRR 425, para. 55.

[37] *Boyle and Rice v. the United Kingdom*, Application Nos. 9659/82 and 9658/82, judgment 27 April 1988, Series A. No. 131, (1988) 10 EHRR 425, para. 52.

[38] See, for example, *Kudla v. Poland*, Application No. 30210/96, Grand Chamber judgment 26 October 2000, (2002) 35 EHRR 11, para. 157; see also *Čonka v. Belgium*, Application No. 51564/99, judgment 5 February 2002, (2002) 34 EHRR 54, para. 75.

[39] *Keenan v. the United Kingdom*, Application No. 27229/95, judgment 3 April 2001, (2001) 33 EHRR 38, para. 130.

the object of the six month time-limit under Article 35 is to promote legal certainty, by ensuring that cases raising issues under the Convention are dealt with within a reasonable time and that past decisions are not continually open to challenge. The rule also affords the prospective applicant a time to consider whether to lodge an application and, if so, to decide on the specific complaints and arguments to be raised . . .[40]

The six month period runs from the day after the final decision in domestic proceedings which are deemed effective.[41] The six months is counted as running from the date of service of the written document in cases where the applicant is entitled, pursuant to domestic law, to be served with a written copy of the final domestic decision, irrespective of whether that judgment was previously delivered orally.[42]

In terms of mental disability cases and the six months rule, the Court has emphasised that the six months rule 'has to be applied without excessive formalism, having regard to the particular circumstances of the case. [. . .] There may, in particular, be special circumstances – for example, where the applicant's mental state rendered him or her incapable of lodging a complaint within the prescribed period – which can interrupt or suspend the running of time for the purposes of limitation'.[43]

If there is no adequate remedy against a particular act or decision that is alleged to be in breach of the Convention, the six months start from the date on which that act or decision took place.[44] If the applicant found out about the particular act or decision afterwards, it is the date of knowledge which is relevant.[45] This might be particularly important to bear in mind in relation to guardianship proceedings that may take place without the person's knowledge, or in proceedings where there are no effective domestic remedies.

An application concerning a continuing violation (such as the law prohibiting a person under guardianship from marrying, or an ongoing unlawful detention) can be submitted to the Court at any time during the ongoing violation or until six months after it or the last effective domestic remedy, because the clock does not start running until the continuing violation stops. In some cases however, it may be advantageous to apply to relevant authorities to obtain an official 'decision' on the matter before applying to the

---

[40] *Vasyl Gavrylovych Koval v. Ukraine*, Application No. 65550/01, decision 30 March 2004.

[41] There is of course a danger in waiting for a domestic court to give a decision in a case and then applying to the Strasbourg Court only to find that the Court declares the case inadmissible because it does not consider the final domestic court an effective remedy. Again, if there are any doubts as to the effectiveness of a particular remedy, practitioners are advised to lodge a pre-application letter to the ECtHR explaining that the case is still going through domestic proceedings which the practitioner is not sure will be effective.

[42] See for example *Worm v. Austria*, Application No. 22714/93, judgment 29 August 1997, (1988) 25 EHRR 454, para. 33 or *Drosopoulos v. Greece* Application No. 40442/98, decision 7 December 2000.

[43] *Storck v. Germany*, Application No. 61603/00, judgment 16 June 2005, para. 95, in which the Court referred to the admissibility decisions of *K. v. Ireland*, Application No. 10416/83, Commission decision of 17 May 1984, Decisions and Reports (DR) 38, p. 160, and *H. v. the United Kingdom and Ireland*, Application No. 9833/82, Commission decision of 7 March 1985, DR 42, p. 57.

[44] *Valašinas v. Lithuania*, Application No. 44558/98, decision 14 March 2000.

[45] See *X. v. the United Kingdom*, Application No. 7379/76, decision 10 December 1976.

Strasbourg Court. If time is tight, practitioners should remember that the Court accepts applications via a 'pre-application letter', which is discussed later in this chapter.

Anonymous applications

The Court does not deal under Article 34 with applications submitted anonymously. The applicant's identity *must* be revealed in the application form. If the applicant would like to have the protection of anonymity remain anonymous during the proceedings, there is a procedure, which will be dealt with below, to allow their identity to remain confidential (see the section on 'Anonymity and confidentiality', below).

Applications substantially the same

Under Article 35(2)(b), the Court is obliged to declare inadmissible any case which has already (a) been examined by the Court[46] or (b) has already been submitted to another procedure of international investigation,[47] and which does not contain any new relevant information. New information which would be relevant may be domestic court judgments which shed new light on the admissibility of an application.

Incompatibility with the Convention

There are four situations in which an application may be found inadmissible because of being incompatible with the Convention under Article 35(3), and these are referred to by their Latin names:

- Incompatible *ratione personae*: The application will be declared inadmissible unless the respondent State is a party to the Convention and is responsible for the alleged violation.[48]
- Incompatible *ratione loci*: The application will be declared inadmissible unless it has taken place within the respondent Government's jurisdiction, including areas where the State has 'effective control' over the territory. States are responsible, under Article 1 of the Convention, for all acts and omissions of their organs, whether these arise from domestic law or from the need to fulfil international legal obligations.[49]
- Incompatible *ratione temporis*: The application will be declared inadmissible unless it has taken place after the Convention came into force, or after a country ratified the Convention. The date of ratification by each State can be found on the Court's website, www.echr.coe.int.

---

[46] Article 35(2)(b).
[47] Article 35(2)(b).
[48] The State may not be responsible if the alleged violation was caused by a non-State actor, or if the State cannot be said to have been responsible. For example, abuses in a private hospital are not controlled by the State, but the applicant may have a claim against the State if it failed to hold an investigation into a credible claim of an Article 3 violation.
[49] See for example the Grand Chamber judgment in *Ilaşcu and Others v. Moldova and Russia*, Application No. 48787/99, judgment 8 July 2004, (2005) 40 EHRR 46, para. 311.

- Incompatible *ratione materiae*: The application will be declared inadmissible unless the alleged violation is one which can be argued under the Convention. Practitioners should remember that the Convention is a living instrument, and that the case-law has developed to include issues which the drafters of the convention probably did not have in mind.[50]

Manifestly ill-founded

Article 35(3) requires the Court to declare applications inadmissible if they are 'manifestly ill-founded'. It may be difficult to distinguish between this limb and the test of *ratione materiae*, above. The Court uses this limb of Article 35 to declare inadmissible those cases which do not raise serious questions of fact and law and are of such limited complexity that their determination should depend only on an examination on the merits. Grounds of inadmissibility are normally of a formal nature (non-exhaustion, six months, etc.). It is frequent for a Committee to decide that an application is inadmissible because it is 'manifestly ill-founded'. Chambers of the Court declare applications inadmissible on this ground less frequently. Cases are declared inadmissible because, for example, they do not have the evidence to substantiate the claim that is being made, the facts do not disclose any breach of the Convention, or the applicant cannot claim to be a victim. The Court often fails to give substantive reasons why it finds cases manifestly ill-founded.

Applicant has not suffered a significant disadvantage (Protocol 14)

Protocol 14 to the Convention, which will come into force three months after the date on which all Parties to the Convention have expressed their consent to be bound by the Protocol. The Protocol inserts a new admissibility criterion into Article 35. Under Article 35(3)(b), the Court will be able to declare inadmissible any individual application where the applicant has not suffered a significant disadvantage. However, cases may not be dismissed on this ground if 'respect for human rights' requires an examination on the merits or where the case has not been duly examined by a domestic tribunal. In the two years following the entry into force of the Protocol, this criterion may be applied only by Chambers and the Grand Chamber.

Applying to the Court

This section briefly describes aspects related to the procedure of taking a case to the European Court of Human Rights.[51]

---

[50]   For example, the State obligation under Article 2 of the Convention to adequately investigate deaths was developed by the judges – it is not something which appears in the Convention. Similarly, an ever-increasing array of issues are held by the Court to engage Article 8.

[51]   Again, this book does not intend to be a comprehensive guide to lodging a case with the European Court of Human Rights, rather to cover issues which may arise when representing people with mental disabilities. Practitioners should read other books such as those recommended *supra* at note 1.

Legal representation

This book has been written, in part at least, for legal representatives. However, applications to the Court can be lodged by the applicant or by a representative who need not be legally qualified.[52] If the applicant has lodged the application without a legal representative and the case is 'communicated' (a procedural issue which is Convention language for 'sent') to the respondent Government, the Court will require the applicant to be represented by a lawyer authorized to practise in any of the Council of Europe Member States and resident in the territory of one of one of the States.[53] If a different person (e.g. a lawyer not qualified to represent people, or a lawyer from outside one of these States) wishes to represent the applicant, he or she must seek permission from the President of the Chamber.[54] Representatives should note that in 'exceptional circumstances and at any stage of the procedure' the Court has the power to direct that the representative may no longer represent or assist the applicant if the advocate's conduct so warrants.[55] Further, '[i]f the representative of a party makes abusive, frivolous, vexatious, misleading or prolix submissions, the President of the Chamber may exclude that representative from the proceedings, refuse to accept all or part of the submissions or make any other order which he or she considers it appropriate to make, without prejudice to Article 35 § 3 of the Convention.'[56]

How to apply

Applications to the Court must be submitted in writing and signed by the applicant or the applicant's representative.[57] The application need not be made using the Court's application form (see Appendix 8 for a copy of the application form), but can be in the form of a letter (see section on 'pre-application letters', below). Practitioners may have good reasons not to submit a full application to the Court. Written applications must be sent to the Court at the following address:

> The Registrar
> European Court of Human Rights
> Council of Europe
> F. 67075 STRASBOURG CEDEX
> France

Applications may also be submitted by fax (number +33 3 88 41 27 30), as long as the original follows within five days.[58] Where applicants are legally or otherwise represented,

---

[52] Rule 36(1) of the Rules of Court (July 2006).
[53] The Rules of Court uses the word 'advocate' but this book uses the term 'lawyer' to avoid confusion with advocates who are not legally qualified.
[54] Rule 36(4) of the Rules of Court (July 2006).
[55] Rule 36(4)(b) of the Rules of Court (July 2006).
[56] Rule 44D of the Rules of Court (July 2006).
[57] Applications cannot be submitted by telephone. See Rule 45(1) of the Rules of Court (July 2006), and section 1(1) of the Practice Direction on Institution of Proceedings (March 2005).
[58] Practice Direction: Institution of Proceedings (March 2005), para. 5.

the application should also contain a power of attorney or written authority to act, although this may be submitted later.[59]

Pre-application letters

As was discussed earlier in this chapter, it sometimes unclear to the applicant or lawyer whether domestic proceedings have been exhausted. The six months time limit may be fast approaching but the lawyer may not have enough evidence or may not have sufficiently researched the law in order to submit a fully argued application. In such situations, practitioners should consider sending a 'pre-application letter' in cases where they want to protect against an eventual finding by the Court that the application is out of time according to Article 35. A pre-application letter can usefully 'stop the clock' for the purposes of the six month rule.

A pre-application letter should contain the applicant's name, address, age, and a summary of the facts of the complaint, as well as outline what domestic legal proceedings have been pursued. The letter should also set out the Articles of the Convention which the applicant claims to have been breached. Practitioners are advised to be as broad as possible in the short argumentation provided to the Court at this stage. Failure to raise a certain Article of the Convention at this stage may, if the time limits have passed, render inadmissible a future application relying on different Articles.

The Court expects a completed application form to be completed within six weeks of sending the pre-application letter,[60] and will destroy the file if there is no correspondence within one year. The Court may declare the case inadmissible if the applicant does not adhere to the time limits set by the Court. A fully completed application form should be submitted as soon as possible after the completion of domestic proceedings. In any event, we recommend keeping the Court updated regularly about the progress of the case.

Application Form

If a pre-application letter has been sent to the Court, an application form should be completed ideally within six weeks, or as soon as practicably possible and sent to the Court. Applicants or their representatives should take great care in being as comprehensive as possible when filling out the application form. This is the first (and in many cases only) chance to provide well thought out legal argumentation to the Court. An application form can be found at appendix 8. An application should be written legibly or preferably typed.[61] If an application exceeds ten pages excluding annexes, the applicant must additionally file a short summary.[62] Documents listed (such as court judgments and applica-

---

[59] Rule 45(3) of the Rules of Court (July 2006).
[60] Practice Direction: Institution of Proceedings (March 2005), para. 4.
[61] Practice Direction: Institution of Proceedings (March 2005), para. 13.
[62] Practice Direction: Institution of Proceedings (March 2005), para. 14.

tions, appeals, etc.) should be listed in date order and numbered consecutively and given a short description (e.g., 'Judgment of Supreme Court of Russia, 16 April 2006').[63]

Letter of authority (power of attorney)

The letter of authority must be completed and signed by an applicant wishing to be represented before the Court and by the lawyer of the applicant. It can be found on the Court's website www.echr.coe.int and is reproduced at appendix 9. The Authority states:

> I (applicant's name), hereby authorize (name, address and occupation of representative) to represent me in the proceedings before the European Court of Human Rights and in any subsequent proceedings under the European Convention on Human Rights concerning my application introduced under Article 34 of the Convention against (respondent State) on (date of letter of introduction).

Whilst this Authority may seem simple, some applicants with mental disabilities may face problems in instructing a lawyer, and signing the authority (see above section on "Victims" and chapter 9 on representation).

Anonymity and confidentiality

All documents relating to a particular case which have been lodged with the Court – whether from the applicant, respondent Government of a third party – are (theoretically at least) open to the public.[64] The hard exception to this rule are firstly Committee decisions and secondly documents in relation to friendly settlements, or where the President of the Chamber decides any document should not be made public.[65] The Rules of Court state that:

> Public access to a document of any part of it may be restricted in the interests of morals, public order or national security in a democratic society, where the interests of juveniles or the protection of the private life of the parties so require, or to the extent strictly necessary in the opinion of the President in special circumstances where publicity would prejudice the interests of justice.[66]

In cases concerning people with mental disabilities, there may often be information which is private in nature and which the applicant would not want the public to know about. Such information could be, for example, diagnoses of mental illness, periods of treatment in psychiatric hospitals or information relating to denial of legal capacity.

---

[63] Practice Direction: Institution of Proceedings (March 2005), para. 15.
[64] Article 40(2) of the European Convention on Human Rights. This is worth bearing in mind when the practitioner knows of similar cases pending. Practitioners can write to the court to request copies of all documents about a particular case.
[65] Rule 33(1).
[66] Rule 33(2).

Practitioners should always discuss these issues with the applicant. If the applicant is uncomfortable with any aspect of the case being available to the public, the advocate should write to the Court at the outset of proceedings or at any time thereafter requesting that the President of the Chamber deny access to a document or part of a document. Such a request must include reasons and specify whether it is requested that all or part of the documents be inaccessible to the public.[67]

Practitioners should also discuss with their client the possibility of requesting the Court not to disclose their identity to the public. The Court has granted this request in many cases including those where the applicant was a person with autism represented by carers,[68] where the applicant is a child,[69] where the application concerns matters of mental health,[70] or famous applicants who might be subject to public retribution.[71]

The Court will only grant such a request 'in exceptional and duly justified cases'.[72] If such a request is made it should contain a statement of the reasons justifying such a departure from the normal rule of public access to information in proceedings before the Court. The request should also state that in the event in the event of anonymity being authorised by the President of the Chamber, he or she wishes to be designated by his or her initials or by a single letter (e.g. X., Y., Z., etc.).[73] It is of course obvious that there is no way to keep the applicant's details anonymous from the respondent State. The respondent Government has the right to defend the case and can only do so if they know who the applicant is. This has implications for vulnerable applicants who, for example, are still detained in psychiatric or other institutions and who may be subject to punishment or intimidation by authorities.

Procedure from application to admissibility

A pre-application letter, or a completed application form, will be processed by the Registry and an application number given to the case. The application number must be cited on all future correspondence. The case will be allocated to a Judge Rapporteur who will examine the case.[74] The Judge Rapporteur remains anonymous to the Applicant. The Judge Rapporteur can decide to refer the case to a Committee of three judges who can

---

[67] Rule 33(3).
[68] For example, *H.L. v. the United Kingdom*, Application No. 45508/99, judgment 5 October 2004,(2005) 40 EHRR 32.
[69] For example, *T. and V. v. the United Kingdom*, Application Nos. 24888/94 and 24724/94, judgment 16 December 1999, (2000) 30 EHRR 121.
[70] For example, *H.M. v. Switzerland*, Application No. 39187/98, judgment 26 February 2002, (2004) 38 EHRR 17.
[71] *T. v. the United Kingdom*, Application No. 24724/94, judgment 16 December 1999, (2000) 30 EHRR 121.
[72] Rule 47(3).
[73] Practice Direction Institution of Proceedings (March 2005), para. 17.
[74] Rule 49.

unanimously declare a case inadmissible.[75] If the Committee declares a case inadmissible the applicant is sent a short letter explaining briefly the reasons for the decision, and informing the applicant that there are no rights of appeal and that the case file will be destroyed in one year.[76] If the Committee does not reach a unanimous decision, the case is referred to a Chamber of seven judges.

The Chamber may do one of a number of things:

- declare the case inadmissible (in which case the Chamber provides a more reasoned decision), or strike the case out of the list;[77]
- request the parties to submit any factual information, documents or other material considered by the Chamber or its President to be relevant;[78]
- give notice of the application to the respondent Government and invite that party to submit written observations on the application.[79]

In taking these steps, the Chamber may ask the parties to make submissions on both admissibility and merits of the case.[80] If the Chamber takes the decision not to declare the case inadmissible, the application will be 'communicated' (sent) to the Government for its comments.[81] The Government's response will be sent to the Applicant and representative, who are given an opportunity to comment within a given time set by the Court. Correspondence by parties after admissibility must be in English or French, unless the President of the Chamber authorises otherwise.[82]

Further written correspondence to the Court should contain the application number and the name of the case as well as a title indicating the nature of the content (e.g. reply to the Government's/the applicant's observations on admissibility [and the merits]).[83] There are further rules about paper size and legibility, numbering of pages and chapter headings.[84] If a pleading exceeds 30 pages, a short summary should accompany it.[85] Where a party produces documents and/or other exhibits together with a pleading, every piece of evidence should be listed in a separate annex.[86]

The parties may request the Chamber to hold an oral hearing on admissibility, or the Chamber may instigate a hearing on its own motion.[87] Nowadays hearings on

---

[75] Article 28, Rule 53.
[76] It is interesting to note that if a domestic court were to send such a brief rejection letter to an applicant, the ECtHR would probably find that the lack of reasons for the court's decision did not meet Article 6 guarantees of fair trial.
[77] Rule 54(1).
[78] Rule 54(2)(a).
[79] Rule 54(2)(b).
[80] Rule 54A.
[81] Some governments have a designated representative based in Strasbourg.
[82] Rule 34 of the Rules of Court (July 2006).
[83] Practice Direction: Written Pleadings (March 2005), para. 8.
[84] Practice Direction: Written Pleadings (March 2005), para. 9.
[85] Practice Direction: Written Pleadings (March 2005), para. 10.
[86] Practice Direction: Written Pleadings (March 2005), para. 11.
[87] Rule 54(3). Oral hearings on admissibility are now rare. However, if the applicant's lawyer thinks there

admissibility, merits or a combination are rare.[88] Whether following a hearing or whether the case has been conducted on the papers, a Chamber decision (on admissibility) or judgment (on the merits) is made public. An admissibility decision contains a summary of the facts, the applicant's complaints and an outline of the law in question, and reasons for the Court's decision.[89]

If a case is declared admissible, the Court will ask the parties to submit further observations. The Court will seek to establish the facts. Whilst the Court has stated that it is not a court of fourth instance and will rarely challenge a factual findings by domestic authorities, it does retain the authority to come to different conclusions from domestic courts.[90] The Court can ask the parties for documentary evidence, to hear witnesses or to obtain expert reports.[91] In some cases the Court will send a delegation to the country where the alleged violation took place in order to investigate the facts and interview witnesses.[92] People with mental disabilities often face difficulties with credibility. The evidence of a person with mental disabilities may not be given the same weight as those without a diagnosis and therefore in appropriate cases legal representatives may consider whether it would be advantageous to the client to ask the Court to carry out a fact-finding delegation during which a Court delegation could interview the applicant and other witnesses and to visit any institutions where violations allegedly took place.

Although the Convention says otherwise,[93] it is now the usual practice in simple for a Chamber to examine both the admissibility and merits at the same time. The Chamber may declare a case admissible and deal with the merits of the case at a later stage.

It should be noted that Article 8 of Protocol 14 to the Convention (which had yet to come into force at the time this book went to print) establishes a fast-track procedure for 'manifestly well-founded' applications. A Committee of three judges will examine admissibility and the merits of a case if the issues in the case concern have already been dealt with by well-established case law.

Effective exercise of the right of application

The Convention itself contains an obligation on States not to hinder a person exercising his or her right to seek access before the European Court of Human Rights. Article 34 of the Convention contains the provision that States undertake not to hinder in any way

---

is an advantage in having an oral hearing, a letter should be sent to the Court detailing the reasons for such a request. Unless there are exceptional circumstances, oral hearings deal with admissibility *and* merits.

[88] Given their rarity, issues which relate to oral hearings are not dealt with further in this book.

[89] Article 45, Rule 56.

[90] See, for example, *Ribitsch v. Austria*, Application No. 18896/91, judgment 4 December 1995, (1996) 21 EHRR 573, para. 33.

[91] Annex to the Rules, Rules A1 and 2.

[92] See an Annex to the Rules of the Court, Rules A1–A8. For more on the fact-finding procedure, see Philip Leach, *op. cit.*, pp. 65–69.

[93] See Article 29(3) of the Convention.

the effective exercise of the right of application. Behaviour which is considered by the Court to hinder the exercise of right of application includes for example interference with the applicant's correspondence,[94] and questions or interviews by State officials regarding Strasbourg applications.[95] In such cases evidence of intimidation will be crucial: it is obviously difficult to document verbal threats, but witness statements written up after the event as well as any other written documentation will assist the Court to make an assessment as to the truth of any claim, and its seriousness.

Applicants and their representatives should also be aware of the existence of the *European Agreement Relating to Persons Participating in Proceedings of the European Court of Human Rights*, 5 March 1996. This Agreement is designed to give persons taking part in proceedings before the Court (whether as parties, their lawyers or advisers, or as witnesses, experts or interveners) immunities and facilities to enable them fully to participate in the proceedings. The main provisions are immunity from legal process in respect of statements made and documents submitted to the Court; a right to correspond freely with the Court, including applicants who are detained; and free and unimpeded movement and travel for the purpose of attending and returning from proceedings before the Court. Somewhat inexplicably, the European Agreement has not been ratified by all States which have ratified the Convention. Nevertheless, the points which it contains can be used to argue a violation of Article 34 of the Convention in cases where there has been intimidation or hindrance of the right of application.

Costs

One of the pleasantly surprising features of the European Court of Human Rights procedure is that the applicant is never at any risk of paying the respondent Government's costs, even if the Court declares a case inadmissible or if it finds no violation of the Convention. If the applicant is successful (meaning that the Court finds one or more violations of the Convention), the applicant can apply to the Court for 'just satisfaction' under Article 41.[96] Just satisfaction may include recuperation of legal costs from the Government, those incurred in the domestic proceedings as well as proceedings before the Court. Applicants do not have to deal with costs at the time of the original application.

There is no formal procedure for assessing the amount of costs, and the Court has wide discretion as to what it allows. The Court generally employs a three-stage test in assessing costs. *First*, such costs must have been actually incurred by the applicant. *Second*, such

---

[94] *Cotlet v. Romania*, Application No. 38565/97, judgment 3 June 2003.
[95] *Akdivar v. Turkey*, Application 21893/93, judgment 16 September 1997, (1997) 23 EHRR 143.
[96] Note the separate right to compensation contained in Article 5(5) of the ECHR for any violation of Article 5: this is discussed in chapter 2 of this volume.

costs must have been necessarily incurred. *Third*, such costs must be reasonable as to quantum.

Costs can only be reclaimed if they are actually incurred by the applicant. This means that a lawyer acting on a *pro bono* basis and who has made it clear that he/she is acting as such will be unable to recover costs because the applicant would not owe the attorney the money.[97] However, the Court has called upon attorneys that take on human rights cases to moderate their fees so that 'applicants [do] not encounter undue financial difficulties in bringing complaints under the Convention'.[98] In keeping with this policy, the Court has found it acceptable if the lawyer presents the client with his fee notes for domestic procedures a fairly long time after the services were rendered, after the European Court of Human Rights has found violations of the Convention.

For example, in *Pakelli v. Germany*,[99] the applicant claimed reimbursement of lawyer's fees for domestic proceedings in 1978. However, the lawyer did not demand the legal fees from his client until 1982, saying that he knew that his client could not afford to pay at that time and he was therefore content to wait. The Court ruled that the lawyer's behaviour did not constitute a waiver of the fees and that such fees were still owed by the applicant. As a result, the respondent Government was required to pay these fees. It is therefore advisable for lawyers to discuss the details of the costs with the client at the outset of proceedings. This would preclude an argument sometimes made by the respondent Governments that the fee notes are false and that the applicant is not actually liable to pay legal fees.[100] It is to be noted that the applicant cannot recover a lawyer's fees paid on contingency basis (no win, no fee) in countries where such a fee arrangement is not legally enforceable.[101]

All costs claimed must be shown to have been necessary in order to seek, through domestic courts, prevention of or remedy for a violation and to have the same established by the Court.[102] Therefore, in a case where the Court makes a finding of violation of only part of the claim, the applicant cannot claim costs related to the unsuccessful part of the claim: in such cases costs may be proportionally reduced. The Court retains a discretion in assessing actual quantum. In one case,[103] the Court found that most of the costs were incurred in respect to the complaint under Article 1 of Protocol 1, which was declared

[97] *McCann v. the United Kingdom*, Application No. 18984/91, judgment 27 September 1995, (1996) 21 EHRR 97, para. 221.

[98] *Young, James and Webster v. the United Kingdom (Article 50)*, Application Nos. 7601/76, 7806/77, judgment 18 October 1982, (1982) 4 EHRR 38, para. 15.

[99] Application No. 8398/78, judgment 25 April 1983, (A/64) (1984) 6 EHRR 1.

[100] See, for example, *Eckle v. Germany (Article 50)*, Application No. 8130/78, judgment 21 June 1983, (1983) 5 EHRR 1, para. 35.

[101] *Dudgeon v. the United Kingdom (Article 50)*, Application No. 7525/76, judgment 24 February 1983, (A/59) (1983) 5 EHRR 573, para. 22.

[102] *Minelli v. Switzerland*, Application No. 8660/79, judgment 25 March 1983 (A/62) (1983) 5 EHRR 554, para. 45.

[103] *Mats Jacobsson v. Sweden*, Application No. 11309/84, judgment 28 June 1990, (A/180-A) (1991) 13 EHRR 79, para. 46.

inadmissible. As a result, the applicant received only 20% of the fees sought. If the applicant's unsuccessful claims constitute only an insubstantial part of the application, the Court may reduce the costs by very little, or not at all.[104]

Legal fees must be reasonable. The Court has dismissed claims for fees for the preparation of documents that the Court did not eventually take into account, sums paid to lawyers for work the Court considered unnecessary (including consultation and research work), and costs connected with an expert's presence in Strasbourg on the day of the hearing.[105] It seems that generally the Court has considered two lawyers to be an appropriate number to represent an applicant in proceedings at the Court.[106] As for actual quantum, the Court is not bound by domestic scales of legal fees, but 'derive[s] some assistance from them'.[107] The Court will assess legal fees with regard to what would be a reasonable figure for lawyers in the country in which they generally practice.[108]

European Legal Aid

In order to enable applicants to be legally represented, the Court allows applicants to apply for Council of Europe legal aid. This will be granted only if it is necessary for the proper conduct of the case and if the applicant has insufficient means to meet all or part of the costs of bringing a case to the Court.[109] Applicants will be asked to compete a 'Declaration of Applicant's Means' form, which is sent to the Court and the domestic authorities for assessment.[110] The Government has an opportunity to comment on the form.[111]

If an applicant receives Council of Europe legal aid, any award of costs is subject to a deduction for the legal aid already received. Thus, the respondent Government is obliged only to pay the net difference. Moreover, the applicant cannot make claims for additional

---

[104] *Eckle v. Germany (Article 50)*, Application No. 8130/78, judgment 21 June 1983, (1983) 5 EHRR 1, para. 51.

[105] *Sporrong and Lönnroth v. Sweden (Article 50)*, Application Nos. 7151/75 and 7152/75, judgment 18 December 1984, (A/85) (1985) 7 EHRR CD256, para. 39; *Dudgeon v. the United Kingdom (Article 50)*, Application No. 7525/76, judgment 24 February 1983, (A/59) (1983) 5 EHRR 573, para. 27.

[106] *Twalib v. Greece*, Application No. 24294/94, judgment 9 June 1998, (2001) 33 EHRR 24, para. 71; *Kokkinakis v. Greece*, Application No. 14307/88, judgment 19 April 1993, (A/260-A) (1994) 17 EHRR 397, para. 60; *Baraona v. Portugal*, Application No. 10092/82, judgment 21 June 1987, (A/122) (1991) 13 EHRR 329, para. 63.

[107] *Tolstoy Miloslavsky v. the United Kingdom*, Application No. 18139/91, judgment 23 June 1995, (1995) 20 EHRR 442, para. 77. See also *Hadjianastassiou v. Greece*, Application No. 12945/87, judgment 21 November 1992, (A/252-A) (1993) 16 EHRR 219, para. 49.

[108] In *Halford v. the United Kingdom*, Application No. 20605/92, judgment 27 May 1997, (1997) 24 EHRR 523, paras. 80–82, for example, the Court held that the attorneys' fees claimed by the applicant were too high (the applicant asked for £239 an hour, while the usual rate for domestic proceedings was £120–150 an hour).

[109] Rule 92.

[110] Rule 93(1).

[111] Rule 93(2).

legal fees if the lawyer accepted the conditions and the scale of fees of Council of Europe legal aid as an adequate payment for his/her services.[112]

Documentation of Costs

At the end of proceedings in which one or more violations of the Convention have been found, the Court requires the applicant to produce receipts and other particulars in order to determine what costs have actually been incurred. The applicant's claim is then forwarded to the respondent Government for comment. While the Court almost always allows the claim if the Government does not dispute it,[113] an objection by the Government can lead to a rejection of the claim in absence of adequate documentation which, for example, justifies the award of any sums additional to the Council of Europe legal aid already awarded.[114]

The Court has been fairly flexible in allowing applicants to recover some costs even when they were not able to carefully document their legal expenses. For example, in the case of *Minelli v. Switzerland* the Court ruled that since the lawyer's fees and expenses claimed by the applicant appeared to be 'plausible and reasonable', it was not necessary for the applicant to produce the relevant documentation as requested by the Government.[115] The applicant in *Merger and Cros v. France* submitted that she could not produce evidence to support her claim for lawyer's fees because the vouchers for such fees disappeared when submitted to the Dijon Court of Appeal.[116] The Court found that the applicant produced sufficient evidence to explain why she was unable to produce invoices and the Court therefore granted the applicant an equitable sum for her lawyer's fees.

In the absence of careful documentation, the Court is likely to make an award of costs that is significantly lower than that claimed, an award that the Court considers reasonable in the circumstances. In *Gillow v. the United Kingdom*,[117] the applicants sought reimbursement for the expenses relating to their visits to Strasbourg for consultations, attendance at the Commission's hearing, attendance at the delivery of the Court's judgment, and lawyer's services in connection with the Court hearing. The applicant did not provide any documentation for these expenses. Instead of denying any costs due to non-documentation, the Court looked at the expenses claimed item-by-item and ruled on the reasonableness and the necessity of each expense. The Court found that the applicants' presence at the consultations in Strasbourg was unnecessary as the matter could have been dealt with by correspondence. On the other hand, the Court found it necessary and rea-

---

[112] *Feldbrugge v. the Netherlands (Article 50)*, Application No. 8562/79, judgment 27 July 1987, (A/124) (1991) 13 EHRR 571, paras. 19–20.
[113] See, for example, *Unterpertinger v. Austria*, Application No. 9120/80, judgment 22 October 1986, (A/110) (1991) 13 EHRR 175, para. 36.
[114] *Milasi v. Italy*, Application No. 10527/83, judgment 19 May 1987, (A/119) (1988) 10 EHRR 333, para. 24.
[115] Application No. 8660/79, judgment 25 March 1983, (A/62) (1983) 5 EHRR 554, para. 49.
[116] Application No. 68864/01, judgment 22 December 2004, paras. 74–78.
[117] Application No. 9063/80, judgment 25 August 1987, (A/124) (1991) 13 EHRR 593, paras. 16–22.

sonable for the applicants to be present at the delivery of the judgment and therefore reimbursed their travel expenses for that visit.[118]

Third party interventions

Article 36(2) of the Convention allows the Court, in the 'interest of the proper administration of justice', to invite any State which is not a party to the proceedings or 'any person concerned who is not the applicant' to submit written comments or take part in hearings.[119] Commonly national or international non-governmental organizations have sought to intervene in important cases, and these interventions are sometimes called *amicus curiae* (friend of the court) briefs. Such organizations must apply to the President of the Chamber within 12 weeks from the case's being sent to the respondent Government.[120] Curiously, at present there is no way for NGOs to find out which cases have been communicated, but Registry lawyers have recently agreed to look into methods of making this data public.[121] Usually intervening organizations are asked to limit their observations in length, and to focus on international and comparative legal perspectives.

In recent years there has been an influx of human rights organizations which have sought to submit third party interventions in cases which are of significant legal or policy importance. However, there is nothing stopping a national NGO from any other country from asking permission from the Court to intervene. Applicants and their lawyers may consider it strategically valuable in appropriate cases to contact relevant NGOs, explain the case, and ask the NGOs to seek permission from the Court to intervene. In cases concerning mental disability issues, applicants and their representatives may wish to contact specialist organizations working in this field.[122]

Under Protocol 14 to the Convention (which at time this book went to print had yet to come into force), the Council of Europe Commissioner for Human Rights may submit written comments and take part in hearings in all cases before a Chamber or the Grand Chamber.[123] Changes to the Convention introduced by Protocol 14 will for the first time mention the Commissioner for Human Rights in the Convention text by formally providing that the Commissioner has the right to intervene as third party. It

---

[118] As no documents were presented, there were no exact figures for the travel expenses. The Court, however, found that the amount claimed by the applicant was reasonable and granted them that amount. See also *Van der Hurk v. the Netherlands*, Application No. 16034/90, judgment 22 March 1994, (A/288) (1994) 18 EHRR 481, paras. 65–67.

[119] Under Article 8 of Protocol 14, which has yet to come into force, the Commissioner of Human Rights of the Council of Europe will be given the authority to submit comments to the Court and take part in hearings.

[120] Rules of Court, Rule 44(2)(b).

[121] Personal communication by Registrars at a meeting organized by the ECtHR for NGOs, 10 April 2006.

[122] For example, the Mental Disability Advocacy Center is an international legal advocacy organization promoting and protecting the rights of people with mental disabilities. See www.mdac.info. (The authors declare an interest as a board member of the organization and its Executive Director.)

[123] Article 13 of Protocol 14 to the Convention will amend Article 36 of the Convention.

remains to be seen how active the Commissioner will be in intervening. We hope that the Commissioner's office will engage with broad consultation to identify those human rights cases which would benefit from the Commissioner's intervention.

Interim measures

The Court has a system for making orders at any stage in the proceedings. Rule 39 of the Rules of Court sets out that the Court may 'at the request of a party or of any other person concerned, or of its own motion, indicate to the parties any interim measure which it considers should be adopted in the interests of the parties or of the proper conduct of the proceedings before it'. Before making such a request, the Court may ask the respondent Government for further information under Rule 54(2) of the Rules of Court.

Requests for interim measures have historically been made when an applicant faces deportation to a country where it is thought that his or her life will be put at risk,[124] whether that country is a Council of Europe Member State or not. Recently, the Court ordered the Russian government to allow access to an applicant who was being detained in a psychiatric hospital without being allowed to meet with his lawyer.[125] The Court has developed a Practice Direction on interim measures which suggests that interim measures are available in cases where there is an urgent need, although interestingly Rule 39 itself does not specify that the interim measures procedure may be used only in urgent cases. In the event that a respondent Government does not comply with interim measures, the Court may find a violation of Article 34 of the Convention depending on whether the failure to follow an interim measure has affected the applicant's right to effective exercise of individual application.[126]

Friendly settlement

When a case is declared admissible the Court invites the parties to reach an agreement by way of 'friendly settlement'.[127] If a friendly settlement is reached, 'the Court shall strike the case out of its list by means of a decision which shall be confined to a brief statement

---

[124] See for example *Shamayev and others v. Georgia and Russia*, Application No. 36378/93, judgment 12 April 2005.

[125] See the case of *S. v. Russia*, being litigated by the Mental Disability Advocacy Center (Application No. 44009/05).

[126] See *Mamatkulov and Abdurasulovic v. Turkey*, Application Nos. 46827/99 and 46951/99, judgments 6 February 2003, (2005) 41 EHRR 25.

[127] Article 38(1)(b). At present a friendly settlement is available only after a case has been declared admissible. However, under Protocol 14 to the Convention, which has not yet come into force, friendly settlements will be available at any stage of the proceedings (see Article 15 of Protocol 14, amending Article 38 of the Convention).

of the facts and of the solution reached'.[128] Communications to the Court in relation of a friendly settlement are made 'without prejudice' to the parties' submissions on the substance of the application.[129] Therefore friendly settlement information must not be revealed or referred to by either of the parties in any of the court documents or during an oral hearing.

The friendly settlement procedure is both an opportunity and a threat. On the one hand it is an opportunity to utilise a *quasi* mediation service provided free of charge, and one which will lead on to an examination of the merits if the negotiations fail. The respondent Government may offer the applicant a certain (and in some cases enormous) amount of money and promise to amend legislation which violates the Convention. This itself can be the threat of friendly settlements: respondent Governments can 'buy off' applicants. In strong cases, Governments may offer money far above that which legal advisors on both sides would predict would be awarded by the Court should the Court find a violation. The Government could also make it clear that such an offer is not an admission of a violation of the Convention. A Government would take such a step thereby in order to prevent the case proceeding further, avoiding the costs of governmental lawyers and the embarrassment and cost of a finding against the Government.

In such situations, the applicant's legal advisor is put in a difficult position. On the one hand, the lawyer has a duty to the client to advise on the best outcome for the client (which clearly includes the financial outcome). On the other hand, a lawyer and client too will be aware of the potentially far-reaching effect of a judgment by the European Court of Human Rights, and if the applicant decides to accept the money offered in friendly settlement, there will be no judgment and therefore the case law of the Court will not have progressed. Some clients have suffered such injustices that no amount of money will sway them from their determination to reject a settlement, and move forward to seek a declaratory remedy from the Court. People with mental disabilities are also often chronically poor, however, and even small offers of settlement can appear generous. There is therefore the fierce temptation for clients to settle their cases, sometimes for considerably less than their lawyers may think appropriate, or less than their lawyers predict the Court would grant if the case were to proceed to judgment. In the mental disability field, like any other, lawyers should take time to go through with their clients the implications of a friendly settlement and to record their client's decision in writing.

Striking out

The Court may strike a case out at any time during the proceedings according to Article 37(1) of the Convention if:

---

[128] Article 39.
[129] Rule 62(2).

a. the applicant does not intend to pursue his application; or
b. the matter has been resolved; or
c. for any other reason established by the Court, it is no longer justified to continue the examination of the application.

Article 37 further provides that the Court may decide to continue the examination of the application if respect for human rights as defined in the Convention and the protocols thereto so requires, and that if a case has been struck out, the Court retains the authority to restore an application to its list of cases if it considers that the circumstances justify such a course.

The *first* situation in which a case will be struck out is where the applicant does not intend to pursue his application. This will occur if the applicant informs the Court of this intention. It may also occur if the Court does not hear from the applicant or representative for an extended period of time, despite letters' having been sent by the Court.

The *second* circumstance in which the Court will strike out a case is where the matter has been resolved. For example, the law has changed in a country and the applicant has been provided with remedies.[130]

The *third* situation in which a case will be struck out gives the Court a broad discretion, because it is 'for any other reason'. A respondent Government may make a unilateral declaration acknowledging the violations and admitting that the case should be struck out under this heading.[131] The Grand Chamber has recently clarified the remit of Article 37(1)(c), articulating relevant factors to be taken into account when deciding to strike out a case. These include the nature of the complaints made, whether the issues raised are comparable to issues determined by the Court in previous cases, the nature and scope of any measures taken by the respondent Government in the context of the execution of judgments delivered by the Court in any such previous cases, and the impact of these measures on the case at issue, whether – and if so, to what extent – the facts are in dispute between the parties.[132]

Judgment and remedies

The European Court of Human Rights delivers over one thousand judgments per year.[133] These are usually advertised in advance via Registry press releases and published on the

---

[130] For example, in *Balikçi v. Turkey* (Application No. 26481/95, judgment 6 January 2004), the Turkish Constitution was amended to recognise the applicant's right as a civil servant to join a trade union, and the applicant had benefited from his record being cleared of a reprimand he had received for joining a trade union.
[131] See *Acar v. Turkey*, Application No. 26307/95, Grand Chamber judgment on a preliminary issue 6 May 2003, (2004) 38 EHRR 2.
[132] See *Acar v. Turkey, op. cit.*
[133] In 2005 the figure was 1,105. See the Court's 'Survey of Activities 2005' available from the Court's website.

Court's website on the day of delivery. Chamber judgments are rarely read out by a judge in open court, unlike Grand Chamber judgments, which are always delivered in this way. Rule 74(1) of the Rules of Court specify what elements must be in the judgment, including details of the judges, parties and representatives, an account of the procedure followed, the facts of the case, summaries of the submissions of the parties, the reasons in points of law, the operative provisions, the decision (if any) in relation to costs. Judges are free to append concurring or dissenting opinions, which are often a well-written critique of the majority's decision.

The ECHR offers limited remedies. Primarily the Convention provides declaratory relief. That is, to declare whether there has been a violation of one or more Articles of the Convention. It is primarily for the State concerned to choose, subject to supervision by the Committee of Ministers, the means to be used in its domestic legal order in order to discharge its obligation under Article 46 of the Convention.[134] However, an applicant's victory at Strasbourg does not mean that a respondent Government is legally obliged under international law to amend legislation or take any other measures beyond paying the 'just satisfaction'. Only in the most egregious cases will the Court order, for example, an applicant's release from unlawful detention.[135]

If the Court finds that there has been a violation of the Convention or its protocols, it may make an award for just satisfaction, under Article 41. 'Just satisfaction' may include compensation for pecuniary and non-pecuniary losses. The Court can also award the respondent Government to pay the applicant's legal costs (see above section on costs). Either the applicant or the respondent Government may, in exceptional cases and within three months of the Chamber's judgment, ask the case to be referred to the Grand Chamber for a re-hearing.[136] If the case is accepted, it is heard afresh, not as an appeal.[137]

Enforcement of judgments

The Council of Europe's Committee of Ministers has the responsibility of supervising the execution of Court judgments. All judgments are transmitted to the Committee of

---

[134] See *Öcalan v. Turkey*, Application No. 46221/99, Judgment (Grand Chamber) 12 May 2005, (2005) 41 EHRR 45, para. 210.
[135] For example, see *Ilaşcu and Others v. Moldova and Russia*, Application No. 48787/99, Grand Chamber judgment 8 July 2004, (2005) 40 EHRR 46, para. 490, in which the Court stated: 'The Court further considers that any continuation of the unlawful and arbitrary detention of the three applicants would necessarily entail a serious prolongation of the violation of Article 5 found by the Court and a breach of the respondent States' obligation under Article 46 § 1 of the Convention to abide by the Court's judgment. Regard being had to the grounds on which they have been found by the Court to be in violation of the Convention (see paragraphs 352 and 393 above), the respondent States must take every measure to put an end to the arbitrary detention of the applicants still detained and to secure their immediate release.'
[136] Article 43 ECHR.
[137] See *Refah Partisi (the Welfare Party) and others v. Turkey*, Application Nos. 41340/98, 41340/98, 41342/98, 41343/98, 41344/98, Grand Chamber judgment 13 February 2003, (2003) 37 EHRR 1.

Ministers,[138] which asks the respondent Government to report on implementation of a judgment, including payment of just satisfaction awarded by the Court. The Committee of Ministers and the Court are increasingly concerned with judgments which are illustrative of systemic issues in a particular country,[139] and pay particular attention to measures which a Government takes to prevent similar violations in the future, for example, introducing new legislation or training of public officials.[140] The Committee of Ministers may issue a resolution condemning a Government which fails to comply with a judgment of the Court. Although there is no procedure for doing so, applicants can write to the Secretariat of the Committee of Ministers if there are any concerns about the Government's compliance with a Court's judgment. In those cases where judgments are ignored by Governments for a long time, the Committee of Legal Affairs of the Parliamentary Assembly of the Council of Europe may discuss the case and make recommendations.[141]

---

[138] Article 46(2) ECHR.
[139] See the Declaration of the Committee of Ministers, 12 May 2004 "Ensuring the effectiveness of the implementation of the European Convention on Human Rights at national and European levels". See also the first case in which the Court responded: *Broniowski v. Poland*, Application No. 31443/96, judgment 22 June 2004, (2005) 40 EHRR 21.
[140] See for example, *Pauwels v. Belgium*: Committee of Ministers Resolution DH(96)676, 15 November 1996 (A/135) (1989) 11 EHRR 238, and *Yagis v. Turkey*: Committee of Ministers Resolution DH(99)20, 18 January 1999, both cited in P. Leach, *op. cit.*
[141] PACE Resolution 1226(2000), Execution of judgments of the European Court of Human Rights, 28 September 2000.

Chapter 9

Representing People with Mental Disabilities

The Lawyer's Role

So far, this book has drawn the landscape of ECHR rights relating to people with mental disabilities. These rights will have become meaningful only if lawyers are effective and dedicated in their representation of people with mental disabilities. In a European context, remarkably little has been written on the particular complexities that such professional relationships create. The North American literature is considerably richer, and European lawyers new to the representation of people with mental disabilities would be well advised to consider it with care.[1] Nonetheless, in the absence of literature directed to a European audience, we provide in appendix 7 to this volume an introductory guide to representation of people with mental disabilities, and to some of the particular problems it raises.

---

[1] See, for example, American Bar Association Commission on the Mentally Disabled, 'How to Prepare for an Involuntary Civil Commitment Hearing', 37 *Prac. Law.* (1991) 39; J. Abisch, 'Mediational Lawyering in the Civil Commitment Context: A Therapeutic Jurisprudence Solution to the Counsel Role Dilemma', 1 *Psychol. Pub. Pol'y & L* (1995) 120, J. Cook, 'Good Lawyers and Bad Role Models: The Role of Respondent's Counsel in a Civil Commitment Hearing' 14 *Geo. J. Legal Ethics* (2000) 179; D. Green, '"I'm OK – You're OK": Educating Lawyers to "Maintain a Normal Client-Lawyer Relationship" with a Client with a Mental Disability', 28 *J. Legal Prof.* (2003–2004) 65; M Perlin, '"You have discussed lepers and crooks": Sanism in clinical teaching', 9 *Clinical L. Rev.* (2003) 683; M. Perlin and R. Sadoff, 'Ethical Issues in the Representation of Individuals in the Commitment Process', 45 *Law & Contemp. Probs.* (1982) 161; D. Romano, 'The Legal Advocate and the Questionably Competent Client in the Context of a Poverty Law Clinic', 35 *Osgoode Hall Law Journal* (1997) 737.

The legal profession is governed primarily by the domestic law in its own jurisdiction. That said, international law does provide some expectations of its own regarding the nature and standard of representation, and the ECHR itself may be breached if representation does not meet a minimal standard.[2]

Lawyers should pursue cases in this field with due diligence, as they would any other case. This is expressly expected in the Principles for Lawyers published by the United Nations:

> 14. Lawyers, in protecting the rights of their clients and in promoting the cause of justice, shall seek to uphold human rights and fundamental freedoms recognized by national and international law and shall at all times act freely and diligently in accordance with the law and recognized standards and ethics of the legal profession.[3]

The UN Basic Principles for Lawyers define the core duties of lawyers as follows:

> 13. The duties of lawyers towards their clients shall include:
>   (a) Advising clients as to their legal rights and obligations, and as to the working of the legal system in so far as it is relevant to the legal rights and obligations of the clients;
>   (b) Assisting clients in every appropriate way, and taking legal action to protect their interests;
>   (c) Assisting clients before courts, tribunals or administrative authorities, where appropriate.[4]

These do not change simply because the client is engaged in the psychiatric or social care system. Similarly, the basic standards of professionalism, including the duty of confidentiality, do not change because the client has or is perceived to have a mental health problem or intellectual disability.

In much of this book, we have been discussing how people with mental disabilities have particular needs in the legal system. Many of those issues remain relevant here. It may take longer to get instructions from a client with some mental disabilities, for example, and it may be necessary to choose vocabulary and simple sentence structures so that that a person with intellectual disabilities can understand the advice offered.

It does not follow from this that the lawyer is justified in taking a paternalistic attitude to his or her client. It is instead appropriate to emphasise how similar many people with mental disabilities are to any other clients. As discussed in chapter 6, it cannot be assumed that because a client has a diagnosis of a mental disability, he or she lacks mental capacity to instruct a lawyer. Large-scale research has shown that most people with psychiatric diagnoses, even most people with quite severe diagnoses, may be as able to make decisions as the general population.[5] When this is the case, there is no justification for ignoring the

---

[2] The scope of the ECHR requirements is discussed later in this chapter.
[3] *Basic Principles on the Role of Lawyers*, Adopted by the Eighth United Nations Congress on the Prevention of Crime and the Treatment of Offenders, Havana, Cuba, 27 August to 7 September 1990, principle 14.
[4] *Basic Principles on the Role of Lawyers*, Adopted by the Eighth United Nations Congress on the Prevention of Crime and the Treatment of Offenders, Havana, Cuba, 27 August to 7 September 1990, principle 13.
[5] T. Grisso and P.S. Appelbaum, 'The MacArthur Treatment Competence Study (III): Abilities of Patients

client when formulating a case strategy. Frequently, clients caught up in the mental health system have coherent and cogent views about what they wish to happen to them. Indeed, some clients have been through various parts of the mental health and social care systems for considerable periods of their lives, giving them particularly relevant experience as to the range of services available to them, and the outcomes they would prefer. In the same way that other clients rightly expect their lawyers to respect their views, clients in the psychiatric system should enjoy the same respect from their legal representatives.

In order for the lawyer appropriately to act for the client, it is vital to meet with the client and to discuss what the client wants. Either before or after that meeting, it will be necessary to review the clinical file and any other documentation relevant to the case.[6] Professionals schooled in law tend to view matters through specific categorical structures relating to legality and rights. Clients do not necessarily share those approaches, and may in particular not agree with an outcome that the lawyer might think is in the client's best interests. Clients often have considerable experience in mental health or social care systems, and understand their situations in very nuanced terms. They may well want a result that is not a simple legal 'win'. A client in an institution may want simply to be free of the whole psychiatric system, for example, but alternatively he or she may want to be out of the institution, but to continue his or her relationship with the institution as an out-patient. A client may want a change of medication, rather than to be free of the system as a whole. A client may understand his or her need to be in an institution, but wish to be in an institution closer to family members, or in a less restrictive department of the existing institution. A client may want to be free of guardianship altogether, or may be happy with partial guardianship even when the lawyer believes that a full release from guardianship may be attainable.

How these possibilities play through in legal terms will depend on the domestic law in question and the human rights law articulated elsewhere in this volume. Some outcomes may be attainable, others not; and explaining what is a legally and practically realistic objective may well form the core of the advice provided by the lawyer. Nonetheless, failure to identify the client's vision of success may well lead to unfortunate consequences. It would be a Pyrrhic victory indeed if a lawyer successfully obtained the complete separation of the client from the mental health system, if what the client really wanted was a change of medication.

Even during domestic court cases, lawyers must be aware that the case could potentially find itself at the ECtHR. Any ECHR points that are within the domestic court's jurisdiction must be argued before that court, and failure to do so may result in the ECtHR declaring an application inadmissible (see chapter 8, above). Further, of course, the

---

To Consent to Psychiatric and Medical Treatments', (1995) 19 *Law & Hum. Behav.* 149 at 169. While the context of this research is capacity to consent to treatment, the methodology tested for impairment of understanding, appreciation and reasoning ability. These criteria would apply similarly to determination of capacity to instruct a lawyer.

[6]   The United Nations Basic Principles for Lawyers require that this information be provided to the lawyer by the authorities in a timely fashion: Principle 21.

ECHR has direct effect in many Member States of the Council of Europe, so it is possible that arguing these issues in domestic courts may yield a suitable remedy for the client.

Clients who lack capacity to instruct a lawyer

All this is clearest when the client has capacity. For that reason, capacity should be determined at the beginning of the client-lawyer relationship, and reviewed on an ongoing basis over the course of events. As discussed in chapter 6, capacity means the ability to understand and appreciate consequences of pursuing the various options available. While clearly there is a standard here, care must be taken to ensure that the standard is not raised too high, and it should certainly not collapse into a determination of the main issue in the case. It cannot be correct that the standard of capacity to instruct a lawyer in a case concerning capacity to consent to treatment would include the ability to understand and appreciate the consequences of treatment, for example. If that were the case, a lawyer believing a client to lack that capacity would be unable to take instructions the client, and the views of the client might be effectively marginalised, even if the court's view of the client's treatment capacity might be different.

Particular difficulties may arise with clients who have been deprived of *legal* capacity by operation of law, usually through the operation of guardianship statutes.[7] In many jurisdictions, such clients lose the legal right to hire and instruct a lawyer, even if they in fact have the practical/functional capacity to do so in a given case. If the case does not raise ECHR issues such as would give an independent right to a lawyer,[8] it is likely that the approval of the guardian will be required to instruct a lawyer, and in law the guardian would become the client. Short of challenging the entire guardianship order, a route which may be unsuccessful if the client lacks the actual capacity to make other relevant decisions, there may be little that can be done to challenge this legal inability to instruct a lawyer. For this reason, ECHR rights that do provide an independent right to legal representation may be of particular significance to an individual with mental disabilities.

The ECtHR has been conspicuously silent on the question of capacity to instruct a lawyer. Certainly, it must be the case that a person who actually has capacity for ECHR litigation may retain and instruct a lawyer for that litigation, even if he or she is under guardianship and therefore has no standing to instruct a lawyer in domestic proceedings.[9] It is difficult to imagine that the ECtHR would allow such a person to be deprived of his or her right to pursue a remedy in a hearing required by the ECtHR itself.

The threshold of capacity is more uncertain; in other words, what does 'capacity to instruct a lawyer' actually mean? It must be the case that the client understands the gen-

---

[7]   See chapter 6 above.
[8]   Such as is probably the case under Article 5(4) of the ECHR (see chapter 2), or in legal representation in guardianship proceedings (see chapter 6).
[9]   A legal block to accessing an attorney could well be a violation of the European Convention on Human Rights itself.

eral subject matter of the litigation (for example detention, treatment, control of decision-making), and to be able to express a clear and reasonably consistent view as to what outcome they would like in that litigation. The client's views on the central question of the result they desire should not be affected by psychosis or similar mental disability, although the presence of such mental disability not affecting their views on this central question should not dissuade the lawyer from taking instructions from the individual. Considerable care should be afforded before a higher standard is imposed on people who have a diagnosis. Otherwise the views of clients will be unduly marginalised. The fact that a client wants an outcome that the lawyer considers to be ill-advised is not of itself evidence of incapacity. The fact that a client may be unrealistic as to their prospects of success at living outside an institution, for example, may be relevant to what advice the lawyer offers, but it does not of itself suggest that the client lacks capacity.

Irrespective of whether the lawyer has instructions in any particular case or not, the ECtHR is clear that people who lack capacity should not be deprived of legal representation. Indeed, it seems that the duty of the State to provide a legal representative may be higher for people whose capacity is reduced, at least where liberty is at stake:

> . . . where a person is confined in a psychiatric institution on the ground of the commission of acts which constituted criminal offences but for which he could not be held responsible on account of mental illness, he should – unless there are special circumstances – receive legal assistance in subsequent proceedings relating to the continuation, suspension or termination of his detention. The importance of what is at stake for him – personal liberty – taken together with the very nature of his affliction – diminished mental capacity – compel this conclusion.[10]

The ECHR offers no guidance as to *how* the lawyer in such cases ought to proceed, however, and it may be that a considerable margin of appreciation may be shown to individual domestic legal systems as to how to approach this difficulty. There are several possibilities, each of which presents its own array of advantages and disadvantages. Some of these options will be considered in turn, namely taking instructions from a 'litigation friend', an outsider 'litigation friend', and the lawyer acting without instructions.

Taking instructions from a 'litigation friend'

One possibility is that the lawyer would take instructions from a 'litigation friend', an individual appointed by a court with particular responsibility for the litigation at issue. This has the advantage that, when it works properly, this individual might be particularly aware of the personal situation of the person lacking capacity, and therefore best able to advise

---

[10] *Megyeri v. Germany*, Application No. 13770/88, judgment 12 May 1992, Series A no. 237–A, (A/237A) (1993) 15 EHRR 584, para. 23. See also *Pereira v. Portugal*, Application No. 44872/98, judgment 26 Feb 2002, (2003) 36 EHRR 49, paras. 58–9. In that case, the applicant was held expressly to be unable to conduct his own legal proceedings notwithstanding his legal training, and the appointment of a lawyer for him was held correspondingly by the Portuguese authorities to be necessary. The lawyer played no active part in the proceedings, and the ECtHR found a violation of Article 5(4) of the ECHR.

regarding the factual situation and the appropriate outcome for that individual. This imports a corresponding difficulty, however: if the litigation friend is so close to the individual lacking capacity, it is likely that the litigation friend will also have his or her own views as to the appropriateness of given outcomes. Indeed, the outcome of the litigation may affect that individual directly: a successful challenge to a detention, for example, may in practice mean that the litigation friend has to assume a markedly increased role in caring for the person lacking capacity. It seems difficult if not impossible to expect that individual to separate out his or her personal views from those of the person lacking capacity. In the result, the risk is that the client in effect becomes the litigation friend rather than the person lacking capacity.

Indeed, it is quite possible that the person exercising the role of litigation friend is part of the problem for the person lacking capacity. No doubt many guardians are selfless and devoted to the care of the person lacking capacity, but particularly if they are in receipt of formal legal powers, they nonetheless have considerable power over that individual. If the guardian's use of those powers (or failure to use them) is at the core of the litigation, his or her appointment as litigation friend would effectively undercut the litigation: the guardian would be both applicant and respondent in the case. Even if the formal respondent were someone else, such as a psychiatric institution, any implicit compliance by the guardian in the course of events complained of would make them inappropriate to direct the litigation on behalf of the person lacking capacity. Even if a different individual from the family or immediate social circle is selected to act as litigation friend, the micropolitics of family relationships may nonetheless make it difficult for that individual to challenge the decisions taken by the guardian up to that point.

Outsider 'litigation friend'

Another possibility is for the state to provide a litigation friend who is not otherwise directly related to the care of the individual, most commonly in the form of a 'public guardian' or similar official. There are advantages to this approach, in that such an individual is likely to have access to professional expertise, and a good knowledge of the array of services that may be available for the person lacking capacity. The other key participants in the litigation might well be state or state-related bodies, and when the case reaches the ECtHR the respondent will by definition be the state, so certainly, clear administrative lines of division would be necessary to ensure that this individual was acting without the influence of the respondents in the litigation. Such clear lines can no doubt be drawn through careful legislative drafting. The real difficulty is that the outsider litigation friend is unlikely to know the individual lacking capacity personally. While that official can interview members of the individual's family and social circle, the resources available may limit such investigations.

Lawyer representing without instructions

Another possibility is to allow the lawyer to represent the individual without further instructions, in effect becoming a *de facto* litigation friend. The question in this context is what the lawyer is permitted to do. Certainly, particularly if the person lacking capacity is objecting to the decisions that have been made about him or her, the lawyer can ensure that a *prima facie* case for those decisions has been made out, based on the facts known to the decision-maker. The lawyer can similarly ensure that there has been compliance with all required procedures for the decision. This nonetheless seems inadequate, as it fails to address whether the decision-maker's view of the facts, and the decisions made as a result of those facts, are appropriate. If these are taken into account, however, the job of the lawyer becomes difficult. Not only must the lawyer investigate the facts, a task that may prove time-consuming, but he or she must also evaluate the decisions. What standard is to be used for such evaluation? If it is best interests of the client, it is not obvious that the lawyer's view is to be preferred to those of others in the system. If it is something else, what? Whatever system is used will import value choices that may or may not reflect the values of the client. If they do not reflect the views of the client, it is difficult to see that it is the client who is being represented.

Being clear about the client-lawyer relationship

All of this serves to emphasise the importance of being clear about the terms of the client-lawyer relationship at the beginning of that relationship. The lawyer must be clear in his or her mind what role they are fulfilling. Even if the client lacks functional or actual capacity to instruct the lawyer, the terms of this role should be explained to the client if at all possible.

A similar confusion of roles may arise if the lawyer is asked to see the person with mental disabilities (whether or not he or she has capacity) not by that person, but by a third party such as a family member, guardian, or a court. The first question is who is the client: the family member, the guardian, the court or the person with the mental disabilities? It is far from obvious that these individuals will have interests that are identical, and this should be clarified at the beginning of the relationship. If the court has appointed the lawyer, what are the terms of the appointment? Is the lawyer to represent the person with mental disability, where that person would be the client, or is the lawyer to advise the court as *amicus curiae* (friend to the court), in which case the court is effectively the client. It is difficult to see that the latter role would meet the requirements of the ECHR for representation in matters of detention, unless there is another lawyer representing that person, or *perhaps* unless that person is choosing to represent himself or herself. This should be clarified with the court at the time of the appointment. In any event, it should be made clear both to the person engaging the lawyer and to the person with mental disability at start of the first meeting with the lawyer just what the role of the lawyer is in this context.

Representation and the ECHR

The provision of an appropriate standard of legal services is not necessarily just a matter of professional ethics. Failure to meet such a standard can also in itself give rise to a violation of the client's rights under the ECHR. For cases concerning detention in psychiatric and related institutions under Article 5, the potential breach flows from jurisprudence regarding the right to challenge the detention under Article 5(4). As early as *Winterwerp v. the Netherlands*, the Court spoke of the individual's right to legal representation in these hearings,[11] and in *Pereira v. Portugal* the Court held that inadequate representation by a state-appointed lawyer in such proceedings constituted a violation of the applicant's rights under Article 5(4).[12] For cases engaging Article 6, a specific right to legal representation is provided only by Article 6(3)(c), for people charged with criminal offences. The Court has held however that the specific rights under Article 6(3) are 'aspects' of the more general right to a fair hearing under Article 6(1).[13] Article 6 requires that the individual be given a reasonable opportunity to present his or her case under conditions that do not place him or her at a substantial disadvantage vis-à-vis the adversary. In appropriate cases, the court has extended this to the provision of legal aid.[14]

It is difficult to see any meaningful difference in the rights to representation provided by Article 6(1) and Article 5(4). In both cases, the court hearings concern fundamental rights of the persons affected, and in both cases the hearing must provide fundamental procedural safeguards to the determination of those rights. Indeed, the ECtHR itself uses Article 6 jurisprudence to inform its reading of Article 5(4).[15] While the ECtHR has also held that court hearings under Article 5(4) need not always have procedural protections identical to those in trials under Article 6, it is difficult to see that such differences manifest themselves on the issue of standard of representation.

The respondent in ECHR litigation is the State, and this creates an awkward dynamic in litigation surrounding the adequacy of provision of legal services. The Court is understandably concerned to ensure that domestic legal professions remain independent from the State; indeed, any over-control by the State of the applicant's lawyer would itself raise

---

[11] *Winterwerp v. the Netherlands*, Application No. 6301/73, judgment 24 October 1979, (1979) 2 EHRR 1, para. 60; see also *Megyeri v. Germany*, Application No. 13770/88, judgment 12 May 1992, (1993) 15 EHRR 584, para. 23. See further chapter 2 above.

[12] *Pereira v. Portugal, op. cit.*, paras 61–3.

[13] See, for example, *Van Geyseghem v. Belgium* [GC], Application No. 26103/95, judgment 21 January 1999, (2001) 32 EHRR 24, para. 27, ECHR 1999–I; *Balliu v. Albania*, Application No. 74727/01, judgment 30 November 2005, para. 25. *Brennan v. the United Kingdom*, Application No. 39846/98, judgment 16 October 2001, (2002) 34 EHRR 18, paras. 45, 48; *Czekalla v. Portugal*, Application No. 38830/97, judgment 10 January 2003, para. 59; *Daud v. Portugal*, Application No. 22600/93, judgment 21 April 1998, (2000) 30 EHRR 400, para. 33; *Lagerblom v. Sweden*, Application No. 26891/95, judgment 14 January 2003, para. 48.

[14] See *Steel and Morris v. the United Kingdom*, Application No. 68416/01, judgment 15 May 2005, (2005) EHRR 41, para. 62; *P., C., and S. v. the United Kingdom*, Application No. 56547/00, judgment 16 July 2002, (2002) 35 EHRR 31.

[15] See, for example, *Winterwerp v. the Netherlands*, Application No. 6301/73, judgment 24 October 1979, (1979) 2 EHRR 1, para. 60; *Pereira v. Portugal*, Application No. 44872/98, judgment 26 February 2002, para. 60.

important human rights concerns. The litigation has concerned only lawyers provided through State legal aid schemes, and therefore lawyers over whom the State is in a position of some responsibility. The ECtHR has not at this time found a Convention violation based on the inadequate practice of a lawyer hired privately. Further, the Court has made it clear that it is concerned with manifest failures of representation, rather than errors in tactics by lawyers. The resulting jurisprudence steers a difficult course between these differing pressures. *Czekalla v. Portugal* provides a clear articulation of the Court's approach:

> While it has frequently observed that the Convention is designed to guarantee not rights that are theoretical or illusory but rights that are practical and effective, assigning counsel does not in itself ensure the effectiveness of the assistance he may afford an accused. Nevertheless, a State cannot be held responsible for every shortcoming on the part of a lawyer appointed for legal-aid purposes. It follows from the independence of the legal profession from the State that the conduct of the defence is essentially a matter between the defendant and his counsel, whether appointed under a legal-aid scheme or privately financed. The competent national authorities are required under Article 6 § 3(c) to intervene only if a failure by legal-aid counsel to provide effective representation is manifest or sufficiently brought to their attention in some other way.[16]

While the client does not have a right under the ECHR to require the government to appoint a lawyer of the client's choosing to represent him or her,[17] it does seem that the Convention requires a certain standard of representation by a lawyer who is appointed by the State. When such a standard is not reached, it is not necessary that the applicant show that the failure of representation caused actual damage to his or her situation. The failure of representation may itself be sufficient to ground a Convention violation.[18]

The approach of the Court raises three questions: when is the State required to appoint a lawyer for the individual; what standard of representation must fail to be met in order for a Convention violation to occur; and what triggers the duty of the State to intervene? This second question in turn raises the issue of how the State ought to intervene, once its duty arises.

The Right to a Lawyer Appointed by the State

While the client has a right to legal representation, it is not yet clear that there is an automatic right under the ECHR for that representation to be provided by the State. In some countries such representation is routinely provided when Article 5 rights are at issue.[19] In other jurisdictions such legal aid is means tested (i.e. such aid depends on the person's financial situation). Even when the government does provide a lawyer, the funding may be insufficient to cover the costs of appropriate preparation for and attendance at the

---

[16] *Czekalla v. Portugal*, Application No. 38830/97, judgment 10 January 2003, para. 60.
[17] *Lagerblom v. Sweden*, Application No. 26891/95, judgment 14 January 2003, para. 55, *Mayzit v. Russia*, Application No. 63378/00, judgment 20 January 2005, para. 66.
[18] *Alimena v. Italy*, Application No. 11910/85, judgment 19 February 1991, para. 20.
[19] For detentions hearings in the Czech Republic, Hungary, Norway, and England and Wales, for example, the state system of legal aid provides the legal fees for an advocate, irrespective of the assets of the client.

court hearing. While the ECtHR has insisted on the right of clients to legal representation, it has further distinguished between cases where representation is needed for the proper conduct of proceedings, for example because of the disability of the client, and when it is not. In cases involving the review of detention, for example, the Court is required to appoint a lawyer only when the representation is 'necessary'. *Pereira v. Portugal* provides an example of this:

> [. . .] where a person is confined in a psychiatric institution on the ground of the commission of acts which constituted criminal offences but for which he could not be held responsible on account of mental illness, he should – unless there are special circumstances – receive legal assistance in subsequent proceedings relating to the continuation, suspension or termination of his detention. The importance of what is at stake for him – personal liberty – taken together with the very nature of his affliction – diminished mental capacity – compel this conclusion. . . .
>
> It is not disputed that the applicant suffered from a mental disability which prevented him from conducting court proceedings satisfactorily despite his legal training. That was, moreover, the conclusion of the [. . .] President of the Criminal Division of the Supreme Court, who decided not to take any further account of the applications lodged by the applicant, given his mentally disturbed state. . . .
>
> The circumstances of the case therefore required a defence lawyer to be appointed to assist the applicant in the proceedings relating to periodic review of the lawfulness of the detention.[20]

This raises the question of when representation is 'necessary' for the satisfactory conduct of proceedings, and when it is not. It has been argued elsewhere in this book that the complexity of detention hearings is now such that no lay person should be expected to negotiate the law without legal representation, and that the importance of what is at stake for the individual – his or her personal liberty – is sufficiently important that legal representation must always be provided in these circumstances.[21] If that is the case, the ECHR jurisprudence regarding the standard of that representation would be engaged.

That would be the case for court hearings under Article 5. A similar requirement would not necessarily apply for other court hearings. Certainly, there is a right to representation under for cases engaging Article 6, but in a criminal context, the provision of representation by the State is required only cases where the client has insufficient means to pay for it.[22] It is arguable that this is insufficient to take account of the needs of people with mental disabilities. Arguably, the right to a fair trial under Article 6(1) should be construed to require the provision of a lawyer paid for by the State in circumstances where it is at least unclear whether the client has functional is of dubious capacity and where the consequences of the court hearing may be intrusive or far-reaching. Guardianship court hearings are a particularly clear example of this. As discussed in chapter 2, these may be of considerable legal and factual complexity, and the consequences can

---

[20] *Pereira v. Portugal, op. cit.*, paras. 56–9. See also *Megyeri v. Germany, op. cit.*
[21] See further chapter 2, regarding court hearings under Article 5(4).
[22] Article 6(3)(c).

be a near-total deprivation of rights for the individual concerned. In the same way that justice may require the provision of legal representation in the context of an Article 5 hearing, it is arguable that the fair trial provisions of Article 6(1) would require representation for these hearings also.

Standards of Representation Under the ECHR

The first case on representation under the ECHR concerned a lawyer who failed to appear at the court hearing at all.[23] The State took the view that once it had appointed a lawyer for the applicant, its duties under Article 6(3) were satisfied. This view was resoundingly rejected by the Court:

> The Court recalls that the Convention is intended to guarantee not rights that are theoretical or illusory but rights that are practical and effective; this is particularly so of the rights of the defence in view of the prominent place held in a democratic society by the right to a fair trial, from which they derive. [. . .] As the Commission's Delegates correctly emphasised, Article 6 par. 3 (c) [. . .] speaks of "assistance" and not of "nomination". Again, mere nomination does not ensure effective assistance since the lawyer appointed for legal aid purposes may die, fall seriously ill, be prevented for a protracted period from acting or shirk his duties. If they are notified of the situation, the authorities must either replace him or cause him to fulfil his obligations. Adoption of the Government's restrictive interpretation would lead to results that are unreasonable and incompatible with both the wording of sub-paragraph (c) [. . .] and the structure of Article 6 [. . .] taken as a whole; in many instances free legal assistance might prove to be worthless.[24]

The Court has found a similar violation when the lawyer attends the hearing, but takes no active part in the proceedings.[25]

As noted above, the Court has been hesitant to delve too deeply into the calibre of representation when it is actually provided. Nonetheless, the Court has been prepared to find Convention violations based on particularly serious shortcomings by lawyers. *Czellaka v. Portugal* provides an indication as to the Court's approach:

> [The Court] notes in the first place, like the Government, that the State cannot be held responsible for any inadequacy or mistake in the conduct of the applicant's defence attributable to his officially appointed lawyer. It considers, however, that in certain circumstances negligent failure to comply with a purely formal condition cannot be equated with an injudicious line of defence or a mere defect of argumentation. That is so when as a result of such negligence a defendant is deprived of a remedy without the situation being put right by a higher court. It should be pointed out in that connection that the applicant was a foreigner who did not know the language in which the proceedings were being conducted and who

---

[23] *Artico v. Italy*, Application No. 6694/74, judgment 13 May 1980, (A/37) (1981) 3 EHRR 1. Given the result in this case, it is unsurprising that the Court has also affirmed the right to be informed of the date and time of hearing: *Alimena v. Italy*, Application No. 11910/85, judgment 24 January 1991, paras. 18, 20.

[24] *Artico v. Italy, op. cit.*, para. 33.

[25] *Pereira v. Portugal, op. cit.*, para. 60.

was facing charges which made him liable to – and indeed led to – a lengthy prison sentence.[26]

This case involved the failure by the lawyer to file particular documents necessary to start the appeal, resulting in the rejection of the appeal on purely formal grounds – a particularly glaring error on the part of the lawyer. While the case opens the door to litigation based on negligent practice in such extreme cases, it is likely that the Court will remain hesitant to interfere in litigation tactics.

While there is hesitancy to second-guess a lawyer's tactics, the jurisprudence does suggest that the Court has implied expectations on what sort of preparation is appropriate. The State is expected to appoint the lawyer in a sufficiently timely fashion to ensure that he or she will have time to interview the client, study the case file, and prepare relevant written and oral arguments.[27] Thus in *Daud v. Portugal*, the Court found that the appointment of a lawyer three days prior to the commencement of a criminal trial did not allow the lawyer sufficient time to study the file, visit the client in prison, and prepare a defence.[28]

Consistent with this, it is expected that the lawyer will have access to those documents that will allow for appropriate preparation of the case, including relevant court files and investigation files.[29] This is required not merely by the ECHR jurisprudence, but also by Principle 21 of the United Nations *Basic Principles on the Role of Lawyers*:

> It is the duty of the competent authorities to ensure lawyers access to appropriate information, files and documents in their possession or control in sufficient time to enable lawyers to provide effective legal assistance to their clients. Such access should be provided at the earliest appropriate time.[30]

The lawyer should be hired in sufficient time to discuss the content of those files with the client prior to formulating submissions.[31] Any restrictions on the rights to see such files must be subject to suitable procedural safeguards.[32] There is further a right to have translations of all documents needed to make sense of defence into a language that the client can understand.[33]

---

[26]   *Czekalla v. Portugal*, Application No. 38830/97, judgment 10 January 2003, para. 65.
[27]   *Goddi v. Italy*, Application No. 8966/80, judgment 9 April 1984, (A/76) (1984) 6 EHRR 457, para. 31; *Daud v. Portugal*, Application No. 22600/93, judgment 21 April 1998, (2000) 30 EHRR 400, para. 39.
[28]   *Daud v. Portugal, op. cit.*, para. 39.
[29]   *Nikolova v. Bulgaria*, Application No. 31195/96, judgment 25 March 1999, (2001) 31 EHRR 3, paras. 58–66; *Kamasinski v. Austria*, Application No. 9783/82, judgment 19 December 1989, (A/168) (1991) 13 EHRR 36.
[30]   Principle 21 of the *Basic Principles on the Role of Lawyers*, Adopted by the Eighth United Nations Congress on the Prevention of Crime and the Treatment of Offenders, Havana, Cuba, 27 August to 7 September 1990.
[31]   *Öcalan v. Turkey*, Application No. 46221/99, judgment 12 March 2003, (2003) 37 EHRR 10, para. 160.
[32]   See, for example, *Rowe and Davis v. the United Kingdom*, Application No. 28901/95, judgment 16 Feb 2000, (2000) 30 EHRR 1, paras. 53–67.
[33]   *Lagerblom v. Sweden*, Application No. 26891/95, judgment 14 January 2003, para. 61.

The lawyer must be able to meet the client sufficiently frequently and for a sufficiently long time to formulate a response to the case.[34] These meetings must occur outside hearing of third parties, such as staff of the institution in which an individual is confined.[35] Correspondence between detained persons and their lawyers are similarly subject to particular protections under Article 8. Letters to or from an individual's lawyer may be opened only if there is reasonable reason to believe that lawyer-client privilege is being abused. They may not be read by institutional staff, and suitable guarantees to this effect must be provided, such as opening the letter in the presence of the detained person.[36]

State Intervention in Cases of Inadequate Representation

This jurisprudence would suggest that the Court expects lawyers to provide that standard of service, and, as will be discussed below, it is certainly reasonable for clients to expect provision of such professional services. When the matter of professional standards is raised before the ECtHR, however, the respondent is the State. The question is thus when it is the State's duty to intervene, and what form that intervention should take.

The jurisprudence focuses on whether the client has taken adequate steps to alert the State, generally through domestic courts, that inadequate representation is an issue. In *Daud v. Portugal*, the client had notified the domestic court of the problems, but in his own language, Spanish, rather than Portuguese. This was held by the ECtHR to be sufficient to put the domestic court on notice of the problems the client was facing.[37] In *Czekalla v. Portugal*, the fact that the client was trying to file documents he had written himself, notwithstanding the fact that a lawyer had been provided for him, was viewed as relevant to determining that notice of the difficulties had been provided to the domestic court.[38]

This approach is problematic for all clients, whether or not they have a mental disability. The ECHR requires that a client be provided with a lawyer only when the interests of justice require. Normally, this will mean when the legal aspects of the case are sufficiently complicated that the client cannot be expected to represent himself or herself. It is difficult to see that the client in that context is appropriately placed to know if there is a significant difficulty with his or her legal representation. In the *Czellaka* case, for example, the lawyer failed to file the proper papers for an appeal. It may be abundantly

---

[34] *Daud v. Portugal, op. cit.*, para. 39; *Öcalan v. Turkey, op. cit.*, para. 157.
[35] European Agreement Relating To Persons Participating In Proceedings Of The European Court Of Human Rights, E.T.S. 161 (Strasbourg, 5 March 1996), Article 3(c). See also *Öcalan v. Turkey, op. cit.*, paras. 146–51; *Lanz v. Austria*, Application No. 24430/94, judgment 31 January 2002, paras. 51–3; *Brennan v. the United Kingdom*, Application No. 39846/98, judgment 16 October 2001, para. 58.
[36] *Campbell v. the United Kingdom* Application No. 13590/88, judgment 25 March 1992, (1993) 15 EHRR 137, para. 124; see also European Agreement Relating To Persons Participating In Proceedings Of The European Court Of Human Rights, E.T.S. 161 (Strasbourg, 5 March 1996), Article 2(a), which requires correspondence between lawyers and detained clients to be delivered without undue delay and without alteration.
[37] *Daud v. Portugal, op. cit.*, paras. 41–2.
[38] *Czekalla v. Portugal*, Application No. 38830/97, judgment 10 January 2003, para. 67.

clear to another lawyer that this is manifestly improper practice; but it is difficult to see that a client can expect to have such knowledge of the technical requirements of law. Even in cases where the failings are not of such a formal legal nature, the Court's approach is problematic. If the problem is that the lawyer never meets the client, it may be that the client realises that there may be a difficulty in representation, but it is not obvious how the client will know what to do about it. To protect his or her rights, the client must notify the relevant authority, generally the domestic court. However, in order to know how to do this the client may well need legal advice which, may be unaffordable. Courts are viewed by many clients as threatening places, approached only through lawyers. It is far from obvious that they will know and have the courage to go to the domestic court directly to complain about their lawyer.

These problems may be amplified where the client has a mental disability. Certainly, some people with mental disabilities will be as capable as the population as a whole to assess the work of their lawyer, but others will not. Consider an individual with an intellectual disability who is engaged in litigation. It may well be the case that they are entirely unable to recognise when they are receiving substandard service, and may certainly be unable to know how to respond if the service is inadequate.

When the domestic court's attention is drawn to representation that is sufficiently inadequate as to constitute an infringement of the ECHR, it must respond. Generally, the ECtHR expects the domestic court to suspend the hearing to allow suitable representation to be provided,[39] although in *Czekalla v. Portugal* the ECtHR held that the domestic court should have invited the lawyer to re-submit the papers, remedying the technical fault.[40]

On the day of the court hearing, it is not obvious what else can be done, but for people detained under Article 5, adjournment of the hearing is not a desirable outcome. The ECtHR has itself increasingly restricted the delay it will allow between an application and a court hearing under Article 5;[41] it is ironic that the result of poor representation would be to increase that delay. It is unfortunate that the Court has not seen fit to examine ways in which poor representation can be remedied prior to the hearing date.

Another Model?

The arguments elsewhere in this volume will make clear that the ECHR jurisprudence has been relatively strong on procedural rights, and weaker on substantive rights. This makes the reticence of the Court in engaging with issues of the calibre of representation

---

[39] *Daud v. Portugal, op. cit.,* para. 42; *Balliu v. Albania* Application No. 74727/01, judgment 30 November 2005, para. 37; *Goddi v. Italy,* Application No. 8966/80, judgment 9 April 1984, (A/76) (1984) 6 EHRR 457, para. 31.
[40] *Czekalla v. Portugal, op. cit.,* para. 68.
[41] See further chapter 2, above.

of particular concern, as high-quality lawyering is the keystone of procedural justice. Equally surprising, given the significant growth in ECHR litigation in issues relating to mental disability in the last decade, is the relative paucity of case law relating to representation. Of the cases cited above, only *Pereira v. Portugal* concerns representation in the context of a client with a mental disability.

It should not be assumed that the absence of litigation means that representation is of a uniformly high standard across the territory of the Council of Europe. Certainly, there are many examples of high quality advocacy, but there are also indications that complacency is inappropriate. A 2004 study of Article 5(4) hearings for persons in a high security psychiatric institution in Hungary found that lawyers met their clients for the first time at the courtroom on the day of the hearing. The lawyers had not examined the files prior to this time. The average time for the hearing itself was eight minutes, with a third of the hearings observed by the research team lasting four minutes or less. Payment to the lawyers was minimal, so the limited services provided are in that sense predictable, but it is difficult to see that this would constitute adequate legal representation by any meaningful standard.[42] While this is a particularly clear example of systemic inadequate representation, there is no reason to believe it is unique. Along with some examples of very good advocacy, the reports of clients indicate some examples of remarkably poor practice: Mr Pereira's experience is by no means unique.

The ECtHR's concern about the independence of the legal profession from the state is understandable. The very nature of an effective legal profession presupposes that the lawyer can represent the client fearlessly and without threat of reprisal. In cases where the state has an interest in the outcome, or where (as in most Article 5(4) hearings) it is the respondent, the very nature of the lawyer-client relationship will be undercut if the state is overly controlling of the individual's lawyer. Certainly, therefore, the Court is right to shy away from second-guessing the tactics of experienced lawyers.

That is not the same thing as introducing safeguards to ensure that lawyers are appropriately aware of the domestic law at issue and appropriately prepared for hearings. By way of comparison, it is illuminating to consider the approach of the Montana Supreme Court in its judgment of *In the matter of the mental health of K.G.F.*[43] This case concerned representation of people under psychiatric detention – essentially, the equivalent of challenges to detention under Article 5(4). The court in that case relied heavily on the *Guidelines for Involuntary Civil Commitment*[44] developed and published by the Center for State Courts in the United States. The criteria adopted by the court in *K.G.F.* included the following:

---

[42] See Mental Disability Advocacy Center, *Liberty Denied: Human Rights Violations in Criminal Psychiatric Detention Reviews in Hungary*, (Budapest: MDAC, 2004) pp. 20–7. This publication is available electronically at http://www.mdac.info.

[43] 2001 MT 140. This case is available electronically at http://www.lawlibrary.state.mt.us.

[44] Center for State Courts, *Guidelines for Involuntary Civil Commitment* (1986), reprinted in 10 *Mental and Physical Disability Law Review* 410. The section of particular interest regarding representation is Part E, at pages 464–475. The *Guidelines* are available electronically at http://www.ncsconline.org.

- To be eligible for appointment, lawyers should have specialised course training, or have received supervised on-the-job training in the duties, skills, and ethics of representing people detained in psychiatric settings;
- At a bare minimum, a lawyer should possess a verifiably competent understanding of the legal process of involuntary detentions, as well as the range of alternative, less-restrictive treatment and care options available;
- The desires of the detained person must be taken into consideration in the . . . confirmation of the appointment of the lawyer;
- Before and after the required meeting with a detained person, the lawyer should conduct a thorough review of all available records. Such inquiry must necessarily involve the detained person's prior medical history and treatment, if and to what extent medication has played a role in the application for a court review, the patient's relationship to family and friends within the community, and the patient's relationship with all relevant medical professionals involved prior to and during the petition process. A detained person's rights, without the assistance of a diligent, competent, and well-informed lawyer at the commencement of the critical investigatory stage of the detention process, would have little meaning;
- A lawyer should be prepared to discuss with his or her client the available options in light of such investigations, as well as the practical and legal consequences of those options. It is important that the lawyer request a reasonable amount of time for such an investigation prior to the court hearing;
- Prior to or following the initial client interview, a lawyer should also attempt to interview all persons who have knowledge of the circumstances surrounding the detention, including family members, acquaintances and any other persons identified by the client as having relevant information, and be prepared to call such persons as witnesses.
- A lawyer shall meet with his or her client, explain the substance of the case, and explain the probable course of the proceedings. The pre-hearing services of a lawyer are an indispensable prerequisite for protecting a respondent's interests.
- The initial client interview should be conducted in private and should be held sufficiently before any scheduled hearings to permit effective preparation and pre-hearing assistance to the client;
- In addition to explaining the legal process and the various rights at issue to the client, a lawyer should also find out, if possible, a clear understanding of what the client would like to see happen in the forthcoming court hearing, whether it be arguing against detention, seeking a change to informal[45] status, formulating and then negotiating with the State a least-restrictive alternative to detention, or agreeing to a State-recommended Court-ordered detention;
- The proper role of the lawyer is to represent the perspective of the respondent [client] and to serve as a vigorous advocate for the respondent's wishes. To the extent that a

---

[45] That is, remaining in hospital without being formally legally detained.

client is unable or unwilling to express personal wishes, the lawyer should advocate the position that best safeguards and advances the client's interest;

- In the courtroom, a lawyer should engage in all aspects of advocacy and vigorously argue to the best of his or her ability for the ends desired by the client;

- The ultimate decision of whether a client should be detained, should not be independently made by a lawyer. Regardless of an attorney's personal opinion, the attorney shall use all reasonable efforts within the bounds of law to advocate the proposed patient's right to avoid Court-ordered mental health services if the proposed patient expresses a desire to avoid the services.[46]

These criteria do not appear to be particularly controversial; indeed a number of them are reflected in the rather limited ECHR jurisprudence on representation.[47] Their primary difference from the ECHR jurisprudence is in specificity and tone. If the ECtHR is hoping to achieve a reasonable standard of advocacy in matters relating to mental disability, adopting this sort of proactive language would be appropriate.

Equally important, the Court must move away from allowing a laissez-faire attitude on the part of the states to poor representation. As noted above, people with mental disabilities who are subjected to substandard legal representation cannot be assumed to have the knowledge or the ability to recognise the difficulties and draw them to the attention of the relevant court authorities. If the Court believes that reasonably competent representation is a part of the client's rights under Articles 5(4) and 6(1), then it should insist that the state be proactive in ensuring such a standard. If the issue is compliance with the Convention, then such a duty flows from the state's general duty to respect human rights under Article 1. In the same way that Article 1 requires the state to take reasonable steps to avoid inhuman treatment prohibited by Article 3, so it must require reasonable steps to avoid poor representation that would violate Articles 5(4) and 6(1).

What does this mean in practice? Certainly, the importance of training in the relevant domestic and ECHR law relating to mental disability is an obvious starting point. Because of the importance of the independence of the legal profession, it is appropriate that this be offered independent of the government; but it should be insisted upon. Legal professional organisations could similarly be required to be more proactive to ensure the appropriate standard of legal services to persons with mental disabilities. It is difficult to see that the insistence upon such standards violates the principle of independence of the legal profession, beyond an insistence that the lawyers meet professional standards that would be uncontroversial in most solicitor-client contexts.

Inevitably, much will depend on funding. Lawyers will be understandably reluctant to perform services for which they are not paid. If a reasonable standard of representation

---

[46] *In the matter of the mental health of K.G.F.*, 2001 MT 140, paras. 71–89.
[47] The overall direction of these criteria is also consistent with the *Basic Principles on the Role of Lawyers*, Adopted by the Eighth United Nations Congress on the Prevention of Crime and the Treatment of Offenders, Havana, Cuba, 27 August to 7 September 1990.

is to be achieved, States must be forthcoming with reasonable funding. Such a duty is buttressed by Article 3 of the United Nations Basic Principles on the Role of Lawyers:

> 3. Governments shall ensure the provision of sufficient funding and other resources for legal services to the poor and, as necessary, to other disadvantaged persons. Professional associations of lawyers shall cooperate in the organization and provision of services, facilities and other resources.[48]

Governments should be expected to live up to that commitment.

---

[48] *Basic Principles on the Role of Lawyers*, Adopted by the Eighth United Nations Congress on the Prevention of Crime and the Treatment of Offenders, Havana, Cuba, 27 August to 7 September 1990.

Chapter 10

Conclusion

The original ratifying countries never anticipated the Convention's detailed reach into their laws that we witness today. Envisaged as an ultimate protection against States lapsing into totalitarianism,[1] the EHCR system has instead become a significant determinant of domestic laws. As it is for other areas of law, so this is increasingly true of the jurisprudence as it relates to mental disability.

It is now quite difficult to see how the Court could ever have performed as originally expected. To maintain that light a touch it would have needed to wrap every guarantee with a near insurmountable margin of appreciation. There would be little judicial pride in such work. With hindsight it is hardly surprising that the Court has been far more activist than its creators expected, and that mental disability should be a fruitful field for Convention law. The three traditional principal components of mental disability law – detention, treatment and guardianship – all involve the use of compulsion or loss of legal autonomy, and all engage Convention rights.

In Chapter 1 we noted that the pace is quickening in the field of mental disability at Strasbourg, with over forty judgments in this field delivered in the period between 2000 and 2004. For those studying the Court's jurisprudence on mental disability this is welcome. It becomes possible to fit a few more of the missing pieces into the jigsaw. But many

---

[1] Woolf et al., *Review of the Working Methods of the European Court of Human Rights* (Strasbourg, ECtHR, 2005), p. 7.

important pieces are still missing. Authors, and, more importantly, the legislators who are expected to enact Convention-compliant statutory law, still have to guess how the Court will decide some core issues. Some guesses are relatively easy, but some of the outstanding issues will present difficult choices for the Court and are therefore much harder to predict.

While the jurisprudence has increased in recent years, one might equally ask why there have been so few mental disability cases? The total to date is still minuscule, set against the number of people with mental disabilities within ECHR territory whose circumstances engage Convention guarantees, and dwarfed by the number of cases involving delays in criminal process brought under Article 6. Criminal law has long been central to human rights discourse, and criminal process usually involves contact with lawyers. Legal advocacy for those detained, involuntarily treated, or deprived of autonomy is still in its infancy in many countries. Only in the last few decades has mental disability law has come into its own as a field of international human rights law. The United Nations Principles for the Protection of Persons with Mental Illness, promulgated at the end of 1991, was the first major international instrument to articulate these rights in any detail.

It is difficult to overstate the importance of legal representation, and fortunate that the Court can make a real difference in this area if it chooses to do so. As we describe in Chapter 2, in *Winterwerp*,[2] *Megyeri*[3] and *Pereira*[4] the Court has been edging ever closer to deciding that legal representation is required for all detained patients at Article 5(4) court hearings. Sooner or later, in our view, it must do so; and the Court must logically take the same approach for court hearings under Article 6 concerned with assumption of guardianship powers.[5] It will also have to address periodic review of guardianship on a parallel with its decisions under Article 5(4). Experience suggests that once lawyers become involved with Article 5(4) hearings they take up other issues. Legal representation is just one strand of the Court's case law, but in this area it is the key to delivering Convention rights.

The Court might not welcome the prospect of a growing number of applications. At the present time it is in real danger of asphyxiating on its burgeoning caseload. The problem is well illustrated by statistics cited in Lord Woolf's *Review of the Working Methods of the European Court of Human Rights* published in December 2005: 404 applications were lodged in 1981, 4,750 in 1997 and 44,100 in 2004, a one hundredfold increase in less than 25 years. The backlog of unresolved cases stood at 82,100 in 2004; it is projected to rise to 250,000 by 2010. Internal and external audits suggest that the staff at the Registry, currently 521 (itself twice that of 6 years ago), needs to be increased to 1,280.[6] There are real doubts as to whether such number can be absorbed. The Court is all too

---

[2] *Winterwerp v. the Netherlands*, Application no. 6301/73, judgment 24 October 1979 (A/33) (1979–80) 2 EHRR 387.
[3] *Megyeri v. Germany*, Application No. 13770/88, judgment 12 May 1992 (1992) 15 EHRR 584.
[4] *Pereira v. Portugal*, Application No. 44872/98, judgment 26 February 2002 (2003) 36 EHRR 49.
[5] See discussion in chapter 6, above.
[6] Woolf et al., *op. cit.*, pp. 4, 7, 11.

aware that any failure to deal with applications promptly would threaten its credibility, particularly because both under Article 5(4) and Article 6(1) it expects speed and promptness from Contracting Parties. It would ill become the Court itself if its own proceedings became known for serious delay.

The Woolf Report sees 'repetitive' cases as a major part of the Court's difficulty, cases that invoke essentially similar points of law, but have traditionally been argued and decided separately.[7] It welcomes the approach adopted in *Broniowski v. Poland* where the Court used the mechanism of a 'pilot judgment' in circumstances where numerous applicants from a single State raised the same Convention issue, in that case a loss of property rights. The Court gave judgment in the lead case on the generic issues raised, and remitted the matter to the Polish Government, with the hope that negotiations between the parties would achieve agreement on compensation both on the lead case and the others.[8] The Report recommends that the Court should be giving priority to and deciding important points of principle rather than attempting to be an ombudsman service for 800 million people.

Major reforms will be required to the Convention system, the scope of which lies outside this book. However much of the 'missing' mental disability case-law does raise issues of real principle, involving the fundamental architecture of Convention law on mental disability. But there is also 'missing' case law applying established principles to facts. The Court has not received applications from those in greatest distress. Reports from the CPT and non-governmental organisations discussed elsewhere in this volume give stark details of the exceedingly grim conditions prevailing in some psychiatric hospitals and care homes, particularly in countries joining the Convention system since the early 1990s. These reports leave no doubt that in some institutions mortality rates have been grossly elevated due to wholly avoidable causes like malnutrition and hypothermia, the clearest possible breaches of Articles 2 and 3. There are no Court judgments in this area.

The Court is of course a reactive body and cannot engineer cases that need to be brought. However its approach to the concept of 'victim' under the Convention places an unjustifiable barrier in the way of those who might seek to call those responsible to account. At the moment only close relatives have been recognised as victims when complaining of an unlawful death under Article 2. Many of the residents in these hospitals and homes have lost all contact with family, and may have graduated to them from orphanages. To confine applications to next of kin excludes the possibility of any claim under the Convention. It would be a small improvement to permit a deceased's guardian to present an Article 2 case. Such a change would nonetheless not be enough because many people have no guardian. For others, staff at the institution assume the role, and are therefore implicated to a greater or lesser extent. The case of *Skjoldager v. Sweden*,[9] one of the last

---

[7]   Woolf et al., *op. cit.*, pp. 19, 38.
[8]   Woolf et al., *op. cit.*, p. 39.
[9]   *Skjoldager v. Sweden*, Application No. 22504/93, decision 17 May 1995. For further discussion of this case, see p. 209 above.

Commission decisions, shows that a concerned outsider, in that case a visiting psychologist, cannot make proxy applications on behalf of living residents. Closed institutions can be very well defended against intervention from outside. If patients or residents can have regular contact with a lawyer for the purposes of an Article 5(4) or Article 6(1) court hearing, there would at least be a chance of bringing legal rights to an isolated and neglected constituency.

While there may be compelling reasons in favour of considering the ECtHR a court of principle, it must somehow continue to have teeth for individuals whose rights are violated. It is clear that States and domestic courts cannot be relied upon to implement the spirit or letter of ECtHR judgments, at least without the continued possibility of ECtHR oversight. Even when advocacy exists it can be almost useless. The extraordinarily poor standard of representations at detention hearings in some parts of Europe serves as an example.[10] These are not marginal cases occurring out of sight and mind; some involve legal systems where lawyers are routinely and manifestly unprepared for the hearings, and it is not credible that the courts before which they appear are unaware of this. There is no new ECHR law here; at issue is a flagrant violation. Yet the domestic courts either choose not to intervene, or consider themselves powerless to do so. Even when States receive unfavourable judgments by the Court, laws sometimes remain unchanged for years; when other States receive such judgments, there seems to be little willingness to apply the relevant judgment, even when it manifestly applies. Any restriction in bringing these cases to the ECtHR because they involve no new 'principle' of law would leave the people whose rights are being violated without redress. We would be left wondering whether the Court is intended to build intellectual castles in the sky, or to bring about real human rights advances to people in the most need.

International bodies increasingly codify human rights principles, with recommendations, standards, principles and conventions. We await with enthusiasm the forthcoming United Nations Convention on the Rights of Persons with Disabilities. Many of these international instruments are referred to in this book, and where there is no Court case-law we cite this 'soft law'. It is drafted as a coherent whole, with consistency between its parts, to a reasonably high degree of detail, and can therefore serve as a legislative model. The Council of Europe's Recommendation No. R(99)4 which concerns incapacity and guardianship is one such example, which assumes importance in the relative absence of Convention decisions on guardianship and capacity. The Court revisits mental disability on an occasional basis, and now finds that many issues have been elaborated in detail in 'soft law'. This might encourage a bolder approach, but it has not happened yet.

The Court's approach is one of cautious incrementalism. Many decisions are made on a very narrow basis, for example deciding issues on one limb of Article 5 but leaving other very important issues under the same Article unresolved. Even when dealing with a one-dimensional issue, the Court can be very tentative. How speedily must a decision be made

---

[10]   See discussion in chapters 2 and 9 of this volume.

under Article 5(4) for a newly detained patient? A reasonable question one might think, but one to which it is still not possible to give an answer after over 55 years. A decision will say that the delay is too lengthy, but decline to reveal the standard, leaving legislators and national courts to guess. The Court will eventually have to reveal its hand under the inevitable flow of applications. It is only then that the standard will have been established. In this sense, the Court can be the author of its own case load misfortune.

There is an obvious contrast with the duty expected of countries to make their domestic laws explicit. Involuntary detention must be 'according to law', and interventions engaging Article 8 must be codified and foreseeable in their impact. Court decisions on the structural features of mental disability law, particularly process requirements, are effectively statutory requirements to the 46 Member States of the Council of Europe. But the Court shows no urgency in dispelling remaining doubts about the Convention's requirements. It tends to prefer a nibble to a bite.

This incrementalist approach risks leaving mental disability picking around the edges of human rights development. This may be an effective approach for some issues involving the right to court process, the traditional mainstay of human rights. It is much less likely to be able to promote other forms of human rights. Exclusion from mainstream education, housing and employment perpetuates the segregation and stigma that have also been a conspicuous feature of lives of persons with mental disabilities across Convention territory. It is much less obvious that the incrementalist approach of the Court can engage with what in essence involves a paradigm shift in human rights thinking and social perceptions; yet without such a paradigm shift, it is difficult to see how the rights we discuss in chapter 7 can be obtainable. In this regard, *D.H. and others v. Czech Republic*,[11] involving a claim by Roma families to inclusive education, does not inspire optimism.

Margins of appreciation, however much derided, are essential to the Court's working. But if they are drawn too wide they can emasculate the Convention's protection. Some of the margins allowed by the Court are threatening to confer discretions so wide as to negate any Convention protection. The margin first identified in *Luberti v. Italy*,[12] but since expanded in *Johnson v. United Kingdom*,[13] is considered further below.

Article 5 has been easily the most productive field for the Court in mental disability, and the broad scheme is in place. However the case law is much stronger on process than substance. The entry criterion that emerged from *Winterwerp* – 'a true mental disorder of a kind or degree warranting compulsory admission'[14] – has remained the Court's oft-cited test ever since 1979. It is entirely circular, and some would say general to the point of banality. Since a 'pressing social need' is a requirement to justify any intervention under

---

[11] Application No. 57325/00, judgment 7 February 2006. See further pp. 189–90, above.
[12] *Luberti v. Italy*, Application No. 9019/80, judgment 23 February 1984, Series A no. 75, pp. 12–13, 1984 6 EHRR 441.
[13] *Johnson v. the United Kingdom*, Application No. 22520/93, judgment 24 October 1997, (1997) 27 EHRR 296.
[14] *Winterwerp v. the Netherlands op. cit.*, para. 39.

Article 8, it must logically also apply to involuntary admission, but that would merely add words of emphasis to the word 'warranting'. The Court of course allows a wide margin of appreciation to the national definition of 'unsoundness of mind', and similarly shows no enthusiasm for questioning on-the-spot assessments, so it may have felt thus far that there is little profit in any further elaboration of the criterion. There are no cases that have seriously tested the limits of the margin allowed.

The jurisprudence on capacity is still very thin. A court finding of incapacity would normally be a prerequisite for any physical treatment given without consent – it clearly determines civil rights – and so it is discriminatory to omit it for mental disability. Justification for treatment over an individual's competent refusal of consent could be found if, taking up the Council of Europe 2004 Recommendations, there was a significant risk of serious harm to the patient or another person, and no less intrusive means of providing appropriate care is available. The CPT Standards similarly uncouple involuntary detention and involuntary treatment, and would allow a legally detained patient who retains capacity the right to refuse treatment unless overridden by clear legal criteria, and only in exceptional circumstances.[15]

Since there is no international legislative consensus on the issue the Court may well allow involuntary admission without an assessment or finding of incapacity, as part of the margin of appreciation. To permit involuntary treatment thereafter without prior determination of capacity would be to bury the issue altogether, and be overtly – and some would say indefensibly – discriminatory. It seems likely that any restriction on an individual's right to consent to treatment for a mental disability will require access to a judicial process under Article 6.[16] If the right to consent can be restricted by incapacity to consent, which seems most likely, then the Court will have to decide how often this should be periodically reviewable. Periodic review of detention appears to be required no more than annually, although institutional staff must keep an ongoing assessment to ensure the continued appropriateness of the detention. This is not necessarily an appropriate guide for capacity determinations. Capacity can change very rapidly, sometimes in the course of a few days as a result of response to medication, and a mere annual right of review would not fit medical reality. The Court will also have to decide whether a court determination under Article 6 should be automatic or only available upon application by the person with mental disability. If the former, there would be a very major extension of Convention-driven process. If the latter, there remains the issue of whether a positive obligation will be created to appoint a guardian. If the guardian is appointed, it then becomes an issue how far he or she would then be required to take proceedings on the person's behalf, and how such an obligation would be enforced. Unless these issues are addressed, the rights of the individual without capacity would be, to use the Court's own language, 'theoretical and illusory'.[17]

---

[15] See further chapter 4.
[16] See further page 160 above.
[17] *Airey v. Ireland*, Application No. 6289/73, judgment 9 October 1979, Series A, No. 32, (1979–80) HRR 305, para. 24.

Mental health services in many countries are skewed towards institutional care, but the overwhelming political movement in service provision has been in favour of community services. It is still uncertain how far the Court will engage with this new thinking and recognise the right to community integration.[18] The Court has declined to specify a level of community services that a State must provide, although we argue above that it has not entirely closed the door to such a determination in the future.[19] Time will tell whether the Court can or will find in the Convention a right that the United States Supreme Court found in the Americans with Disabilities Act 1990 in *Olmstead v. LC.*[20]

The Court gives those seeking discharge from hospitals or care homes virtually no assistance. In cases such as *Kolanis v. the United Kingdom*[21] and *I.H. v. the United Kingdom*,[22] where issues of risk arose, the Court was not prepared to find that continued detention violated Article 5 when conditions set for discharge by a Tribunal had not been met. In *Ashingdane v. the United Kingdom*, the Court decided that Article 5 did not control the place of detention, only the fact of detention.[23] Where a country's mental health services include high, medium and low security institutions the individual therefore cannot look to the Convention for protection against improper placement. Psychiatric opinion, to which the Court will give respect, usually regards release from high security as requiring progression first to medium or low security institutions, and probably conditional release thereafter.

Kolanis shows that the Court is extremely reluctant to adjudicate when a discharge raises a conflict of medical opinion. In the United Kingdom, courts do not order doctors to carry out treatment with which they disagree, and the Court at Strasbourg was content to follow that principle. But there are grave dangers down this path. The objection by psychiatrists approached to provide community supervision in *Kolanis* was not to the idea of a conditional discharge per se, but to the tribunal's proposed condition of residence with family, in other words to the setting in which treatment would be given. In *I.H.* the objection essentially went to the wisdom of the Tribunal's decision. A potential receiving psychiatrist is thus given a power that the Court was not prepared to allow a government minister in *X. v. United Kingdom*.[24] The Tribunal's decision becomes a mere recommendation. The ECtHR was influenced by the fact that local authorities and psychiatrists were susceptible to judicial review if they failed to use 'best efforts' or were 'unreasonable'. However it is perfectly possible for a tribunal and receiving psychiatrist

---

[18]   See discussion in Chapter 7.

[19]   See discussion at pp. 45–6 of *Kolanis v. the United Kingdom*, Application No. 517/02, judgment 21 June 2005, (2006) 42 EHRR 12.

[20]   *Olmstead v. L.C.* (1999) 527 US 581. This case is discussed at pp. 185–6 above.

[21]   *Kolanis v. the United Kingdom, op. cit.*

[22]   *I.H. v. the United Kingdom*, Application No. 17111/04, decision 21 June 2005.

[23]   See *Ashingdane v. the United Kingdom*, Application No. 8225/78, judgment 28 May 1985 (A/93) (1985) 7 EHRR 528, paras. 41–2.

[24]   *X. v. United Kingdom*, Application No. 7215/75, judgment 5 November 1981, (1981) 4 EHRR 188, para. 41.

to disagree, with both being legally 'reasonable'. Following *Kolanis*, the receiving psychiatrist's objection prevails over the Article 5(4) court.

In *Luberti v. Italy*[25] the Court allowed a margin of appreciation for a State when it assessed the speed with which an Article 5(4) decision was reached for an Applicant who had previously been found to be of 'unsound mind' and to present a danger to society. In *Johnson v. the United Kingdom*[26] the Court extended this in two ways. It held that there was no obligation immediately to release a patient following a favourable 5(4) decision, even when a patient has been found not to be suffering from any mental disorder at all. Moreover the language of the judgment in *Johnson* no longer restricted the margin to those posing a risk to society. The Court's judgment in *Winterwerp* gave reason to believe that the discharge criteria under Article 5 would be the logical mirror-image of the entry criteria. As a result of these cases the two are now far apart, and Article 5 detention has acquired some of the characteristics of a lobster-pot, easier to enter than escape. At every stage a patient's quest for tangible rights confronts either a wide margin of appreciation or an absence of Article 5 protection altogether. No one would deny that the Court faces difficult choices with issues involving release, nor that some margin may be necessary, but the current state of jurisprudence cedes an astonishing degree of power to detaining authorities. It urgently requires some re-balancing.

The Court's decision in *H.L. v. the United Kingdom*[27] is highly significant. Mr. H.L. was admitted informally (not in law detained) to an intensive behaviour unit of a psychiatric hospital. He evidenced no objection, and could not in practice have done so due to his autism. The Court decided he was nonetheless detained in the unit, and that Article 5 applied to his case. This case has many implications that will take time to resolve. Some of these are analogous to those related to determination of capacity, noted above: how are rights to be made real for a group of people who, by definition, cannot be assumed to have the ability to initiate proceedings themselves? Equally, the Court did not explore what has been called the 'horizontal impact' of its decision. Some of the factors that led the Court to conclude that he was Article 5 detained may apply just as much to those living with paid carers in the community, as the Applicant had been prior to his admission, or indeed with family. An individual might well, for example, be prevented from leaving his home if he sought to do so. Does this mean that such people are similarly detained in a community setting, or is the fact of institutional placement decisive? The Court has always regarded detention as a multi-factorial issue, and so it may try to draw a line between those in institutions and those in the community. At the same time, the Court has already held that Article 5 applies to detentions in private clinics, even when these are not pursuant to judicial order. A dividing line between private clinics and other care structures in the private sector would seem somewhat arbitrary.

---

[25] *Luberti v. Italy, op. cit.*
[26] *Johnson v. the United Kingdom, op. cit.*
[27] *H.L. v. the United Kingdom*, Application No. 45508/99, judgment 5 October 2004, (2005) 40 EHRR 32. This case is discussed in detail at pp. 36–7 and 68–9, above.

The question of 'speed' for a newly detained patient under Article 5(4) has been referred to above[28] as an example of the Court's tentativeness, and as exemplifying its preference for a case-by-case approach. Although the Court may be hesitant to establish an inflexible rule, there is definite scope for enunciating some firmer guidelines. The time under consideration is between the date of application and a court's decision. Hospitals preparing their response may need to contact other agencies or family, or to hold a case conference. Multi-member tribunals will have to be empanelled. If the time allowed is very short, it may not be possible in time for the hearing to identify an alternative community placement to one that may have broken down. However the Court has now accepted that adjournments sought by the applicant may constitute a waiver of the speed requirement, and so the required speed can be to some extent at the patient's election. The protection established by Article 5 was undoubtedly intended, amongst other things, to guard against wholly unjustified involuntary admission due to misjudgement, misinformation, misidentification, or even improper motive. In such cases it is vital that the time be very short indeed, and to allow two weeks would be generous to the authorities involved. Significantly the United Nations Human Rights Committee has suggested that two weeks would be too long,[29] and the Court may not wish to lag behind a sister organisation. The likelihood, we think, is that it will eventually settle on seven days in a case without special features, but perhaps leaving scope for some case-by-case variation.

By contrast, there appears to be no need to leave any room for case-by-case variation for legal representation. Once the Court said in *Pereira* that it was 'self-evident' that legal issues can arise at an Article 5(4) court hearing[30] it became hardly imaginable that any patient could be left unrepresented. Systems of legal representation remain a rarity across Convention territory, and the Court's reluctance to state a rule has the unfortunate consequence of reducing the impact of its jurisprudence on this issue. Where the Court can properly state a rule of general application it should surely do so. Once declared, other cases in breach of the rule can be regarded as 'repetitive', and tracked through a speedier form of resolution. If the Court can steel itself to declaring a rule, it could properly give attention to cases involving inadequate representation, setting standards for a service whose existence should be taken for granted.

Across Convention territory 'guardianship' takes many forms, with widely different application. In some countries the proportion of the population whose right to make decisions for themselves has been supplanted by a formal judicial decision is very small, perhaps as little as one in 2000 people in the United Kingdom. In others that proportion can be as high as one in 130. There is therefore a wide variation in the capacity of those who are under some form of guardianship. The dearth of case-law in this area is sure to

---

[28] See pp. 66–7, above.

[29] See, for example, *Concluding observations of the Human Rights Committee: Estonia*, 15 March 2003, CCPR/CO/77/EST, para. 10, discussed on p. 66, above.

[30] *Pereira v. Portugal*, Application No. 44872/98, judgment 26 February 2002, (2003) 36 EHRR 49, para. 61.

change, and there are numerous issues that the Court will have to tackle. At the threshold point, the Court needs to cement the need for legal representation, and to clarify rights to periodic review. It will need to ensure that review cannot be a casual endorsement of the appointed guardian's role, and therefore possibly to build in an element of challenge to the status quo. It will certainly need to tackle what we have called 'plenary' guardianship, whereby all autonomy is removed, and no recognition is given to the possibility that a person has capacity in one area although not in another. Conferring on guardians the exclusive right to initiate legal proceedings can lock the individual concerned out of all access to domestic courts, and place the guardian in a position of being able to thwart challenge to his or her appointment. It can also be used to achieve involuntary placement, and the question for the Court will be whether this can bring Article 5 into play. It would seem entirely artificial to distinguish such controls from overt involuntary admission. The years to date are rich in Article 5 cases but thin on Article 6. The coming years need to redress that balance.

We would clearly not have written this book unless we were committed to the possibilities offered by the ECHR to give life to the rights of people with mental disabilities, and we are similarly firm in our belief that these possibilities must as a matter of priority become realised. For too long, people with disabilities, and people with mental health problems and intellectual disabilities in particular, were left at the margins of human rights discourse. A change has commenced, but only commenced.

APPENDICES

Appendix 1

Convention for the Protection of Human Rights and Fundamental Freedoms

213 U.N.T.S. 222, entered into force Sept. 3, 1953, as amended by Protocols Nos 3, 5, 8, and 11 which entered into force on 21 September 1970, 20 December 1971, 1 January 1990, and 1 November 1998 respectively.

Rome, 4.XI.1950

The text of the Convention had been amended according to the provisions of Protocol No. 3 (ETS No. 45), which entered into force on 21 September 1970, of Protocol No. 5 (ETS No. 55), which entered into force on 20 December 1971 and of Protocol No. 8 (ETS No. 118), which entered into force on 1 January 1990, and comprised also the text of Protocol No. 2 (ETS No. 44) which, in accordance with Article 5, paragraph 3 thereof, had been an integral part of the Convention since its entry into force on 21 September 1970. All provisions which had been amended or added by these Protocols are replaced by Protocol No. 11 (ETS No. 155), as from the date of its entry into force on 1 November 1998. As from that date, Protocol n° 9 (ETS No. 140), which entered into force on 1 October 1994, is repealed and Protocol n° 10 (ETS No. 146), which has not entered into force, has lost its purpose.

The governments signatory hereto, being members of the Council of Europe,

Considering the Universal Declaration of Human Rights proclaimed by the General Assembly of the United Nations on 10th December 1948;

Considering that this Declaration aims at securing the universal and effective recognition and observance of the Rights therein declared;

Considering that the aim of the Council of Europe is the achievement of greater unity between its members and that one of the methods by which that aim is to be pursued is the maintenance and further realisation of human rights and fundamental freedoms;

Reaffirming their profound belief in those fundamental freedoms which are the foundation of justice and peace in the world and are best maintained on the one hand by an effective political democracy and on the other by a common understanding and observance of the human rights upon which they depend;

Being resolved, as the governments of European countries which are like-minded and have a common heritage of political traditions, ideals, freedom and the rule of law, to take the first steps for the collective enforcement of certain of the rights stated in the Universal Declaration,

Have agreed as follows:

Article 1 – Obligation to respect human rights

The High Contracting Parties shall secure to everyone within their jurisdiction the rights and freedoms defined in Section I of this Convention.

Section I – Rights and freedoms

Article 2 – Right to life

1. Everyone's right to life shall be protected by law. No one shall be deprived of his life intentionally save in the execution of a sentence of a court following his conviction of a crime for which this penalty is provided by law.
2. Deprivation of life shall not be regarded as inflicted in contravention of this article when it results from the use of force which is no more than absolutely necessary: (a) in defence of any person from unlawful violence; (b) in order to effect a lawful arrest or to prevent the escape of a person lawfully detained; (c) in action lawfully taken for the purpose of quelling a riot or insurrection.

Article 3 – Prohibition of torture

No one shall be subjected to torture or to inhuman or degrading treatment or punishment.

Article 4 – Prohibition of slavery and forced labour

1. No one shall be held in slavery or servitude.
2. No one shall be required to perform forced or compulsory labour.
3. For the purpose of this article the term "forced or compulsory labour" shall not include:

    a. any work required to be done in the ordinary course of detention imposed according to the provisions of Article 5 of this Convention or during conditional release from such detention;
    b. any service of a military character or, in case of conscientious objectors in countries where they are recognised, service exacted instead of compulsory military service;
    c. any service exacted in case of an emergency or calamity threatening the life or well-being of the community;
    d. any work or service which forms part of normal civic obligations.

Article 5 – Right to liberty and security

1. Everyone has the right to liberty and security of person. No one shall be deprived of his liberty save in the following cases and in accordance with a procedure prescribed by law:

    a. the lawful detention of a person after conviction by a competent court;
    b. the lawful arrest or detention of a person for non-compliance with the lawful order of a court or in order to secure the fulfilment of any obligation prescribed by law;
    c. the lawful arrest or detention of a person effected for the purpose of bringing him before the competent legal authority on reasonable suspicion of having committed an offence or when it is reasonably considered necessary to prevent his committing an offence or fleeing after having done so;
    d. the detention of a minor by lawful order for the purpose of educational supervision or his lawful detention for the purpose of bringing him before the competent legal authority;
    e. the lawful detention of persons for the prevention of the spreading of infectious diseases, of persons of unsound mind, alcoholics or drug addicts or vagrants;
    f. the lawful arrest or detention of a person to prevent his effecting an unauthorised entry into the country or of a person against whom action is being taken with a view to deportation or extradition.

2 . Everyone who is arrested shall be informed promptly, in a language which he understands, of the reasons for his arrest and of any charge against him.

3. Everyone arrested or detained in accordance with the provisions of paragraph 1.c of this article shall be brought promptly before a judge or other officer authorised by law to exercise judicial power and shall be entitled to trial within a reasonable time or to release pending trial. Release may be conditioned by guarantees to appear for trial.

4. Everyone who is deprived of his liberty by arrest or detention shall be entitled to take proceedings by which the lawfulness of his detention shall be decided speedily by a court and his release ordered if the detention is not lawful.

5. Everyone who has been the victim of arrest or detention in contravention of the provisions of this article shall have an enforceable right to compensation.

Article 6 – Right to a fair trial

1. In the determination of his civil rights and obligations or of any criminal charge against him, everyone is entitled to a fair and public hearing within a reasonable time by an independent and impartial tribunal established by law. Judgment shall be pronounced publicly but the press and public may be excluded from all or part of the trial in the interests of morals, public order or national security in a democratic society, where the interests of juveniles or the protection of the private life of the parties so require, or to the extent strictly necessary in the opinion of the court in special circumstances where publicity would prejudice the interests of justice.

2. Everyone charged with a criminal offence shall be presumed innocent until proved guilty according to law.

3. Everyone charged with a criminal offence has the following minimum rights:

    a. to be informed promptly, in a language which he understands and in detail, of the nature and cause of the accusation against him;

    b. to have adequate time and facilities for the preparation of his defence;

    c. to defend himself in person or through legal assistance of his own choosing or, if he has not sufficient means to pay for legal assistance, to be given it free when the interests of justice so require;

    d. to examine or have examined witnesses against him and to obtain the attendance and examination of witnesses on his behalf under the same conditions as witnesses against him;

    e. to have the free assistance of an interpreter if he cannot understand or speak the language used in court.

Article 7 – No punishment without law

1. No one shall be held guilty of any criminal offence on account of any act or omission which did not constitute a criminal offence under national or international law at the time when it was committed. Nor shall a heavier penalty be imposed than the one that was applicable at the time the criminal offence was committed.

2. This article shall not prejudice the trial and punishment of any person for any act or omission which, at the time when it was committed, was criminal according to the general principles of law recognised by civilised nations.

Article 8 – Right to respect for private and family life

1. Everyone has the right to respect for his private and family life, his home and his correspondence.
2. There shall be no interference by a public authority with the exercise of this right except such as is in accordance with the law and is necessary in a democratic society in the interests of national security, public safety or the economic well-being of the country, for the prevention of disorder or crime, for the protection of health or morals, or for the protection of the rights and freedoms of others.

Article 9 – Freedom of thought, conscience and religion

1. Everyone has the right to freedom of thought, conscience and religion; this right includes freedom to change his religion or belief and freedom, either alone or in community with others and in public or private, to manifest his religion or belief, in worship, teaching, practice and observance.
2. Freedom to manifest one's religion or beliefs shall be subject only to such limitations as are prescribed by law and are necessary in a democratic society in the interests of public safety, for the protection of public order, health or morals, or for the protection of the rights and freedoms of others.

Article 10 – Freedom of expression

1. Everyone has the right to freedom of expression. This right shall include freedom to hold opinions and to receive and impart information and ideas without interference by public authority and regardless of frontiers. This article shall not prevent States from requiring the licensing of broadcasting, television or cinema enterprises.
2. The exercise of these freedoms, since it carries with it duties and responsibilities, may be subject to such formalities, conditions, restrictions or penalties as are prescribed by law and are necessary in a democratic society, in the interests of national security, territorial integrity or public safety, for the prevention of disorder or crime, for the protection of health or morals, for the protection of the reputation or rights of others, for preventing the disclosure of information received in confidence, or for maintaining the authority and impartiality of the judiciary.

Article 11 – Freedom of assembly and association

1. Everyone has the right to freedom of peaceful assembly and to freedom of association with others, including the right to form and to join trade unions for the protection of his interests.

2. No restrictions shall be placed on the exercise of these rights other than such as are prescribed by law and are necessary in a democratic society in the interests of national security or public safety, for the prevention of disorder or crime, for the protection of health or morals or for the protection of the rights and freedoms of others. This article shall not prevent the imposition of lawful restrictions on the exercise of these rights by members of the armed forces, of the police or of the administration of the State.

Article 12 – Right to marry

Men and women of marriageable age have the right to marry and to found a family, according to the national laws governing the exercise of this right.

Article 13 – Right to an effective remedy

Everyone whose rights and freedoms as set forth in this Convention are violated shall have an effective remedy before a national authority notwithstanding that the violation has been committed by persons acting in an official capacity.

Article 14 – Prohibition of discrimination

The enjoyment of the rights and freedoms set forth in this Convention shall be secured without discrimination on any ground such as sex, race, colour, language, religion, political or other opinion, national or social origin, association with a national minority, property, birth or other status.

Article 15 – Derogation in time of emergency

1. In time of war or other public emergency threatening the life of the nation any High Contracting Party may take measures derogating from its obligations under this Convention to the extent strictly required by the exigencies of the situation, provided that such measures are not inconsistent with its other obligations under international law.
2. No derogation from Article 2, except in respect of deaths resulting from lawful acts of war, or from Articles 3, 4 (paragraph 1) and 7 shall be made under this provision.
3. Any High Contracting Party availing itself of this right of derogation shall keep the Secretary General of the Council of Europe fully informed of the measures which it has taken and the reasons therefor. It shall also inform the Secretary General of the Council of Europe when such measures have ceased to operate and the provisions of the Convention are again being fully executed.

Article 16 – Restrictions on political activity of aliens

Nothing in Articles 10, 11 and 14 shall be regarded as preventing the High Contracting Parties from imposing restrictions on the political activity of aliens.

Article 17 – Prohibition of abuse of rights

Nothing in this Convention may be interpreted as implying for any State, group or person any right to engage in any activity or perform any act aimed at the destruction of any of the rights and freedoms set forth herein or at their limitation to a greater extent than is provided for in the Convention.

Article 18 – Limitation on use of restrictions on rights

The restrictions permitted under this Convention to the said rights and freedoms shall not be applied for any purpose other than those for which they have been prescribed.

Section II – European Court of Human Rights

Article 19 – Establishment of the Court

To ensure the observance of the engagements undertaken by the High Contracting Parties in the Convention and the Protocols thereto, there shall be set up a European Court of Human Rights, hereinafter referred to as "the Court". It shall function on a permanent basis.

Article 20 – Number of judges

The Court shall consist of a number of judges equal to that of the High Contracting Parties.

Article 21 – Criteria for office

1. The judges shall be of high moral character and must either possess the qualifications required for appointment to high judicial office or be jurisconsults of recognised competence.
2. The judges shall sit on the Court in their individual capacity.
3. During their term of office the judges shall not engage in any activity which is incompatible with their independence, impartiality or with the demands of a full-time office; all questions arising from the application of this paragraph shall be decided by the Court.

Article 22 – Election of judges

1. The judges shall be elected by the Parliamentary Assembly with respect to each High Contracting Party by a majority of votes cast from a list of three candidates nominated by the High Contracting Party.
2. The same procedure shall be followed to complete the Court in the event of the accession of new High Contracting Parties and in filling casual vacancies.

Article 23 – Terms of office

1. The judges shall be elected for a period of six years. They may be re-elected. However, the terms of office of one-half of the judges elected at the first election shall expire at the end of three years.
2. The judges whose terms of office are to expire at the end of the initial period of three years shall be chosen by lot by the Secretary General of the Council of Europe immediately after their election.
3. In order to ensure that, as far as possible, the terms of office of one-half of the judges are renewed every three years, the Parliamentary Assembly may decide, before proceeding to any subsequent election, that the term or terms of office of one or more judges to be elected shall be for a period other than six years but not more than nine and not less than three years.
4. In cases where more than one term of office is involved and where the Parliamentary Assembly applies the preceding paragraph, the allocation of the terms of office shall be effected by a drawing of lots by the Secretary General of the Council of Europe immediately after the election.
5. A judge elected to replace a judge whose term of office has not expired shall hold office for the remainder of his predecessor's term.
6. The terms of office of judges shall expire when they reach the age of 70.
7. The judges shall hold office until replaced. They shall, however, continue to deal with such cases as they already have under consideration.

Article 24 – Dismissal

No judge may be dismissed from his office unless the other judges decide by a majority of two-thirds that he has ceased to fulfil the required conditions.

Article 25 – Registry and legal secretaries

The Court shall have a registry, the functions and organisation of which shall be laid down in the rules of the Court. The Court shall be assisted by legal secretaries.

Article 26 – Plenary Court

The plenary Court shall (a) elect its President and one or two Vice-Presidents for a period of three years; they may be re-elected; (b) set up Chambers, constituted for a fixed period of time; (c) elect the Presidents of the Chambers of the Court; they may be re-elected; (d) adopt the rules of the Court, and (e) elect the Registrar and one or more Deputy Registrars.

Article 27 – Committees, Chambers and Grand Chamber

1. To consider cases brought before it, the Court shall sit in committees of three judges, in Chambers of seven judges and in a Grand Chamber of seventeen judges. The Court's Chambers shall set up committees for a fixed period of time.

2. There shall sit as an ex officio member of the Chamber and the Grand Chamber the judge elected in respect of the State Party concerned or, if there is none or if he is unable to sit, a person of its choice who shall sit in the capacity of judge.
3. The Grand Chamber shall also include the President of the Court, the Vice-Presidents, the Presidents of the Chambers and other judges chosen in accordance with the rules of the Court. When a case is referred to the Grand Chamber under Article 43, no judge from the Chamber which rendered the judgment shall sit in the Grand Chamber, with the exception of the President of the Chamber and the judge who sat in respect of the State Party concerned.

Article 28 – Declarations of inadmissibility by committees

A committee may, by a unanimous vote, declare inadmissible or strike out of its list of cases an application submitted under Article 34 where such a decision can be taken without further examination. The decision shall be final.

Article 29 – Decisions by Chambers on admissibility and merits

1. If no decision is taken under Article 28, a Chamber shall decide on the admissibility and merits of individual applications submitted under Article 34.
2. A Chamber shall decide on the admissibility and merits of inter-State applications submitted under Article 33.
3. The decision on admissibility shall be taken separately unless the Court, in exceptional cases, decides otherwise.

Article 30 – Relinquishment of jurisdiction to the Grand Chamber

Where a case pending before a Chamber raises a serious question affecting the interpretation of the Convention or the protocols thereto, or where the resolution of a question before the Chamber might have a result inconsistent with a judgment previously delivered by the Court, the Chamber may, at any time before it has rendered its judgment, relinquish jurisdiction in favour of the Grand Chamber, unless one of the parties to the case objects.

Article 31 – Powers of the Grand Chamber

The Grand Chamber shall a determine applications submitted either under Article 33 or Article 34 when a Chamber has relinquished jurisdiction under Article 30 or when the case has been referred to it under Article 43; and b consider requests for advisory opinions submitted under Article 47.

Article 32 – Jurisdiction of the Court

1. The jurisdiction of the Court shall extend to all matters concerning the interpretation and application of the Convention and the protocols thereto which are referred to it as provided in Articles 33, 34 and 47.

2. In the event of dispute as to whether the Court has jurisdiction, the Court shall decide.

Article 33 – Inter-State cases

Any High Contracting Party may refer to the Court any alleged breach of the provisions of the Convention and the protocols thereto by another High Contracting Party.

Article 34 – Individual applications

The Court may receive applications from any person, non-governmental organisation or group of individuals claiming to be the victim of a violation by one of the High Contracting Parties of the rights set forth in the Convention or the protocols thereto. The High Contracting Parties undertake not to hinder in any way the effective exercise of this right.

Article 35 – Admissibility criteria

1. The Court may only deal with the matter after all domestic remedies have been exhausted, according to the generally recognised rules of international law, and within a period of six months from the date on which the final decision was taken.
2. The Court shall not deal with any application submitted under Article 34 that (a) is anonymous; or (b) is substantially the same as a matter that has already been examined by the Court or has already been submitted to another procedure of international investigation or settlement and contains no relevant new information.
3. The Court shall declare inadmissible any individual application submitted under Article 34 which it considers incompatible with the provisions of the Convention or the protocols thereto, manifestly ill-founded, or an abuse of the right of application.
4. The Court shall reject any application which it considers inadmissible under this Article. It may do so at any stage of the proceedings.

Article 36 – Third party intervention

1. In all cases before a Chamber or the Grand Chamber, a High Contracting Party one of whose nationals is an applicant shall have the right to submit written comments and to take part in hearings.
2. The President of the Court may, in the interest of the proper administration of justice, invite any High Contracting Party which is not a party to the proceedings or any person concerned who is not the applicant to submit written comments or take part in hearings.

Article 37 – Striking out applications

1. The Court may at any stage of the proceedings decide to strike an application out of its list of cases where the circumstances lead to the conclusion that

   a. the applicant does not intend to pursue his application; or
   b. the matter has been resolved; or
   c. for any other reason established by the Court, it is no longer justified to continue the examination of the application.

   However, the Court shall continue the examination of the application if respect for human rights as defined in the Convention and the protocols thereto so requires.

2. The Court may decide to restore an application to its list of cases if it considers that the circumstances justify such a course.

Article 38 – Examination of the case and friendly settlement proceedings

1. If the Court declares the application admissible, it shall

   a. pursue the examination of the case, together with the representatives of the parties, and if need be, undertake an investigation, for the effective conduct of which the States concerned shall furnish all necessary facilities;
   b. place itself at the disposal of the parties concerned with a view to securing a friendly settlement of the matter on the basis of respect for human rights as defined in the Convention and the protocols thereto.

2. Proceedings conducted under paragraph 1.b shall be confidential.

Article 39 – Finding of a friendly settlement

If a friendly settlement is effected, the Court shall strike the case out of its list by means of a decision which shall be confined to a brief statement of the facts and of the solution reached.

Article 40 – Public hearings and access to documents

1. Hearings shall be in public unless the Court in exceptional circumstances decides otherwise.
2. Documents deposited with the Registrar shall be accessible to the public unless the President of the Court decides otherwise.

Article 41 – Just satisfaction

If the Court finds that there has been a violation of the Convention or the protocols thereto, and if the internal law of the High Contracting Party concerned allows only partial reparation to be made, the Court shall, if necessary, afford just satisfaction to the injured party.

Article 42 – Judgments of Chambers

Judgments of Chambers shall become final in accordance with the provisions of Article 44, paragraph 2.

Article 43 – Referral to the Grand Chamber

1. Within a period of three months from the date of the judgment of the Chamber, any party to the case may, in exceptional cases, request that the case be referred to the Grand Chamber.
2. A panel of five judges of the Grand Chamber shall accept the request if the case raises a serious question affecting the interpretation or application of the Convention or the protocols thereto, or a serious issue of general importance.
3. If the panel accepts the request, the Grand Chamber shall decide the case by means of a judgment.

Article 44 – Final judgments

1. The judgment of the Grand Chamber shall be final.
2. The judgment of a Chamber shall become final

   a. when the parties declare that they will not request that the case be referred to the Grand Chamber; or
   b. three months after the date of the judgment, if reference of the case to the Grand Chamber has not been requested; or
   c. when the panel of the Grand Chamber rejects the request to refer under Article 43.

3. The final judgment shall be published.

Article 45 – Reasons for judgments and decisions

1. Reasons shall be given for judgments as well as for decisions declaring applications admissible or inadmissible.
2. If a judgment does not represent, in whole or in part, the unanimous opinion of the judges, any judge shall be entitled to deliver a separate opinion.

Article 46 – *Binding force and execution of judgments*

1. The High Contracting Parties undertake to abide by the final judgment of the Court in any case to which they are parties.
2. The final judgment of the Court shall be transmitted to the Committee of Ministers, which shall supervise its execution.

Article 47 – *Advisory opinions*

1. The Court may, at the request of the Committee of Ministers, give advisory opinions on legal questions concerning the interpretation of the Convention and the protocols thereto.
2. Such opinions shall not deal with any question relating to the content or scope of the rights or freedoms defined in Section I of the Convention and the protocols thereto, or with any other question which the Court or the Committee of Ministers might have to consider in consequence of any such proceedings as could be instituted in accordance with the Convention.
3. Decisions of the Committee of Ministers to request an advisory opinion of the Court shall require a majority vote of the representatives entitled to sit on the Committee.

Article 48 – *Advisory jurisdiction of the Court*

The Court shall decide whether a request for an advisory opinion submitted by the Committee of Ministers is within its competence as defined in Article 47.

Article 49 – *Reasons for advisory opinions*

1. Reasons shall be given for advisory opinions of the Court.
2. If the advisory opinion does not represent, in whole or in part, the unanimous opinion of the judges, any judge shall be entitled to deliver a separate opinion.
3. Advisory opinions of the Court shall be communicated to the Committee of Ministers.

Article 50 – *Expenditure on the Court*

The expenditure on the Court shall be borne by the Council of Europe.

Article 51 – *Privileges and immunities of judges*

The judges shall be entitled, during the exercise of their functions, to the privileges and immunities provided for in Article 40 of the Statute of the Council of Europe and in the agreements made thereunder.

Section III – Miscellaneous provisions

Article 52 – Inquiries by the Secretary General

On receipt of a request from the Secretary General of the Council of Europe any High Contracting Party shall furnish an explanation of the manner in which its internal law ensures the effective implementation of any of the provisions of the Convention.

Article 53 – Safeguard for existing human rights

Nothing in this Convention shall be construed as limiting or derogating from any of the human rights and fundamental freedoms which may be ensured under the laws of any High Contracting Party or under any other agreement to which it is a Party.

Article 54 – Powers of the Committee of Ministers

Nothing in this Convention shall prejudice the powers conferred on the Committee of Ministers by the Statute of the Council of Europe.

Article 55 – Exclusion of other means of dispute settlement

The High Contracting Parties agree that, except by special agreement, they will not avail themselves of treaties, conventions or declarations in force between them for the purpose of submitting, by way of petition, a dispute arising out of the interpretation or application of this Convention to a means of settlement other than those provided for in this Convention.

Article 56 – Territorial application

1. Any State may at the time of its ratification or at any time thereafter declare by notification addressed to the Secretary General of the Council of Europe that the present Convention shall, subject to paragraph 4 of this Article, extend to all or any of the territories for whose international relations it is responsible.
2. The Convention shall extend to the territory or territories named in the notification as from the thirtieth day after the receipt of this notification by the Secretary General of the Council of Europe.
3. The provisions of this Convention shall be applied in such territories with due regard, however, to local requirements.
4. Any State which has made a declaration in accordance with paragraph 1 of this article may at any time thereafter declare on behalf of one or more of the territories to which the declaration relates that it accepts the competence of the Court to receive applications from individuals, non-governmental organisations or groups of individuals as provided by Article 34 of the Convention.

Article 57 – Reservations

1. Any State may, when signing this Convention or when depositing its instrument of ratification, make a reservation in respect of any particular provision of the Convention to the extent that any law then in force in its territory is not in conformity with the provision. Reservations of a general character shall not be permitted under this article.
2. Any reservation made under this article shall contain a brief statement of the law concerned.

Article 58 – Denunciation

1. A High Contracting Party may denounce the present Convention only after the expiry of five years from the date on which it became a party to it and after six months' notice contained in a notification addressed to the Secretary General of the Council of Europe, who shall inform the other High Contracting Parties.
2. Such a denunciation shall not have the effect of releasing the High Contracting Party concerned from its obligations under this Convention in respect of any act which, being capable of constituting a violation of such obligations, may have been performed by it before the date at which the denunciation became effective.
3. Any High Contracting Party which shall cease to be a member of the Council of Europe shall cease to be a Party to this Convention under the same conditions.
4. The Convention may be denounced in accordance with the provisions of the preceding paragraphs in respect of any territory to which it has been declared to extend under the terms of Article 56.

Article 59 – Signature and ratification

1. This Convention shall be open to the signature of the members of the Council of Europe. It shall be ratified. Ratifications shall be deposited with the Secretary General of the Council of Europe.
2. The present Convention shall come into force after the deposit of ten instruments of ratification.
3. As regards any signatory ratifying subsequently, the Convention shall come into force at the date of the deposit of its instrument of ratification.
4. The Secretary General of the Council of Europe shall notify all the members of the Council of Europe of the entry into force of the Convention, the names of the High Contracting Parties who have ratified it, and the deposit of all instruments of ratification which may be effected subsequently.

Done at Rome this 4th day of November 1950, in English and French, both texts being equally authentic, in a single copy which shall remain deposited in the archives of the Council of Europe. The Secretary General shall transmit certified copies to each of the signatories.

Protocol 1

Protocol to the Convention for the Protection of Human Rights and Fundamental Freedoms

Paris, 20.III.1952

The governments signatory hereto, being members of the Council of Europe,

Being resolved to take steps to ensure the collective enforcement of certain rights and freedoms other than those already included in Section I of the Convention for the Protection of Human Rights and Fundamental Freedoms signed at Rome on 4 November 1950 (hereinafter referred to as the Convention),

Have agreed as follows:

Article 1. Protection of property

Every natural or legal person is entitled to the peaceful enjoyment of his possessions. No one shall be deprived of his possessions except in the public interest and subject to the conditions provided for by law and by the general principles of international law.

The preceding provisions shall not, however, in any way impair the right of a State to enforce such laws as it deems necessary to control the use of property in accordance with the general interest or to secure the payment of taxes or other contributions or penalties.

Article 2. Right to education

No person shall be denied the right to education. In the exercise of any functions which it assumes in relation to education and to teaching, the State shall respect the right of parents to ensure such education and teaching in conformity with their own religious and philosophical convictions.

Article 3. Right to free elections

The High Contracting Parties undertake to hold free elections at reasonable intervals by secret ballot, under conditions which will ensure the free expression of the opinion of the people in the choice of the legislature.

Article 4. Territorial application

Any High Contracting Party may at the time of signature or ratification or at any time thereafter communicate to the Secretary General of the Council of Europe a declaration stating the extent to which it undertakes that the provisions of the present Protocol shall apply to such of the territories for the international relations of which it is responsible as are named therein.

Any High Contracting Party which has communicated a declaration in virtue of the preceding paragraph may from time to time communicate a further declaration modifying the terms of any former declaration or terminating the application of the provisions of this Protocol in respect of any territory.

A declaration made in accordance with this article shall be deemed to have been made in accordance with paragraph 1 of Article 56 of the Convention.

Article 5. Relationship to the Convention

As between the High Contracting Parties the provisions of Articles 1, 2, 3 and 4 of this Protocol shall be regarded as additional articles to the Convention and all the provisions of the Convention shall apply accordingly.

Article 6. Signature and ratification

This Protocol shall be open for signature by the members of the Council of Europe, who are the signatories of the Convention; it shall be ratified at the same time as or after the ratification of the Convention. It shall enter into force after the deposit of ten instruments of ratification. As regards any signatory ratifying subsequently, the Protocol shall enter into force at the date of the deposit of its instrument of ratification.

The instruments of ratification shall be deposited with the Secretary General of the Council of Europe, who will notify all members of the names of those who have ratified.

Done at Paris on the 20th day of March 1952, in English and French, both texts being equally authentic, in a single copy which shall remain deposited in the archives of the Council of Europe. The Secretary General shall transmit certified copies to each of the signatory governments.

Protocol 2

[ETS No. 44, Strasbourg, 6 May 1963. This protocol is superseded by protocol 11.]

Protocol 3

[ETS No. 45, Strasbourg, 6 May 1963. This protocol replaced the former Article 29 of the Convention, and amended Articles 30 and 34. These amendments are reflected in the amended version of the Convention, above.]

Protocol 4

Protocol No. 4 to the Convention for the Protection of Human Rights and Fundamental Freedoms securing certain rights and freedoms other than those already included in the Convention and in the first Protocol thereto

Strasbourg, 16.IX.1963

The governments signatory hereto, being members of the Council of Europe,

Being resolved to take steps to ensure the collective enforcement of certain rights and freedoms other than those already included in Section I of the Convention for the Protection of Human Rights and Fundamental Freedoms signed at Rome on 4th November 1950 (hereinafter referred to as the Convention) and in Articles 1 to 3 of the First Protocol to the Convention, signed at Paris on 20th March 1952,

Have agreed as follows:

Article 1 – Prohibition of imprisonment for debt

No one shall be deprived of his liberty merely on the ground of inability to fulfil a contractual obligation.

Article 2 – Freedom of movement

1. Everyone lawfully within the territory of a State shall, within that territory, have the right to liberty of movement and freedom to choose his residence.
2. Everyone shall be free to leave any country, including his own.
3. No restrictions shall be placed on the exercise of these rights other than such as are in accordance with law and are necessary in a democratic society in the interests of national security or public safety, for the maintenance of ordre public, for the prevention of crime, for the protection of health or morals, or for the protection of the rights and freedoms of others.
4. The rights set forth in paragraph 1 may also be subject, in particular areas, to restrictions imposed in accordance with law and justified by the public interest in a democratic society.

Article 3 – Prohibition of expulsion of nationals

1. No one shall be expelled, by means either of an individual or of a collective measure, from the territory of the State of which he is a national.
2. No one shall be deprived of the right to enter the territory of the state of which he is a national.

Article 4 – Prohibition of collective expulsion of aliens

Collective expulsion of aliens is prohibited.

Article 5 – Territorial application

1. Any High Contracting Party may, at the time of signature or ratification of this Protocol, or at any time thereafter, communicate to the Secretary General of the Council of Europe a declaration stating the extent to which it undertakes that the provisions of this Protocol shall apply to such of the territories for the international relations of which it is responsible as are named therein.
2. Any High Contracting Party which has communicated a declaration in virtue of the preceding paragraph may, from time to time, communicate a further declaration modifying the terms of any former declaration or terminating the application of the provisions of this Protocol in respect of any territory.
3. A declaration made in accordance with this article shall be deemed to have been made in accordance with paragraph 1 of Article 56 of the Convention.
4. The territory of any State to which this Protocol applies by virtue of ratification or acceptance by that State, and each territory to which this Protocol is applied by virtue of a declaration by that State under this article, shall be treated as separate territories for the purpose of the references in Articles 2 and 3 to the territory of a State.
5. Any State which has made a declaration in accordance with paragraph 1 or 2 of this Article may at any time thereafter declare on behalf of one or more of the territories to which the declaration relates that it accepts the competence of the Court to receive applications from individuals, non-governmental organisations or groups of individuals as provided in Article 34 of the Convention in respect of all or any of Articles 1 to 4 of this Protocol.

Article 6 – Relationship to the Convention

As between the High Contracting Parties the provisions of Articles 1 to 5 of this Protocol shall be regarded as additional Articles to the Convention, and all the provisions of the Convention shall apply accordingly.

Article 7 – Signature and ratification

1. This Protocol shall be open for signature by the members of the Council of Europe who are the signatories of the Convention; it shall be ratified at the same time as or after the ratification of the Convention. It shall enter into force after the deposit of five instruments of ratification. As regards any signatory ratifying subsequently, the Protocol shall enter into force at the date of the deposit of its instrument of ratification.
2. The instruments of ratification shall be deposited with the Secretary General of the Council of Europe, who will notify all members of the names of those who have ratified.

In witness whereof the undersigned, being duly authorised thereto, have signed this Protocol.

Done at Strasbourg, this 16th day of September 1963, in English and in French, both texts being equally authoritative, in a single copy which shall remain deposited in the archives of the Council of Europe. The Secretary General shall transmit certified copies to each of the signatory states.

Protocol 5

[ETS No. 114, Strasbourg, 28 April 1983. This protocol concerns the abolition the death penalty.]

Protocol 6

Protocol No. 6 to the Convention for the Protection of Human Rights and Fundamental Freedoms concerning the abolition of the death penalty

Strasbourg, 28.IV.1983

The member States of the Council of Europe, signatory to this Protocol to the Convention for the Protection of Human Rights and Fundamental Freedoms, signed at Rome on 4 November 1950 (hereinafter referred to as the Convention),

Considering that the evolution that has occurred in several member States of the Council of Europe expresses a general tendency in favour of abolition of the death penalty;

Have agreed as follows:

Article 1 – Abolition of the death penalty

The death penalty shall be abolished. No-one shall be condemned to such penalty or executed.

Article 2 – Death penalty in time of war

A State may make provision in its law for the death penalty in respect of acts committed in time of war or of imminent threat of war; such penalty shall be applied only in the instances laid down in the law and in accordance with its provisions. The State shall communicate to the Secretary General of the Council of Europe the relevant provisions of that law.

Article 3 – Prohibition of derogations

No derogation from the provisions of this Protocol shall be made under Article 15 of the Convention.

Article 4 – Prohibition of reservations

No reservation may be made under Article 57 of the Convention in respect of the provisions of this Protocol.

Article 5 – Territorial application

1. Any State may at the time of signature or when depositing its instrument of ratification, acceptance or approval, specify the territory or territories to which this Protocol shall apply.
2. Any State may at any later date, by a declaration addressed to the Secretary General of the Council of Europe, extend the application of this Protocol to any other territory specified in the declaration. In respect of such territory the Protocol shall enter into force on the first day of the month following the date of receipt of such declaration by the Secretary General.
3. Any declaration made under the two preceding paragraphs may, in respect of any territory specified in such declaration, be withdrawn by a notification addressed to the Secretary General. The withdrawal shall become effective on the first day of the month following the date of receipt of such notification by the Secretary General.

Article 6 – Relationship to the Convention

As between the States Parties the provisions of Articles 1 and 5 of this Protocol shall be regarded as additional articles to the Convention and all the provisions of the Convention shall apply accordingly.

Article 7 – Signature and ratification

The Protocol shall be open for signature by the member States of the Council of Europe, signatories to the Convention. It shall be subject to ratification, acceptance or approval. A member State of the Council of Europe may not ratify, accept or approve this Protocol unless it has, simultaneously or previously, ratified the Convention. Instruments of ratification, acceptance or approval shall be deposited with the Secretary General of the Council of Europe.

Article 8 – Entry into force

1. This Protocol shall enter into force on the first day of the month following the date on which five member States of the Council of Europe have expressed their consent to be bound by the Protocol in accordance with the provisions of Article 7.
2. In respect of any member State which subsequently expresses its consent to be bound by it, the Protocol shall enter into force on the first day of the month following the date of the deposit of the instrument of ratification, acceptance or approval.

Article 9 – Depositary functions

The Secretary General of the Council of Europe shall notify the member States of the Council of:

a.   any signature;
b.   the deposit of any instrument of ratification, acceptance or approval;
c.   any date of entry into force of this Protocol in accordance with articles 5 and 8;
d.   any other act, notification or communication relating to this Protocol.

In witness whereof the undersigned, being duly authorised thereto, have signed this Protocol. Done at Strasbourg, this 28th day of April 1983, in English and in French, both texts being equally authentic, in a single copy which shall be deposited in the archives of the Council of Europe. The Secretary General of the Council of Europe shall transmit certified copies to each member State of the Council of Europe.

Protocol 7

Protocol No. 7 to the Convention for the Protection of Human Rights and Fundamental Freedoms

Strasbourg, 22.XI.1984

The member States of the Council of Europe signatory hereto,

Being resolved to take further steps to ensure the collective enforcement of certain rights and freedoms by means of the Convention for the Protection of Human Rights and Fundamental Freedoms signed at Rome on 4 November 1950 (hereinafter referred to as the Convention),

Have agreed as follows:

Article 1 – Procedural safeguards relating to expulsion of aliens

1. An alien lawfully resident in the territory of a State shall not be expelled therefrom except in pursuance of a decision reached in accordance with law and shall be allowed:

   a. to submit reasons against his expulsion,
   b. to have his case reviewed, and
   c. to be represented for these purposes before the competent authority or a person or persons designated by that authority.

2. An alien may be expelled before the exercise of his rights under paragraph 1.a, b and c of this Article, when such expulsion is necessary in the interests of public order or is grounded on reasons of national security.

Article 2 – Right of appeal in criminal matters

1. Everyone convicted of a criminal offence by a tribunal shall have the right to have his conviction or sentence reviewed by a higher tribunal. The exercise of this right, including the grounds on which it may be exercised, shall be governed by law.
2. This right may be subject to exceptions in regard to offences of a minor character, as prescribed by law, or in cases in which the person concerned was tried in the first instance by the highest tribunal or was convicted following an appeal against acquittal.

Article 3 – Compensation for wrongful conviction

When a person has by a final decision been convicted of a criminal offence and when subsequently his conviction has been reversed, or he has been pardoned, on the ground that a new or newly discovered fact shows conclusively that there has been a miscarriage of justice, the person who has suffered punishment as a result of such conviction shall be compensated according to the law or the practice of the State concerned, unless it is proved that the non-disclosure of the unknown fact in time is wholly or partly attributable to him.

Article 4 – Right not to be tried or punished twice

1. No one shall be liable to be tried or punished again in criminal proceedings under the jurisdiction of the same State for an offence for which he has already been finally acquitted or convicted in accordance with the law and penal procedure of that State.
2. The provisions of the preceding paragraph shall not prevent the reopening of the case in accordance with the law and penal procedure of the State concerned, if there is evidence of new or newly discovered facts, or if there has been a fundamental defect in the previous proceedings, which could affect the outcome of the case.
3. No derogation from this Article shall be made under Article 15 of the Convention.

Article 5 – Equality between spouses

Spouses shall enjoy equality of rights and responsibilities of a private law character between them, and in their relations with their children, as to marriage, during marriage and in the event of its dissolution. This Article shall not prevent States from taking such measures as are necessary in the interests of the children.

Article 6 – Territorial application

1. Any State may at the time of signature or when depositing its instrument of ratification, acceptance or approval, specify the territory or territories to which the Protocol shall apply and state the extent to which it undertakes that the provisions of this Protocol shall apply to such territory or territories.
2. Any State may at any later date, by a declaration addressed to the Secretary General of the Council of Europe, extend the application of this Protocol to any other territory specified in the declaration. In respect of such territory the Protocol shall enter into force on the first day of the month following the expiration of a period of two months after the date of receipt by the Secretary General of such declaration.
3. Any declaration made under the two preceding paragraphs may, in respect of any territory specified in such declaration, be withdrawn or modified by a notification addressed to the Secretary General. The withdrawal or modification shall become effective on the first day of the month following the expiration of a period of two months after the date of receipt of such notification by the Secretary General.
4. A declaration made in accordance with this Article shall be deemed to have been made in accordance with paragraph 1 of Article 56 of the Convention.
5. The territory of any State to which this Protocol applies by virtue of ratification, acceptance or approval by that State, and each territory to which this Protocol is applied by virtue of a declaration by that State under this Article, may be treated as separate territories for the purpose of the reference in Article 1 to the territory of a State.
6. Any State which has made a declaration in accordance with paragraph 1 or 2 of this Article may at any time thereafter declare on behalf of one or more of the territories

to which the declaration relates that it accepts the competence of the Court to receive applications from individuals, non- governmental organisations or groups of individuals as provided in Article 34 of the Convention in respect of Articles 1 to 5 of this Protocol.

Article 7 – Relationship to the Convention

As between the States Parties, the provisions of Article 1 to 6 of this Protocol shall be regarded as additional Articles to the Convention, and all the provisions of the Convention shall apply accordingly.

Article 8 – Signature and ratification

This Protocol shall be open for signature by member States of the Council of Europe which have signed the Convention. It is subject to ratification, acceptance or approval. A member State of the Council of Europe may not ratify, accept or approve this Protocol without previously or simultaneously ratifying the Convention. Instruments of ratification, acceptance or approval shall be deposited with the Secretary General of the Council of Europe.

Article 9 – Entry into force

1. This Protocol shall enter into force on the first day of the month following the expiration of a period of two months after the date on which seven member States of the Council of Europe have expressed their consent to be bound by the Protocol in accordance with the provisions of Article 8.
2. In respect of any member State which subsequently expresses its consent to be bound by it, the Protocol shall enter into force on the first day of the month following the expiration of a period of two months after the date of the deposit of the instrument of ratification, acceptance or approval.

Article 10 – Depositary functions

The Secretary General of the Council of Europe shall notify all the member States of the Council of Europe of:

a. any signature;
b. the deposit of any instrument of ratification, acceptance or approval;
c. any date of entry into force of this Protocol in accordance with Articles 6 and 9;
d. any other act, notification or declaration relating to this Protocol.

In witness whereof the undersigned, being duly authorised thereto, have signed this Protocol.

Done at Strasbourg, this 22nd day of November 1984, in English and French, both texts being equally authentic, in a single copy which shall be deposited in the archives of the Council of Europe. The Secretary General of the Council of Europe shall transmit certified copies to each member State of the Council of Europe.

Protocol 8

[ETS No. 118, Strasbourg, 19 March 1985. This protocol amends a variety of procedural Articles of the Convention. These amendments are reflected in the amended version of the Convention, above. Protocol 8 is in any event superseded by Protocol 11.]

Protocol 9

[ETS No. 140, Strasbourg, 6 November 1990. This protocol amended a variety of procedural Articles of the Convention. It was superseded by Protocol 11.]

Protocol 10

[ETS No. 146, Strasbourg, 25 March 1992. This protocol amended the former Article 32 of the Convention. It was superseded by Protocol 11.]

Protocol 11

[ETS No. 155, Strasbourg, 11 May 1994. This protocol fundamentally re-structured the administration of the Court, abolishing the European Commission of Human Rights and establishing the current system of judicial appointments and decision-making. The provisions of this protocol are reflected in the amended version of the Convention, above.]

Protocol 12

Protocol No. 12 to the Convention for the Protection of Human Rights and Fundamental Freedoms

Rome, 4.XI.2000

The member States of the Council of Europe signatory hereto,

Having regard to the fundamental principle according to which all persons are equal before the law and are entitled to the equal protection of the law;

Being resolved to take further steps to promote the equality of all persons through the collective enforcement of a general prohibition of discrimination by means of the Convention for the Protection of Human Rights and Fundamental Freedoms signed at Rome on 4 November 1950 (hereinafter referred to as the Convention);

Reaffirming that the principle of non-discrimination does not prevent States Parties from taking measures in order to promote full and effective equality, provided that there is an objective and reasonable justification for those measures,

Have agreed as follows:

Article 1 – General prohibition of discrimination

1. The enjoyment of any right set forth by law shall be secured without discrimination on any ground such as sex, race, colour, language, religion, political or other opinion, national or social origin, association with a national minority, property, birth or other status.
2. No one shall be discriminated against by any public authority on any ground such as those mentioned in paragraph 1.

Article 2 – Territorial application

1. Any State may, at the time of signature or when depositing its instrument of ratification, acceptance or approval, specify the territory or territories to which this Protocol shall apply.
2. Any State may at any later date, by a declaration addressed to the Secretary General of the Council of Europe, extend the application of this Protocol to any other territory specified in the declaration. In respect of such territory the Protocol shall enter into force on the first day of the month following the expiration of a period of three months after the date of receipt by the Secretary General of such declaration.
3. Any declaration made under the two preceding paragraphs may, in respect of any territory specified in such declaration, be withdrawn or modified by a notification addressed to the Secretary General of the Council of Europe. The withdrawal or modification shall become effective on the first day of the month following the expiration of a period of three months after the date of receipt of such notification by the Secretary General.
4. A declaration made in accordance with this article shall be deemed to have been made in accordance with paragraph 1 of Article 56 of the Convention.
5. Any State which has made a declaration in accordance with paragraph 1 or 2 of this article may at any time thereafter declare on behalf of one or more of the territories

to which the declaration relates that it accepts the competence of the Court to receive applications from individuals, non-governmental organisations or groups of individuals as provided by Article 34 of the Convention in respect of Article 1 of this Protocol.

Article 3 – Relationship to the Convention

As between the States Parties, the provisions of Articles 1 and 2 of this Protocol shall be regarded as additional articles to the Convention, and all the provisions of the Convention shall apply accordingly.

Article 4 – Signature and ratification

This Protocol shall be open for signature by member States of the Council of Europe which have signed the Convention. It is subject to ratification, acceptance or approval. A member State of the Council of Europe may not ratify, accept or approve this Protocol without previously or simultaneously ratifying the Convention. Instruments of ratification, acceptance or approval shall be deposited with the Secretary General of the Council of Europe.

Article 5 – Entry into force

1. This Protocol shall enter into force on the first day of the month following the expiration of a period of three months after the date on which ten member States of the Council of Europe have expressed their consent to be bound by the Protocol in accordance with the provisions of Article 4.
2. In respect of any member State which subsequently expresses its consent to be bound by it, the Protocol shall enter into force on the first day of the month following the expiration of a period of three months after the date of the deposit of the instrument of ratification, acceptance for approval.

Article 6 – Depositary functions

The Secretary General of the Council of Europe shall notify all the member States of the Council of Europe of:

a. any signature;
b. the deposit of any instrument of ratification, acceptance or approval;
c. any date of entry into force of this Protocol in accordance with Articles 2 and 5;
d. any other act, notification or communication relating to this Protocol.

In witness whereof the undersigned, being duly authorised thereto, have signed this Protocol.

Done at Rome, this 4th day of November 2000, in English and in French, both texts being equally authentic, in a single copy which shall be deposited in the archives of the Council of Europe. The Secretary General of the Council of Europe shall transmit certified copies to each member State of the Council of Europe.

Protocol 13

[Vilnius, 3 May 2002. Protocol 13 abolishes the death penalty in all circumstances.]

Table of Accessions

[As of 31 January 2006. The Table of Accessions is kept up-to-date on the ECtHR web site, http://www.coe.echr.int.]

Dates of ratification of the European Convention on Human Rights and Additional Protocols
Note: CETS = "Council of Europe Treaty Series" Dates of entry into force

States	Convention CETS No. 005	Protocol No. 1 CETS No. 009	Protocol No. 4 CETS No. 046	Protocol No. 6 CETS No. 114	Protocol No. 7 CETS No. 117	Protocol No. 12 CETS No. 177	Protocol No. 13 CETS No. 187
Albania	02/10/96	02/10/96	02/10/96	01/10/00	01/01/97	01/04/05	
Andorra	22/01/96			01/02/96			01/07/03
Armenia	26/04/02	26/04/02	26/04/02	01/10/03	01/07/02	01/04/05	
Austria	03/09/58	03/09/58	18/09/69	01/03/85	01/11/88		01/05/04
Azerbaijan	15/04/02	15/04/02	15/04/02	01/05/02	01/07/02		
Belgium	14/06/55	14/06/55	21/09/70	01/01/99			01/10/03
Bosnia-Herzegovina	12/07/02	12/07/02	12/07/02	01/08/02	01/10/02	01/04/05	01/11/03
Bulgaria	07/09/92	07/09/92	04/11/00	01/10/99	01/02/01		01/07/03
Croatia	05/11/97	05/11/97	05/11/97	01/12/97	01/02/98	01/04/05	01/07/03
Cyprus	06/10/62	06/10/62	03/10/89	01/02/00	01/12/00	01/04/05	01/07/03
Czech Republic	01/01/93	01/01/93	01/01/93	01/01/93	01/01/93		01/11/04
Denmark	03/09/53	18/05/54	02/05/68	01/03/85	01/11/88		01/07/03
Estonia	16/04/96	16/04/96	16/04/96	01/05/98	01/07/96		01/06/04
Finland	10/05/90	10/05/90	10/05/90	01/06/90	01/08/90	01/04/05	01/03/05
France	03/05/74	03/05/74	03/05/74	01/03/86	01/11/88		
Georgia	20/05/99	07/06/02	13/04/00	01/05/00	01/07/00	01/04/05	01/09/03
Germany	03/09/53	13/02/57	01/06/68	01/08/89			01/02/05
Greece	28/11/74	28/11/74		01/10/98	01/11/88		01/06/05
Hungary	05/11/92	05/11/92	05/11/92	01/12/92	01/02/93		01/11/03
Iceland	03/09/53	18/05/54	02/05/68	01/06/87	01/11/88		01/03/05
Ireland	03/09/53	18/05/54	29/10/68	01/07/94	01/11/01		01/07/03
Italy	26/10/55	26/10/55	27/05/82	01/01/89	01/02/92		
Latvia	27/06/97	27/06/97	27/06/97	01/06/99	01/09/97		

Table (*cont.*)

States	Convention CETS No. 005	Protocol No. 1 CETS No. 009	Protocol No. 4 CETS No. 046	Protocol No. 6 CETS No. 114	Protocol No. 7 CETS No. 117	Protocol No. 12 CETS No. 177	Protocol No. 13 CETS No. 187
Liechtenstein	08/09/82	14/11/95		01/12/90	01/05/05		01/07/03
Lithuania	20/06/95	24/05/96	20/06/95	01/08/99	01/09/95		01/05/04
Luxembourg	03/09/53	18/05/54	02/05/68	01/03/85	01/07/89		
Malta	23/01/67	23/01/67	05/06/02	01/04/91	01/04/03		01/07/03
Moldova	12/09/97	12/09/97	12/09/97	01/10/97	01/12/97		
Monaco	30/11/05		30/11/05	01/12/05	01/02/05		01/03/06
Netherlands	31/08/54	31/08/54	23/06/82	01/05/86		01/04/05	
Norway	03/09/53	18/05/54	02/05/68	01/11/88	01/01/89		01/12/05
Poland	19/01/93	10/10/94	10/10/94	01/11/00	01/03/03		
Portugal	09/11/78	09/11/78	09/11/78	01/11/86			01/02/04
Romania	20/06/94	20/06/94	20/06/94	01/07/94	01/09/94		01/08/03
Russia	05/05/98	05/05/98	05/05/98		01/08/98		
San Marino	22/03/89	22/03/89	22/03/89	01/04/89	01/06/89	01/04/05	01/08/03
Serbia and Montenegro	03/03/04	03/03/04	03/03/04	01/04/04	01/06/04	01/04/05	01/07/04
Slovakia	01/01/93	01/01/93	01/01/93	01/01/93	01/01/93		01/12/05
Slovenia	28/06/94	28/06/94	28/06/94	01/07/94	01/09/94		01/04/04
Spain	04/10/79	27/11/90		01/03/85			
Sweden	03/09/53	18/05/54	02/05/68	01/03/85	01/11/88		01/08/03
Switzerland	28/11/74			01/11/87	01/11/88		01/07/03
The former Yugoslav Republic of Macedonia	10/04/97	10/04/97	10/04/97	01/05/97	01/07/97		01/11/04
Turkey	18/05/54	18/05/54		01/12/03			
Ukraine	11/09/97	11/09/97	11/09/97	01/05/00	01/12/97		01/07/03
United Kingdom	03/09/53	18/05/54		01/06/99			01/02/04

Appendix 2

European Convention for the Prevention of Torture and Inhuman or Degrading Treatment or Punishment [ETS No. 126]

CPT/Inf/C (2002) 1 [EN] (Part 1) –

Strasbourg, 26.XI.1987.

Text amended according to the provisions of Protocols No. 1 (ETS No. 151) and No. 2 (ETS No. 152) which entered into force on 1 March 2002.

The member States of the Council of Europe, signatory hereto,

Having regard to the provisions of the Convention for the Protection of Human Rights and Fundamental Freedoms,

Recalling that, under Article 3 of the same Convention, "no one shall be subjected to torture or to inhuman or degrading treatment or punishment";

Noting that the machinery provided for in that Convention operates in relation to persons who allege that they are victims of violations of Article 3;

Convinced that the protection of persons deprived of their liberty against torture and inhuman or degrading treatment or punishment could be strengthened by non-judicial means of a preventive character based on visits,

Have agreed as follows:

Chapter I

Article 1

There shall be established a European Committee for the Prevention of Torture and Inhuman or Degrading Treatment or Punishment (hereinafter referred to as "the Committee"). The Committee shall, by means of visits, examine the treatment of persons deprived of their liberty with a view to strengthening, if necessary, the protection of such persons from torture and from inhuman or degrading treatment or punishment.

Article 2

Each Party shall permit visits, in accordance with this Convention, to any place within its jurisdiction where persons are deprived of their liberty by a public authority.

Article 3

In the application of this Convention, the Committee and the competent national authorities of the Party concerned shall co-operate with each other.

Chapter II

Article 4

1. The Committee shall consist of a number of members equal to that of the Parties.
2. The members of the Committee shall be chosen from among persons of high moral character, known for their competence in the field of human rights or having professional experience in the areas covered by this Convention.
3. No two members of the Committee may be nationals of the same State.
4. The members shall serve in their individual capacity, shall be independent and impartial, and shall be available to serve the Committee effectively.

Article 5

1. The members of the Committee shall be elected by the Committee of Ministers of the Council of Europe by an absolute majority of votes, from a list of names drawn

up by the Bureau of the Consultative Assembly of the Council of Europe; each national delegation of the Parties in the Consultative Assembly shall put forward three candidates, of whom two at least shall be its nationals. Where a member is to be elected to the Committee in respect of a non-member State of the Council of Europe, the Bureau of the Consultative Assembly shall invite the Parliament of that State to put forward three candidates, of whom two at least shall be its nationals. The election by the Committee of Ministers shall take place after consultation with the Party concerned.

2. The same procedure shall be followed in filling casual vacancies.
3. The members of the Committee shall be elected for a period of four years. They may be re-elected twice. However, among the members elected at the first election, the terms of three members shall expire at the end of two years. The members whose terms are to expire at the end of the initial period of two years shall be chosen by lot by the Secretary General of the Council of Europe immediately after the first election has been completed.
4. In order to ensure that, as far as possible, one half of the membership of the Committee shall be renewed every two years, the Committee of Ministers may decide, before proceeding to any subsequent election, that the term or terms of office of one or more members to be elected shall be for a period other than four years but not more than six and not less than two years.
5. In cases where more than one term of office is involved and the Committee of Ministers applies the preceding paragraph, the allocation of the terms of office shall be effected by the drawing of lots by the Secretary General, immediately after the election.

Article 6

1. The Committee shall meet in camera. A quorum shall be equal to the majority of its members. The decisions of the Committee shall be taken by a majority of the members present, subject to the provisions of Article 10, paragraph 2.
2. The Committee shall draw up its own rules of procedure.
3. The Secretariat of the Committee shall be provided by the Secretary General of the Council of Europe.

Chapter III

Article 7

1. The Committee shall organise visits to places referred to in Article 2. Apart from periodic visits, the Committee may organise such other visits as appear to it to be required in the circumstances.
2. As a general rule, the visits shall be carried out by at least two members of the Committee. The Committee may, if it considers it necessary, be assisted by experts and interpreters.

Article 8

1. The Committee shall notify the Government of the Party concerned of its intention to carry out a visit. After such notification, it may at any time visit any place referred to in Article 2.
2. A Party shall provide the Committee with the following facilities to carry out its task:

   a. access to its territory and the right to travel without restriction;
   b. full information on the places where persons deprived of their liberty are being held;
   c. unlimited access to any place where persons are deprived of their liberty, including the right to move inside such places without restriction;
   d. other information available to the Party which is necessary for the Committee to carry out its task. In seeking such information, the Committee shall have regard to applicable rules of national law and professional ethics.

3. The Committee may interview in private persons deprived of their liberty.
4. The Committee may communicate freely with any person whom it believes can supply relevant information.
5. If necessary, the Committee may immediately communicate observations to the competent authorities of the Party concerned.

Article 9

1. In exceptional circumstances, the competent authorities of the Party concerned may make representations to the Committee against a visit at the time or to the particular place proposed by the Committee. Such representations may only be made on grounds of national defence, public safety, serious disorder in places where persons are deprived of their liberty, the medical condition of a person or that an urgent interrogation relating to a serious crime is in progress.
2. Following such representations, the Committee and the Party shall immediately enter into consultations in order to clarify the situation and seek agreement on arrangements to enable the Committee to exercise its functions expeditiously. Such arrangements may include the transfer to another place of any person whom the Committee proposed to visit. Until the visit takes place, the Party shall provide information to the Committee about any person concerned.

Article 10

1. After each visit, the Committee shall draw up a report on the facts found during the visit, taking account of any observations which may have been submitted by the Party concerned. It shall transmit to the latter its report containing any recommendations

it considers necessary. The Committee may consult with the Party with a view to suggesting, if necessary, improvements in the protection of persons deprived of their liberty.

2. If the Party fails to co-operate or refuses to improve the situation in the light of the Committee's recommendations, the Committee may decide, after the Party has had an opportunity to make known its views, by a majority of two-thirds of its members to make a public statement on the matter.

Article 11

1. The information gathered by the Committee in relation to a visit, its report and its consultations with the Party concerned shall be confidential.
2. The Committee shall publish its report, together with any comments of the Party concerned, whenever requested to do so by that Party.
3. However, no personal data shall be published without the express consent of the person concerned.

Article 12

Subject to the rules of confidentiality in Article 11, the Committee shall every year submit to the Committee of Ministers a general report on its activities which shall be transmitted to the Consultative Assembly and to any non-member State of the Council of Europe which is a party to the Convention, and made public.

Article 13

The members of the Committee, experts and other persons assisting the Committee are required, during and after their terms of office, to maintain the confidentiality of the facts or information of which they have become aware during the discharge of their functions.

Article 14

1. The names of persons assisting the Committee shall be specified in the notification under Article 8, paragraph 1.
2. Experts shall act on the instructions and under the authority of the Committee. They shall have particular knowledge and experience in the areas covered by this Convention and shall be bound by the same duties of independence, impartiality and availability as the members of the Committee.
3. A Party may exceptionally declare that an expert or other person assisting the Committee may not be allowed to take part in a visit to a place within its jurisdiction.

Chapter IV

Article 15

Each Party shall inform the Committee of the name and address of the authority competent to receive notifications to its Government, and of any liaison officer it may appoint.

Article 16

The Committee, its members and experts referred to in Article 7, paragraph 2 shall enjoy the privileges and immunities set out in the annex to this Convention.

Article 17

1. This Convention shall not prejudice the provisions of domestic law or any international agreement which provide greater protection for persons deprived of their liberty.
2. Nothing in this Convention shall be construed as limiting or derogating from the competence of the organs of the European Convention on Human Rights or from the obligations assumed by the Parties under that Convention.
3. The Committee shall not visit places which representatives or delegates of Protecting Powers or the International Committee of the Red Cross effectively visit on a regular basis by virtue of the Geneva Conventions of 12 August 1949 and the Additional Protocols of 8 June 1977 thereto.

Chapter V

Article 18

1. This Convention shall be open for signature by the member States of the Council of Europe. It is subject to ratification, acceptance or approval. Instruments of ratification, acceptance or approval shall be deposited with the Secretary General of the Council of Europe.
2. The Committee of Ministers of the Council of Europe may invite any non-member State of the Council of Europe to accede to the Convention.

Article 19

1. This Convention shall enter into force on the first day of the month following the expiration of a period of three months after the date on which seven member States of the Council of Europe have expressed their consent to be bound by the Convention in accordance with the provisions of Article 18.

2. In respect of any State which subsequently expresses its consent to be bound by it, the Convention shall enter into force on the first day of the month following the expiration of a period of three months after the date of the deposit of the instrument of ratification, acceptance, approval or accession.

Article 20

1. Any State may at the time of signature or when depositing its instrument of ratification, acceptance, approval or accession, specify the territory or territories to which this Convention shall apply.
2. Any State may at any later date, by a declaration addressed to the Secretary General of the Council of Europe, extend the application of this Convention to any other territory specified in the declaration. In respect of such territory the Convention shall enter into force on the first day of the month following the expiration of a period of three months after the date of receipt of such declaration by the Secretary General.
3. Any declaration made under the two preceding paragraphs may, in respect of any territory specified in such declaration, be withdrawn by a notification addressed to the Secretary General. The withdrawal shall become effective on the first day of the month following the expiration of a period of three months after the date of receipt of such notification by the Secretary General.

Article 21

No reservation may be made in respect of the provisions of this Convention.

Article 22

1. Any Party may, at any time, denounce this Convention by means of a notification addressed to the Secretary General of the Council of Europe.
2. Such denunciation shall become effective on the first day of the month following the expiration of a period of twelve months after the date of receipt of the notification by the Secretary General.

Article 23

The Secretary General of the Council of Europe shall notify the member States and any non-member State of the Council of Europe party to the Convention of:
   a.   any signature;
   b.   the deposit of any instrument of ratification, acceptance, approval or accession;
   c.   any date of entry into force of this Convention in accordance with Articles 19 and 20;
   d.   any other act, notification or communication relating to this Convention, except for action taken in pursuance of Articles 8 and 10.

In witness whereof, the undersigned, being duly authorised thereto, have signed this Convention. Done at Strasbourg, the 26 November 1987, in English and in French, both texts being equally authentic, in a single copy which shall be deposited in the archives of the Council of Europe. The Secretary General of the Council of Europe shall transmit certified copies to each member State of the Council of Europe.

Annex Privileges and Immunities (Article 16)

1. For the purpose of this annex, references to members of the Committee shall be deemed to include references to experts mentioned in Article 7, paragraph 2.
2. The members of the Committee shall, while exercising their functions and during journeys made in the exercise of their functions, enjoy the following privileges and immunities:

   a. immunity from personal arrest or detention and from seizure of their personal baggage and, in respect of words spoken or written and all acts done by them in their official capacity, immunity from legal process of every kind;
   b. exemption from any restrictions on their freedom of movement on exit from and return to their country of residence, and entry into and exit from the country in which they exercise their functions, and from alien registration in the country which they are visiting or through which they are passing in the exercise of their functions.

3. In the course of journeys undertaken in the exercise of their functions, the members of the Committee shall, in the matter of customs and exchange control, be accorded:

   a. by their own Government, the same facilities as those accorded to senior officials travelling abroad on temporary official duty;
   b. by the Governments of other Parties, the same facilities as those accorded to representatives of foreign Governments on temporary official duty.

4. Documents and papers of the Committee, in so far as they relate to the business of the Committee, shall be inviolable. The official correspondence and other official communications of the Committee may not be held up or subjected to censorship.
5. In order to secure for the members of the Committee complete freedom of speech and complete independence in the discharge of their duties, the immunity from legal process in respect of words spoken or written and all acts done by them in discharging their duties shall continue to be accorded, notwithstanding that the persons concerned are no longer engaged in the discharge of such duties.
6. Privileges and immunities are accorded to the members of the Committee, not for the personal benefit of the individuals themselves but in order to safeguard the inde-

pendent exercise of their functions. The Committee alone shall be competent to waive the immunity of its members; it has not only the right, but is under a duty, to waive the immunity of one of its members in any case where, in its opinion, the immunity would impede the course of justice, and where it can be waived without prejudice to the purpose for which the immunity is accorded.

Appendix 3

CPT Standards, Part V: Involuntary Placement in Psychiatric Establishments

[Extract from the 8th General Report [CPT/Inf (98) 12]; reprinted in *CPT Standards*, CPT/Inf/E (2002) 1 – Rev. 2004]

A. Preliminary remarks

25. The CPT is called upon to examine the treatment of all categories of persons deprived of their liberty by a public authority, including persons with mental health problems. Consequently, the Committee is a frequent visitor to psychiatric establishments of various types.

Establishments visited include mental hospitals accommodating, in addition to voluntary patients, persons who have been hospitalised on an involuntary basis pursuant to civil proceedings in order to receive psychiatric treatment. The CPT also visits facilities (special hospitals, distinct units in civil hospitals, etc.) for persons whose admission to a psychiatric establishment has been ordered in the context of criminal proceedings. Psychiatric facilities for prisoners who develop a mental illness in the course of their imprisonment, whether located within the prison system or in civil psychiatric institutions, also receive close attention from the CPT.

26. When examining the issue of health-care services in prisons in its 3rd General Report (cf. CPT/Inf (93) 12, paragraphs 30 to 77), the CPT identified a number of general criteria which have guided its work (access to a doctor; equivalence of care; patient's consent and confidentiality; preventive health care; professional independence and professional competence). Those criteria also apply to involuntary placement in psychiatric establishments.

In the following paragraphs, some of the specific issues pursued by the CPT in relation to persons who are placed involuntarily in psychiatric establishments are described.[1] The CPT hopes in this way to give a clear advance indication to national authorities of its views concerning the treatment of such persons; the Committee would welcome comments on this section of its General Report.

B. Prevention of ill-treatment

27. In view of its mandate, the CPT's first priority when visiting a psychiatric establishment must be to ascertain whether there are any indications of the deliberate ill-treatment of patients. Such indications are seldom found. More generally, the CPT wishes to place on record the dedication to patient care observed among the overwhelming majority of staff in most psychiatric establishments visited by its delegations. This situation is on occasion all the more commendable in the light of the low staffing levels and paucity of resources at the staff's disposal.

Nevertheless, the CPT's own on-site observations and reports received from other sources indicate that the deliberate ill-treatment of patients in psychiatric establishments does occur from time to time. A number of questions will be addressed subsequently which are closely-linked to the issue of the prevention of ill-treatment (e.g. means of restraint; complaints procedures; contact with the outside world; external supervision). However, some remarks should be made at this stage as regards the choice of staff and staff supervision.

28. Working with the mentally ill and mentally handicapped will always be a difficult task for all categories of staff involved. In this connection it should be noted that health-care staff in psychiatric establishments are frequently assisted in their day-to-day work by orderlies; further, in some establishments a considerable number of personnel are assigned to security-related tasks. The information at the CPT's disposal suggests that when deliberate ill-treatment by staff in psychiatric establishments

---

[1] As regards psychiatric care for prisoners, reference should also be made to paragraphs 41 to 44 of the Committee's 3rd General Report.

does occur, such auxiliary staff rather than medical or qualified nursing staff are often the persons at fault.

Bearing in mind the challenging nature of their work, it is of crucial importance that auxiliary staff be carefully selected and that they receive both appropriate training before taking up their duties and in-service courses. Further, during the performance of their tasks, they should be closely supervised by – and be subject to the authority of – qualified health-care staff.

29. In some countries, the CPT has encountered the practice of using certain patients, or inmates from neighbouring prison establishments, as auxiliary staff in psychiatric facilities. The Committee has serious misgivings about this approach, which should be seen as a measure of last resort. If such appointments are unavoidable, the activities of the persons concerned should be supervised on an on-going basis by qualified health-care staff.

30. It is also essential that appropriate procedures be in place in order to protect certain psychiatric patients from other patients who might cause them harm. This requires inter alia an adequate staff presence at all times, including at night and weekends. Further, specific arrangements should be made for particularly vulnerable patients; for example, mentally handicapped and/or mentally disturbed adolescents should not be accommodated together with adult patients.

31. Proper managerial control of all categories of staff can also contribute significantly to the prevention of ill-treatment. Obviously, the clear message must be given that the physical or psychological ill-treatment of patients is not acceptable and will be dealt with severely. More generally, management should ensure that the therapeutic role of staff in psychiatric establishments does not come to be considered as secondary to security considerations.

Similarly, rules and practices capable of generating a climate of tension between staff and patients should be revised accordingly. The imposition of fines on staff in the event of an escape by a patient is precisely the kind of measure which can have a negative effect on the ethos within a psychiatric establishment.

C. Patients' living conditions and treatment

32. The CPT closely examines patients' living conditions and treatment; inadequacies in these areas can rapidly lead to situations falling within the scope of the term "inhuman and degrading treatment". The aim should be to offer material conditions which are conducive to the treatment and welfare of patients; in psychiatric terms, a positive therapeutic environment. This is of importance not only for patients but also for staff working in psychiatric establishments. Further, adequate treatment and

care, both psychiatric and somatic, must be provided to patients; having regard to the principle of the equivalence of care, the medical treatment and nursing care received by persons who are placed involuntarily in a psychiatric establishment should be comparable to that enjoyed by voluntary psychiatric patients.

33. The quality of patients' living conditions and treatment inevitably depends to a considerable extent on available resources. The CPT recognises that in times of grave economic difficulties, sacrifices may have to be made, including in health establishments. However, in the light of the facts found during some visits, the Committee wishes to stress that the provision of certain basic necessities of life must always be guaranteed in institutions where the State has persons under its care and/or custody. These include adequate food, heating and clothing as well as – in health establishments – appropriate medication.

Living conditions

34. Creating a positive therapeutic environment involves, first of all, providing sufficient living space per patient as well as adequate lighting, heating and ventilation, maintaining the establishment in a satisfactory state of repair and meeting hospital hygiene requirements.

Particular attention should be given to the decoration of both patients' rooms and recreation areas, in order to give patients visual stimulation. The provision of bedside tables and wardrobes is highly desirable, and patients should be allowed to keep certain personal belongings (photographs, books, etc.). The importance of providing patients with lockable space in which they can keep their belongings should also be underlined; the failure to provide such a facility can impinge upon a patient's sense of security and autonomy.

Sanitary facilities should allow patients some privacy. Further, the needs of elderly and/or handicapped patients in this respect should be given due consideration; for example, lavatories of a design which do not allow the user to sit are not suitable for such patients. Similarly, basic hospital equipment enabling staff to provide adequate care (including personal hygiene) to bedridden patients must be made available; the absence of such equipment can lead to wretched conditions.

It should also be noted that the practice observed in some psychiatric establishments of continuously dressing patients in pyjamas/nightgowns is not conducive to strengthening personal identity and self-esteem; individualisation of clothing should form part of the therapeutic process.

35. Patients' food is another aspect of their living conditions which is of particular concern to the CPT. Food must be not only adequate from the standpoints of quantity and quality, but also provided to patients under satisfactory conditions. The necessary equipment should exist enabling food to be served at the correct temperature. Further, eating arrangements should be decent; in this regard it should be stressed

that enabling patients to accomplish acts of daily life – such as eating with proper utensils whilst seated at a table – represents an integral part of programmes for the psycho-social rehabilitation of patients. Similarly, food presentation is a factor which should not be overlooked.

The particular needs of disabled persons in relation to catering arrangements should also be taken into account.

36. The CPT also wishes to make clear its support for the trend observed in several countries towards the closure of large-capacity dormitories in psychiatric establishments; such facilities are scarcely compatible with the norms of modern psychiatry. Provision of accommodation structures based on small groups is a crucial factor in preserving/restoring patients' dignity, and also a key element of any policy for the psychological and social rehabilitation of patients. Structures of this type also facilitate the allocation of patients to relevant categories for therapeutic purposes.

Similarly, the CPT favours the approach increasingly being adopted of allowing patients who so wish to have access to their room during the day, rather than being obliged to remain assembled together with other patients in communal areas.

Treatment

37. Psychiatric treatment should be based on an individualised approach, which implies the drawing up of a treatment plan for each patient. It should involve a wide range of rehabilitative and therapeutic activities, including access to occupational therapy, group therapy, individual psychotherapy, art, drama, music and sports. Patients should have regular access to suitably-equipped recreation rooms and have the possibility to take outdoor exercise on a daily basis; it is also desirable for them to be offered education and suitable work.

The CPT all too often finds that these fundamental components of effective psychosocial rehabilitative treatment are underdeveloped or even totally lacking, and that the treatment provided to patients consists essentially of pharmacotherapy. This situation can be the result of the absence of suitably qualified staff and appropriate facilities or of a lingering philosophy based on the custody of patients.

38. Of course, psychopharmacologic medication often forms a necessary part of the treatment given to patients with mental disorders. Procedures must be in place to ensure that medication prescribed is in fact provided, and that a regular supply of appropriate medicines is guaranteed. The CPT will also be on the look-out for any indications of the misuse of medication.

39. Electroconvulsive therapy (ECT) is a recognised form of treatment for psychiatric patients suffering from some particular disorders. However, care should be taken that ECT fits into the patient's treatment plan, and its administration must be accompanied by appropriate safeguards.

The CPT is particularly concerned when it encounters the administration of ECT in its unmodified form (i.e. without anaesthetic and muscle relaxants); this method can no longer be considered as acceptable in modern psychiatric practice. Apart from the risk of fractures and other untoward medical consequences, the process as such is degrading for both the patients and the staff concerned. Consequently, ECT should always be administered in a modified form.

ECT must be administered out of the view of other patients (preferably in a room which has been set aside and equipped for this purpose), by staff who have been specifically trained to provide this treatment. Further, recourse to ECT should be recorded in detail in a specific register. It is only in this way that any undesirable practices can be clearly identified by hospital management and discussed with staff.

40. Regular reviews of a patient's state of health and of any medication prescribed is another basic requirement. This will inter alia enable informed decisions to be taken as regards a possible dehospitalisation or transfer to a less restrictive environment.

A personal and confidential medical file should be opened for each patient. The file should contain diagnostic information (including the results of any special examinations which the patient has undergone) as well as an ongoing record of the patient's mental and somatic state of health and of his treatment. The patient should be able to consult his file, unless this is unadvisable from a therapeutic standpoint, and to request that the information it contains be made available to his family or lawyer. Further, in the event of a transfer, the file should be forwarded to the doctors in the receiving establishment; in the event of discharge, the file should be forwarded – with the patient's consent – to a treating doctor in the outside community.

41. Patients should, as a matter of principle, be placed in a position to give their free and informed consent to treatment. The admission of a person to a psychiatric establishment on an involuntary basis should not be construed as authorising treatment without his consent. It follows that every competent patient, whether voluntary or involuntary, should be given the opportunity to refuse treatment or any other medical intervention. Any derogation from this fundamental principle should be based upon law and only relate to clearly and strictly defined exceptional circumstances.

Of course, consent to treatment can only be qualified as free and informed if it is based on full, accurate and comprehensible information about the patient's condition and the treatment proposed; to describe ECT as "sleep therapy" is an example of less than full and accurate information about the treatment concerned. Consequently, all patients should be provided systematically with relevant information about their condition and the treatment which it is proposed to prescribe for them. Relevant information (results, etc.) should also be provided following treatment.

D. Staff

42. Staff resources should be adequate in terms of numbers, categories of staff (psychiatrists, general practitioners, nurses, psychologists, occupational therapists, social workers, etc.), and experience and training. Deficiencies in staff resources will often seriously undermine attempts to offer activities of the kind described in paragraph 37; further, they can lead to high-risk situations for patients, notwithstanding the good intentions and genuine efforts of the staff in service.

43. In some countries, the CPT has been particularly struck by the small number of qualified psychiatric nurses among the nursing staff in psychiatric establishments, and by the shortage of personnel qualified to conduct social therapy activities (in particular, occupational therapists). The development of specialised psychiatric nursing training and a greater emphasis on social therapy would have a considerable impact upon the quality of care. In particular, they would lead to the emergence of a therapeutic milieu less centred on drug-based and physical treatments.

44. A number of remarks concerning staff issues and, more particularly, auxiliary staff, have already been made in an earlier section (cf. paragraphs 28 to 31). However, the CPT also pays close attention to the attitude of doctors and nursing staff. In particular, the Committee will look for evidence of a genuine interest in establishing a therapeutic relationship with patients. It will also verify that patients who might be considered as burdensome or lacking rehabilitative potential are not being neglected.

45. As in other health-care services, it is important that the different categories of staff working in a psychiatric unit meet regularly and form a team under the authority of a senior doctor. This will allow day-to-day problems to be identified and discussed, and guidance to be given. The lack of such a possibility could well engender frustration and resentment among staff members.

46. External stimulation and support are also necessary to ensure that the staff of psychiatric establishments do not become too isolated. In this connection, it is highly desirable for such staff to be offered training possibilities outside their establishment as well as secondment opportunities. Similarly, the presence in psychiatric establishments of independent persons (e.g. students and researchers) and external bodies (cf. paragraph 55) should be encouraged.

E. Means of restraint

47. In any psychiatric establishment, the restraint of agitated and/or violent patients may on occasion be necessary. This is an area of particular concern to the CPT, given the potential for abuse and ill-treatment.

The restraint of patients should be the subject of a clearly-defined policy. That policy should make clear that initial attempts to restrain agitated or violent patients should, as far as possible, be non-physical (e.g. verbal instruction) and that where physical restraint is necessary, it should in principle be limited to manual control.

Staff in psychiatric establishments should receive training in both non-physical and manual control techniques vis-à-vis agitated or violent patients. The possession of such skills will enable staff to choose the most appropriate response when confronted by difficult situations, thereby significantly reducing the risk of injuries to patients and staff.

48. Resort to instruments of physical restraint (straps, strait-jackets, etc.) shall only very rarely be justified and must always be either expressly ordered by a doctor or immediately brought to the attention of a doctor with a view to seeking his approval. If, exceptionally, recourse is had to instruments of physical restraint, they should be removed at the earliest opportunity; they should never be applied, or their application prolonged, as a punishment.

The CPT has on occasion encountered psychiatric patients to whom instruments of physical restraint have been applied for a period of days; the Committee must emphasise that such a state of affairs cannot have any therapeutic justification and amounts, in its view, to ill-treatment.

49. Reference should also be made in this context to the seclusion (i.e. confinement alone in a room) of violent or otherwise "unmanageable" patients, a procedure which has a long history in psychiatry.

There is a clear trend in modern psychiatric practice in favour of avoiding seclusion of patients, and the CPT is pleased to note that it is being phased out in many countries. For so long as seclusion remains in use, it should be the subject of a detailed policy spelling out, in particular: the types of cases in which it may be used; the objectives sought; its duration and the need for regular reviews; the existence of appropriate human contact; the need for staff to be especially attentive.

Seclusion should never be used as a punishment.

50. Every instance of the physical restraint of a patient (manual control, use of instruments of physical restraint, seclusion) should be recorded in a specific register estab-

lished for this purpose (as well as in the patient's file). The entry should include the times at which the measure began and ended, the circumstances of the case, the reasons for resorting to the measure, the name of the doctor who ordered or approved it, and an account of any injuries sustained by patients or staff.

This will greatly facilitate both the management of such incidents and the oversight of the extent of their occurrence.

F. Safeguards in the context of involuntary placement

51. On account of their vulnerability, the mentally ill and mentally handicapped warrant much attention in order to prevent any form of conduct – or avoid any omission – contrary to their well-being. It follows that involuntary placement in a psychiatric establishment should always be surrounded by appropriate safeguards. One of the most important of those safeguards – free and informed consent to treatment – has already been highlighted (cf. paragraph 41).

The Initial Placement Decision

52. The procedure by which involuntary placement is decided should offer guarantees of independence and impartiality as well as of objective medical expertise.

As regards, more particularly, involuntary placement of a civil nature, in many countries the decision regarding placement must be taken by a judicial authority (or confirmed by such an authority within a short time-limit), in the light of psychiatric opinions. However, the automatic involvement of a judicial authority in the initial decision on placement is not foreseen in all countries. Committee of Ministers Recommendation N° R (83) 2 on the legal protection of persons suffering from mental disorder placed as involuntary patients allows for both approaches (albeit setting out special safeguards in the event of the placement decision being entrusted to a non-judicial authority). The Parliamentary Assembly has nevertheless reopened the debate on this subject via its Recommendation 1235 (1994) on psychiatry and human rights, calling for decisions regarding involuntary placement to be taken by a judge.

In any event, a person who is involuntarily placed in a psychiatric establishment by a non-judicial authority must have the right to bring proceedings by which the lawfulness of his detention shall be decided speedily by a court.

Safeguards During Placement

53. An introductory brochure setting out the establishment's routine and patients' rights should be issued to each patient on admission, as well as to their families. Any patients unable to understand this brochure should receive appropriate assistance.

Further, as in any place of deprivation of liberty, an effective complaints procedure is a basic safeguard against ill-treatment in psychiatric establishments. Specific arrangements should exist enabling patients to lodge formal complaints with a clearly-designated body, and to communicate on a confidential basis with an appropriate authority outside the establishment.

54. The maintenance of contact with the outside world is essential, not only for the prevention of ill-treatment but also from a therapeutic standpoint.

Patients should be able to send and receive correspondence, to have access to the telephone, and to receive visits from their family and friends. Confidential access to a lawyer should also be guaranteed.

55. The CPT also attaches considerable importance to psychiatric establishments being visited on a regular basis by an independent outside body (e.g. a judge or supervisory committee) which is responsible for the inspection of patients' care. This body should be authorised, in particular, to talk privately with patients, receive directly any complaints which they might have and make any necessary recommendations.

Discharge

56. Involuntary placement in a psychiatric establishment should cease as soon as it is no longer required by the patient's mental state. Consequently, the need for such a placement should be reviewed at regular intervals.

When involuntary placement is for a specified period, renewable in the light of psychiatric evidence, such a review will flow from the very terms of the placement. However, involuntary placement might be for an unspecified period, especially in the case of persons who have been compulsorily admitted to a psychiatric establishment pursuant to criminal proceedings and who are considered to be dangerous. If the period of involuntary placement is unspecified, there should be an automatic review at regular intervals of the need to continue the placement.

In addition, the patient himself should be able to request at reasonable intervals that the necessity for placement be considered by a judicial authority.

57. Although no longer requiring involuntary placement, a patient may nevertheless still need treatment and/or a protected environment in the outside community. In this connection, the CPT has found, in a number of countries, that patients whose mental state no longer required them to be detained in a psychiatric establishment nevertheless remained in such establishments, due to a lack of adequate care/accommodation in the outside community. For persons to remain deprived of their liberty as a result of the absence of appropriate external facilities is a highly questionable state of affairs.

G. Final remarks

58. The organisational structure of health-care services for persons with psychiatric disorders varies from country to country, and is certainly a matter for each State to determine. Nevertheless, the CPT wishes to draw attention to the tendency in a number of countries to reduce the number of beds in large psychiatric establishments and to develop community-based mental health units. The Committee considers this is a very favourable development, on condition that such units provide a satisfactory quality of care.

It is now widely accepted that large psychiatric establishments pose a significant risk of institutionalisation for both patients and staff, the more so if they are situated in isolated locations. This can have a detrimental effect on patient treatment. Care programmes drawing on the full range of psychiatric treatment are much easier to implement in small units located close to the main urban centres.

Appendix 4

Recommendation Rec(2004)10 of the Committee of Ministers to member States concerning the protection of the human rights and dignity of persons with mental disorder

(Adopted by the Committee of Ministers on 22 September 2004 at the 896th meeting of the Ministers' Deputies. Pursuant to Art 10.2c of the Rules of Procedure for the meetings of Ministers' Deputies, the Government of the United Kingdom has reserved the right to comply or not comply with the recommendation as a whole.)

The Committee of Ministers, under the terms of Article 15.*b* of the Statute of the Council of Europe,

Considering that the aim of the Council of Europe is to achieve a greater unity between its members, in particular through harmonising laws on matters of common interest;

Having regard, in particular:

- to the Convention for the Protection of Human Rights and Fundamental Freedoms of 4 November 1950 and to its application by the organs established under that Convention;

- to the Convention for the Protection of Human Rights and Dignity of the Human Being with regard to the Application of Biology and Medicine ("Convention on Human Rights and Biomedicine") of 4 April 1997;
- to Recommendation No. R (83)2 concerning the legal protection of persons suffering from mental disorder placed as involuntary patients;
- to Recommendation No. R (87)3 on the European Prison Rules;
- to Recommendation No. R (98)7 concerning the ethical and organisational aspects of health care in prison;
- to Recommendation 1235 (1994) of the Parliamentary Assembly of the Council of Europe on psychiatry and human rights;

Having regard to the work of the European Committee for the Prevention of Torture and Inhuman or Degrading Treatment or Punishment;

Having regard to the public consultation on the protection of the human rights and dignity of persons suffering from mental disorder, initiated by the Steering Committee on Bioethics;

Considering that common action at European level will promote better protection of the human rights and dignity of persons with mental disorder, in particular those subject to involuntary placement or involuntary treatment;

Considering that both mental disorder and certain treatments for such disorder may affect the essence of a person's individuality;

Stressing the need for mental health professionals to be aware of such risks, to act within a regulatory framework and to regularly review their practice;

Stressing the need to ensure that persons with mental disorder are never emotionally, physically, financially or sexually exploited;

Conscious of the responsibility of mental health professionals to guarantee, as far as they are able, the implementation of the principles enshrined in these guidelines;

Recommends that the governments of member states should adapt their laws and practice to the guidelines contained in this Recommendation;

Recommends that the governments of member states should review their allocation of resources to mental health services so that the provisions of these guidelines can be met.

Guidelines

Chapter I – Object and scope

Article 1 – Object

1. This Recommendation aims to enhance the protection of the dignity, human rights and fundamental freedoms of persons with mental disorder, in particular those who are subject to involuntary placement or involuntary treatment.
2. The provisions of this Recommendation do not limit or otherwise affect the possibility for a member state to grant persons with mental disorder a wider measure of protection than is stipulated in this Recommendation.

Article 2 – Scope and definitions

Scope

1. This Recommendation applies to persons with mental disorder defined in accordance with internationally accepted medical standards.
2. Lack of adaptation to the moral, social, political or other values of a society, of itself, should not be considered a mental disorder.

Definitions

3. For the purpose of this Recommendation, the term:

– "competent body" means an authority, or a person or body provided for by law which is distinct from the person or body proposing an involuntary measure, and that can make an independent decision;
– "court" includes reference to a court-like body or tribunal;
– "facility" encompasses facilities and units;
– "personal advocate" means a person helping to promote the interests of a person with mental disorder and who can provide moral support to that person in situations in which the person feels vulnerable;
– "representative" means a person provided for by law to represent the interests of, and take decisions on behalf of, a person who does not have the capacity to consent;
– "therapeutic purposes" includes prevention, diagnosis, control or cure of the disorder, and rehabilitation;
– "treatment" means an intervention (physical or psychological) on a person with mental disorder that, taking into account the person's social dimension, has a therapeutic purpose in relation to that mental disorder. Treatment may include measures to improve the social dimension of a person's life.

Chapter II – General provisions

Article 3 – Non-discrimination

1. Any form of discrimination on grounds of mental disorder should be prohibited.
2. Member states should take appropriate measures to eliminate discrimination on grounds of mental disorder.

Article 4 – Civil and political rights

1. Persons with mental disorder should be entitled to exercise all their civil and political rights.
2. Any restrictions to the exercise of those rights should be in conformity with the provisions of the Convention for the Protection of Human Rights and Fundamental Freedoms and should not be based on the mere fact that a person has a mental disorder.

Article 5 – Promotion of mental health

Member states should promote mental health by encouraging the development of programmes to improve the awareness of the public about the prevention, recognition and treatment of mental disorders.

Article 6 – Information and assistance on patients' rights

Persons treated or placed in relation to mental disorder should be individually informed of their rights as patients and have access to a competent person or body, independent of the mental health service, that can, if necessary, assist them to understand and exercise such rights.

Article 7 – Protection of vulnerable persons with mental disorders

1. Member states should ensure that there are mechanisms to protect vulnerable persons with mental disorders, in particular those who do not have the capacity to consent or who may not be able to resist infringements of their human rights.
2. The law should provide measures to protect, where appropriate, the economic interests of persons with mental disorder.

Article 8 – Principle of least restriction

Persons with mental disorder should have the right to be cared for in the least restrictive environment available and with the least restrictive or intrusive treatment available, taking into account their health needs and the need to protect the safety of others.

Article 9 – Environment and living conditions

1. Facilities designed for the placement of persons with mental disorder should provide each such person, taking into account his or her state of health and the need to protect the safety of others, with an environment and living conditions as close as possible to those of persons of similar age, gender and culture in the community. Vocational rehabilitation measures to promote the integration of those persons in the community should also be provided.
2. Facilities designed for the involuntary placement of persons with mental disorder should be registered with an appropriate authority.

Article 10 – Health service provision

Member states should, taking into account available resources, take measures:

    i. to provide a range of services of appropriate quality to meet the mental health needs of persons with mental disorder, taking into account the differing needs of different groups of such persons, and to ensure equitable access to such services;

    ii. to make alternatives to involuntary placement and to involuntary treatment as widely available as possible;

    iii. to ensure sufficient provision of hospital facilities with appropriate levels of security and of community-based services to meet the health needs of persons with mental disorder involved with the criminal justice system;

    iv. to ensure that the physical health care needs of persons with mental disorder are assessed and that they are provided with equitable access to services of appropriate quality to meet such needs.

Article 11 – Professional standards

1. Professional staff involved in mental health services should have appropriate qualifications and training to enable them to perform their role within the services according to professional obligations and standards.
2. In particular, staff should receive appropriate training on:

    i. protecting the dignity, human rights and fundamental freedoms of persons with mental disorder;

    ii. understanding, prevention and control of violence;

    iii. measures to avoid the use of restraint or seclusion;

    iv. the limited circumstances in which different methods of restraint or seclusion may be justified, taking into account the benefits and risks entailed, and the correct application of such measures.

Article 12 – General principles of treatment for mental disorder

1. Persons with mental disorder should receive treatment and care provided by adequately qualified staff and based on an appropriate individually prescribed treatment plan. Whenever possible the treatment plan should be prepared in consultation with the person concerned and his or her opinion should be taken into account. The plan should be regularly reviewed and, if necessary, revised.
2. Subject to the provisions of chapter III and Articles 28 and 34 below, treatment may only be provided to a person with mental disorder with his or her consent if he or she has the capacity to give such consent, or, when the person does not have the capacity to consent, with the authorisation of a representative, authority, person or body provided for by law.
3. When because of an emergency situation the appropriate consent or authorisation cannot be obtained, any treatment for mental disorder that is medically necessary to avoid serious harm to the health of the individual concerned or to protect the safety of others may be carried out immediately.

Article 13 – Confidentiality and record-keeping

1. All personal data relating to a person with mental disorder should be considered to be confidential. Such data may only be collected, processed and communicated according to the rules relating to professional confidentiality and personal data protection.
2. Clear and comprehensive medical and, where appropriate, administrative records should be maintained for all persons with mental disorder placed or treated for such a disorder. The conditions governing access to that information should be clearly specified by law.

Article 14 – Biomedical research

Biomedical research on a person with mental disorder should respect the provisions of this Recommendation and the relevant provisions of the Convention on Human Rights and Biomedicine, its additional Protocol on Biomedical Research and the other legal provisions ensuring the protection of persons in research contexts.

Article 15 – Dependants of a person with mental disorder

The needs of family members, in particular children, who are dependent on a person with mental disorder should be given appropriate consideration.

Chapter III – Involuntary placement in psychiatric facilities, and involuntary treatment, for mental disorder

Article 16 – Scope of chapter III

The provisions of this chapter apply to persons with mental disorder:

   i.   who have the capacity to consent and are refusing the placement or treatment concerned; or
   ii. who do not have the capacity to consent and are objecting to the placement or treatment concerned.

Article 17 – Criteria for involuntary placement

1. A person may be subject to involuntary placement only if all the following conditions are met:

   i.   the person has a mental disorder;
   ii. the person's condition represents a significant risk of serious harm to his or her health or to other persons;
   iii. the placement includes a therapeutic purpose;
   iv. no less restrictive means of providing appropriate care are available;
   v.   the opinion of the person concerned has been taken into consideration.

2. The law may provide that exceptionally a person may be subject to involuntary placement, in accordance with the provisions of this chapter, for the minimum period necessary in order to determine whether he or she has a mental disorder that represents a significant risk of serious harm to his or her health or to others if:

   i.   his or her behaviour is strongly suggestive of such a disorder;
   ii. his or her condition appears to represent such a risk;
   iii. there is no appropriate, less restrictive means of making this determination; and
   iv. the opinion of the person concerned has been taken into consideration.

Article 18 – Criteria for involuntary treatment

A person may be subject to involuntary treatment only if all the following conditions are met:

   i.   the person has a mental disorder;
   ii. the person's condition represents a significant risk of serious harm to his or her health or to other persons;
   iii. no less intrusive means of providing appropriate care are available;
   iv. the opinion of the person concerned has been taken into consideration.

Article 19 – Principles concerning involuntary treatment

1. Involuntary treatment should:

    i.   address specific clinical signs and symptoms;
    ii. be proportionate to the person's state of health;
    iii. form part of a written treatment plan;
    iv. be documented;
    v.   where appropriate, aim to enable the use of treatment acceptable to the person as soon as possible.

2. In addition to the requirements of Article 12.1 above, the treatment plan should:

    i.   whenever possible be prepared in consultation with the person concerned and the person's personal advocate or representative, if any;
    ii. be reviewed at appropriate intervals and, if necessary, revised, whenever possible in consultation with the person concerned and his or her personal advocate or representative, if any.

3. Member states should ensure that involuntary treatment only takes place in an appropriate environment.

Article 20 – Procedures for taking decisions on involuntary placement and/or involuntary treatment

Decision

1. The decision to subject a person to involuntary placement should be taken by a court or another competent body. The court or other competent body should:

    i.   take into account the opinion of the person concerned;
    ii. act in accordance with procedures provided by law based on the principle that the person concerned should be seen and consulted.

2. The decision to subject a person to involuntary treatment should be taken by a court or another competent body. The court or other competent body should:

    i.   take into account the opinion of the person concerned;
    ii. act in accordance with procedures provided by law based on the principle that the person concerned should be seen and consulted.

However, the law may provide that when a person is subject to involuntary placement the decision to subject that person to involuntary treatment may be taken by a doctor having the requisite competence and experience, after examination of the person concerned and taking into account his or her opinion.

3.   Decisions to subject a person to involuntary placement or to involuntary treatment should be documented and state the maximum period beyond which, according to law, they should be formally reviewed. This is without prejudice to the person's rights to reviews and appeals, in accordance with the provisions of Article 25.

Procedures prior to the decision

4.   Involuntary placement, involuntary treatment, or their extension should only take place on the basis of examination by a doctor having the requisite competence and experience, and in accordance with valid and reliable professional standards.
5.   That doctor or the competent body should consult those close to the person concerned, unless the person objects, it is impractical to do so, or it is inappropriate for other reasons.
6.   Any representative of the person should be informed and consulted.

Article 21 – Procedures for taking decisions on involuntary placement and/or involuntary treatment in emergency situations

1.   Procedures for emergency situations should not be used to avoid applying the procedures set out in Article 20.
2.   Under emergency procedures:

   i.   involuntary placement or involuntary treatment should only take place for a short period of time on the basis of a medical assessment appropriate to the measure concerned;
   ii.   paragraphs 5 and 6 of Article 20 should be complied with as far as possible;
   iii.   decisions to subject a person to involuntary placement or to involuntary treatment should be documented and state the maximum period beyond which, according to law, they should be formally reviewed. This is without prejudice to the person's rights to reviews and appeals, in accordance with the provisions of Article 25.

3.   If the measure is to be continued beyond the emergency situation, a court or another competent body should take decisions on the relevant measure, in accordance with Article 20, as soon as possible.

Article 22 – Right to information

1.   Persons subject to involuntary placement or involuntary treatment should be promptly informed, verbally and in writing, of their rights and of the remedies open to them.

2. They should be informed regularly and appropriately of the reasons for the decision and the criteria for its potential extension or termination.
3. The person's representative, if any, should also be given the information.

Article 23 – Right to communication and to visits of persons subject to involuntary placement

The right of persons with mental disorder subject to involuntary placement:

i.   to communicate with their lawyers, representatives or any appropriate authority should not be restricted. Their right to communicate with their personal advocates or other persons should not be unreasonably restricted;
ii. to receive visits should not be unreasonably restricted, taking into account the need to protect vulnerable persons or minors placed in or visiting a psychiatric facility.

Article 24 – Termination of involuntary placement and/or involuntary treatment

1. Involuntary placement or involuntary treatment should be terminated if any of the criteria for the measure are no longer met.
2. The doctor in charge of the person's care should be responsible for assessing whether any of the relevant criteria are no longer met unless a court has reserved the assessment of the risk of serious harm to others to itself or to a specific body.
3. Unless termination of a measure is subject to judicial decision, the doctor, the responsible authority and the competent body should be able to take action on the basis of the above criteria in order to terminate that measure.
4. Member states should aim to minimise, wherever possible, the duration of involuntary placement by the provision of appropriate aftercare services.

Article 25 – Reviews and appeals concerning the lawfulness of involuntary placement and/or involuntary treatment

1. Member states should ensure that persons subject to involuntary placement or involuntary treatment can effectively exercise the right:

i.   to appeal against a decision;
ii. to have the lawfulness of the measure, or its continuing application, reviewed by a court at reasonable intervals;
iii. to be heard in person or through a personal advocate or representative at such reviews or appeals.

2. If the person, or that person's personal advocate or representative, if any, does not request such review, the responsible authority should inform the court and ensure

that the continuing lawfulness of the measure is reviewed at reasonable and regular intervals.

3.   Member states should consider providing the person with a lawyer for all such proceedings before a court. Where the person cannot act for him or herself, the person should have the right to a lawyer and, according to national law, to free legal aid. The lawyer should have access to all the materials, and have the right to challenge the evidence, before the court.

4.   If the person has a representative, the representative should have access to all the materials, and have the right to challenge the evidence, before the court.

5.   The person concerned should have access to all the materials before the court subject to the protection of the confidentiality and safety of others according to national law. If the person has no representative, he or she should have access to assistance from a personal advocate in all procedures before a court.

6.   The court should deliver its decision promptly. If it identifies any violations of the relevant national legislation it should send these to the relevant body.

7.   A procedure to appeal the court's decision should be provided.

Chapter IV – Placement of persons not able to consent in the absence of objection

Article 26 – Placement of persons not able to consent in the absence of objection

Member states should ensure that appropriate provisions exist to protect a person with mental disorder who does not have the capacity to consent and who is considered in need of placement and does not object to the placement.

Chapter V – Specific situations

Article 27 – Seclusion and restraint

1.   Seclusion or restraint should only be used in appropriate facilities, and in compliance with the principle of least restriction, to prevent imminent harm to the person concerned or others, and in proportion to the risks entailed.

2.   Such measures should only be used under medical supervision, and should be appropriately documented.

3.   In addition:

    i.   the person subject to seclusion or restraint should be regularly monitored;
    ii.   the reasons for, and duration of, such measures should be recorded in the person's medical records and in a register.

4.   This Article does not apply to momentary restraint.

Article 28 – Specific treatments

1. Treatment for mental disorder that is not aimed at producing irreversible physical effects but may be particularly intrusive should be used only if no less intrusive means of providing appropriate care is available. Member states should ensure that the use of such treatment is:

   i.   subject to appropriate ethical scrutiny;
   ii. in accordance with appropriate clinical protocols reflecting international standards and safeguards;
   iii. except in emergency situations as referred to in Article 12, with the person's informed, written consent or, in the case of a person who does not have the capacity to consent, the authorisation of a court or competent body;
   iv. fully documented and recorded in a register.

2. Use of a treatment for mental disorder with the aim of producing irreversible physical effects should be exceptional, and should not be used in the context of involuntary placement. Such a treatment should only be carried out if the person concerned has given free, informed and specific consent in writing. The treatment should be fully documented and recorded in a register, and used only:

   i.   in accordance with the law;
   ii. subject to appropriate ethical scrutiny;
   iii. in accordance with the principle of least restriction;
   iv. if an independent second medical opinion agrees that it is appropriate; and
   v.   in accordance with appropriate clinical protocols reflecting international standards and safeguards.

Article 29 – Minors

1. The provisions of this Recommendation should apply to minors unless a wider measure of protection is provided.
2. In decisions concerning placement and treatment, whether provided involuntarily or not, the opinion of the minor should be taken into consideration as an increasingly determining factor in proportion to his or her age and degree of maturity.
3. A minor subject to involuntary placement should have the right to assistance from a representative from the start of the procedure.
4. A minor should not be placed in a facility in which adults are also placed, unless such a placement would benefit the minor.
5. Minors subject to placement should have the right to a free education and to be reintegrated into the general school system as soon as possible. If possible, the minor should be individually evaluated and receive an individualised educational or training programme.

Article 30 – Procreation

The mere fact that a person has a mental disorder should not constitute a justification for permanent infringement of his or her capacity to procreate.

Article 31 – Termination of pregnancy

The mere fact that a person has a mental disorder should not constitute a justification for termination of her pregnancy.

Chapter VI – Involvement of the criminal justice system

Article 32 – Involvement of the police

1. In the fulfilment of their legal duties, the police should coordinate their interventions with those of medical and social services, if possible with the consent of the person concerned, if the behaviour of that person is strongly suggestive of mental disorder and represents a significant risk of harm to him or herself or to others.
2. Where other appropriate possibilities are not available the police may be required, in carrying out their duties, to assist in conveying or returning persons subject to involuntary placement to the relevant facility.
3. Members of the police should respect the dignity and human rights of persons with mental disorder. The importance of this duty should be emphasised during training.
4. Members of the police should receive appropriate training in the assessment and management of situations involving persons with mental disorder, which draws attention to the vulnerability of such persons in situations involving the police.

Article 33 – Persons who have been arrested

If a person whose behaviour is strongly suggestive of mental disorder is arrested:

   i.   the person should have the right to assistance from a representative or an appropriate personal advocate during the procedure;
   ii.   an appropriate medical examination should be conducted promptly at a suitable location to establish:

      a. the person's need for medical care, including psychiatric care;
      b. the person's capacity to respond to interrogation;
      c. whether the person can be safely detained in non-health care facilities.

Article 34 – Involvement of the courts

1. Under criminal law, courts may impose placement or treatment for mental disorder whether the person concerned consents to the measure or not. Member states should ensure that the person can effectively exercise the right to have the lawfulness of the measure, or its continuing application, reviewed by a court at reasonable intervals. The other provisions of chapter III should be taken into account in such placements or treatments; any non-application of those provisions should be justifiable.
2. Courts should make sentencing decisions concerning placement or treatment for mental disorder on the basis of valid and reliable standards of medical expertise, taking into consideration the need for persons with mental disorder to be treated in a place appropriate to their health needs. This provision is without prejudice to the possibility, according to law, for a court to impose psychiatric assessment and a psychiatric or psychological care programme as an alternative to imprisonment or to the delivery of a final decision.

Article 35 – Penal institutions

1. Persons with mental disorder should not be subject to discrimination in penal institutions. In particular, the principle of equivalence of care with that outside penal institutions should be respected with regard to their health care. They should be transferred between penal institution and hospital if their health needs so require.
2. Appropriate therapeutic options should be available for persons with mental disorder detained in penal institutions.
3. Involuntary treatment for mental disorder should not take place in penal institutions except in hospital units or medical units suitable for the treatment of mental disorder.
4. An independent system should monitor the treatment and care of persons with mental disorder in penal institutions.

Chapter VII – Quality assurance and monitoring

Article 36 – Monitoring of standards

1. Member states should ensure that compliance with the standards set by this recommendation and by mental health law is subject to appropriate monitoring. That monitoring should cover:

    i.   compliance with legal standards;
    ii. compliance with technical and professional standards.

2. The systems for conducting such monitoring should:

    i.   have adequate financial and human resources to perform their functions;

    ii.   be organisationally independent from the authorities or bodies monitored;

    iii.   involve mental health professionals, lay persons, persons with mental disorder and those close to such persons;

    iv.   be coordinated, where appropriate, with other relevant audit and quality assurance systems.

Article 37 – Specific requirements for monitoring

1.   Monitoring compliance with standards should include:

    i.   conducting visits and inspections of mental health facilities, if necessary without prior notice, to ensure:

        a. that persons are only subject to involuntary placement in facilities registered by an appropriate authority, and that such facilities are suitable for that function;

        b. that suitable alternatives to involuntary placement are provided;

    ii.   monitoring compliance with professional obligations and standards;

    iii.   ensuring powers exist to investigate the death of persons subject to involuntary placement or involuntary treatment, and that any such death is notified to the appropriate authority and is subject to an independent investigation;

    iv.   reviewing situations in which communication has been restricted;

    v.   ensuring that complaints procedures are provided and complaints responded to appropriately.

2.   Appropriate follow-up of the results of monitoring should be ensured.

3.   In respect of persons subject to provisions of mental health law, the persons conducting monitoring should be entitled:

    i.   to meet privately with such persons, and with their consent or that of their representatives, have access to their medical file at any time;

    ii.   to receive confidential complaints from such persons;

    iii.   to obtain from authorities or staff responsible for the treatment or care of such persons any information that may reasonably be considered necessary for the performance of their functions, including anonymised information from medical records.

Article 38 – Statistics, advice and reporting

1.   Systematic and reliable anonymised statistical information on the application of mental health law and on complaints should be collected.

2. Those responsible for the care of persons with mental disorder should:

    i.   receive from those responsible for quality assurance and monitoring:

         a. regular reports, and where possible publish those reports;
         b. advice on the conditions and facilities appropriate to the care of persons with mental disorder;

    ii. respond to questions, advice and reports arising from the quality assurance and monitoring systems.

3. Information on the implementation of mental health law and actions concerning compliance with standards should be made available to the public.

Appendix 5

Recommendation No. R (99) 4 of the Committee of Ministers to Member States on Principles Concerning the Legal Protection of Incapable Adults

(Adopted by the Committee of Ministers on 23 February 1999 at the 660th meeting of the Ministers' Deputies. When adopting this decision, the Representative of Ireland indicated that, in accordance with Article 10.2c of the Rules of Procedure for the meetings of the Ministers' Deputies, he reserved the right of his Government to comply or not with principles 5 and 6 of the Recommendation. When adopting this decision, the Representative of France indicated that, in accordance with Article 10.2c of the Rules of Procedure for the meetings of the Ministers' Deputies, the following reservation should be made: France considers that the application of principle 23, para. 3 should be subject to a request by the person concerned.)

The Committee of Ministers, under the terms of Article 15.*b* of the Statute of the Council of Europe,

Bearing in mind the Universal Declaration of Human Rights proclaimed by the General Assembly of the United Nations on 10 December 1948;

Bearing in mind the International Covenant on Civil and Political Rights and the International Covenant on Economic, Social and Cultural Rights of 16 December 1966;

Bearing in mind the Convention for the Protection of Human Rights and Fundamental Freedoms of 4 November 1950;

Bearing in mind the Convention for the Protection of Human Rights and Dignity of the Human Being with regard to the Application of Biology and Medicine: Convention on Human Rights and Biomedicine of 4 April 1997;

Considering that the aim of the Council of Europe is to achieve a greater unity between its members, in particular by promoting the adoption of common rules in legal matters;

Noting that demographic and medical changes have resulted in an increased number of people who, although of full age, are incapable of protecting their interests by reason of an impairment or insufficiency of their personal faculties;

Noting also that social changes have resulted in an increased need for adequate legislation to ensure the protection of such people;

Noting that legislative reforms on the protection, by representation or assistance, of incapable adults have been introduced or are under consideration in a number of member states and that these reforms have common features;

Recognising, however, that wide disparities in the legislation of member states in this area still exist;

Convinced of the importance in this context of respect for human rights and for the dignity of each person as a human being,

Recommends the governments of member states to take or reinforce, in their legislation and practice, all measures they consider necessary with a view to the implementation of the following principles:

Principles

Part I – Scope of application

1. The following principles apply to the protection of adults who, by reason of an impairment or insufficiency of their personal faculties, are incapable of making, in an autonomous way, decisions concerning any or all of their personal or economic

affairs, or understanding, expressing or acting upon such decisions, and who consequently cannot protect their interests.

2. The incapacity may be due to a mental disability, a disease or a similar reason.
3. The principles apply to measures of protection or other legal arrangements enabling such adults to benefit from representation or assistance in relation to those affairs.
4. In these principles "adult" means a person who is treated as being of full age under the applicable law on capacity in civil matters.
5. In these principles "intervention in the health field" means any act performed professionally on a person for reasons of health. It includes, in particular, interventions for the purposes of preventive care, diagnosis, treatment, rehabilitation or research.

Part II – Governing principles

Principle 1 – Respect for human rights

In relation to the protection of incapable adults the fundamental principle, underlying all the other principles, is respect for the dignity of each person as a human being. The laws, procedures and practices relating to the protection of incapable adults shall be based on respect for their human rights and fundamental freedoms, taking into account any qualifications on those rights contained in the relevant international legal instruments.

Principle 2 – Flexibility in legal response

1. The measures of protection and other legal arrangements available for the protection of the personal and economic interests of incapable adults should be sufficient, in scope or flexibility, to enable a suitable legal response to be made to different degrees of incapacity and various situations.
2. Appropriate measures of protection or other legal arrangements should be available in cases of emergency.
3. The law should provide for simple and inexpensive measures of protection or other legal arrangements.
4. The range of measures of protection should include, in appropriate cases, those which do not restrict the legal capacity of the person concerned.
5. The range of measures of protection should include those which are limited to one specific act without requiring the appointment of a representative or a representative with continuing powers.
6. Consideration should be given to the inclusion of measures under which the appointed person acts jointly with the adult concerned, and of measures involving the appointment of more than one representative.
7. Consideration should be given to the need to provide for, and regulate, legal arrangements which a person who is still capable can take to provide for any subsequent incapacity.

8. Consideration should be given to the need to provide expressly that certain decisions, particularly those of a minor or routine nature relating to health or personal welfare, may be taken for an incapable adult by those deriving their powers from the law rather than from a judicial or administrative measure.

Principle 3 – Maximum preservation of capacity

1. The legislative framework should, so far as possible, recognise that different degrees of incapacity may exist and that incapacity may vary from time to time. Accordingly, a measure of protection should not result automatically in a complete removal of legal capacity. However, a restriction of legal capacity should be possible where it is shown to be necessary for the protection of the person concerned.
2. In particular, a measure of protection should not automatically deprive the person concerned of the right to vote, or to make a will, or to consent or refuse consent to any intervention in the health field, or to make other decisions of a personal character at any time when his or her capacity permits him or her to do so.
3. Consideration should be given to legal arrangements whereby, even when representation in a particular area is necessary, the adult may be permitted, with the representative's consent, to undertake specific acts or acts in a specific area.
4. Whenever possible the adult should be enabled to enter into legally effective transactions of an everyday nature.

Principle 4 – Publicity

The disadvantage of automatically giving publicity to measures of protection or similar legal arrangements should be weighed in the balance against any protection which might be afforded to the adult concerned or to third parties.

Principle 5 – Necessity and subsidiarity

1. No measure of protection should be established for an incapable adult unless the measure is necessary, taking into account the individual circumstances and the needs of the person concerned. A measure of protection may be established, however, with the full and free consent of the person concerned.
2. In deciding whether a measure of protection is necessary, account should be taken of any less formal arrangements which might be made, and of any assistance which might be provided by family members or by others.

Principle 6 – Proportionality

1. Where a measure of protection is necessary it should be proportional to the degree of capacity of the person concerned and tailored to the individual circumstances and needs of the person concerned.

2. The measure of protection should interfere with the legal capacity, rights and freedoms of the person concerned to the minimum extent which is consistent with achieving the purpose of the intervention.

Principle 7 – Procedural fairness and efficiency

1. There should be fair and efficient procedures for the taking of measures for the protection of incapable adults.
2. There should be adequate procedural safeguards to protect the human rights of the persons concerned and to prevent possible abuses.

Principle 8 – Paramountcy of interests and welfare of the person concerned

1. In establishing or implementing a measure of protection for an incapable adult the interests and welfare of that person should be the paramount consideration.
2. This principle implies, in particular, that the choice of any person to represent or assist an incapable adult should be governed primarily by the suitability of that person to safeguard and promote the adult's interests and welfare.
3. This principle also implies that the property of the incapable adult should be managed and used for the benefit of the person concerned and to secure his or her welfare.

Principle 9 – Respect for wishes and feelings of the person concerned

1. In establishing or implementing a measure of protection for an incapable adult the past and present wishes and feelings of the adult should be ascertained so far as possible, and should be taken into account and given due respect.
2. This principle implies, in particular, that the wishes of the adult as to the choice of any person to represent or assist him or her should be taken into account and, as far as possible, given due respect.
3. It also implies that a person representing or assisting an incapable adult should give him or her adequate information, whenever this is possible and appropriate, in particular concerning any major decision affecting him or her, so that he or she may express a view.

Principle 10 – Consultation

In the establishment and implementation of a measure of protection there should be consultation, so far as reasonable and practicable, with those having a close interest in the welfare of the adult concerned, whether as representative, close family member or otherwise. It is for national law to determine which persons should be consulted and the effects of consultation or its absence.

Part III – Procedural principles

Principle 11 – Institution of proceedings

1. The list of those entitled to institute proceedings for the taking of measures for the protection of incapable adults should be sufficiently wide to ensure that measures of protection can be considered in all cases where they are necessary. It may, in particular, be necessary to provide for proceedings to be initiated by a public official or body, or by the court or other competent authority on its own motion.
2. The person concerned should be informed promptly in a language, or by other means, which he or she understands of the institution of proceedings which could affect his or her legal capacity, the exercise of his or her rights or his or her interests unless such information would be manifestly without meaning to the person concerned or would present a severe danger to the health of the person concerned.

Principle 12 – Investigation and assessment

1. There should be adequate procedures for the investigation and assessment of the adult's personal faculties.
2. No measure of protection which restricts the legal capacity of an incapable adult should be taken unless the person taking the measure has seen the adult or is personally satisfied as to the adult's condition and an up-to-date report from at least one suitably qualified expert has been submitted. The report should be in writing or recorded in writing.

Principle 13 – Right to be heard in person

The person concerned should have the right to be heard in person in any proceedings which could affect his or her legal capacity.

Principle 14 – Duration, review and appeal

1. Measures of protection should, whenever possible and appropriate, be of limited duration. Consideration should be given to the institution of periodical reviews.
2. Measures of protection should be reviewed on a change of circumstances and, in particular, on a change in the adult's condition. They should be terminated if the conditions for them are no longer fulfilled.
3. There should be adequate rights of appeal.

Principle 15 – Provisional measures in case of emergency

If a provisional measure is needed in a case of emergency, principles 11 to 14 should be applicable as far as possible according to the circumstances.

Principle 16 – Adequate control

There should be adequate control of the operation of measures of protection and of the acts and decisions of representatives.

Principle 17 – Qualified persons

1. Steps should be taken with a view to providing an adequate number of suitably qualified persons for the representation and assistance of incapable adults.
2. Consideration should be given, in particular, to the establishment or support of associations or other bodies with the function of providing and training such people.

Part IV – The role of representatives

Principle 18 – Control of powers arising by operation of law

1. Consideration should be given to the need to ensure that any powers conferred on any person by operation of law, without the intervention of a judicial or administrative authority, to act or take decisions on behalf of an incapable adult are limited and their exercise controlled.
2. The conferment of any such powers should not deprive the adult of legal capacity.
3. Any such powers should be capable of being modified or terminated at any time by a measure of protection taken by a judicial or administrative authority.
4. Principles 8 to 10 apply to the exercise of such powers as they apply to the implementation of measures of protection.

Principle 19 – Limitation of powers of representatives

1. It is for national law to determine which juridical acts are of such a highly personal nature that they can not be done by a representative.
2. It is also for national law to determine whether decisions by a representative on certain serious matters should require the specific approval of a court or other body.

Principle 20 – Liability

1. Representatives should be liable, in accordance with national law, for any loss or damage caused by them to incapable adults while exercising their functions.
2. In particular, the laws on liability for wrongful acts, negligence or maltreatment should apply to representatives and others involved in the affairs of incapable adults.

Principle 21 – Remuneration and expenses

1. National law should address the questions of the remuneration and the reimbursement of expenses of those appointed to represent or assist incapable adults.

2. Distinctions may be made between those acting in a professional capacity and those acting in other capacities, and between the management of personal matters of the incapable adult and the management of his or her economic matters.

Part V – Interventions in the health field

Principle 22 – Consent

1. Where an adult, even if subject to a measure of protection, is in fact capable of giving free and informed consent to a given intervention in the health field, the intervention may only be carried out with his or her consent. The consent should be solicited by the person empowered to intervene.
2. Where an adult is not in fact capable of giving free and informed consent to a given intervention, the intervention may, nonetheless, be carried out provided that:

    – it is for his or her direct benefit, and
    – authorisation has been given by his or her representative or by an authority or a person or body provided for by law.

3. Consideration should be given to the designation by the law of appropriate authorities, persons or bodies for the purpose of authorising interventions of different types, when adults who are incapable of giving free and informed consent do not have a representative with appropriate powers. Consideration should also be given to the need to provide for the authorisation of a court or other competent body in the case of certain serious types of intervention.
4. Consideration should be given to the establishment of mechanisms for the resolution of any conflicts between persons or bodies authorised to consent or refuse consent to interventions in the health field in relation to adults who are incapable of giving consent.

Principle 23 – Consent (alternative rules)

1. If the government of a member state does not apply the rules contained in paragraphs 1 and 2 of Principle 22, the following rules should be applicable:

    Where an adult is subject to a measure of protection under which a given intervention in the health field can be carried out only with the authorisation of a body or a person provided for by law, the consent of the adult should nonetheless be sought if he or she has the capacity to give it.

2. Where, according to the law, an adult is not in a position to give free and informed consent to an intervention in the health field, the intervention may nonetheless be carried out if:

– it is for his or her direct benefit, and
– authorisation has been given by his or her representative or by an authority or a person or body provided for by law.

3. The law should provide for remedies allowing the person concerned to be heard by an independent official body before any important medical intervention is carried out.

Principle 24 – Exceptional cases

1. Special rules may be provided by national law, in accordance with relevant international instruments, in relation to interventions which, because of their special nature, require the provision of additional protection for the person concerned.
2. Such rules may involve a limited derogation from the criterion of direct benefit provided that the additional protection is such as to minimise the possibility of any abuse or irregularity.

Principle 25 – Protection of adults with a mental disorder

Subject to protective conditions prescribed by law, including supervisory, control and appeal procedures, an adult who has a mental disorder of a serious nature may be subjected, without his or her consent, to an intervention aimed at treating his or her mental disorder only where, without such treatment, serious harm is likely to result to his or her health.

Principle 26 – Permissibility of intervention in emergency situation

When, because of an emergency situation, the appropriate consent or authorisation cannot be obtained, any medically necessary intervention may be carried out immediately for the benefit of the health of the person concerned.

Principle 27 – Applicability of certain principles applying to measures of protection

1. Principles 8 to 10 apply to any intervention in the health field concerning an incapable adult as they apply to measures of protection.
2. In particular, and in accordance with principle 9, the previously expressed wishes relating to a medical intervention by a patient who is not, at the time of the intervention, in a state to express his or her wishes should be taken into account.

Principle 28 – Permissibility of special rules on certain matters

Special rules may be provided by national law, in accordance with relevant international instruments, in relation to interventions which are necessary in a democratic society in the interest of public safety, for the prevention of crime, for the protection of public health or for the protection of the rights and freedom of others.

Appendix 6

Internet Resources

Council of Europe

Council of Europe
http://www.coe.int
   Complex website with links to all organs of the Council of Europe.

European Court of Human Rights
http://www.echr.coe.int
   Contains all information about the working of the Court: Rules of Court, Practice
   Directions, annual reports, names and biographies of judges.

Searchable database of ECtHR decisions and judgments ('HUDOC')
http://cmiskp.echr.coe.int/
   User-friendly database. Note that some judgments are only available in one of the
   Court's official languages of English and French. If searching for an admissibility
   decision, users must ensure that they tick the 'decisions' box on the top right corner.
   Also has a French interface.

European Committee for the Prevention of Torture
http://cpt.coe.int
>   Contains information about membership and functioning of the CPT and all pub-
>   lished reports of visits. Also includes the CPT standards under 'documents'.

European Social Charter
http://www.coe.int/T/E/Human_Rights/Esc/
>   Contains links to the texts, European Committee on Social Rights, reporting proce-
>   dure and collective complaints procedure.

Treaty Office
http://conventions.coe.int
>   This lists all of the Council of Europe's conventions. The ECHR is listed, and sepa-
>   rately all its protocols. Users can download all conventions and view signatures and
>   ratifications.

Commissioner for Human Rights
http://www.coe.int/commissioner
>   Information about the Office of the Commissioner, currently Thomas Hammarberg.

Committee of Ministers
http://www.coe.int/cm
>   Includes information about execution of the judgments of the European Court of
>   Human Rights, as well as Recommendations (such as those referred to in this book).

United Nations

Office of the High Commissioner for Human Rights
http://www.ohchr.org
>   All information on the High Commissioner, currently Louise Arbour. Also links to all
>   UN human rights instruments and monitoring mechanisms.

UN Enable
http://www.un.org/esa/socdev/enable/
>   The UN's site for disability issues.

Special Rapporteur on the right of everyone to the enjoyment of the highest attainable stan-
dard of physical and mental health
http://www.ohchr.org/english/issues/health/right/
>   Information about the Special Rapporteur, currently Paul Hunt, including his report
>   on mental disability and the right to health.

World Health Organization, mental health program
http://www.who.int/mental_health
> Contains a wealth of information on mental health and related issues, including the manual on human rights and legislation, as well as manuals on mental health advocacy, financing, resources, organisation.

World Health Organization Regional Office for Europe, mental health program
http://www.euro.who.int/mentalhealth
> All information on mental health initiatives at the European office, based in Copenhagen.

Academic Institutions

University of Virginia Institute of Law, Psychiatry and Public Policy
http://www.ilppp.virginia.edu/
> Home of the MacArthur risk assessment and capacity studies

Non-Governmental Organizations

The European Coalition for Community Living
http://www.community-living.info

European Disability Forum
http://www.edf-feph.org

European Network on Users, Ex-Users and Survivors of Psychiatry
http://www.enusp.org

Global Initiative on Psychiatry
www.gip-global.org

Inclusion Europe
http://www.inclusion-europe.org

Mental Disability Advocacy Center
http://www.mdac.info

Mental Disability Rights International
http://www.mdri.org

Open Society Institute Mental Health Initiative
http://www.soros.org/initiatives/mhi

World Network on Users, Ex-Users and Survivors of Psychiatry
http://www.wnusp.org/

Appendix 7

Practical Issues in Advocacy

This appendix is intended to provide practical advice for lawyers new to representing people with mental disabilities. North America has spawned a significant body of writing on this subject, and Europeans would be well advised to consider it with care.[1] We are unaware of any comparable literature in a European context, however, and certainly of none relating to ECHR applications. The following pragmatic points are drawn in part from experience, and in part from the framework provided by the Montana Supreme Court in *In the matter of the mental health of K.G.F*,[2] discussed further in chapter 9 above. As the ECHR requires the exhaustion of domestic remedies, however, ECHR applications are likely to begin with domestic litigation. The following comments are written with advocacy in both these contexts in mind. The comments are designed primarily with

---

[1] See, for example, American Bar Association Commission on the Mentally Disabled, 'How to Prepare for an Involuntary Civil Commitment Hearing', 37 *Prac. Law*. (1991) 39; J. Abisch, 'Mediational Lawyering in the Civil Commitment Context: A Therapeutic Jurisprudence Solution to the Counsel Role Dilemma', 1 *Psychol. Pub. Pol'y & L* (1995) 120, J. Cook, 'Good Lawyers and Bad Role Models: The Role of Respondent's Counsel in a Civil Commitment Hearing', 14 *Geo. J. Legal Ethics* (2000) 179; D. Green, '"I'm OK – You're OK": Educating Lawyers to "Maintain a Normal Client-Lawyer Relationship" with a Client with a Mental Disability', 28 *J. Legal Prof*. (2003-2004) 65; M Perlin, '"You have discussed lepers and crooks": Sanism in clinical teaching', 9 *Clinical L. Rev*. (2003) 683; M. Perlin and R. Sadoff, 'Ethical Issues in the Representation of Individuals in the Commitment Process', 45 *Law & Contemp. Probs*. (1982) 161; D. Romano, 'The Legal Advocate and the Questionably Competent Client in the Context of a Poverty Law Clinic', 35 *Osgoode Hall Law Journal* (1997) 737.

[2] *In the matter of the mental health of K.G.F*., 2001 MT 140.

court hearings regarding detention[3] or concerning legal incapacity or guardianship arrangements[4] in mind. That said, many of the matters under consideration will be relevant to any court hearing or advocacy on behalf of persons with mental disabilities.

In chapter 9, we make the point that the fundamental role of a lawyer does not change because the client has a mental disability. The lawyer is still expected to act diligently in representing that client, on the client's instructions if the client has capacity to instruct. This is fundamental to respect for the client's autonomy. Describing this classic adversarial role of the lawyer, one commentator has written:

> . . . consideration for the clients militates in favour of representing their subjective wishes; in a world in which mentally disabled persons are confined, treated, disenfranchised, unemployed, and zoned out of neighborhoods, they suffer as much from such indignities as they do from their disabilities. If lawyers do not listen to their clients, respect their views, and assist them to achieve some measure of self-determination, it is not clear who will.[5]

Establishing rapport with the client is as important in this branch of law as in any other, and that in turn means developing an understanding of the way the client perceives the world. As all clients are different, so all clients with mental disabilities are different; but some advice on establishment of that rapport may be helpful. Michael Perlin, an American academic lawyer with a long history of advocacy for people with mental disabilities, provides a list of how lawyers misunderstand their mentally disabled clients:

- Lawyers frequently presume that persons with metal illness are incompetent to engage in autonomous decision-making, applying that presumption to matters directly involving mental disability law issues (commitment, treatment, etc.), choice of trial strategy, and external 'life decisions' (choice of housing, employment, etc.).
- Lawyers often complain, in referring to their clients with mental disabilities, that the 'clients should try harder', not believing that a mental impairment should be considered disabling in the same way that certain physical impairments may be.
- Lawyers look for visual clues as an indicator of whether a client is 'truly' mentally disabled, based on their views of what people with mental disabilities 'ought' to look like. Such visual clues are not a helpful guide as to whether a client is able to provide instructions.
- Lawyers express fear of their client's potential dangerousness, rejecting the rich database that has proven conclusively that mental illness is only a modest risk factor for dangerous behaviour and that an overwhelming proportion of the population with mental illness is not dangerous.
- Lawyers assume that 'quality of life' concerns are less significant for persons with mental disabilities, and that issues such as housing, family relationships, and job satisfaction do not 'count' as much.

---

[3] See also chapter 2.
[4] See further chapter 6.
[5] J. Abisch, 'Mediational Lawyering in the Civil Commitment Context: A Therapeutic Jurisprudence Solution to the Counsel Role Dilemma,' 1 *Psychology, Public Policy and Law* (1995) 120 at 126.

- Lawyers tend to disbelieve what their mentally disabled clients tell them if the information does not conform to their stereotype of what a mentally disabled person 'is like'.
- Lawyers express discomfort about representing people with mental disabilities when the court-ordered outcome of a case might not be in the client's 'best interests'.[6]

Further, while every client deserves a lawyer's attention whilst interviewing and asking questions, people with mental disabilities may require special attention. For example, some people with mental health problems may have 'disordered' speech patterns that the lawyer is not used to. A person may have a paranoia and not trust the lawyer, or may weave the lawyer into a paranoid world, saying things which the lawyer thinks have absolutely no relevance to the conversation.

People with intellectual disabilities often have cognitive difficulties and lawyers are advised to adapt their language to speak in simple terms, without jargon and without using complex and confusing sentences. Abstract concepts and double negatives should be avoided and only one question should be asked at a time. People with intellectual disabilities may be eager to please the questioner, especially if the questioner is someone in authority (like a police officer, doctor, or a lawyer). Therefore the use of leading questions should be avoided, and understanding checked in a variety of ways. Some people with intellectual disabilities affirm the statement which has been suggested to them last,[7] so questions like "Did it happen on Monday, Tuesday or Wednesday?", which would inevitably give the answer Wednesday, should be avoided. Occasionally the presence of another adult might be helpful in supporting the person with intellectual disabilities in what might be an anxiety provoking experience.

The Initial Meeting with the Client

Timing and Location

The initial meeting with the client ought to occur well in advance of the court hearing date if at all possible. As will be clear from the discussion that follows, it may well be necessary for the lawyer to chase up independent evidence to support the case. That can only be accomplished if reasonable time is provided between the initial interview and the hearing.

The site of the initial meeting with the client with mental health problems or intellectual disabilities may well depend on the client's circumstances. If he or she is living in the community or has the right to leave the institution during the day, it can occur at the

---

[6] M. Perlin, "'You have discussed lepers and crooks': Sanism in clinical teaching" (2003) 9 *Clinical Law Review* 683 at 722-3.

[7] D. Green, "'I'm OK – You're OK': Educating Lawyers to "Maintain a Normal Client-Lawyer Relationship" with a Client with a Mental Disability', 28 *J. Legal Prof.* (2003-4) 65 at 84.

lawyer's office, as it would with any other client. This has considerable advantages if it is possible. It re-enforces to the client that he or she will be treated like a regular client, and it ensures that a place will be available that is suitable for the client interview. At the same time, law offices can be intimidating places, and lawyers planning on developing a practice in this area of law would be well-advised to keep this in mind in selecting location and décor. Similar issues arise when the lawyer is consider what to wear to see the client: some lawyers take the view that a better rapport can be built with the client if the lawyer is dressed informally. Other lawyers find that wearing a suit has the advantage that the client perceives the lawyer as trustworthy and worthy of being treated with respect, and – ultimately perhaps more importantly – that the court would have trust in the lawyer.

Clients with intellectual disabilities need to be given time and, if possible, should be interviewed in familiar surroundings. If this is not possible, such clients should be allowed to visit the court beforehand to familiarise themselves with the environment. Because many people with intellectual disabilities have low self-esteem and high social anxiety, it is important to put them at ease before the interview.

On other occasions, and almost invariably for cases involving detention, the client will be in a locked hospital unit or department, or in a closed institution, and it will not be possible to visit the lawyer's office. In these cases, the lawyer will have to go to the client. This raises a number of complexities.

Gaining access

The first issue is simply getting access to the institution. Depending on the state of development of mental disability law in a jurisdiction, and the frequency with which lawyers visit a given institution, the arrival of a lawyer requesting to see an individual may be something of a novelty. If the institution is not used to lawyers, a mixture of tact and tenacity may be necessary simply to get to the client. The issues here are analogous to those relating to other institutional environments such as prisons, although those institutions tend to be more accustomed to visits by lawyers. A few tips may be helpful.

- Unless there is reason to the contrary, the lawyer should go to the institution in business hours, ideally during visiting hours.
- Some institutions, particularly those with strict security régimes, require official identification such as national identification papers or a passport for entry. The lawyer may also require some form of identification that identifies himself or herself as an advocate for people with mental disabilities, or as a lawyer. It may be appropriate to consult the institution in advance to determine what identification is required.
- Some high security facilities have intensive searches of visitors, and restrict the presence of many items, from guns and knives to candy bars, from being brought into the institution. While it may be reasonable for the institution to ensure that contraband is not being brought in by the lawyer, the lawyer should of course also ensure that the content of any client files are not disclosed to the institutional staff.

- Similarly, while the lawyer will need to disclose the name of the person he or she is visiting, the nature of the legal problem in question should not be disclosed without the permission of the client: there is no exception to the general duty regarding confidentiality here.

Meeting the client

Once access has been obtained, it will be necessary to find a place for the interview. The place should be quiet and private, without staff or other people in the institution in a position to overhear the conversation. Hallways or common areas are thus undesirable for this purpose. A small private room is ideal, although the individual's bedroom, particularly if any people sharing the room agree to stay away, may also be suitable.

If the lawyer has spoken with the client by telephone beforehand, it may be possible to get instructions on how much may be disclosed to the institution in advance of the first visit. If the client is content for the lawyer to do so, it may solve many access problems for the lawyer to notify the institution in advance by telephone that he or she will be visiting, and arrange that a room suitable for the initial interview be made available.

Once a lawyer enters an institution, it is good practice to talk with the client immediately, before discussing the case with professionals, even if the lawyer knows that he or she will need to speak with the staff and look at the client's medical records. Making the client the first port of call will go some way to reassuring the client that he or she is the most important person, and that the lawyer is there for the client, not for the staff. The lawyer should explain to the client what the lawyer proposes to do during the visit, for example, to speak with the staff and to look at the medical records, then to return to the client and explain what the staff have said, in order to build up a picture of what aspects the client agrees with and which information is contested. The lawyer should ask permission from the client to speak with staff, and look at the medical records. In most jurisdictions, the client must sign an authority before the lawyer is permitted to look at the medical records, and it is likely to be most convenient for this to be done at this initial interview.

Interviewing the client

A number of issues to be sorted out at the initial meeting have already been noted. The lawyer will wish to use the meeting for at least the following purposes:

- Introduction

  The lawyer should introduce himself or herself, clearly identifying his or her role. Assuming the lawyer is to represent the client, he or she should make that clear, explaining that he or she is independent from (for example) the psychiatric hospital or the guardianship authority. In the event that the lawyer is instead representing the Court or a guardian, this should also be made clear to the client (and the advice that follows below may vary accordingly).

- Determine capacity of client to instruct, and confirm the nature of the client-lawyer relationship
  - The lawyer should determine whether the individual has the factual capacity to provide instructions. As discussed above, this concerns whether the individual has sufficient understanding about the nature of the proceedings. This is not necessarily a single determination. Capacity can vary over time. Further, as interviews with the client progress, it may become clearer what the client is and is not able to understand. With this in mind, it is often helpful to ask the client open-ended questions related to the information (e.g., 'what do you think about that?' or 'is that how you remember it?' rather than 'do you understand?', as this last question invites a simple yes or no answer.) Early in the interview, it may also be helpful to ask the client to explain a short piece of advice or of the lawyer's introduction to the client back to the lawyer in the client's own words, as this ability can give a sense of the strength of the client's ability to absorb and synthesise ideas.
  - The lawyer should find out whether the client has the legal capacity to instruct a lawyer. As noted above, this may be separate from factual capacity if, for example, the individual is under a guardianship régime that has removed his or her right to hire a lawyer.
  - If the client *has* legal and factual capacity, a letter of authority can be signed (see below). The form of authority for proceedings in domestic courts will be determined under domestic law. If the case is to go to the ECtHR, a Letter of Authority valid at the European Court of Human Rights will be required (see chapter 8, and appendices 8 and 9). If the client has been deprived of his or her legal capacity the lawyer should obtain the contact details of the legal guardian. If the lawyer thinks that the client can actually give instructions, the lawyer should consider asking the client to sign a letter of authority in any event. This is particularly important for cases that may go to the ECtHR, where the domestic restrictions on hiring a lawyer will not apply.
  - In the light of the foregoing, clarify with the client what the lawyer's role is. Is the lawyer representing the person present, or someone else? Will the lawyer be taking instructions from the client or from someone else? Does the lawyer *have* to consult with someone else, for example, a guardian? The lawyer should explain the scope of the representation, and probably that the lawyer will be unable to assist in all areas of the client's life. The lawyer should also speak clearly about the fact that the lawyer will act on the client's instructions, but that others (e.g. a court) may find what the client is saying to result from a mental disability. Lawyers should not be afraid to raise the mental disability issues straight away: experience shows that clients appreciate this frankness.

- Determination of legal issues
  - Find out what the issues are. During this crucial preliminary phase, the lawyer should ask open-ended questions to find out what exactly the issues are, and what the client wants the lawyer to do about it.

- Detention. The lawyer should also find out whether the client is detained in the institution? If so, under which law? What is recorded in the medical records about the legal status of the client? Has the client been subject to any other measures (such as involuntary medication, seclusion, restraints).
  - Chronology. The lawyer should ask the client to explain as clearly as possible what has happened to him or her from the time when the legal problem was created until now. For example, ask the client to explain the circumstances in which he had an argument with his wife that precipitated the hospital admission, or (in a guardianship case) when the client found out that an application had been made to place his under guardianship. The lawyer may have to assist the client to remember things in order, and ask some questions for clarification.
  - Reports. The lawyer should go through any medial or social reports with the client, noting anything which the client does not agree with.

- Possible outcomes

  After listening to the chronology carefully, the lawyer should clearly explain the options and outcomes. The lawyer should go through each of these and ensure that the client understands. The lawyer should then make sure that *the client* makes the decision (e.g. in a hospital, does the client want to leave, does the client want a change of medication? In guardianship proceedings, does the client want to retain his legal capacity?)

- Next steps

  The lawyer should consider writing or dictating letters to the hospital or other authorities in the presence of the client.[8] The lawyer should explain to the client what the next steps are. These may include receiving letters, instructing experts, being at the next court hearing, receiving a telephone call, etc. The client should also be made aware of the likely progress in the case. In some cases, the launch of legal proceedings may have social ramifications in the institution, either between residents or, more likely, between the client and staff. Those issues should be considered with the client.

- When the lawyer gets back to the office, the lawyer should write an attendance note of the meeting with the client and send it to him or her. It is worth copying the client on all correspondence to any authorities or any witnesses in the case, so the client can see what steps the lawyer is taking in the case, and also to protect the lawyer against any future criticism about the handling of the case.

Routine contact should then be kept with the client. As noted above, in some institutions repercussions have arisen when people have contacted lawyers and commenced

---

[8] Thanks to Lucy Scott-Moncrieff for this advice. The advantage of dictating correspondence relating to the case in front of the client is that (a) the client can immediately correct any mistakes, and (b) the client is at the heart of the litigation, and (c) the client need not be suspicious of any sides the lawyer might be taking.

proceedings involving staff. Ongoing contact with the client may be necessary to minimise the risk of these repercussions.

Going through evidence with the client

Although it is ethically inappropriate to coach (ie. tell the client what to say), it is good practice to allow the client to go through his or her evidence with the lawyer.

In court reviews of a client's detention in a psychiatric hospital, the court should essentially be interested in whether the hospital can prove that the client meets the statutory criteria for detention. In formulating an opinion, a court is likely to be interested in the following issues:

- Insight. To what extent does the client recognise that he or she has a mental illness (or whatever phrase is used in the law)? This is sometimes troublesome, because psychiatrists can say that a lack of insight is merely a symptom of that person's mental illness. If the client denies having a mental disability, he or she may be in a stronger position if there is evidence that corroborates this. Alternatively, a position could be that the client recognises that he or she has a mental disability, but that it is not of sufficient severity warranting detention, or that the client does not pose a threat to his or her own health or safety or that or others. Lawyers are advised to look carefully at the wording of the domestic law.
- Medication and compliance. What sorts of medication is the client receiving? How invasive is the medication? Does it actually help (the lawyer can consider asking the client to explain how he or she felt just before being admitted to hospital and how s/he is feeling now, and what factors were involved in any changes). What are the adverse effects? What is the client's medication history? Has the client been 'compliant' with medication before – that is, has the client actually taken the medication for a long period of time, and why? This is often a concern by psychiatrists who say that the client needs to be in hospital because the client cannot be trusted to take the medication at home. This is a stereotype that must be challenged. People with mental disabilities are often very much aware of their difficulty and their need for treatment, and quite content to take treatment for it. If the client is not prepared to do this, it is worth finding out why. Is it adverse effects of the medication, or are there other reasons?
- Factual basis of admission to hospital. This is an area where there is often huge confusion and conflicting statements. The police or other agencies may also have been involved. Often admission to hospital has followed from an argument, where of course, there are always two sides to a story. The client may have a very different version of events than that recorded in the medical records. This is the key area where hospital authorities can say "the patient is reported to have threatened neighbours with violence". In order to counter such arguments, the lawyer should carefully listen to the client's version of events, and should chase up any useful witnesses.

In incapacity/guardianship hearings, the lawyer should look carefully at the statutory criteria for depriving a person of legal capacity, or however the domestic legal provisions are phrased. In many countries people are placed under guardianship without a vigorous analysis of the evidence. The following issues may be important to present to the court:

- Competence. This is a huge area. Essentially, can the person fulfil those tasks specified by law. Where the law is unclear, the lawyer should break down the issues into small pieces and examine each one in turn. For example, can the client use money (does the client go to the market, does she go to the post office to pick up a pension, does the client know how to handle money, can the client make basic calculations)?
- Expert evidence. If there is a psychiatric report, questions to ask could include the training and competence of the 'expert', what aspect of the expert's training included making capacity assessments, the length of time which the expert spent with the client, the factual basis on which the opinion of incapacity was reached, and whether any objective psychometric or similar tests of capacity were used.
- Diagnosis. The expert might not be aware of the tenuous link between someone's diagnosis and capacity.

Access to information

As with any case, preparation is vital to success. Lawyers should read all relevant documents, including the client's medical records. The UN Basic Principles for Lawyers make it clear that the lawyer has a right to this information:

> 21. It is the duty of the competent authorities to ensure lawyers access to appropriate information, files and documents in their possession or control in sufficient time to enable lawyers to provide effective legal assistance to their clients. Such access should be provided at the earliest appropriate time.[9]

In order to understand the evidence contained in medical records kept by hospitals on a patient, to understand mental health staff speak about the diagnosis, treatment and prognosis of the client, and to make an assessment about whether to instruct an expert opinion, the lawyer needs to have some understanding of the basics of medical and psychiatric terminology.

The lawyer will invariably need to meet the client more than once before the court hearing. Depending on legality and funding, the lawyer should consider asking for an independent (psychiatrist, psychologist, social worker etc.) expert opinion. The lawyer will have to think about what questions the expert should provide an opinion on. If an expert writes a report, it is clearly more than merely courteous to go to the client and go through the expert's report with the client. At this stage it is worth considering whether

---

[9] *Basic Principles on the Role of Lawyers*, Adopted by the Eighth United Nations Congress on the Prevention of Crime and the Treatment of Offenders, Havana, Cuba, 27 August to 7 September 1990, principle 21.

or not there is enough evidence to continue with the application. If the expert witness supports what the client wants, it would be worth calling the expert to give evidence before the court.

With the client's permission, the lawyer should contact relevant witnesses to ascertain their knowledge of the relevant circumstances of the case. The lawyer will also want to assess whether these witnesses would be useful to call to give evidence to the court.

As would be usual with other cases, lawyers may wish to speak with the opposing party or their legal representatives, to determine what sorts of evidence will be brought by them and to focus legal issues. How far evidence must be disclosed by the various parties will in part be a matter for domestic evidence law. For issues regarding detention, however, Article 5(2) of the European Convention on Human Rights provides the detained person a right to be informed of the reasons for any deprivation of liberty.[10] As such, Article 5(2) provides a right at least to know the general nature of the evidence on which the person is detained, and therefore the issues which need to be addressed in the subsequent court hearing.

The ECHR contains no corresponding obligation on the part of the detained individual or lawyer to disclose the evidence or arguments that they will lead in the eventual court hearing. How far the lawyer may wish to advise the client to do so may be a matter of tactics. Depending on the facts of the situation, the powers of the Court, and the result the client wants, the best technique may be to use the threat of the court hearing by way of leverage to reach a settlement. If the client wishes a transfer to a institution closer to his or her home, for example, such a result may be difficult to achieve through domestic or ECtHR litigation. The lawyer could offer to attempt to broker some sort of agreed resolution, which would get the client into a more convenient institution. If such settlement is the objective, it may be appropriate to be considerably more open with the other parties and their legal representatives than would be the case if the best result was expected to be obtained in court.

If a good result for the client is to be achieved, it may be necessary to expand outside the traditional realm of legal advocacy. If the objective is to get the client out of an institution, for example, the lawyer must be knowledgeable about local alternatives so that he or she can ensure that arrangements are in place for the client's accommodation and provision of appropriate services in the event that the application is successful. That may be important both to ensure that practically the client has somewhere to go, and also as a litigation strategy, as courts and tribunals seem often to be more content to release people if an alternative plan is in place. In some jurisdictions, social services or services run by non-governmental organisations can be used to develop these plans. Such assistance is not required by the ECHR, however, and in the end it may be up to the lawyer to organise such programmes.

---

[10] See Chapter 2 on detention.

Similarly, the client's chances of success before a court or tribunal are likely to be markedly increased if his or her position is supported by the report and testimony of others. Mental disability cases often involve an expert whose opinion is contrary to the client's wishes. In these situations the lawyer should explain to the client that it may be advantageous to instruct an independent medical expert such as a psychiatrist (or in some cases a psychologist), ideally with a speciality in the sort of disorder the client has, be it mental illness, personality disorder, developmental disability, or other mental disability. Further, if there is a longer term plan for the individual, the report or testimony of any doctors or other professionals who will be implicated in that plan is important. At the very least, evidence should be presented of their willingness to do their part in the plan. Similarly, if the client's family members or friends will be central to the success of the plan, evidence should be provided from them that they support it.

The Hearing

The specifics of the hearing will be governed by domestic law relating to the nature of the case. Once again, however, preparation is pivotal.

Legal cultures vary, and in some jurisdictions it is still unusual for issues relating to mental disability to be litigated. However, there is at least on paper some judicial control of issues such as detention in psychiatric institutions and determination legal incapacity in all Council of Europe jurisdictions. It may well be the case that local judges are as prejudiced about mental disability issues as anyone else, and not used to dealing with cases involving what may be perceived as complex (and non-legal) issues of medicine. If the judge is not used to hearing these issues, it may be necessary to explain the law in question from first principles. Indeed, it may be necessary to explain to the judge why the issue is important at all: sadly, people with psychiatric or intellectual disabilities still do not routinely enjoy respect from judges (or lawyers for that matter) in all Council of Europe jurisdictions. A certain amount of tenacity may be necessary on this point.

Court hearings that do not raise ECHR issues are governed exclusively by domestic law, but where the ECHR requires a court hearing, as for issues under Articles 5 or 6 of the Convention, for example, the client has a right to be present, to give testimony and to make representations either individually or through counsel.[11] As with any other client, presentation is significant. In some jurisdictions, particularly where a judge or tribunal comes to the institution to conduct court proceedings, there are anecdotal accounts of clients being brought into the hearing in their pyjamas. Such presentation is demeaning to the client and undercuts his or her credibility in the hearing. The lawyer should arrive in time to ensure that this does not occur. When possible, the client should be presented in a decent set of clothes, appropriately washed and, if a man without a beard, shaved.

---

[11]   See chapters 2 detention and chapter 6 on guardianship.

It is in theory a matter of tactics as to whether to call the client as a witness, but even when not formally required, it is in general desirable if not essential to do so. Even if the points raised in argument are solely legal, experience would suggest a general reluctance of courts and tribunals to accede to applications by people with mental disabilities without hearing from those individuals. The client should be prepared by the lawyer much as any other client would be, prior to offering testimony. This should include describing the layout of the court or room where the hearing will take place, explaining who everyone is, and explaining the sorts of things which the client will be asked about.

Clients with psychoses raise particular tactical issues in this regard. On the one hand, the client may believe strongly in their delusion, and it may be relevant to the story they have to tell on the witness stand. On the other, the psychosis may very much undermine the client's credibility before the tribunal. Several comments are appropriate here. First, astonishingly bizarre things can turn out to be true, or at least not as manifestly false as might at first be assumed, and delusions that are viewed as indicative of particular mental disorders may be based in fact. An individual with a psychiatric history who complains that his neighbours are 'out to get him' or are threatening him is likely to be characterised as suffering from paranoia. This may be true, but it is also true that people with mental disabilities are often stereotyped and misunderstood, and subject to aggression by others as a result. Such 'delusions' may well turn out to be true. If in any doubt, the lawyer should investigate prior to the hearing whether the 'psychotic delusion' has any basis in reality. If it does, he or she should have evidence ready to that effect. If it does not, it may be appropriate to discuss the approach to the issue with the client in advance of the hearing, explaining the potential disadvantages of leading that evidence. Lawyers should not be frightened of speaking about the client's mental health issues with the client. That said, it is likely that the opposing side is well aware of the delusion, and may raise it in cross-examination. This is a difficult situation. The lawyer is under a duty not to mislead the court, and cannot coach the client to do so, even if it would be beneficial. How to proceed in this context will depend on the individual case. It may tactically be best to address a delusion in direct examination, so the client's lawyer can control the terms of its introduction. Lastly, it is of course obvious that a delusion may not be directly relevant to the issue in question. When that is the case, the lawyer should make that clear in his or her submissions to the court.

Dealing with difficult situations

Suicidal clients

Although it is rare, there may be situations when a client tells a lawyer that he or she is suicidal. Lawyers do not generally have training to deal with such situations. Although the lawyer may feel that it is irrational to contemplate suicide, the lawyer will of course be aware that suicide is not a crime in most jurisdictions. That being said, most lawyers will be anxious to protect the client and prevent a loss of life. The appropriate response will depend on the domestic law regarding client-lawyer confidentiality, and the facts of the individual case.

Different jurisdictions deal with client-lawyer confidentiality differently. In some jurisdictions a lawyer is allowed to breach the usual client-lawyer confidentiality if there is an immediate threat to a specific person or group of people. This may or may not include a threat to the client himself or herself.

If it is consistent with professional ethics to break confidentiality in the situation in question, there is still the issue of whom to notify. If the client is already in a psychiatric hospital or similar institution, the lawyer could ask the staff what the procedures are for assessing risk of suicide. There should be written procedures on assessment and management of people contemplating or suspected of contemplating suicide in these environments. If the client is living in the community, the lawyer may be in a difficult position about who, if anyone, should be told.

The decision to pass on the information must therefore be made in the light of applicable laws and ethical guidelines for lawyers. Before making a decision like this it is always a good idea to discuss next steps with a more experienced lawyer. Any action that a lawyer makes should be recorded in detail and signed.

Threats to others

People with mental disabilities are more likely to be the victims of violence than the perpetrators. However, the statistics do not help when a lawyer is faced with a situation when a client is threatening to be violent. It is extremely rare for a client with mental disabilities to be violent to a lawyer who the client knows is on their side. It is therefore important for a lawyer to explain his or her name and role when meeting any new client. A client may behave in a manner that is intimidating or uncomfortable for the lawyer. In these situations it is clear that the lawyer's safety is paramount. Tips for these situations are to meet with the client in a room where there is a table, with the lawyer taking a seat close to the door. The lawyer can ask a member of staff to look through the window of a meeting room – ensuring of course that this staff member cannot hear the conversation.

If the threat is to a person other than the lawyer, the lawyer will have to make a determination whether or not to breach the client-lawyer confidentiality and disclose this information to a third party. The situation raises issues analogous to those discussed above regarding suicide. Again, national laws and ethical guidelines vary, and it is the lawyer's responsibility to know about these.

Voir Note explicative
See Explanatory Note

| Numéro de dossier |
| *File-number* |

COUR EUROPÉENNE DES DROITS DE L'HOMME
EUROPEAN COURT OF HUMAN RIGHTS

Conseil de l'Europe – *Council of Europe*
Strasbourg, France

REQUÊTE
APPLICATION

présentée en application de l'article 34 de la Convention européenne des Droits de l'Homme, ainsi que des articles 45 et 47 du règlement de la Cour

under Article 34 of the European Convention on Human Rights and Rules 45 and 47 of the Rules of Court

IMPORTANT: La présente requête est un document juridique et peut affecter vos droits et obligations.
This application is a formal legal document and may affect your rights and obligations.

I. LES PARTIES
THE PARTIES

A. LE REQUÉRANT/LA REQUÉRANTE
THE APPLICANT

(Renseignements à fournir concernant le/la requérant(e) et son/sa représentant(e) éventuel(le))
(Fill in the following details of the applicant and the representative, if any)

1. Nom de famille .... 2. Prénom(s)
   Surname   *First names(s)*

            Sexe : masculin / féminin   *Sex: male / female*

3. Nationalité .... 4. Profession
   Nationality   *Occupation*

5. Date et lieu de naissance
   Date and place of birth

6. Domicile
   Permanent address

7. Tel. N°

8. Adresse actuelle (si différente de 6.)
   Present address (if different from 6.)

9. Nom et prénom du/de la représentant(e)[1]
   *Name of representative**

10. Profession du/de la représentant(e)
    Occupation of representative

11. Adresse du/de la représentant(e)
    Address of representative

12. Tel. N° .... Fax N°

B. LA HAUTE PARTIE CONTRACTANTE
THE HIGH CONTRACTING PARTY

(Indiquer ci-après le nom de l'Etat/des Etats contre le(s)quel(s) la requête est dirigée)
(Fill in the name of the State(s) against which the application is directed)

13.

---

[1] Si le/la requérant(e) est représenté(e), joindre une procuration signée par le/la requérant(e) et son/sa représentant(e).
If the applicant appoints a representative, attach a form of authority signed by the applicant and his or her representative.

II. EXPOSÉ DES FAITS
STATEMENT OF THE FACTS

(Voir chapitre II de la note explicative)
(See Part II of the Explanatory Note)

14.

III. EXPOSÉ DE LA OU DES VIOLATION(S) DE LA CONVENTION ET/OU DESPROTOCOLES ALLÉGUÉE(S), AINSI QUE DES ARGUMENTS À L'APPUI
STATEMENT OF ALLEGED VIOLATION(S) OF THE CONVENTION AND/OR PROTOCOLS AND OF RELEVANT ARGUMENTS

(Voir chapitre III de la note explicative)
(See Part III of the Explanatory Note)

15.

IV. EXPOSÉ RELATIF AUX PRESCRIPTIONS DE L'ARTICLE 35 § 1 DE LA CONVENTION
STATEMENT RELATIVE TO ARTICLE 35 § 1 OF THE CONVENTION

(Voir chapitre IV de la note explicative. Donner pour chaque grief, et au besoin sur une feuille séparée, les renseignements demandés sous les points 16 à 18 ci-après)
(See Part IV of the Explanatory Note. If necessary, give the details mentioned below under points 16 to 18 on a separate sheet for each separate complaint)

16. Décision interne définitive (date et nature de la décision, organe – judiciaire ou autre – l'ayant rendue)
Final decision (date, court or authority and nature of decision)

17. Autres décisions (énumérées dans l'ordre chronologique en indiquant, pour chaque décision, sa date, sa nature et l'organe – judiciaire ou autre – l'ayant rendue)
Other decisions (list in chronological order, giving date, court or authority and nature of decision for each of them)

18. Dispos(i)ez-vous d'un recours que vous n'avez pas exercé? Si oui, lequel et pour quel motif n'a-t-il pas été exercé?
Is there or was there any other appeal or other remedy available to you which you have not used? If so, explain why you have not used it.

V.   EXPOSÉ DE L'OBJET DE LA REQUÊTE
STATEMENT OF THE OBJECT OF THE APPLICATION

(Voir chapitre V de la note explicative)
(See Part V of the Explanatory Note)

19.

VI.   AUTRES INSTANCES INTERNATIONALES TRAITANT OU AYANT TRAITÉ L'AFFAIRE
STATEMENT CONCERNING OTHER INTERNATIONAL PROCEEDINGS

(Voir chapitre VI de la note explicative)
(See Part VI of the Explanatory Note)

20.   Avez-vous soumis à une autre instance internationale d'enquête ou de règlement les griefs énoncés dans la présente requête ? Si oui, fournir des indications détaillées à ce sujet.
Have you submitted the above complaints to any other procedure of international investigation or settlement? If so, give full details.

VII. PIÈCES ANNEXÉES (PAS D'ORIGIAUX,
UNIQUEMENT DES COPIES ;
PRIÈRE DE N'UTILISER NI AGRAFE,
NI ADHÉSIF, NI LIEN D'AUCUNE SORTE)

LIST OF DOCUMENTS *(NO ORIGINAL DOCUMENTS,
ONLY PHOTOCOPIES,
DO NOT STAPLE, TAPE OR BIND DOCUMENTS)*

(Voir chapitre VII de la note explicative. Joindre copie de toutes les décisions mentionnées sous ch. IV
et VI ci-dessus. Se procurer, au besoin, les copies nécessaires, et, en cas d'impossibilité, expliquer
pourquoi celles-ci ne peuvent pas être obtenues. Ces documents ne vous seront pas retournés.)
*(See Part VII of the Explanatory Note. Include copies of all decisions referred to in Parts IV and VI above.
If you do not have copies, you should obtain them. If you cannot obtain them, explain why not. No documents will be returned to you.)*

21. a)

    b)

    c)

VIII.   DÉCLARATION ET SIGNATURE
DECLARATION AND SIGNATURE

(Voir chapitre VIII de la note explicative)
(See Part VIII of the Explanatory Note)

Je déclare en toute conscience et loyauté que les renseignements qui figurent sur la présente formule de requête sont exacts.
I hereby declare that, to the best of my knowledge and belief, the information I have given in the present application form is correct.

Lieu/*Place*

Date/*Date*

(Signature du/de la requérant(e) ou du/de la représentant(e))
(Signature of the applicant or of the representative)

EUROPEAN COURT OF HUMAN RIGHTS

AUTHORITY[1]
(Rule 36 of the Rules of Court)

I, ...

....

(name and address of applicant)

hereby authorise ....

....

....

(name, address and occupation of representative)

to represent me in the proceedings before the European Court of Human Rights, and in any subsequent proceedings under the European Convention on Human Rights, concerning my application introduced under Article 34 of the Convention against

....

(respondent State)

on ....
(date of letter of introduction)

....
        (place and date)

                                          ....
                                                (signature of applicant)

I herebey accept the above appointment

....
        (signature of representative)

---

1. This form <u>must</u> be completed and signed by any applicant wishing to be represented before the Court and by the lawyer or other person appointed.

Index

50. A. Spiliopoulou Akermark: *Justi.cations of Minority Protection in International Law.* 1997
ISBN 90-411-0424-0

51. A. Boulesbaa: *The U.N. Convention on Torture and the Prospects for Enforcement.* 1997
ISBN 90-411-0457-7

52. S. Bowen (ed.): *Human Rights, Self-Determination and Political Change in the Occupied Palestinian Territories.* 1997
ISBN 90-411-0502-6

53. M. O'Flaherty and G. Gisvold (eds.): *Post-War Protection of Human Rights in Bosnia and Herzegovina.* 1998
ISBN 90-411-1020-8

54. A.-L. Svensson-McCarthy: *The International Law of Human Rights and States of Exception.* With Special Reference to the Travaux Préparatoires and the Case-Law of the International Monitoring Organs. 1998
ISBN 90-411-1021-6

55. G. Gilbert: *Transnational Fugitive Offenders in International Law.* Extradition and Other Mechanisms. 1998
ISBN 90-411-1040-2

56. M. Jones and L.A. Basser Marks (eds.): *Disability, Divers-ability and Legal Change.* 1998
ISBN 90-411-1086-0

57. T. Barkhuysen, M.L. van Emmerik and RH.P.H.M.C. van Kempen (eds.): *The Execution of Strasbourg and Geneva Human Rights Decisions in the National Legal Order.* 1999
ISBN 90-411-1152-2

58. S. Coliver, P. Hoffman, J. Fitzpatrick and S. Bowen (eds.): *Secrecy and Liberty: National Security, Freedom of Expression and Access to Information.* 1999
ISBN 90-411-1191-3

59. W.S. Heinz and H. Fruhling: *Determinants of Gross Human Rights Violations by State and State-Sponsored Actors in Brazil, Uruguay, Chile, and Argentina.* 1960-1990. 1999
ISBN 90-411-1202-2

60. M. Kirilova Eriksson: *Reproductive Freedom.* In the Context of International Human Rights and Humanitarian Law. 1999
ISBN 90-411-1249-9

61. M.B. Eryilmaz: *Arrest and Detention Powers in English and Turkish Law and Practice in the Light of the European Convention on Human Rights.* 1999
ISBN 90-411-1269-3

62. K. Henrard: *Devising and Adequate System of Minority Protection.* Individual Human Rights, Minority Rights and the Right to Self-Determination. 2000
ISBN 90-411-1359-2

63. K. Tomasevski: *Responding to Human Rights Violations.* 1946-1999. 2000
ISBN 90-411-1368-1

64. L.-V.N. Tran: *Human Rights and Federalism.* A Comparative Study on Freedom, Democracy and Cultural Diversity. 2000
ISBN 90-411-1492-0

65. C. Tiburcio: *The Human Rights of Aliens under International and Comparative Law*. 2001
ISBN 90-411-1550-1

66. E. Brems: Human Rights: *Universality and Diversity*. 2001 ISBN 90-411-1618-4

67. C. Bourloyannis-Vrailas and L.-A. Sicilianos: *The Prevention of Human Rights Violations*.
2001 ISBN 90-411-1672-9

68. G. Ulrich and K. Hastrup: *Discrimination and Toleration*. New Perspectives. 2001
ISBN 90-411-1711-3

69. V.O. Orlu Nmehielle: *African Human Rights System*. Its Laws, Practice and Institutions.
2001 ISBN 90-411-1731-8

70. B.G. Ramcharan: *Human Rights and Human Security*. 2002 ISBN 90-411-818-7

71. B.G. Ramcharan: *The United Nations High Commissioner for Human Rights*. The Challenges
of International Protection. 2002 ISBN 90-411-1832-2

72. C. Breen: *The Standard of the Best Interests of the Child*. A Western Tradition in International and Comparative Law. 2002 ISBN 90-411-1851-9

73. M. Katayanagi: *Human Rights Functions of United Nations Peacekeeping Operations*. 2002
ISBN 90-411-1910-8

74. O.M. Arnadottir: *Equality and Non-Discrimination under the European Convention on Human Rights*. 2002 ISBN 90-411-1912-4

75. B.G. Ramcharan: *The Security Council and the Protection of Human Rights*. 2002
ISBN 90-411-1878-0

76. E. Fierro: *The EU's Approach to Human Rights Conditionality in Practice*. 2002
ISBN 90-411-1936-1

77. Natan Lerner: *Group Rights and Discrimination in International Law*. Second Edition. 2002
ISBN 90-411-1982-5

78. S. Leckie (ed.): *National Perspectives on Housing Rights*. 2003 ISBN 90-411-2013-0

79. L.C. Reif: *The Ombudsman, Good Governance and the International Human Rights System*. 2004
ISBN 90-04-13903-6

80. Mary Dowell-Jones: *Contextualising the International Covenant on Economic, Social and Cultural Rights: Assessing the Economic Deficit*. 2004 ISBN 90-04-13908-7

81. Li-ann Thio: *Managing Babel: The International Legal Protection of Minorities in the Twentieth Century*
ISBN 90-04-14198-7

INTERNATIONAL STUDIES IN HUMAN RIGHTS

82. K.D. Beiter: *The Protection of the Right to Education by International Law.* 2006
ISBN 90 04 14704 7

83. J.H. Gerards: *Judicial Review in Equal Treatment Cases.* 2005 ISBN 90 04 14379 3

84. V.A.Leary and D. Warner: *Social Issues, Globalization and International Institutions. Labour Rights and the EU, ILO, OECD and WTO.* 2005 ISBN 90 04 14579 6

85. J.K.M. Gevers, E.H. Hondius and J.H. Hubben (eds.): *Health Law, Human Rights and the Biomedicine Convention.* Essays in Honour of Henriette Roscam Abbing. 2005
ISBN 90 04 14822 1

86. C. Breen: *Age Discrimination and Children's Rights.* Ensuring Equality and Acknowledging Difference. 2006 ISBN 90 04 14827 2

87. B.G. Ramcharan (ed.): *Human Rights Protection in the Field.* 2006 ISBN 90 04 14847 7

88. G. Gilbert: *Responding to International Crime.* Second Edition. 2006
ISBN-13 978 90 04 15276 2. ISBN-10 90 04 15276 8

89. T. Obokata: *Trafficking of Human Beings from a Human Rights Perspective.* Towards a Holistic Approach. 2006 ISBN-13 978 90 04 15405 6. ISBN-10 90 04 15405 1

90. P. Bartlett, O. Lewis and O. Thorold: *Mental Disability and the European Convention on Human Rights.* 2007 ISBN-13 978 90 04 15423 0. ISBN-10 90 04 15423 X

91. R. Craig: *Systemic Discrimination in Employment and the Promotion of Ethnic Equality.* 2007
ISBN-13 978 90 04 15462 9. ISBN-10 90 04 15462 0

This series is designed to shed light on current legal and political aspects of process and organization in the field of human rights

MARTINUS NIJHOFF PUBLISHERS – LEIDEN • BOSTON